the Gates of Paradise

BY THE SAME AUTHOR

Anthologies

Black Water: The Anthology of Fantastic Literature
Other Fires: Short Fiction by Latin American Women
Black Water II: Further Fantastic Literature
The Oxford Book of Canadian Ghost Stories
The Oxford Book of Canadian Mystery Stories
Soho Square III
Seasons: Poems for Children
Evening Games: Stories for Parents and Children
Dark Arrows: Stories of Revenge

Fiction

News From a Foreign Country Came

Other

The Dictionary of Imaginary Places
(with Gianni Guadalupi)

the Gates of Paradise

THE ANTHOLOGY OF
EROTIC SHORT FICTION

EDITED BY
ALBERTO MANGUEL

QUALITY PAPERBACK BOOK CLUB
NEW YORK

See Sources (beginning on page 685) for copyright information on individual stories.

Printed in the United States of America

Dedicated to:

*The Canada Customs officials,
the Alberta Ministry of Education,
U.S. Senator Jesse Helms of North Carolina,
Mrs Mary Whitehouse of the National Listeners
and Viewers Association of Great Britain,
and censor boards the world over, who so
diligently remind us of the importance
of things forbidden.*

"For the sexes: The Gates of Paradise."

— WILLIAM BLAKE

"The Erotic Literature Section at the Bibliothèque Nationale in Paris is called Hell."

— REPORT ON THE BIBLIOTHÈQUE NATIONALE, 1954

"Children of the future age,
Reading this indignant page,
Know that in a former time
Love, sweet love, was thought a crime."

— WILLIAM BLAKE

Thanks for their generous help to:

Craig Stephenson, Jonathan Warner,
Catherine Yolles, Richard Outram,
Gary Ross, Lucinda Vardey, and above all,
to Jan Walter, whose idea it was
in the first place.

Contents

Introduction

ONE OF THE oldest versions of *Beauty and the Beast,* told in Latin by Apuleius sometime in the second century, is the story of a princess ordered by an oracle to become the wife of a dragon. Fearing for her life, dressed in mourning, abandoned by her family, she waited at the top of a mountain for her winged husband. The monster never came. Instead, a breeze lifted her and bore her down into a peaceful valley, in which stood a house of gold and silver. Disembodied voices welcomed her, and offered her food and drink, and sang to her. When night fell, no lights were lit and in the darkness she felt someone near her. "I am your lover and your husband," a voice said, and mysteriously she was no longer afraid. The princess lived with her unseen spouse for many days.

One evening, the voices told her that her sisters were approaching the house, searching for her, and she felt a great desire to see them once again and tell them of the wonderful things that had taken place. The voices warned her not to go but her longing was too great. Calling out their names, she hurried to meet them. At first the sisters seemed overjoyed, but when they heard her story they cried and called her a fool for allowing herself to be deceived by a husband who required the cover of darkness. "There must be something monstrous about him, if he will not show himself to you in the light," they said, and felt pity for her.

That night, steeling herself for a hideous revelation, the princess lit an oil lamp and crept to where her husband was sleeping. What she saw was not a dragon, but a young man of extraordinary beauty, breathing softly into the pillow. Overjoyed, she was about to extinguish the lamp, when a drop of hot oil fell on the sleeper's left shoulder. He awoke, saw the light, said not a word, and fled.

Eros vanishes when Psyche tries to perceive him.

As an adolescent, reading about Eros and Psyche one hot afternoon at home in Buenos Aires, I didn't believe in the moral of the story. I was convinced that in my father's almost unused library, where I had found so many secret pleasures, I would find, by magic chance, the startling and unspoken thing that crept into my dreams and was the butt of schoolyard jokes. I wasn't disappointed. I glimpsed at Eros through the chiffonerie of *Forever Amber,* in a tattered translation of *Peyton Place,* in certain poems of García Lorca, in the sleeping-car chapter of Moravia's *The Conformist* which I read haltingly at thirteen, in Roger Peyrefitte's *Particular Friendships.*

And Eros didn't vanish.

When a couple of years later, I was able to compare my readings to the actual sensation of my hand brushing for the first time over a lover's body, I had to admit that, for once, literature had fallen short. And yet, the thrill of those forbidden pages remained. The panting adjectives, the brazen verbs were perhaps not useful to describe my own confused emotions, but they conveyed to me, then and there, something brave and astonishing and unique.

This uniqueness, I was to discover, brands all our essential experiences. "We live together, we act on, and react to, one another," wrote Aldous Huxley in *The Doors of Perception,* "but always and in all circumstances we are by ourselves. The martyrs go hand in hand into the arena; they are crucified alone. Embraced, the lovers desperately try to fuse their insulated ecstasies into a single self-transcendence; in vain. By its very nature every embodied spirit is doomed to suffer and enjoy in solitude." Even in the moment of greatest intimacy, the erotic act is a solitary act.

Throughout the ages, writers have attempted to make this solitude a shared one. Through ponderous hierarchies (essays on gender etiquette, texts of medieval love-courts), through mechanics (love-making manuals, anthropological studies), through examples (fables, narratives of one kind or another), every culture has sought to comprehend the erotic experience in the hope that perhaps, if faithfully depicted in words, the reader might be able to relive it or even learn it, in the same way that we expect a certain object to preserve a memory or a monument to bring the dead to life.

It's amazing to think how distinguished a universal library of this wishful erotic literature would be. It would include, I imagine, the Platonic dialogues of ancient Greece in which Socrates discusses the types and merits of love, Ovid's *Ars Amatoria* of Imperial Rome in which Eros is considered a social function like table-manners, the *Song of Songs* in which the loves of King Solomon and the black Queen of Sheba become reflections of the world around them, the Hindu *Kamasutra* and the *Kalyana Malla* in which pleasure is regarded as an element of ethics, the Arcipreste de Hita's *Book of Loving Well* in fourteenth-century Spain, which pretends to draw its wisdom from popular sources, the fifteenth-century *Perfumed Garden* of Sheik al-Nefzawi which codifies the erotic acts according to Muslim law, the German *Minnereden* or medieval amatory discourses in which love, like politics, is given its own rhetoric, and poetic allegories such as the *Roman de la Rose* in France and *The Faerie Queene* in England in which the abstract noun "Love" acquires once again, as Eros had, a human or divine face.

There would be other, even stranger works, in this ideal library: the ten-volume novel *Clélie* (1654-60) by Mademoiselle de Scudéry, which includes the *Carte de Tendre,* a map charting the erotic course with its rewards and perils; the writings of the Marquis de Sade who, in tedious catalogues, noted the sexual variations to which a human group can be subjected; the theoretical books of his near-contemporary Charles Fourier, who devised entire utopian societies centred around the sexual activities of its citizens; the intimate journals of Giacomo Casanova, Ihara Saikaku, Benvenuto Cellini, Frank Harris, Anaïs Nin, Henry Miller, John Rechy, all of whom tried to recapture Eros in autobiographical memoirs.

Curled up in an armchair in my father's library, and in other, later armchairs in more houses than I care to remember, I found that in spite of their singularity, certain of these experiences touched me, aroused me, whispered secrets to me. And Eros kept appearing in all sorts of unexpected places.

We may not share experiences, but we can share symbols. Transported into another realm, distracted from its subject, erotic writing at times achieves something of that essentially private act, as when the swoons and agonies of erotic desire become a vast metaphorical vocabulary for the mystical encounter. I remember the excitement with which I read, for the first time, the erotic union described by St John of the Cross:

Oh night that was my guide!
Oh darkness dearer than the morning's pride,
Oh night that joined the lover
To the beloved bride
Transfiguring them each into the other.

Lost to myself I stayed
My face upon my lover having laid
From all endeavour ceasing:
And all my cares releasing
Threw them amongst the lilies there to fade.

(Transl. by Roy Campbell)

And then John Donne, for whom the erotic/mystic act is also an act of exploration:

Licence my roving hands and let them go,
Before, behind, between, above, below.
O my America! my new-found-land.

William Cartwright, the nebulous seventeenth-century

author of *The Royal Slave* (a play which once received praise from both Charles I and Ben Jonson), deserves to be better remembered for the following lines which return spiritual love to its authentic source:

I was that silly thing that once was wrought
    To Practise this thin Love;
I climb'd from Sex to Soul, from Soul to Thought;
    But thinking there to move,
Headlong I rowl'd from Thought to Soul, and then
From Soul I lighted at the Sex agen.

Occasionally, in my haphazard reading, I found that a single image could make a poem successful. These are lines composed by a Sumerian poet *circa* 1700 B.C. She writes:

Going to my young husband –
I'll become the apple
clinging to the bough,
surrounding the stem
with my sweet flesh.

In a few cases, all that is required is an *absence* of description to convey the erotic power of that which has been lost. An anonymous English poet wrote this quatrain sometime in the late Middle Ages:

Western wind, when will thou blow,
The small rain down can rain?

Christ, that my love were in my arms,
And I in my bed again.

Fiction is another matter.

Of all the erotic literary genres, fiction, I think, has the hardest time of it. To tell an erotic story, a story whose subject is outside words and outside time, seems not only a futile task but an impossible one. It is arguable that any subject, in its sheer complexity or simplicity, makes its own telling impossible; that the description of a chair or a cloud or a childhood memory are just as ineffable as lovemaking, as a dream, as music.

Not so.

We have, in most languages, a varied and rich vocabulary that conveys reasonably well, in the hands of an experienced craftsperson, the actions and the elements with which society is comfortable, the daily bric-à-brac of its political animals. But that which society fears or fails to understand, that which forced me to keep a wary eye on the door of my father's library, that which becomes forbidden, even unmentionable in public, is given no proper words with which to approach it. "To write a dream, which shall resemble the real course of a dream, with all its inconsistency, its eccentricities and aimlessness," complained Nathaniel Hawthorne in his *American Notebooks,* "up to this old age of the world, no such thing has ever been written." He could have said the same of the erotic act.

The English language in particular makes things difficult

by simply not having an erotic vocabulary. The sexual organs, the sexual acts borrow the words to define them from either the science of biology or the lexicon of vituperation. Clinical or coarse, the words to describe the marvels of physical beauty and the exultation of pleasure condemn, asepticise or deride that which should be celebrated in wonder. Spanish, German, Italian, and Portuguese suffer from this same weakness. French is, perhaps, a little more fortunate. "*Baiser*" for copulate, which borrows its semantics from the word "kiss"; "*verge*" for penis, the same word for "birch," which in its association with "trees" gives "*verger*" or "orchard"; "*petite mort,*" "little death," for the moment of ecstasy after achieving orgasm, in which the diminutive endearment takes the eternity out of dying, but retains the sense of blissfully leaving this world – have little of the nudge-nudge wink-wink quality of "fuck," "prick," and "come." The vagina (surprise, surprise) receives in French as little respect as it does in English, and "*con*" is hardly better than "cunt." To write an erotic story in English, or to translate one into English, requires from the writer new and crafty ways of making use of the medium, so that the reader is led, against the grain of meaning or through an entirely separate imagination of language, into an experience which society has decreed will remain unspoken. "We have placed sex," said the wise Montaigne, "in the precincts of silence."

But why have we decided that Psyche mustn't look upon Eros?

In the Judeo-Christian world, the banning of Eros finds its canonical voice in St Augustine, a voice that echoes throughout the entire Middle Ages and still rings, distorted, in the censor boardrooms of our day. After a youth of womanizing and carousing (to make use of these fine preacherly words), looking back on his quest for a happy life, Augustine concludes that ultimate happiness, *eudaimonia,* cannot be achieved unless we allow the body to be subordinate to the spirit, and the spirit to God. Bodily love, *eros,* is infamous, and only *amor,* spiritual love, can lead to the enjoyment of God, to *agape,* the feast of love itself that transcends both human body and spirit. Two centuries after Augustine, St Maximus of Constantinople put it into these words: "Love is that good disposition of the soul in which it prefers nothing that exists to knowledge of God. But no man can come to such a state of love if he be attached to anything earthly. Love," concludes St Maximus, "is born from lack of erotic passion." This is a far cry from Plato's contemporaries who saw Eros as the binding force (in a real physical sense) that keeps the universe together.

Condemnation of erotic passion, of the flesh itself, allows most patriarchal societies to brand Woman as the temptress, as Mother Eve, guilty of Adam's daily fall. Because she is to blame, man has a natural right to rule over her, and any deviance from this law – by woman or by man – is punished as treacherous and sinful. As a result, misogyny and homophobia are both justified and encouraged, and an entire apparatus of censorship is constructed to protect male-defined heterosexual stereotypes by assigning women and homosexuals restrictive and pejorative roles. (And children: we excise the sexuality of children from social life, while allowing it to appear in seemingly innocuous guises on the screen and in the fashion pages – as Graham

Greene noted when he reviewed the films of Shirley Temple.)

Pornography requires this double standard. In pornography, the erotic must not be an integral part of a world in which both men and women, homosexual and heterosexual, seek a deeper comprehension of themselves and of the other. To be pornographic, the erotic must be amputated from its context and adhere to strict clinical definitions of that which is condemned. Pornography must faithfully embrace official normality in order to contravene it for no other purpose than immediate arousal. Pornography – or "licentiousness," as it was called – cannot exist without these official standards. "Licentious," meaning "sexually immoral," comes from "license," permission granted (to depart from the rules). That is why our societies allow pornography, which embraces official notions of "normal" or "decent" behaviour, to exist in specific contexts, but zealously persecute artistic erotic expressions in which the authority of those in power is brought implicitly into question. "Girlie" magazines could be bought in neat brown paper bags while *Ulysses* was being tried on charges of obscenity; hard-core porno films are shown in theatres a few steps away from others at which *The Last Temptation of Christ* or *How to Make Love to a Negro* are being picketed.

Erotic literature is subversive; pornography is not. Pornography, in fact, is reactionary to change. "In pornographic novels," says Nabokov in his post-scriptum to *Lolita*, "action has to be limited to the copulation of clichés. Style, structure, imagery should never distract the reader from his tepid lust." Pornography follows the conventions of all dogmatic literature – religious tracts, political bombast, commercial advertising. Erotic literature, if it is to be successful, must establish new conventions, lend the words of the society that condemns it new meaning, and inform its readers of a knowledge that in its very nature must remain intimate. This exploration of the world from a central and utterly private place gives erotic literature its formidable power.

Confronted with the task of making art out of a bewildering variety of objects and subjects, acts and variations, feelings and fears; limited by a vocabulary specifically designed for other purposes; walking the perilous edge between pornography and sentimentality, biology and purple prose, the coy and the over-explicit; threatened by societies intent on preserving the aristocracies of established power through the censoring forces of politics, education and religion, it is a miracle that erotic literature has not only survived this long but become braver, brighter, more confident, pursuing a multi-coloured infinity of objects of desire.

For the mystic, the whole universe is one erotic object, and the whole body the subject of erotic pleasure. The same can be said of every human being who discovers that not only penis and clitoris are places of pleasure but also the hands, the anus, the mouth, the hair, the soles of the feet, every inch of our astounding bodies. That which physically and mentally excites the senses and opens for us what William Blake called the

Gates of Paradise, is always something mysterious and, as we all eventually find out, its shape is dictated by laws of which we know nothing. We admit to loving a woman, a man, a child. Why not a gazelle, a stone, a shoe, the sky at night?

In D. H. Lawrence's *Women in Love,* Rupert Birkin's object of desire is the vegetation itself:

> To lie down and roll in the sticky, cool young hyacinths, to lie on one's belly and cover one's back with handfuls of fine wet grass, soft as a breath, soft and more delicate and more beautiful than the touch of any woman; and then to sting one's thigh against the living dark bristles of the fir-boughs; and then to feel the light whip of the hazel on one's shoulders, stinging, and then to clasp the silvery birch-trunk against one's breast, its smoothness, its hardness, its vital knots and ridges – this was good, this was all very good, very satisfying.

In John Collier's *His Monkey Wife,* Eros is a chimp called Emily with whom an English schoolmaster, Mr Fatigay, falls madly in love:

> "Emily!" he said. "My Angel! My Own! My Love!"
>
> At this last word, Emily raised her eyes, and extended to him her hand.
>
> Under her long and scanty hair he caught glimpses of a plum-blue skin. Into the depths of those all-dark lustrous eyes, his spirit slid with no sound of splash. She uttered a few low words, rapidly, in her native tongue. The candle, guttering beside the bed, was strangled in

the grasp of prehensile foot, and the darkness received, like a ripple in velvet, the final happy sigh.

In Cynthia Ozick's *The Pagan Rabbi,* Eros is an oak-tree:

> I busied my fingers in the interstices of the bark's cuneiform. Then with forehead flat on the tree, I embraced it with both arms to measure it. My hands united on the other side. It was a young narrow weed, I did not know of what family. I reached to the lowest branch and plucked a leaf and made my tongue marvel meditatively along its periphery to assess its shape: oak. The taste was sticky and exaltingly bitter. I then placed one hand (the other I kept around the tree's waist, as it were) in the bifurcation (disgustingly termed crotch) of that lowest limb and the elegant and devoutly firm torso, and caressed that miraculous juncture with a certain languor, which gradually changed to vigor.

This is Marian Engel describing an amorous encounter between a woman and a beast in *Bear*:

> He licked. He probed. She might have been a flea he was searching for. He licked her nipples stiff and scoured her navel. With little nickerings she moved him south.
>
> She swung her hips and made it easy for him.
>
> "Bear, bear," she whispered, playing with his ears. The tongue that was muscular but also capable of lengthening itself like an eel found all her secret places.

> And like no human being she had ever known it persevered in her pleasure. When she came, she whimpered, and the bear licked away her tears.

And the English writer J. R. Ackerley describes in these words his love for his dog Tulip:

> I go to bed early to end the dismal day, but she is instantly beside me, sitting upright against my pillow, her back turned, shifting, licking, panting, shifting, peering at my face, pulling at my arm. Sweet creature, what am I doing to you? I stretch out my hand in the gloom and stroke the small nipples ... Panting, she slackly sits while my hand caresses her, her ears flattened, her head dropped, gazing with vacant eyes into the night beyond the windows. Gradually, she relaxes, subsides. Gradually, my hand upon her, she sleeps ...

Even the lover's severed head can become an erotic object, as when Stendhal has Mathilde, in *The Red and the Black,* seek out Julien's remains:

> He heard Mathilde move hurriedly around the room. She was lighting a number of candles. When Fouque gathered enough strength to look, he saw that she had placed in front of her, on a little marble table, Julien's head, and was kissing its brow ...

A postscript: I believe that, like the erotic act, the act of reading should ultimately be anonymous. We should be able to enter the book or the bed like Alice entering the Nameless Wood on the other side of the Looking-Glass, no longer carrying with us the prejudices of our past, and relinquishing for that instant of intercourse our social trappings. Reading or making love, we should be able to lose ourselves in the other, into whom – to borrow St John's image – we are transformed: reader into writer into reader, lover into lover into lover. *Jouir de la lecture,* "to enjoy reading," say the French for whom reaching orgasm and deriving blissful pleasure are both expressed in a single common word.

Alberto Manguel
Toronto, summer of 1992

ISABEL ALLENDE

WICKED GIRL

During a book-signing in San Diego, California, an old lady came up to Isabel Allende. "I have a question," she said, blinking through two-inch-thick glasses. "All those love scenes you describe, did you really experience them or did you make them up?" Allende didn't have the courage to disappoint her. "Of course I made them up!" she answered. "These things never happen like that!" "Thank God!" the woman cried, and much relieved shook Allende's hand. She had feared that Allende's fiction portrayed a real experience which the reader should have shared.

In Allende's imaginary countries – modelled on the Chile she escaped during Pinochet's dictatorship when free speech and thought were brutally repressed – the erotic act becomes an expression of individual freedom through which the characters, especially her female characters, construct for themselves extraordinary lives. For Allende, the erotic act is an act of resistance.

AT THE AGE of eleven, Elena Mejías was still a scrawny whelp of a girl with the dull skin of solitary children, a mouth revealing gaps still unfilled by second teeth, mouse-colored hair, and a prominent skeleton, much too large for the rest of her, that threatened to poke through at the elbows and knees. Nothing about her betrayed her torrid dreams, nor presaged the sensuous creature she would become. Among the nondescript furnishings and faded draperies of her mother's boardinghouse, she went completely unnoticed. She was like a melancholy little waif playing among the dusty geraniums and enormous ferns in the patio, or trooping back and forth between kitchen range and dining room tables to serve the evening meal. On the rare occasion some boarder took notice of her, it was only to ask her to spray for cockroaches or to fill the watertank in the bathroom when the creaking pump failed to draw water to the second floor. Her mother, exhausted by heat and the grind of running her boardinghouse, had no energy for tenderness or time to devote to her daughter, so she failed to notice when Elena began to change into a different creature. She had always been a quiet, shy child absorbed in mysterious games, talking to herself in corners and sucking her thumb. She emerged from the house only to go to school or the market; she seemed uninterested in the noisy children of her own age playing in the street.

The transformation of Elena Mejías coincided with the arrival of Juan José Bernal, the Nightingale, as he liked to call himself and as a poster he tacked to the wall of his room loudly proclaimed. Most of the boarders were students or employees in some obscure division of city government. Real ladies and gentlemen, Elena's mother always said, for she prided herself on not taking just anyone under her roof, only respectable persons with a visible means of support, good manners, and enough money to pay a month's room and board in advance, who were also disposed to live by the regulations of her boardinghouse – more fitting for a seminary than a hotel. A widow has to think of her reputation and be able to command respect; I don't want my home turned into a haven for bums and perverts, her mother frequently repeated, so no one, especially Elena, would ever forget. One of the girl's responsibilities was to spy on the guests and keep her mother informed of any suspicious behavior. Eternal stealth exaggerated the ethereal air of the child who moved in an aura of silence, vanishing in the shadows of a room only to appear suddenly as if returning from another dimension. Mother and daughter shared the many chores of the boardinghouse, each immersed in her silent routine, feeling no need to communicate with the other. In truth, they spoke very little, and when they did, during the brief freedom of the hour of the siesta, it was about the clients. Sometimes Elena tried to embellish the gray lives of those transitory men and women who passed through the house leaving no trace of a memory by attributing to them some extraordinary event, coloring their lives through the gift of some clandestine love affair or tragedy, but her mother had an infallible instinct for detecting her fantasies. She also knew when her daughter was hiding something from her. She had an unassailable practical sense and a clear notion of everything that went on under her roof. She knew exactly what each lodger was doing at any hour of the night or day, how much sugar was left in the pantry, who was being called when the telephone rang, and where the last person had left the scissors. She had once been a cheerful, even pretty, young woman; her frumpy dresses barely restrained the impatience of a still-young body, but all the years spent scratching out a living had slowly drained away her spirit and zest for life. When Juan José Bernal came to inquire about a room, however, all that changed for her, and for Elena as well. The mother, seduced by the Nightingale's pretentious manner of speaking and the hint of fame represented by the poster, ignored her own rules and accepted him as a guest, despite the fact he did not in any way fit her image of the ideal boarder. Bernal told her that he sang at night and therefore needed to rest during the day; that he was between engagements and thus could not pay the month in advance; and that he was extremely fussy about his food and hygiene – he was a vegetarian, and he needed to shower twice a day. Amazed, Elena watched, without comment or question, as her mother wrote the name of the new guest in her book and then showed him to his room, struggling with his heavy suitcase while he bore the guitar case and the cardboard tube containing his treasured poster. Camouflaged against the wall, Elena followed them up the stairs, noting the new guest's intense appraisal of the cotton skirt clinging to her mother's sweaty buttocks. As she went into the room Elena flipped the switch, and the great blades of the ceiling fan began to turn with the screech of rusted metal.

Bernal's arrival signaled an immediate change in the household routine. There was more work now, because Bernal slept until the other guests had left for their various employments; he tied up the bath for hours on end; he consumed an astounding quantity of rabbit food, which had to be prepared especially for him; he was constantly on the telephone; and he made liberal use of the iron for touching up his dress shirts – without any charge for this unusual privilege. Elena came home at siesta, when the sun was blazing and the day languishing beneath a terrible white glare, but even at that hour Juan José Bernal would still be fast asleep. As her mother had ordered, Elena would remove her shoes to keep from disturbing the artificial quiet of the house. She was aware that her mother was changing day by day. She could see the signs from the very beginning, long before the residents began to whisper behind her mother's back. First it was the fragrance that clung to her mother and lingered in the rooms as she passed through. Elena knew every corner of the house, and her long training in spying led her to the perfume bottle behind the packets of rice and tins of conserves on the pantry shelf. Next she noticed the dark pencil outlining her mother's eyelids, the touch of red on her lips, the new underclothes, the immediate smile when finally Bernal came down in the evening, his hair still wet from the bath, and sat in the kitchen to wolf down strange dishes fit for a fakir. Her mother would sit across from him and listen while he recounted episodes from his life as an artist, punctuating every adventure with a deep laugh.

For several weeks, Elena hated that man who was claiming all the space in the house and all her mother's attention. She was repelled by the brilliantine-slick hair, the polished nails, the excessive zeal with a toothpick, the pedantry, the brazen assumption they all would serve him. She wondered what her mother could see in the man: he was nothing but a small-time adventurer, a bar entertainer whom no one had ever heard of, why, he might be an out-and-out scoundrel, as *señorita* Sofía, one of their oldest boarders, had suggested in whispers. But then one warm Sunday evening when there was nothing to do and time seemed to have stopped within the walls of the house, Juan José Bernal appeared in the patio with his guitar; he installed himself on a bench beneath the fig tree and began to strum a few chords. The sound drew all the guests, who peered out one by one, at first with a certain timidity – unsure of the reason for this unusual occurrence – and then with increasing enthusiasm; they hauled out the dining room chairs and set them in a circle around the Nightingale. The man had an ordinary voice, but he had a good ear, and sang with a certain charm. He knew all the stock boleros and rural ballads of the popular repertoire, and a few songs from the Revolution sprinkled with blasphemies and four-letter words that made the ladies blush. For the first time that Elena could remember, there was a festive air in the house. When it grew dark, they lighted two kerosene lamps and hung them in the trees, and brought beer and the bottle of rum reserved for treating colds. Elena was trembling as she filled the glasses; she felt the heartrending words of the songs and the lament of the guitar in every fiber of her body, like a fever. Her mother was tapping her toe to the rhythm. Suddenly she stood up, took Elena's hands, and the two began to dance, immediately followed by all the others, including *señorita* Sofía, all fluttering and nervous giggles. For an endless moment Elena danced, moving to the cadence of Bernal's voice, held tight against her mother's body, breathing in the new flowery scent, blissfully happy. Then she felt her mother gently pushing her away, pulling back to dance alone. With her eyes closed and her head tipped back, her mother swayed like a sheet drying in the breeze. Elena stepped from the floor, and all the dancers returned to their seats, leaving the mistress of the boardinghouse alone in the center of the patio, lost in her dance.

After that night, Elena saw Bernal through new eyes. She forgot that she had detested his brilliantine, his toothpicks, and his arrogance, and whenever she saw him or heard his voice she remembered the songs he had sung the night of that impromptu fiesta and again felt the flush on her skin and the confusion in her heart, a fever she did not know how to put into words. She watched him when he was not looking, and little by little noticed things she had not at first appreciated, his shoulders, his strong, muscular neck, the sensual curve of his heavy lips, his perfect teeth, the elegance of his long, fine hands. She was filled with an insupportable longing to be close enough to him to bury her face against his dark-skinned chest, to hear the resonance of the air in his lungs and the beating of his heart, to smell his scent, a scent she knew would be sharp and penetrating, like good leather or tobacco. She imagined herself playing with his hair, examining the muscles of his back and legs, discovering the shape of his foot, dissolving into smoke and filtering down his throat to inhabit his entire body. But if he happened to look up and meet her eyes, Elena, trembling, would run and hide in the farthest and densest corner of the patio. Bernal had taken possession of her thoughts; she could not bear how time stopped when she was away from him. In school, she moved as if in a nightmare, blind and deaf to anything except her inner thoughts, where there was room only for him. What was he doing at that moment? Perhaps he was sleeping face down on the bed with the shutters closed, the room in darkness, the warm air stirred by the blades of the fan, a trail of sweat marking his spine, his face sunk in the pillow. At the first sound of the bell marking the end of the day, she ran home, praying he was not yet awake and she would be able to wash and put on a clean dress and sit down to wait for him in the kitchen, pretending to do homework so her mother would not burden her with household chores. Later, when she heard him leaving his bath, whistling, she was tormented by impatience and fear, sure that she would die of pleasure if he touched her, even spoke to her, dying for him to do just that but at the same time ready to fade into the furniture, because although she could not live without him, neither could she endure his burning presence. Stealthily, she followed him everywhere, waited on him hand and foot, tried to divine his wishes and offer whatever he needed before he asked, but always moving like a wraith, not wanting to reveal her existence.

Elena could not sleep at night because he was not in the house. She would get up from her hammock and roam the first floor like a ghost, working up courage finally to tiptoe into Bernal's room. She would close the door behind her and open the shutter a crack to let in the reflection from the street to light the ceremonies she invented to enable her to claim the bits of the man's soul left behind in his belongings. She stood staring at herself in the oval of a mirror as black and shiny as a pool of dark mud, because he had looked at himself there and the vestiges of their two images could blend together in an embrace. She walked toward the glass, eyes staring, seeing herself through his eyes, kissing her own lips with a cold hard kiss that she imagined warm as Bernal's lips. She felt the surface of the mirror against her breast and the tiny grapes of her nipples hardened, generating a dull pain that flowed downward to an exact point between her legs. She sought that pain, again and again. She took a shirt and boots from Bernal's clothespress and put them on. She walked a few steps around the room, very careful not to make any noise. Still in his clothes, she burrowed through his drawers, combed her hair with his comb, sucked his toothbrush, licked his shaving cream, caressed his dirty clothes. Then, without knowing why, she took off her nightdress, his boots and shirt, and lay naked on Bernal's bed, greedily inhaling his scent, invoking his warmth to wrap herself in. She touched every inch of her body, beginning with the strange shape of her skull, the translucent cartilage of her ears, the sockets of her eyes, the opening of her mouth, and continued down her body, sketching all the bones, folds, angles, and curves of the insignificant whole of herself, wishing she were as immense and heavy as a whale. She imagined her body filling with a sweet, sticky liquid like honey, swelling, expanding to the size of a mammoth doll, until she overflowed the bed and the room, until her tumescence filled the entire house. Exhausted, she would doze for a few minutes, weeping.

Then one Saturday morning, watching from her window, Elena saw Bernal walk up to where her mother was bent over the trough scrubbing clothes. He laid his hand on her waist and she did not move, as if the weight of that hand were part of her body. Even from a distance, Elena could see his gesture of possession, her mother's attitude of surrender, their intimacy, the current that joined them in a formidable secret. Elena broke out in a sweat, she could not breathe, her heart was a frightened bird in her rib cage, her hands and feet tingled, her blood rushed until she thought it would burst her fingers. That was when she began to spy on her mother.

One after another, she discovered the clues she sought; at first it was only a glance, an overly long greeting, a complicitous smile, the suspicion that beneath the table their legs were touching and that they were inventing pretexts to be alone. Finally, one night as she was returning from Bernal's room after performing her lover's ritual, she heard a sound like the whisper of an underground stream coming from her mother's room, and she realized that all that time, every night while she believed Bernal was out singing for a living, the man had been just across the hall, and while she was kissing his memory in the mirror and breathing in the trace of his presence in the sheets, he had been with her mother. With the skill learned from many years of making herself invisible, she glided into the room and saw them locked in their pleasure. The fringed lampshade glowed with a warm light that exposed the lovers on the bed. Her mother was transformed into a round, rosy, moaning, opulent siren, an undulating sea anemone, all tentacles and suckers, all mouth and hands and legs and orifices, rolling and turning and cleaving to the large body of Bernal, who by contrast seemed rigid and clumsy, moving spasmodically like a piece of wood tossed by inexplicable high winds. Until that moment the girl had never seen a man naked, and she was taken back by the essential differences. His masculinity seemed brutal to her, and it was a long time before she could overcome the terror and force herself to look. Soon, however, she was conquered by fascination and watched with absolute attention to learn from her mother the formula she had used to snatch Bernal from her, a formula more powerful than all Elena's love, all her prayers, her dreams, her silent summons, all her magic ceremonies contrived to draw him to her. She was sure that her mother's caresses and sighs held the key to the secret, and if she could learn them, Juan José Bernal would sleep with her in the hammock hung every night from two large hooks in the room of the cupboards.

Elena spent the following days in a haze. She lost interest in everything around her, even Bernal himself, whom she stored in a spare compartment of her mind, and she submerged herself in a fanciful reality that completely replaced the world of the living. She continued to follow her routines by force of habit, but her heart was not in anything she did. When her mother noticed her lack of appetite, she attributed it to oncoming puberty – though Elena still looked too young – and she found time to sit alone with her and explain to her the joke of having been born a woman. Elena listened in sullen silence to the peroration about biblical curses and menstrual flow, convinced that none of that would ever happen to her.

On Wednesday Elena felt hungry for the first time in almost a week. She went into the pantry with a can opener and a spoon and devoured the contents of three cans of green peas, then peeled the red wax from a Dutch cheese and ate it as she would an apple. Immediately after, she ran to the patio, doubled over, and vomited a vile green soup over the geraniums. The pain in her belly and the bitter taste in her mouth restored her sense of reality. That night she slept tranquilly, rolled up in her hammock, sucking her thumb as she had in her cradle. Thursday morning she woke happy; she helped her mother prepare coffee for the boarders and ate breakfast with her in the kitchen. Once at school, however, she complained of terrible pains in her stomach, and she writhed so and asked so often to go to the bathroom that by midmorning her teacher gave her permission to go home.

Elena made a long detour, consciously avoiding familiar streets, and approached the house from the back wall, which overlooked a ravine. She managed to scale the wall and jump into the patio with less difficulty than she had expected. She had calculated that at that hour her mother would be in the market and, as it was the day for fresh fish, it would be a while before she returned. The house was empty except for Juan José Bernal and *señorita* Sofía, who had been home from work a week because of an attack of arthritis.

Elena hid her books and shoes under some bushes and slipped into the house. She climbed the stairway, hugging the wall and holding her breath, until she heard the radio thundering from the room of *señorita* Sofía and felt more calm. The door to Bernal's room opened with a push. It was dark inside, and for a moment, having just come from the brilliant daylight outside, she could see nothing. She knew the room from memory, however; she had measured that space many times and knew where each object was, the precise place the floor squeaked, how many steps it was from the door to the bed. She waited, nevertheless, until her eyes adjusted to the darkness and she could see the outlines of the furniture. A few moments more and she could see the man on the bed. He was not sleeping face down, as she had imagined so often, but lying on his back on top of the sheets, wearing only his undershorts; one arm was outflung and the other across his chest, and a lock of hair had fallen over his eyes. Instantly, all the fear and impatience that had accumulated for days disappeared, leaving Elena cleansed, with the calm of one who knows what she has to do. It seemed to her she had lived that moment many times; she told herself she had nothing to fear, this was a ceremony only slightly different from those that had gone before. Slowly, she stripped off her school uniform down to the cotton panties she dared not remove. She walked to the bed. She could see Bernal better now. Gingerly, she sat on the edge of the bed near his hand, concentrating on not adding even one wrinkle to the sheets. She leaned forward slowly, until her face was only a few centimeters from his and she could sense the warmth of his breath and the sweet scent of his body; then with infinite care she lay down beside him, extending each leg so cautiously he did not even stir. She waited, listening to the silence, until she resolved to rest her hand on his belly in an almost imperceptible caress. With that touch a suffocating wave flooded her body; she feared the sound of her heart was echoing through the house and would surely wake Bernal. It was several minutes before she recovered, and when she realized he had not moved, she relaxed, and let her arm fall limp – its weight, in any case, so slight it did not alter his sleep. Recalling her mother's movements, as her fingers crept beneath the elastic waist of his undershorts, Elena sought Bernal's lips and kissed him as she had so often kissed the mirror. Still asleep, Bernal moaned, he wrapped one arm around the girl's waist while his free hand took hers to guide her and his mouth opened to return her kiss, as he whispered his lover's name. Elena heard him name her mother, but rather than drawing back, she pressed even more closely to him. Bernal took her by the waist and pulled her atop him, settling her on his body as he began the first movements of love. Then, sensing the extreme fragility of that birdlike skeleton on his chest, a spark of awareness flashed through the cottony fog of sleep, and he opened his eyes. Elena felt his body tense, felt herself seized by the ribs and thrown aside so violently she fell to the floor, but she sprang to her feet and ran back to the bed to embrace him again. Bernal slapped her full in the face and leapt from the bed, terrorized by who knows what ancient prohibitions and nightmares.

"Wicked, *wicked* girl!" he screamed.

The door opened, and *señorita* Sofía was standing in the threshold.

Elena spent the next seven years with the nuns, three more attending college in the capital, and then began working in a bank. In the meantime, her mother married her lover and the two of them continued to run the boardinghouse until they had saved enough money to retire to a small house in the country, where they grew carnations and chrysanthemums to sell in the city. The Nightingale hung the poster proclaiming his artistry in a gilt frame, but he never sang in a nightclub again, and no one missed him. He never accompanied his wife when she visited his stepdaughter, and he never asked about her – not wanting to stir up doubts in his own mind – but he thought of her constantly. The child's image had stayed with him, intact, untouched by the years; she was still the passionate girl he had rejected. If truth were known, as the years went by, the memory of those light bones, that childish hand on his belly, that baby tongue in his mouth, grew to be an obsession. When he embraced the heavy body of his wife, he had to concentrate on those visions, meticulously invoking Elena's image to awaken the always more diffuse impulse of pleasure. Now in his middle years, he went to stores that sold children's clothing and bought cotton underpants and pleasured himself, stroking them and stroking himself. Then he would be ashamed of such salacious moments and he would burn the panties or bury them in a deep hole in the patio in a vain attempt to put them out of his mind. He began to loiter around schools and parks where he could stand at a distance and watch the prepubescent girls who for an all-too-brief moment bore him to the abyss of that unforgettable Thursday.

Elena was twenty-six when she visited her mother for the first time, bringing her boyfriend, an army captain who for years had been begging her to marry him. The two young people – he, not wanting to seem arrogant, in civilian clothes, she laden with presents – arrived on one of those cool November afternoons. Bernal had awaited that visit like a jittery teenager. He stared at himself in the mirror at every opportunity, scrutinizing his image, wondering whether Elena would see any change, or whether in her mind the Nightingale had remained immune to the ravages of time. He had prepared for the meeting, practicing every word and imagining every possible answer. The only possibility he failed to consider was that in the place of the smoldering child who had consigned him to a life of torment he would find an insipid and quite shy young woman. Bernal felt betrayed.

As it grew dark, after the euphoria of the arrival had worn off and mother and daughter had exchanged all their latest news, they carried chairs to the patio to enjoy the cool of evening. The air was heavy with the perfume of carnations. Bernal suggested a glass of wine, and Elena followed him into the house to bring glasses. For a few moments, they were alone, face to face in the narrow kitchen. Bernal, who had waited so long for this opportunity, held Elena by the arm while he told her how it had all been a terrible mistake, how he had been half asleep that morning and had no idea what he was doing, how he had never meant to throw her to the floor or call her what he did, and would she please take pity on him and forgive him, and maybe then he could come to his senses, because for what seemed a lifetime he had been consumed by a constant burning desire for her that fired his blood and poisoned his mind. She stared at him, speechless, not knowing what to answer. What wicked girl was he talking about? She had left her childhood far behind, and the pain of that first rejected love was locked in some sealed compartment of memory. She did not remember any particular Thursday in her past.

Translated by
Margaret Sayers Peden

JAMES BALDWIN

JUST ABOVE MY HEAD

"It is a terrible, an inexorable, law that one cannot deny the humanity of another without diminishing one's own," wrote James Baldwin in 1960. "In the face of one's victim, one sees oneself." Baldwin's entire work echoes this conviction, in a precise yet impassioned voice influenced, he said, by "the rhetoric of the storefront church." His fiction confronts both racism and homophobia, those circles of intolerance that sometimes contain one another, but ultimately his characters find redemption in the fulfilment of their own selves, in the assertion of their rights beyond their colour and their sex.

"Black slavery," wrote the American novelist Toni Morrison, "enriched the country's creative possibilities. For in that construction of blackness and *enslavement could be found not only the not-free but also, with the dramatic polarity created by skin colour, the projection of the not-me. The result was a playground for the imagination." It is in this playground that Baldwin reigns supreme.*

The following story, a blissful celebration of erotic love, is a self-contained chapter from one of Baldwin's finest novels, Just Above My Head.

IT WAS A HEAVY, slow Saturday afternoon in Atlanta, and they were free until Sunday morning. Webster had disappeared early, with many a vivid warning, and they were glad to be on their own; but his warnings remained with them, and the heat was as heavy as the region's molasses. They would have liked to discover the town, and they walked awhile, but they did not dare walk very far. If they got lost, they would have to ask someone for directions, and so they panicked whenever they saw more white faces than black faces. They had been made to know that they were from the North, and that their accents betrayed them and might land them on the chain gang. It happened every day down here, and, the Lord knew, Webster wouldn't be able to help them.

And the city was like a checkerboard. They would walk a block which was all black, then suddenly turn a corner and find themselves surrounded by nothing but white faces. They wanted to run, but, of course, to run meant that the white mob would run after them and they would, then, be lynched. At such moments, they smiled aimlessly, looked in a store window, if there was one, or else elaborately admired the view, slowing their walk to a shuffle. Then, as though the same idea had hit them at the same moment – which it had – they slowly turned and slowly walked back the way they had come. Sometimes they nearly exploded with the terrified laughter they had not dared release until they were again surrounded by black people, or back in the rooming house.

So this Saturday afternoon, they returned to the café, next to the rooming house. Webster had prepaid their Saturday lunch and dinner. They had a little money in their pockets – not very much, for they had not been paid yet. Webster had all their money. This frightened them, too, but they did not know what to do about it. They had to trust Webster. Wordlessly, though, they trusted Crunch, who was the only one of them who might be able to intimidate Webster.

They sat down in the café, which was nearly empty – they had not yet realized that Southerners move about as little as possible on hot summer afternoons: in general, that is, due to imponderables to which they were reacting but did not understand – and Peanut and Crunch went to the counter, and brought back four Pepsi-Colas.

"Tell you," said Red. "This trip is starting to fuck with my nerves. Can't wait to get back to Seventh Avenue."

"When you was there," said Arthur, smiling, "you couldn't wait to get away." He lit a cigarette and put the pack on the table. "But I know how you feel."

"We just ain't used to it," Peanut said. "And we don't know nobody. Be different, next time."

"How?" asked Red. "How we going to get to know somebody *next* time? You going to write a letter to the governor?"

Crunch laughed, and picked up the pack of cigarettes, and lit one.

"Well," said Peanut, "if we keep coming back, we *bound* to get to know – *somebody* –"

They all laughed, and, after a moment, Peanut laughed. Crunch said, "Well, *you* know somebody – at least, you *knew* somebody – them cousins of yours in Charlotte –"

Peanut sighed and looked down at the table. "Yeah. I'm sorry about that."

Crunch leaned across the table and clapped Peanut on the shoulder. "What *you* sorry about? *You* can't help it if your cousins are fools."

Peanut is the lightest of us, and Crunch is the darkest, and Peanut's cousins *proved* that they did not like dark meat. They hurt Crunch's feelings, and they reminded Peanut of his bewildering grandmother.

"Oh, little by little, we'll figure out how to move," Red said cheerfully. "I'll find me a swinging chick at one of these church socials and make her be our guide."

"These chicks all looking to get married, man," Crunch said. "And they don't want to marry none of us. What do a bank president's daughter want with – a wandering *troubador*?"

"Oh, hell, Crunch," said Peanut. "Love will find a way."

"Not down here, in the land of cotton," Arthur said, and they laughed.

"Anyway," Crunch said after a moment, "little Arthur's the only one liable to come down here next time."

They all looked at Crunch. "Why?" asked Arthur.

Crunch looked at Arthur. "Where's your brother?"

Arthur said, "My brother?" and stared at Crunch. His heart thundered like an express train, stopped.

"Oh, shit," said Red. "You right."

"Right about what?" Arthur asked. But he knew. He had never thought of it.

"Uncle Sam is saving some people over yonder," Crunch said. "He's making the world safe for democracy again, and he needs some niggers for the latrine detail."

The table became very silent.

"Shit," Red said again.

Arthur said nothing. He did not know what to say. He did not dare look up. He looked at the white marble table, and the brown rings made by the Pepsi-Cola bottles. Then he looked very carefully at the flypaper suspended from the ceiling, with flies sticking, stuck, on the yellow paper. He wondered how many flies there were, and thought of counting them. He was suddenly aware that there was an electric fan whirring nearby – if you put your fingers in the fan, the blades would chop your fingers off. He did not think of me at all – he was not thinking.

"Well, let's not sit here like this," Peanut said shakily. "Let's do something."

Yes, but what? A movie would have been ideal, but then, there was the question of whether black people sat in the balcony, or came in through the back door. None of them knew how it worked down here – they had forgotten to ask, or couldn't remember the answers.

"Hell," Red said, suddenly, "there's a black pool hall on the corner, let's go shoot some pool."

"Okay," Crunch said, and everybody rose except Arthur. They all looked at him.

"Ain't you coming?"

"Look," Arthur said calmly, with a smile, "you all go ahead.

I might pick you up later. I got a little headache, I just want to lie down."

Crunch raised that eyebrow at him. "You sure?"

"Yeah, I'm all right. You cats go on, I'll dig you later."

"OK."

The three of them pranced out into the sun, paused for a moment, laughing, before the great glass window. Arthur waited until they had disappeared. Then he rose slowly, leaning lightly on the table, and walked outside. The sun was like a blow. He looked in the direction the boys had taken – saw them, on the still, far corner, ambling across the street.

Then he turned in the opposite direction. The rooming house was next door, really more like a hotel, a narrow, three-storey building. Peanut and Red and Webster were on the ground floor. He and Crunch were on the top floor. He walked into the long, dark, narrow hall, which was absolutely silent, and slowly, shaking, climbed the stairs.

He was covered with cold sweat by the time he reached the top floor, and his hands were shaking so hard he could hardly get the key in the lock, but, at last, the door swung open. Sunlight hammered on the room, and he crossed to the window and pulled down the shade. He ran cold water in the sink, and plunged his face and head under, blindly found the towel, and dried himself. He kicked off his shoes, unpeeled his socks, took off his shirt and trousers, and lay down on Crunch's bed. *Korea.*

He lay there for a long time, numb, as empty as the listening silence, stunned. He lay on his back. The air did not move. He did not move. The sun would not move, the earth, the stars, the moon, the planets, whatever held it all together, the big wheel and the little wheel, and the boulder of his sorrow, which had dropped on him and pinned him to his bed, nothing would move, until he saw Crunch. *Korea.* He fell asleep.

Crunch shook him gently. The room was half dark, not dark yet. Crunch sat on the edge of the bed, looking at him carefully, with that eyebrow raised, half smiling, half frowning.

"You feel better?"

Arthur stared, saying nothing, then he smiled.

"You're back."

"Of course I'm back. You feel better?"

Arthur moved and put his head in Crunch's lap, holding on to him and staring up at him.

The room grew darker. They were alone. Crunch leaned down, and kissed him. Arthur held on to Crunch with all his strength, with all his tears, tears he had not yet begun to shed. Crunch leaned up.

"Let me lock the door," he whispered.

Arthur sat up, and watched Crunch lock the door.

He did it very elaborately, and then turned, grinning, with one finger to his lips.

"We all alone, now, little fellow. Ain't nobody on this floor but us. And it's Saturday night, anyway, *everybody's* out." He grinned, and then his face changed, he stood at the door, looking at Arthur.

"Where's Peanut and Red?"

Arthur was whispering, and Crunch whispered, "I left them in the pool hall. They found some friends."

"They coming back?"

"I told them I was taking you someplace."

He sat down on the bed again, and started taking off his shoes. He looked over at Arthur. "Did I do right?"

"Sure."

"Get under the covers."

Arthur watched as Crunch stripped – Crunch was whistling, low in his throat: and it came to Arthur, with great astonishment, that Crunch was whistling because he was happy – was happy to be here, with Arthur. Arthur watched as Crunch unbuttoned his shirt, watched the long, dark fingers against the buttons and the cloth, watched the cloth fly across the room to land on the other bed, watched as he unbuckled his belt, dropped his trousers, raising one knee then the other, sitting on the bed again to pull the trousers past the big feet, then folding the trousers, and rising to place them on the other bed, pulling off his undershirt, kicking off his shorts, his whole, long, black self padding to the small sink, where he looked, briefly, into the mirror, ran cold water, gargled, his dark body glowing in the darkening room, a miracle of spinal column, neck to buttocks, shoulders and shoulder blades, elbows, wrists, thighs, ankles, a miracle of bone and blood and muscle and flesh and music. Arthur was still wearing his undershirt and his shorts. He hated being naked in front of anyone, even me – perhaps, especially me; I had sometimes given him his bath: but that had been under another condition, for which he had not been responsible, and which he was not compelled to remember. Nakedness had not, then, been a confession, or a vow. Arthur was frightened; then, he wasn't frightened; but he found that he could not move. He could not take off his undershirt. He could not take off his shorts. Crunch turned, and Arthur, in a kind of peaceful terror, watched as the face, and the eyes in that face, and the neck and the chest, and the nipples on the chest, and the ribs and the long flat belly and the belly button and the jungle of hair spinning upward from the long, dark, heavy, swinging sex approached, and Crunch got under the covers, and took Arthur in his arms.

Crunch sighed, a weary, trusting sigh, and put his hands under Arthur's undershirt and pulled it over Arthur's head, and, suddenly, they both laughed, a whispering laugh. Crunch dropped the undershirt on the floor.

"That's called progress," Crunch whispered. "And now," he said, "let's see what we can do down yonder."

He put his hands at Arthur's waist, pulled the shorts down, got them past one foot. Arthur's prick rose.

Crunch stroked it, and grinned. "That's enough progress, for now," he said, but he put his rigid sex against Arthur's, and then they simply lay there, holding on to each other, unable to make another move. They really did not know where another move might carry them. Arthur was afraid in one way, and Crunch in another. It was also as though they had expended so much energy to arrive at this moment that they had to fall out and catch their breath, this moment was almost enough. But it was only a moment: the train was boarded, the engine ready to roll. They held on to each other. This might be the beginning; it might be the beginning of the end. The train was boarded, the engine pulsing, great doors were slamming shut behind them, the train would soon be moving, a journey had begun. They might lose each other on this journey; nothing could be hidden on this journey. They might look at each other, miles from now, when the train stopped at some unimaginable place, and wish never to see each other again. They might be ashamed – they might be debased: they might be for ever lost.

Arthur was less frightened than Crunch. He simply held on to Crunch and stroked him and kissed him, for in the centre of his mind's eye, there was Crunch in uniform, Crunch gone, Crunch forever gone, and, now that he had found him, his mind became as still and empty as the winter sky, at the thought of losing him. He held this blankness as far inside him as he held his tears – for, something told him that Crunch could not bear his tears, could not bear anybody's tears. Tears were a weapon you could use against Crunch.

And Crunch – ah, Crunch. He held my brother, falling in love – falling in love with the little fellow. Crunch was older than Arthur, lonelier than Arthur, knew more about himself than Arthur knew. He had never been on this train, true; but he had been landed in some desolate places. He held him closer, falling in love, his prick stiffening, his need rising, his hope rising; the train began to move, Arthur held him closer, and Crunch moved closer, becoming more naked, praying that Arthur would receive his nakedness.

His long self covered Arthur, his tongue licked Arthur's nipples, his armpits, his belly button. He did not dare go further, yet; shaking, he raised himself to Arthur's lips. He took Arthur's sex in his fist.

"Do me like I do you," he whispered. "Little fellow, come on, this is just the beginning," and Arthur, with a kind of miraculous understanding, kissed Crunch's nipples, slid down to kiss his sex, moved up to his lips again. As he felt Crunch pulsing, he pulsed with Crunch, coaxed the pulsing vein at the underside of the organ as Crunch coaxed his, scarcely breathing. Crunch groaned, *little fellow,* groaned again, they seemed to hang for a second in a splintered, blinding air, then Crunch's sperm shot out against Arthur's belly, Arthur's shot against his, it was as though each were coming through the other's sex.

They lay in each other's arms.

Crunch looked into his Arthur's eyes.

"Hi."

"Hi, yourself."

Their breathing slowed. Neither wanted to move.

"You think we making progress?"

"I'm with you."

They laughed, holding on to each other, wet with each other.

Crunch asked shyly, "Do you still love me?"

"Maybe we should make some more progress."

Crunch shook with laughter, silently, and Arthur shook with joy, watching him. "Right now?"

"Whenever you ready."

"Oh – come on – !" said Crunch.

"That's what I said."

"You – you something –"

"I love you. I'd do anything for you," said Arthur.

Crunch watched him. "For true?"

"For true."

Crunch held him tighter.

"I want to make love with you – every way possible – I don't care what happens – as long as I can hold you." He watched Arthur's eyes; but he was beginning to feel at peace.

"You want to make progress, *I'll* make progress. We'll make progress together."

Crunch asked, “You and me, then?”

“You and me.”

The room was dark. They heard the night outside. They did not want to leave each other’s arms.

Crunch asked, “You hungry?”

“No – not now.”

“You want to wash up?”

“No. Not yet.”

“What you want to do then?”

“Maybe sleep a little – next to you.”

“OK.”

They curled into each other, spoon fashion, Arthur cradled by Crunch.

They did not sleep long. Arthur woke up, and peed in the sink, as quietly as possible. He ran the water as quietly as possible. He lifted the shade, and looked out of the window. It was night, he guessed it to be around nine or ten o’clock; there were not as many people in the street as there would have been on a Saturday night in Harlem. Most of the people were already inside some place, or they were on their way, and their voices, and their music, muffled, filled the air, filled the room. He dropped the shade.

Crunch lay as he had left him. One arm was at his side, one arm lay stretched where Arthur had been. His breathing was deep and slow – yet Arthur sensed that Crunch was not entirely lost in sleep. Arthur crawled back into bed, pulling the covers back up. The moment he crawled into bed, Crunch, still sleeping, pulled Arthur into his arms.

And yet, Crunch lay as one helpless. Arthur was incited by this helplessness, the willing helplessness of the body in his arms. He kissed Crunch, who moaned, but did not stir. He ran his hands up and down the long body. He seemed to discover the mystery of geography, of space and time, the lightning flash of tension between one – moment? – one breath and the next breath. The breathing in – the breathing out. The miracle of air, entering, and the chest rose: the miracle of air transformed into the miracle of breath, coming out, into your face, mixed with Pepsi-Cola, hamburgers, mustard, whatever was in the bowels: and the chest fell. He lay in this urgency for a while, terrified, and happy.

He held Crunch closer, running his fingers up and down the barely tactile complex telegraph system of the spine. His hands dared to discover Crunch's beautiful buttocks, his ass, his behind. He stroked the gift between his legs which held the present and the future. Their sex became rigid. Crunch growled, turned on his back, still holding Arthur.

Arthur moved, in Crunch's arms, belly to belly. Pepsi-Cola, mustard, and onions and hamburgers and Crunch's rising prick: Crunch moaned. Arthur knew something that he did not know he knew – he did not know that he knew that Crunch waited for Arthur's lips at his neck, Arthur's tongue at the nipples of his chest. Pepsi-Cola, mustard, hamburgers, ice cream, surrendered to funkier, unknown odours; Crunch moaned again, surrendering, surrendering, as Arthur's tongue descended Crunch's long black self, down to the raging penis. He licked the underside of the penis, feeling it leap, and he licked the balls. He was setting Crunch free – he was giving Crunch what he, somehow, knew that Crunch longed and feared to give him. He took the penis into his mouth, it moved, with the ease of satin, past his lips, into his throat. For a moment, he was terrified: what now? For the organ was hard and huge and throbbing, Crunch's hands came down, but lightly, on Arthur's head, he began to thrust upward, but carefully, into Arthur's mouth.

Arthur understood Crunch's terror – the terror of someone in the water, being carried away from the shore – and this terror, which was his own terror, soon caused him to gasp, to attempt to pull away, at the same time that he held on. His awareness of Crunch's terror helped him to overcome his own. He had never done this before. In the same way that he knew how Crunch feared to be despised – by him – he knew, too, that he, now, feared to be despised by Crunch. *Cocksucker.*

Well. It was Crunch's cock, and so he sucked it; with all the love that was in him, and a moment came when he felt that love being trusted, and returned. A moment came when he felt Crunch pass from a kind of terrified bewilderment into joy. A friendly, a joyful movement, began. *So high, you can't get over him.*

Sweat from Arthur's forehead fell onto Crunch's belly.

So low – and Crunch gasped as Arthur's mouth left his prick standing in the cold, cold air, as Arthur's tongue licked his sacred balls – *you can't get under him.* Arthur rose, again, to Crunch's lips. *So wide. You can't get around him.* It was as though, with this kiss, they were forever bound together. Crunch moaned, in an absolute agony, and Arthur went down again.

"Little fellow. Baby. Love."

You must come in at the door.

He held the prick in his mouth again, sensing, awaiting, the eruption. He, and he alone, had dragged it up from the depths of his lover.

"Oh. Little fellow."

Then, shaking like an earthquake, "Oh, my love. Oh, love."

Atlanta was still. The world was still. Nothing moved in the heavens.

"Oh. Love."

Curious, the taste, as it came, leaping, to the surface: of Crunch's prick, of Arthur's tongue, into Arthur's mouth and throat. He was frightened, but triumphant. He wanted to sing. The taste was volcanic. This taste, the aftertaste, this anguish, and this boy had changed all tastes for ever. The bottom of his throat was sore, his lips were weary. Every time he swallowed, from here on, he would think of Crunch, and this thought made him smile as, slowly, now, and in a peculiar joy and panic, he allowed Crunch to pull him up, upward, into his arms.

He dared to look into Crunch's eyes. Crunch's eyes were wet and deep *deep like a river,* and Arthur found that he was smiling *peace like a river.*

Arthur asked Crunch, "All right? do you feel all right?"

Crunch put Arthur's head on his chest, ran one long hand up and down Arthur.

"You're the most beautiful thing ever happened to me, baby," he said. "That's how I feel." Then, "Thank you, Arthur."

"For what?" Arthur asked – teasing, bewildered, triumphant – and safe in Crunch's arms.

"For loving me," Crunch said.

After a moment, he pulled up the covers. They went to sleep, spoon fashion, Arthur cradling Crunch.

HONORÉ DE BALZAC

A PASSION IN THE DESERT

"My soul flies to you with these pages," wrote Honoré de Balzac in a letter to his mistress, the Countess Hanska, on October 31, 1843. "I say to them a thousand things, as if I were a madman; and as if I were a madman I think that they go and repeat these things to you; it is impossible for me to understand how these pages impregnated by me will be, in eleven days, in your hands, and why I remain here ..." In hundreds of letters and in the vast cycle of novels we know as The Human Comedy, *Balzac poured out his seemingly endless passions. He described love in countless forms – between men and women, between parents and children, between courtesans and their clients, between men, between women – often borrowing the imagery of politics and economics. "Thrifty love is never true love." "A great love is open to a voracious credit line, and bankruptcy always follows." "Marriage is a political act."*

Balzac's more than 2,000 characters all pursue some form of desire: as if to complete the erotic catalogue, his story

"A Passion in the Desert" depicts not the relationship between two human beings but between a man and what society has chosen to call "a wild beast."

DURING the expedition undertaken in Upper Egypt by General Desaix, a Provençal soldier, who had fallen into the hands of the Maugrabins, was taken by these Arabs into the desert beyond the cataracts of the Nile. In order to put between them and the French army a distance to assure their safety, the Maugrabins made a forced march, and did not halt till night. They then camped by the side of a well, surrounded by a clump of palm trees, where they had before buried some provisions. Never dreaming that their prisoner would think of flight, they merely bound his hands, and all of them, after eating a few dates, and giving barley to their horses, went to sleep. When the Provençal saw his enemies incapable of watching him, he picked up a scimitar with his teeth, and then with the blade fixed between his knees, cut the cords that lashed his wrists, and found himself at liberty. He at once seized a carbine and a dagger; provided himself with some dry dates and a small bag of barley, powder and balls; girded on the scimitar, sprang on a horse, and pressed forward in the direction where he fancied the French army must be found. Impatient to regain the bivouac, he so urged the weary horse, that the poor beast fell dead, its sides torn with the spurs, leaving the Frenchman alone in the midst of the desert.

After wandering for some time amidst the sand with the desperate courage of an escaping convict, the soldier was forced to stop. Night was closing in. Despite the beauty of the Eastern night he had not strength sufficient to go on. Fortunately he had reached a height on the top of which were palm trees, whose leaves, for some time visible far off, had awakened in his heart a hope of safety. He was so weary that he lay down on a granite stone, oddly shaped like a camp bed, and went to sleep, without taking the precaution to protect himself in his slumber. He had sacrificed his life, and his last thought was a regret for having left the Maugrabins, whose wandering life began to please him, now that he was far from them and from all hope of succour.

He was awakened by the sun, whose pitiless rays falling vertically upon the granite made it intolerably hot. For the Provençal had been so careless as to cast himself upon the ground in the direction opposite to that on which the green majestic palm-tops threw their shadow. He looked at these solitary trees and shuddered! They reminded him of the graceful shafts surmounted by long foils that distinguish the Saracenic columns of the Cathedral of Arles. He counted the few palms; and then looked about him. A terrible despair seized upon his soul. He saw a boundless ocean. The melancholy sands spread round him, glittering like a blade of steel in a bright light, as far as the eye could see. He knew not whether he was gazing on an ocean, or a chain of lakes as lustrous as a mirror. A fiery mist shimmered, in little ripples, above the tremulous landscape. The sky possessed an Oriental blaze, the brilliancy which brings despair, seeing that it leaves the imagination nothing to desire. Heaven and earth alike were all aflame. The silence was terrible in its wild and awful majesty. Infinity, immensity, oppressed the soul on all sides; not a cloud was in the sky, not a breath was in the air, not a movement on the bosom of the sand, which undulated into tiny waves. Far away, the horizon was marked off, as on a summer day at sea, by a line of light as bright and narrow as a sabre's edge.

The Provençal clasped his arms about a palm tree as if it had been the body of a friend; then, sheltered by the straight and meagre shadow, he sat down weeping on the granite, and looking with deep dread upon the lonely scene spread out before his eyes. He cried aloud as if to tempt the solitude. His voice, lost in the hollows of the height, gave forth far-off a feeble sound that woke no echo.

The Provençal was twenty-two years old. He loaded his carbine.

"Time enough for that!" he muttered to himself, placing the weapon of deliverance on the ground.

Looking by turns at the melancholy waste of sand and at the blue expanse of sky, the soldier dreamed of France. With delight he fancied that he smelt the Paris gutters, and recalled the towns through which he had passed, the faces of his comrades, and the slightest incidents of his life. Then, his Southern imagination made him fancy, in the play of heat quivering above the plain, the pebbles of his own dear Provence. But fearing all the dangers of this cruel mirage, he went down in the direction opposite to that which he had taken when he had climbed the hill the night before. Great was his joy on discovering a kind of grotto, naturally cut out of the enormous fragments of granite that formed the bottom of the hill. The remnants of a mat showed that this retreat had once been inhabited. Then, a few steps further, he saw palm trees with a load of dates. Again the instinct which attaches man to life awoke within his heart. He now hoped to live until the passing of some Maugrabin; or perhaps he would soon hear the boom of cannon, for at that time Buonaparte was overrunning Egypt. Revived by this reflection, the Frenchman cut down a few bunches of ripe fruit, beneath whose weight the date trees seemed to bend, and felt sure, on tasting this unhoped-for manna, that the inhabitant of this grotto had cultivated the palm trees. The fresh and luscious substance of the date bore witness to his predecessor's care.

The Provençal passed suddenly from dark despair to well-nigh insane delight. He climbed the hill again; and spent the remainder of the day in cutting down a barren palm tree, which the night before had served him for shelter.

A vague remembrance made him think of the wild desert beasts; and, foreseeing that they might come to seek the spring which bubbled through the sand among the rocks, he resolved to secure himself against their visits by placing a barrier at the door of his hermitage. In spite of his exertions, in spite of the strength with which the fear of being eaten during sleep endued him, it was impossible for him to cut the palm to pieces in one day; but he contrived to bring it down. When, towards evening, the monarch of the desert fell, the thunder of its crash resounded far, as if the mighty Solitude had given forth a moan. The soldier shuddered as if he had heard a voice that prophesied misfortune. But like an heir who does not long bewail the death of a relation, he stripped the tree of the broad, long, green leaves, and used them to repair the mat on which he was about to lie. At length, wearied by the heat and by his labours, he fell asleep beneath the red roof of his murky grotto.

In the middle of the night he was disturbed by a strange noise. He sat up; in the profound silence he could hear a creature breathing – a savage respiration which resembled nothing human. Terror, intensified by darkness, silence, and the fancies of one suddenly awakened, froze his blood. He felt the sharp contraction of his scalp, when, as the pupils of his eyes dilated, he saw in the shadow two faint and yellow lights. At first he thought these lights were some reflection of his eyeballs, but soon, the clear brightness of the night helping him to distinguish objects in the grotto, he saw lying at two paces from him an enormous beast.

Was it a lion? – a tiger? The Provençal was not sufficiently educated to know the species of his enemy, but his terror was all the greater; since his ignorance assisted his imagination. He bore the cruel torture of listening, of marking the caprices of this awful breathing, without losing a sound of it, or venturing to make the slightest movement. A smell as pungent as a fox's, but more penetrating, filled the grotto; and when it entered his nostrils his terror passed all bounds; he could no longer doubt the presence of the terrible companion whose royal den was serving him for bivouac. Presently the moon, now sinking, lighted up the den, and in the moon-rays gradually shone out a panther's spotted skin.

The lion of Egypt was sleeping, curled up like a great dog who is the peaceable possessor of a sumptuous kennel at a mansion door; its eyes, which had been opened for one moment, were now closed again. Its face was turned towards the Frenchman.

A thousand troubled thoughts passed through the mind of the panther's prisoner. At first he thought of shooting it; but there was not enough room between them to adjust his gun; the barrel would have reached beyond the animal. And what if he awoke it! This supposition made him motionless. Listening in the silence to the beating of his heart, he cursed the loud pulsations, fearing to disturb the sleep that gave him time to seek some means of safety. Twice he placed his hand upon his scimitar, with the intention of cutting off the head of his enemy; but the difficulty of cutting through the short, strong fur compelled him to abandon the idea. To fail was certain death. He preferred the odds of conflict, and determined to await the daybreak. And daylight was not long in coming. The Frenchman was able to examine the panther. Its muzzle was stained with blood.

"It has eaten plenty," he reflected, without conjecturing that the feast might have been composed of human flesh; "it will not be hungry when it wakes."

It was a female. The fur upon her breast and thighs shone with whiteness. A number of little spots like velvet looked like charming bracelets around her paws. The muscular tail was also white, but tipped with black rings. The upper part of her coat, yellow as old gold, but very soft and smooth, bore those characteristic marks, shaded into the form of roses, which serve to distinguish the panther from the other species of the genus *Felis.* This fearful visitor was snoring tranquilly in an attitude as graceful as that of a kitten lying on the cushions of an ottoman. Her sinewy, blood-stained paws, with powerful claws, were spread beyond her head, which rested on them, and from which stood out the thin, straight whiskers with a gleam like silver wires.

If she had been imprisoned in a cage, the Provençal would assuredly have admired the creature's sensual grace, and the vivid contrasts of colour that gave her garment an imperial lustre; but at this moment he felt his sight grow dim at her sinister aspect. The presence of the panther, even sleeping, made him experience the effect which the magnetic eyes of the serpent are said to exercise upon the nightingale.

In the presence of this danger the courage of the soldier faltered, although without doubt it would have risen at the cannon's mouth. A desperate thought, however, filled his mind, and dried up at its source the chilly moisture which was rolling down his forehead. Acting as men do who, driven to extremities, at last defy their fate, and nerve themselves to meet their doom, he saw a tragedy in this adventure, and resolved to play his part in it with honour to the last.

"Two days ago," he argued with himself, "the Arabs might have killed me."

Considering himself as good as dead, he waited bravely, yet with restless curiosity, for the awakening of his enemy.

When the sun shone out, the panther opened her eyes suddenly; then she spread out her paws forcibly, as if to stretch them and get rid of cramp. Then she yawned, showing an alarming set of teeth and an indented, rasp-like tongue. "She is like a dainty lady!" thought the Frenchman, as he saw her rolling over with a gentle and coquettish movement. She licked off the blood that stained her paws and mouth, and rubbed her head with movements full of charm. "That's it! Just make yourself pretty!" the Frenchman said, his gaiety returning with his courage. "Then we must say good-morning." And he took up the short dagger of which he had relieved the Maugrabins.

At this moment the panther turned her head towards the Frenchman, and looked at him fixedly, without advancing. The rigidity of those metallic eyes, and their unbearable brightness, made the Provençal shudder. The beast began to move towards him. He looked at her caressingly, and fixing her eyes as if to magnetise her, he let her come close up to him; then, with a soft and gentle gesture, he passed his hand along her body, from head to tail, scratching with his nails the flexible vertebrae that divide a panther's yellow back. The beast put up her tail with pleasure; her eyes grew softer; and when for the third time the Frenchman accomplished this self-interested piece of flattery, she broke into a purring like a cat. But this purr proceeded from a throat so deep and powerful that it re-echoed through the grotto like the peals of a cathedral organ. The Provençal, realising the success of his caresses, redoubled them, until the imperious beauty was completely soothed and lulled.

When he felt sure that he had perfectly subdued the ferocity of his capricious companion, whose hunger had been satisfied so cruelly the night before, he got up to leave the grotto. The panther let him go; but when he had climbed the hill, she came bounding after him with the lightness of a sparrow hopping from branch to branch, and rubbed herself against the soldier's leg, arching her back after the fashion of a cat. Then looking at her guest with eyes whose brightness had grown less inflexible, she uttered that savage cry which naturalists have compared to the sound of a saw.

"What a beauty!" cried the Frenchman, smiling. He set himself to play with her ears, to caress her body, and to scratch her head hard with his nails. Then, growing bolder with success, he tickled her skull with the point of his dagger, watching for the spot to strike her. But the hardness of the bones made him afraid of failing.

The sultana of the desert approved the action of her slave by raising her head, stretching her neck, and showing her delight by the quietness of her attitude. The Frenchman suddenly reflected that in order to assassinate this fierce princess with one blow he need only stab her in the neck. He had just raised his knife for the attempt, when the panther, with a graceful action, threw herself upon the ground before his feet, casting him from time to time a look in which, in spite of its ferocity of nature, there was a gleam of tenderness.

The poor Provençal, with his back against a palm tree, ate his dates, while he cast inquiring glances, now towards the desert for deliverers, now upon his terrible companion, to keep an eye upon her dubious clemency. Every time he threw away a date-stone, the panther fixed her eyes upon the spot with inconceivable mistrust. She scrutinised the Frenchman with a business-like attention; but the examination seemed favourable, for when he finished his poor meal, she licked his boots, and with her rough, strong tongue removed the dust incrusted in their creases.

"But when she becomes hungry?" thought the Provençal.

Despite the shudder this idea caused him, the soldier began examining with curiosity the proportions of the panther, certainly one of the most beautiful specimens of her kind. She was three feet high and four feet long, without the tail. This powerful weapon, as round as a club, was nearly three feet long. The head – large as that of a lioness – was distinguished by an expression of rare delicacy; true, the cold cruelty of the tiger dominated, but there was also a resemblance to the features of a wily woman. In a word, the countenance of the solitary queen wore at this moment an expression of fierce gaiety, like that of Nero flushed with wine; she had quenched her thirst in blood, and now desired to play.

The soldier tried to come and go, and the panther let him, content to follow him with her eyes, but less after the manner of a faithful dog than of a great Angora cat, suspicious even of the movements of its master. When he turned round he saw beside the fountain the carcase of his horse; the panther had dragged the body all that distance. About two-thirds had been devoured. This sight reassured the Frenchman. He was thus easily able to explain the absence of the panther, and the respect which she had shown for him while he was sleeping.

This first piece of luck emboldened him about the future. He conceived the mad idea of setting up a pleasant household life, together with the panther, neglecting no means of pacifying her and of conciliating her good graces. He returned to her, and saw, to his delight, that she moved her tail with an almost imperceptible motion. Then he sat down beside her without fear, and began to play with her; he grasped her paws, her muzzle, pulled her ears, threw her over on her back, and vigorously scratched her warm and silky sides. She let him have his way, and when the soldier tried to smooth the fur upon her paws she carefully drew in her claws, which had the curve of a Damascus blade. The Frenchman, who kept one hand upon his dagger, was still thinking of plunging it into the body of the too-confiding panther; but he feared lest she should strangle him in her last convulsions. And besides, within his heart there was a movement of remorse that warned him to respect an inoffensive creature. It seemed to him that he had found a friend in this vast desert. Involuntarily he called to mind a woman whom he once had loved, whom he sarcastically had nicknamed "Mignonne," from her jealousy, which was so fierce that during the whole time of their acquaintance he went in fear that she would stab him. This memory of his youth suggested the idea of calling the young panther by this name, whose lithe agility and grace he now admired with less terror.

Towards evening he had become so far accustomed to his perilous position, that he almost liked the hazard of it. At last his companion had got into the habit of looking at him when he called in a falsetto voice "Mignonne."

At sun-down Mignonne uttered several times a deep and melancholy cry.

"She has been properly brought up," thought the light-hearted soldier; "she says her prayers!" But it was, no doubt, her peaceful attitude which brought the jest into his mind.

"All right, my little pet; I will let you get to sleep first," he said, relying on his legs to get away as soon as she was sleeping and to seek some other shelter for the night.

The soldier waited with patience for the hour of flight, and when it came, set out full speed in the direction of the Nile. But he had only gone a quarter of a league across the sand when he heard the panther bounding after him, uttering at intervals that saw-like cry, more terrible even than the thudding of her leaps.

"Well!" he said to himself, "she must have taken a fancy to

me. Perhaps she has never yet met anyone. It is flattering to be her first love!" At this moment the Frenchman fell into a shifting quicksand, so dangerous to the traveller in the desert, escape from which is hopeless. He felt that he was sinking; he gave a cry of terror. The panther seized him by the collar with her teeth, and springing backwards with stupendous vigour drew him from the gulf as if by magic.

"Ah! Mignonne!" cried the soldier, enthusiastically caressing her, "we are friends now for life and death. But no tricks, eh?" and he retraced his steps.

Henceforth the desert was as though it had been peopled. It contained a being with whom he could converse, and whose ferocity had been softened for him, without his being able to explain so strange a love affair.

However great was his desire to keep awake and on his guard, he feel asleep. On awakening, Mignonne was no longer to be seen. He climbed the hill, and then perceived her afar off, coming along by leaps and bounds, according to the nature of these creatures, the extreme flexibility of whose vertebrae prevents their running.

Mignonne came up, her jaws besmeared with blood. She received the caresses of her companion with deep purrs of satisfaction. Her eyes, now full of softness, were turned, with even greater tenderness than the night before, to the Provençal, who spoke to her as to a pet.

"Ah! Beauty! you are a respectable young woman, are you not? You like petting, don't you? Are you not ashamed of yourself? You have been eating a Maugrabin! Well! they're animals, as you are. But don't you go and gobble up a Frenchman. If you do, I shall not love you!"

She played as a young pup plays with its master, letting him roll her over, beat and pet her; and sometimes she would coax him to caress her with a movement of entreaty.

A few days passed thus. This companionship revealed to the Provençal the sublime beauties of the desert. From the moment when he found within it hours of fear and yet of calm, a sufficiency of food, and a living creature who absorbed his thoughts, his soul was stirred by new emotions. It was a life of contrasts. Solitude revealed to him her secrets, and involved him in her charm. He discovered in the rising and the setting of the sun a splendour hidden from the world of men. His frame quivered when he heard above his head the soft whirr of a bird's wings – rare wayfarer; or when he saw the clouds – those changeful, many-coloured voyagers – mingle in the depth of heaven. In the dead of night he studied the effects of the moon upon the sea of sand, which the simoon drove in ever-changing undulations. He lived with the Oriental day; he marvelled at its pomp and glory; and often, after having watched the grandeur of a tempest in the plain, in which the sands were whirled in dry red mists of deadly vapour, he beheld with ecstasy the coming on of night, for then there fell upon him the benignant coolness of the stars. He heard imaginary music in the sky. Solitude taught him all the bliss of reverie. He spent whole hours in calling trifles to remembrance, in comparing his past life with his strange present. To his panther he grew passionately attached, for he required an object of affection. Whether by a strong effort of his will he had really changed the character of his companion, or whether, thanks to the constant warfare of the deserts, she found sufficient food, she showed no disposition to attack him, and at last, in her perfect tameness, he no longer felt the slightest fear.

He spent a great part of his time in sleeping, but ever, like a spider in its web, with mind alert, that he might not let deliverance escape him, should any chance to pass within the sphere described by the horizon. He had sacrificed his shirt to make a flag, which he had hoisted to the summit of a palm tree stripped of leaves. Taught by necessity, he had found the means to keep it spread by stretching it with sticks, lest the wind should fail to wave it at the moment when the hoped-for traveller might be travelling the waste of sand.

It was during the long hours when hope abandoned him that he amused himself with his companion. He had learnt to understand the different inflexions of her voice, and the expression of her glances; he had studied the varying changes of the spots that starred her robe of gold. Mignonne no longer growled, even when he seized her by the tuft with which her terrible tail ended, to count the black and white rings which adorned it, and which glittered in the sun like precious gems. It delighted him to watch the delicate soft lines of her snowy breast and graceful head. But above all when she was gambolling in her play he watched her with delight, for the agility, the youthfulness of all her movements filled him with an ever-fresh surprise. He admired her suppleness in leaping, climbing, gliding, pressing close against him, swaying, rolling over, crouching for a bound. But however swift her spring, however slippery the block of granite, she would stop short, without motion, at the sound of the word "Mignonne!"

One day, in the most dazzling sunshine, an enormous bird was hovering in the air. The Provençal left his panther to examine this new visitor; but after waiting for a moment the deserted sultana uttered a hoarse growl.

"Blessed if I don't believe that she is jealous!" he exclaimed, perceiving that her eyes were once more hard and rigid. "A woman's soul has passed into her body, that is certain!"

The eagle disappeared in air, while he admired afresh the rounded back and graceful outlines of the panther. She was as pretty as a woman. The blonde fur blended in its delicate gradations into the dull white colour of the thighs. The brilliant sunshine made this vivid gold, with spots of brown, take on a lustre indescribable. The Provençal and the panther looked at one another understandingly; the beauty of the desert quivered when she felt the nails of her admirer on her skull. Her eyes gave forth a flash like lightning, and then she closed them hard.

"She *has* a soul," he cried, as he beheld the desert queen in her repose, golden as the sands, white as their blinding lustre, and, like them, fiery and alone.

The end of the story is difficult to tell. It ended as all great passions end – through a misunderstanding. Each thought the other guilty of a falsity, each was too proud to give an explanation, and obstinacy brought about a rupture.

Somehow, one day while they were playing together, the Provençal must have hurt her, and she turned on him as if mad and with her sharp teeth seized his thigh. The action was not savage, but fancying that she meant to kill him, he plunged his dagger in her throat. She rolled over with a heart-rending cry, and stared at him in her last struggles, without anger. Later, he said that he would have given everything on earth, even his cross – which he had not then won – to bring her back to life. It was, he said, as if he had slain another human being.

And when the soldiers who had seen his flag hastened to his rescue, they found the Provençal kneeling by the panther's body, his face bathed in tears.

Translator anonymous

GEORGES BATAILLE

THE DEAD MAN

When the Argentinian writer Julio Cortázar first read Georges Bataille in the mid-fifties, he believed he had discovered the true inheritor of the Marquis de Sade, a writer capable of sounding the foulest recesses of the soul. A few years later he was introduced to a slim, elegantly dressed, elderly gentleman who looked, Cortázar said, "like a cross between a haberdasher and a head waiter at Maxim's," and he had enormous difficulty in reconciling this innocent-looking figure with the author of such sexual nightmares as Story of the Eye *and* Madame Edwarda. *"It is literature that is not innocent," Bataille explained. "It is guilty and should admit itself so."*

"I belong to a turbulent generation," Bataille wrote of himself, "born to literary life in the tumult of surrealism." Philosopher, novelist and brilliant critic, converted to Catholicism in his adolescence, the first French writer to undergo Freudian psychoanalysis, in 1927, Bataille brought to the reader's attention the erotic significance of everyday

acts and invented monstrous fables, such as "The Dead Man," to advocate what he called "the practise of joy in the face of death."

Marie Remains Alone with the Dead Edward

WHEN EDWARD fell back dead, a void opened in her, a long shudder ran down her, which lifted her up like an angel. Her naked breasts stood up in an imaginary church where the feeling of the irretrievable emptied her. Standing, near the dead man, absent, outside herself, in a slow ecstasy, overwhelmed. Edward, as he died, had begged her to strip herself naked.

She hadn't had the time to do it! She was there, in disarray: only her breasts jutted out of the ripped dress.

Marie Goes Out of the House Naked

The time had come to deny the laws to which fear subjects us. She pulled off her dress and put her coat on her arm. She was crazy and naked. She rushed outside and ran into the night in the downpour. Her shoes smacked in the mud and the rain eddied down her. She had to go very badly, but she held it in. In the softness of the woods, Marie stretched out on the ground. She pissed for a long time, urine covered her legs. On the ground she sang in a crazy impossible voice:

> ... there is some nudity
> and some atrocity ...

Then she got up, put her raincoat back on and ran through Quilly up to the door of the inn.

Marie Waits in Front of the Inn

Dazed, she remained in front of the door, lacking the courage to go in. She heard, coming from inside, screams, the songs of whores and drunks. She felt herself trembling, but she took pleasure in this trembling.

She thought, "I'll go in, they'll see me naked." She had to lean against the wall. She opened her coat and put her long fingers in her slit. She listened, fixed with anxiety, she breathed in the smell of her ill-washed sex. In the inn, they were screeching away, then everything went silent. It was raining: in a cellarlike darkness, a warmish wind slanted the rain. The voice of a whore sang a sad song about the working class districts on the edge of town. Heard outside, in the night, the dark voice veiled by the walls was excruciating. It went silent. Applause and the stamping of feet followed, then clapping in rhythm.

Marie was sobbing in the darkness. She cried in her helplessness, the back of her hand against her teeth.

Marie Goes into the Inn

Knowing that she would be going in, Marie trembled. She opened the door, took three steps into the room: a gust of wind closed the door behind her. The farmboys, the woman who kept the bar, and the whores all stared at her. She stood motionless at the entrance; muddy, hair streaming with water, and just generally looking bad. She looked as if she had floated up on the squall of the night (they could hear the wind outside). Her coat covered her, but she pulled back the collar.

Marie Drinks with the Farmboys

She asked in a quiet voice:

– Got anything to drink?

The barkeeper answered from behind the bar:

– Calva?

She poured a shot at the bar.

Marie wouldn't take it.

– I want a bottle and some glasses she said.

Her quiet voice was firm. She added:

– I'm drinking with them.

She paid.

One of the farmboys with dirt on his boots said timidly:

– You just dropped in for some entertainment?

– That's right, said Marie.

She tried to smile: the smile bored right through her.

She took a seat by the boy, rubbed her leg up against his,

took his hand and placed it between her thighs.

When the boy touched the slit, he moaned:

– In the Name of God!

Excited, the others kept quiet.

One of the girls, getting up, lifted up one of her coattails.

– Take a look at this, she said, she's naked as the day she was born.

Marie let her go on and emptied a glass of liquor.

– She's used to milk, said the woman behind the bar.

Marie belched bitterly.

Marie Pulls out the Dick of a Drunkard

Marie said sadly:

– That's a fact.

Her wet black curls stuck to her face in ringlets. She shook her pretty head, got up, took off her coat.

A lout who had been drinking in the inn moved toward her. He staggered, beating the air with his arms. He screeched out:

– All naked ladies up for grabs!

The woman behind the bar warned him:

– I'll twist your ugly beak …

She grabbed his nose and twisted it.

He screeched.

– No, try there, said Marie, it works better.

She walked up to the drunk and unbuttoned his fly: she pulled out of his trousers his half-limp dick.

The dick raised a great burst of laughter.

In one gulp, Marie, bold as a beast, sucked down a second glass.

The barkeeper, eyes like searchlights, gently touched her behind near the cleft.

– Good enough to eat, she said.

Marie filled her glass again. The liquor gurgled out.

She slugged it down like she was dying. The glass fell from her hands. Her behind was flat and nicely cleft. Her softness lit up the room.

Marie Dances with Pierrot

One of the farmboys was standing over in the corner with a hateful look on his face.

He was just a little too good-looking a man, in high crepe rubber boots, that were just a little too new.

Marie came up to him with the bottle in her hand. She was feeling good and she was excited. Her legs swayed in her floating stockings. The boy took the bottle and took a slug. He screamed out in a fierce, unthinkable voice:

– Enough!

Slamming the empty bottle straight down on the table.

Marie asked him:

– Want another?

He answered with a smile: he was treating her like a conquest.

He started up the player piano. He pretended, when it began to play, to dance a little dance with his arms curved out in front of him.

He took Marie by the hand, they danced an obscene java.

Marie gave herself up to it completely, nauseated, her head thrown back.

Marie Falls Down Dead Drunk

The barkeeper all of a sudden jumped up screaming:

– Pierrot!

Marie was falling: she escaped from the arms of the beautiful boy who tripped.

The thin body, which had been gliding along, fell to the floor with the noise of a beast.

– The little whore! said Pierrot.

He wiped his mouth with the back of his sleeve.

The barkeeper rushed over. She knelt down and raised her head with care: saliva, or rather drool, was running from her lips.

One girl brought a moistened napkin.

In a short time, Marie came to. She asked weakly:

– Liquor!

– Give her a glass, said the barkeeper to one of the girls.

They gave her a glass. She drank and said:

– More!

The girl filled her glass. Marie lifted it out of her hands. She drank as if she was running out of time.

Nestling in the arms of one of the girls and the barkeeper, she lifted her head:

– More! she said.

Marie Tries to Speak

The farmboys, the girls and the barkeeper surrounded Marie waiting to see what she was going to say.

Marie murmured only one word:

... the dawn, she said.

Then her head fell back heavily. Sick, very sick ...

The barkeeper asked:

– What'd she say?

No one knew what to answer.

Marie Is Sucked by Pierrot

Then the barkeeper said to pretty Pierrot:

– Suck her.

– Should we put her on a chair? said one girl.

Several of them grabbed her body at once and managed to get her ass onto the chair.

Pierrot, kneeling down, slipped her legs over his shoulders. The young stud had a smile of conquest and darted his tongue into her crotch hair.

Sick, lit-up, Marie seemed happy, she smiled without opening her eyes.

Marie Kisses the Barkeeper on the Mouth

She felt lit-up, frozen over, but endlessly emptying, emptying her life into the sewer.

A helpless desire maintained a tension in her: she would have liked to let that tension in her belly go. She imagined the horror of the others. She was no longer separated from Edward.

Her cunt and her ass naked: the smell of her ass and her wet cunt freed her heart and the tongue of Pierrot, which wet her, seemed as cold as death to her.

Drunk with liquor and with tears and not crying, she drank in this cold, her mouth open: she pulled over to her the head of the barkeeper, opening to the woman's decaying teeth the voluptuous abyss of her lips.

Marie Drinks in Huge Gulps

Marie pushed the woman away and she saw her head, hair dishevelled, twisted out of itself with joy. The face of the virago radiated drunken tenderness. She was drunk too, sentimental drunk: devoted tears came to her eyes.

Looking at these tears and seeing nothing, Marie was living bathed in the light of the dead man. She said:

– I'm thirsty.

Pierrot was sucking hard enough to take his breath away.

Hurriedly, the barkeeper gave her a bottle.

Marie drank in long gulps and emptied it.

Marie Comes

… Scuffling, a cry of terror, a confusion of broken bottles, Marie's thighs twitched like a frog's. The boys were screaming and shoving for position. The barkeeper helped Marie, laid her out on the bench.

Her eyes remained empty, ecstatic.

The wind, the squall, outside, were going crazy. In the night, the shutters banged away.

– Listen, said the barkeeper.

They heard the howling of the wind in the trees, long and moaning like the cry of a mad woman.

The door was wide open, a gust of wind blew into the room. Instantly, naked Marie found herself standing up.

She cried out:

– *Edward*!

And the anguish made her voice a prolonging of the wind.

Marie Encounters a Dwarf

From this bad night came a man, struggling to close an umbrella: his rat-like silhouette stood out in the doorway.

– Quickly, your lordship! come in, said the barkeeper.

She staggered.

The dwarf came forward without answering.

– You're soaked, the woman continued, closing the door.

The little man was possessed of a surprising gravity, enormous and hunchbacked, with a huge head crowning his shoulders.

He greeted Marie, then turned towards the farmboys.

– Good day, Pierrot, he said shaking his hand, take my coat if you would.

Pierrot helped the count to remove his overcoat. The count gave him a pinch on the ass.

Pierrot smiled. The count shook people's hands amicably.

– May, I? he asked as he bowed.

He took a seat at Marie's table across from her.

– A few bottles, would you, said the count.

– I've drunk, said one girl, so much I could piss on my chair.

– Drink enough to shit, my child …

He stopped crisply, rubbing his hands.

Not without a certain detachment.

Marie Sees the Ghost of Edward

Marie remained motionless looking at the count and his head turned toward her.

– Pour, she said.

The count filled the glasses.

She said again, very wisely:

– I'm going to die at dawn …

The count's steely look moved up and down her.

His blond eyebrows went up, accentuating the wrinkles in his excessively wide forehead.

Marie lifted her glass and said:

– Drink!

The count also lifted his glass and drank: they greedily emptied their glasses in unison.

The barkeeper came and sat down near Marie.

– I'm afraid, Marie said to her.

Her eyes never left the count.

She made a kind of coughing: she murmured in a crazed voice into the ear of the old woman:

– It's the ghost of Edward.

– Edward? asked the woman quietly.

– He's dead, said Marie in the same voice.

She took the other woman's hand and bit it.

– You bitch, screamed the woman who'd been bitten.

But freeing her hand, she caressed Marie; kissing her on the shoulder, she said to the count:

– All the same, she's sweet.

Marie Gets Up on Top of the Bench

The count in his turn asked:

– Who is Edward?

– You no longer know who you are, said Marie.

This time her voice broke.

– Make him drink, she demanded of the barkeeper.

She seemed to be at the end of her rope.

The count snorted down his glass but admitted:

– Liquor has very little effect on me.

The enormous little man with the excessively large head scanned Marie with a mournful eye, as if he had had the intention of annoying her.

He scanned everything in the same way, his head stiff between his shoulders.

He called out:

– Pierrot!

The boy approached.

– This young child, said the dwarf, has given me a hard-on. How about sitting yourself down here.

– Be nice, Pierrot, jerk me off. I don't dare ask this child …

He smiled.

– She isn't accustomed, as you are, to monsters.

At this point, Marie got up on top of the bench.

Marie Pisses on the Count

– I'm afraid, said Marie. You look like a fence post.

He didn't answer. Pierrot grabbed his prick.

He was in fact impassive as a fence post.

– Go away, Marie told him, or I'll piss on you …

She got up on the table and squatted down.

– I'd be only too delighted, responded the monster. His neck had no freedom of movement; if he spoke, his chin alone moved.

Marie pissed.

Pierrot vigorously jerked off the count who was struck in the face with urine.

The count turned red and urine drenched him. Pierrot was jerking him off like someone fucking and his prick spat cum on his waistcoat. The dwarf was emitting a death rattle, convulsing from head to foot.

Marie Sprinkles Herself with Urine

Marie kept pissing.

On the table amidst the bottles and the glasses, she sprinkled herself with urine with her hands.

She drenched her legs, her ass, her face.

– Look how pretty I am, she said.

Squatting down, with her cunt at the level of the monster's head, she made her lips open horribly.

Marie Falls onto the Monster

Marie had a bitter smile.

A vision of bad horror …

One of her legs slipped: her cunt struck the count in the head.

He lost his balance and fell.

The two of them crashed down screaming, in an incredible din.

Marie Bites the Dwarf on the Dick

On the ground there was a horrible scuffle.

Marie broke loose, bit the dwarf on the dick and he screeched. Pierrot knocked her to the ground. He spread out her arms to form a cross: the others held her legs.

Marie wailed:

– Leave me alone.

Then she fell silent.

By the end she was panting, her eyes closed.

She opened her eyes. Pierrot, red, sweaty, was on top of her.

– Fuck me, she said.

Marie Is Poked by Pierrot

– Fuck her, Pierrot, said the barkeeper.

The others moved excitedly around the victim.

Marie let her head fall back, annoyed by these preparations.

The others laid her out, opened her legs. She was breathing quickly, her breath was burning.

The scene in its slowness evoked the slaughter of a pig, or the burial of a god.

Pierrot had his pants off, the count required that he be naked.

The delicate young man stamped like a bull: the count facilitated the entrance of his cock. The victim quivered and struggled: bodies locked with incredible hatred.

The others watched, their lips dry, stunned by this frenzy.

The bodies knotted together by Pierrot's prick rolled on the ground struggling. At the end, arching forward to the breaking point, completely out of breath, the farmboy howled, slobbering all over himself. Marie responded with a death spasm.

Marie Listens to the Birds in the Woods

... Marie came to.

She heard the songs of birds on the branch of a tree.

The songs, of an incredible delicacy, flitted whistling from tree to tree. Stretched out on the moist grass she saw the sky was light: the day was being born at that very moment.

She was cold, seized by a frozen happiness, suspended in an unintelligible emptiness. However much she would have liked to gently lift up her head, and in spite of the fact that she fell back in exhaustion on the ground, she remained faithful to the light, to the foliage, to the birds that peopled the woods. For an instant, occasions of childhood shyness brushed lightly over her, in memory. She recognized, bent over her, the great and massive head of the count.

Marie Vomits

What Marie read in the eyes of the dwarf was the insistence of death ... this face expressed only an infinite disillusionment, that a frightful obsession made cynical. Hate leapt up in her, and death approaching, she got very frightened.

She raised herself up clinching her teeth in front of the kneeling monster.

Standing, she trembled.

She took a step back, looked at the count and vomited.

– You see, she said.

– Relieved? asked the count.

– No, she said.

She saw the vomit in front of her. Her torn coat barely covered her.

– Where are we going? she said.

– Your place, answered the count.

Marie Shits on the Vomit

– My place, groaned Marie. Once again his head turned toward her.

– Are you the devil himself to want to go to my place? she asked.

– Yes, the dwarf came back, they've sometimes told me I was the devil himself.

– The devil? said Marie, I'd shit in the devil's face!

– Just a moment ago you vomited.

– I'd shit.

She squatted down and shit on the vomit.

The monster was still kneeling.

Marie leaned against an oak. She was sweating, in a trance. She said:

– All that, it's just nothing. But *at my place* you'll be scared … Too late …

She shook her head and, wild, marched roughly up to the dwarf, pulled him by the collar and screamed:

– You coming?

– My pleasure, said the count.

He added, almost quietly:

– She's worth it to me.

Marie Leads Off the Count

Marie, who heard him, looked directly at the count. He got up:

– No one, he murmured, ever speaks to me that way.

– You can leave, she said. But if you come …

The count interrupted her curtly.

– I follow. You're going to give yourself to me.

She remained violent.

– It's time, she said. Come.

The Gnome Enters the House

They walked swiftly.

Day was breaking when they arrived. Marie pushed on the gate. They took a path lined with old trees: the sun made their heads golden.

Marie in all her surliness knew she was in accord with the sun. She led the count into the room.

– It's over, she said to herself. She was at once weak, full of hatred, indifferent.

– Undress yourself, she said, I'll wait in the next room.

The count undressed unhurriedly.

The sun through a clump of leaves speckled the wall and the speckles of light were dancing.

Marie Dies

The count got a hard-on.

His dick was long and reddish.

His naked body and his dick had a devilish deformity. His head in his angular shoulders, which were raised too far up, was pale and mocking.

He desired Marie and limited his thoughts to his desire.

He pushed open the door. Sadly naked, she waited for him in front of a bed, provocative and ugly: drunkenness and fatigue had beaten her down.

– What's wrong? said Marie.

The dead man, in disorder, filled the room …

The count stammered gently.

– … I didn't know.

He had to steady himself on a piece of furniture: *he lost his hard-on.*

Marie had a hideous smile.

– *It is accomplished!* she said.

She looked stupid, holding out a broken phial in her right hand. Finally, she fell.

Marie Follows the Dead Man into the Earth

… Finally *the count noticed the two hearses in a row, heading slowly toward the cemetery.*

The dwarf hissed between his teeth:

– I was had …

He didn't see the canal and let himself slip.

A loud noise, for an instant, disturbed the silence of the water.

The sun remained.

Translated by
Jayne Austen

ANNE BILLAT

HOW ISHMAEL AND ISAAC CAME TO BE BORN

The daughter of an obscure French poet exiled in the Middle East and of a Lebanese singer, Anne Billat was born in 1957 in Damiya, on the edge of the Jordan. At sixteen, to escape the sudden rages of her mother and the hashish-induced deliriums of her father, Billat became a prostitute. A few years later she met an English businessman, Sir S. Roissy, and married him. Their marriage was not a happy one. In 1990, in Monte Carlo, Anne Billat committed suicide.

Billat published a single book during her lifetime, The Blue Dress, *which was hailed as "an erotic masterpiece with biblical echoes." She wrote in French, considered herself a Palestinian citizen, and regarded the Bible as the source of both her language and her imagery. At her death, she left behind numerous erotic texts (among them "How Ishmael and Isaac Came to Be Born") which have not yet found a publisher.*

Sarah's barrenness

THROUGH AN OPENING in the tent, Sarah observed the deep blue sky where her husband lodged his futile god who had promised them the earth and all its wonders.

In Ur, her city, she had been honoured. She had expected Abraham to make her fruitful. Now she was old. And still they were childless.

It was not because she found no pleasure in their couplings. But what can a woman do when her man cannot send his seed deep down into her depths, however divine the seed's essence might be? Because Abraham, in spite of being both a prophet and a patriarch, never crossed her downy threshold; his staff grew soft, like a snake in front of her burning bush. They said she was barren when in fact she lay fallow. The shepherds never imagined that their leader might be bereft of power. Not fully bereft, of course, since Agar had given birth to Ishmael, Abraham's son. But powerless in her presence.

She needed to silence her belly which was claiming its due. In Ur, Sarah had studied the strokes that straighten the rod and make the milk of life burst forth, brutal and hot. From the shepherds' wives, Sarah had learned the gestures needed to awaken strong desire and make it last, to cause the trunk of the tree of peace to spread its vertiginous roots.

Sarah's sighs

Many times she had kneaded the loaf in search of nourishment, but manna would not come either from her man nor from the deceiving heavens. Why had she abandoned the old gods for a powerless new one?

She remembered the God of Volcanoes, the God of Eruptions. She remembered Baal, the Devouring God, the God of Horrors. She remembered all these cruel gods, devourers of children and creators of orgies.

But now, there would be no children, no future generations, and Sarah grieved as she waited, seeing, through the bearded opening of the tent, Ra's ray fall like a fiery spear. She lifted her dress and offered her dark triangle to the sunlight in the hopes that the ancient god would make her fruitful.

Sarah stopped pretending, because at ninety years of age, she was short of breath.

She could console herself with nothing except a few brave memories.

Abraham's serpent

Sarah remembered her wedding night. Abraham had leaned over her, sweating somewhat and certainly drunk. Abraham had leaned over her and whispered, very tenderly:

"My child, sister mine."

It is true that he was ten years her senior. It is true that they had known one another for a very long time. But to be thought of as his child? To be called his sister? She had smiled. Had it been that smile that had troubled Abraham?

So Sarah took the rod with both hands and drew it towards her sacred triangle. As if it were a goat's udder, she milked the rod with strong and regular movements, crushing the ophidian head against her pubis. In vain.

How she had feared – but also hoped for – that feast of pain, of blood and of showers that her sisters and cousins had bragged about!

Abraham had felt disgust. And ever since he had been unable to pay hommage to his sister-wife.

Sarah's endeavours

It was not as if she had not tried. How many artifices, how many concoctions were experimented with! One evening, as Abraham returned stinking of the flock he had just herded, Sarah fell to her knees, put her arms around the man's waist and, her chin against his failing member, had begged:

"My lord and master, may your wrath not fall upon your servant. I'll take you in my mouth, O Abraham; I'll draw out your vigour to give you the strength of the Oak of Mamre. I'll place my hands upon you, my fingers shall trace like asps the furrows of your body and sail like ships in your valley. My fingers will know that hollow common to men and women, and the most daring, the slimmest or the stoutest, whichever pleases you, will delve inside you to knead your walls, O Master Mine, like the wave kneads the cliffs. My lord and master, may our wrath not fall upon your servant who chooses to become a whore so that you may be a husband."

Abraham's daydream

Sarah matched actions to words. Abraham lent himself to the ploy because he too anxiously sought a solution. He conjured up the image of Sarah's handmaid, Agar, the young Egyptian, whom he had surprised contemplating herself. The young girl may have noticed that Abraham was watching her, and yet she carried on as if she had been alone. She took some ointment and smeared it gently over her breasts. Then she brushed her breasts with a soft brush to help them grow, as well as the insides of her thighs which felt slightly downy to the touch.

So it was that Abraham, caught in his daydream, became virile. Sarah imagined that her charms and her dexterity had worked at last. She moved Abraham towards her.

But Abraham, coming out of his dream, softened once again. It was over. Abraham rose and went out to piss. Sarah wept.

Agar's arrival

Sarah said to Abraham:

"See, I am barren for all eternity. Go, I beseech you, to my handmaid. Perhaps through her I shall be able to bear a child!"

Abraham listened to Sarah's voice, and acquiesced.

So it was that Sarah, Abraham's wife, gave Agar the Egyptian, her handmaid, as wife to her husband, after they had lived for ten years in the land of Canaan.

It was Sarah herself who led Abraham to the handmaid. It was she who undressed Agar, slowly, gradually revealing the young woman's breasts. The breasts held the cloth for a moment, then they let the cloth slide and they sprang upwards, free, towards the sky. Abraham fell to his knees, his legs weak and his loins in flames.

Then Sarah pulled the tunic off the arms and, like the sun rises from behind the hills, the sacred mount appeared, barely dusky, and the lips, faintly underlined with down. The Egyptian body rose, the wild copper beauty of the Nile was revealed. Sarah was a priestess, her mission was holy.

All three knew it.

On his knees, the patriarch held his ploughshare in his hands.

"Fertile land of the Nile, O delta. I'll sow you, I'll be the crocodile diving in the living shade of your waters. Silt-laden land, sacred mouth of the river, I'll spill myself inside your banks, I'll drown myself as I drown you, O overflowing torrent which devastates me and brings me back to life! Promised land, you whore! I'll take you from every port, I'll make you tremble like a beast of burden! Ruined land, O earthquake, O Agar!"

Abraham chanted, Abraham prayed, Abraham gave thanks to God. But to which God?

Sarah's defeat

Then Sarah said:

"Come near, you old goat."

She grabbed hold of the venerable head of hair and forced the old man to sink his generous nose in the young girl's lips. The virgin belly gave way under pressure from the bone. Sarah guided the patriarch and the Egyptian held the hoary head and gave it the desired rhythm. She closed her eyes and didn't notice Sarah bending over her. She didn't see but felt her mistress's tongue glide between her buttocks. She didn't see but felt the hands of the one who was almost her mother caressing her breasts. Agar was transported. Mad Sarah. She broke up the communion and rose to her feet.

She made Agar kneel and then covered her with a lamb's skin, wishing to humiliate her.

"Smell her," she said to Abraham.

Abraham smelled.

"Lick her."

Abraham licked.

"Take her."

Abraham approached, all muscles taut. Sarah interposed herself. In her woman's rage, she wished to change places with the Egyptian at the very last minute. But Abraham was rutting, and like a goat who knows exactly what he wants, he cast aside his wife before God and entered Egypt. And there were tremors along the land of the Nile, belly and loins struck by the belly of bronze.

He moved to and fro inside Agar and she became pregnant. And thus was Ishmael born.

The three men

Deep inside the tent, Sarah bemoaned her lot. Recalling what she had done, she felt hurt. She felt so alone, so empty.

Outside, Abraham was warming his old bones and rekindling his hopes. He lifted his eyes and saw three men standing beside him, as if sprung from his thoughts.

He bowed to them and said:

"Rest under that tree. I offer you my hospitality. I beg you wait, while I prepare a meal."

Through the opening in the tent, he whispered to his wife:

"Don't you see? This is the chance of our lifetime. These three are a gift from heaven."

Then, leaving Sarah to her astonishment, he ran to the pen and ordered that a tender lamb be sacrificed, and that prayers be spoken during the slaughter. While the lamb was being chosen, he returned to sit with his guests. They were given some food, because Abraham knew well the laws of hospitality.

"Where is Sarah, your wife?"

"She is there, inside the tent," Abraham answered.

"Good. Now return to your offerings and don't come back until we call you."

And one of the men added, as if he were reciting a text:

"It is written, *I shall return to you at that same time and Sarah, your wife, shall bear a child.*"

Abraham left to sacrifice the lamb himself and pronounce the appropriate prayers. The men entered the tent.

Abraham returned to the place that the three angels had sanctified with their presence – if they were indeed three angels. Through an opening, he saw what God was seeing: his old wife, ecstatic as if she had already attained the seventh heaven. A Tower of Babel complete at last, she seemed to be touching God himself.

The alliance

Old Sarah could still be beautiful. Or at least, she seemed younger, she was younger, transfigured in that very instant. Perhaps the angels' aura shed its light on her.

The first of the men had undressed. He appeared suddenly naked and Sarah was astounded by the young sapling. The second placed himself behind her, glued to her back, lifted her breasts holding them with full soft hands, caressing them, pinching her nipples while the mouth drowned in her neck. Sarah abandoned herself, closed her eyes.

The miracle took place, and the miracle was that her soul, her entire body were being renewed, reborn, made young again. And in front of Abraham's very eyes, his wife shed seventy-five years! The angels, youthful and comely, required her youth and beauty to make it all happen.

The third, the one who had spoken to Abraham, remained to one side, in the depths of the tent. Impossible as it might seem, he was the most perfect of the three. He watched, a fine happy smile on his lips. On Sarah's lips, the same smile. She slid, stretching her hands towards the first one's rod, which was approaching her with divine languor. The other, at Sarah's back, followed her in a slow-paced fall. Sarah felt against her buttocks the column of fire holding her up, a pillar between herself and the ground. And the pillar was the staff of life. It slid between her thighs and rammed against her sex while the man's hands made love to her breasts, becoming like an octopus, fondling her, while the man's lips sucked at her neck.

At last the second angel reached her. She grasped his sex and held it in her youthful hands; then she pressed it against her belly, flat. The angel behind her stepped back a little and Sarah was able to take the sapling inside her. And the angel entered her without ever reaching the end, opening her painlessly. The other's sex was beating against her narrow door. Sarah saw stars. She opened her mouth to breathe in the ether she had now reached and here was the third angel, pushing tenderly into her mouth his divine ray of light.

The God was there, and He was three.

The Chief of Angels

Now the Chief of Angels knew that Abraham was watching him. He bared his buttocks completely and Abraham saw the magnificent ass quiver, contract, spread and reveal, fascinating as God's eye fixed in the tomb of great-grandfather Cain, a woman's slit, an unfathomable marvel. The Chief of Angels was man or woman alternatively, and sometimes both at once.

For it wasn't a rod that Sarah was breathing in now, but lips. And her tongue entered a cavern, lit brightly behind her closed eyes. And Sarah sailed through the ether.

The Chief of Angels gestured to Abraham, pointing to his own body. And the gesture meant: Abraham, old goat, come take your God.

Abraham ran to him, casting off his clothes. He ran,

rutting, eyes wide open, as mad as when Agar had been offered to him. That was how he was: he required a sign from on high for the act to be fulfilled. He required a ceremony. Because for this man, for this solitary being, this founder, love could be nothing except a trial, an offering to God.

Genesis

Abraham reached the very core of the sacrifice. And then the only true miracle took place. The three apparitions suddenly vanished and Abraham, the very old Abraham, and Sarah, ancient Sarah, were united at last, for all eternity.

The names had changed, and the course of events had changed.

And old Sarah opened her eyes and saw Abraham.

And old Abraham opened his eyes and saw Sarah.

And they remained together for a very long time because, at their age, pleasure is slow in coming.

And thus was Isaac born.

Translated by
Alberto Manguel

HAROLD BRODKEY

INNOCENCE

The notion that love can be codified into rituals is an ancient one. The Middle Ages established amatory rules and courts of love as strict as those of law, and problems were set to these courts for learned ladies to judge according to this erotic justice. If a lover, ordered by his lady to cease serving her, speaks in her defence upon hearing her defamed, is he guilty of disobedience? The Countess of Champagne ruled that he was not, because the lady's command was a wrong one and therefore had no binding force.

Love treatises were common in China, in India, in the world of Islam, in Japan. In our less poetic times, they take the form of self-help books and quizzes in fashion magazines. But the need to believe that lovemaking can follow established systems of communication is still strongly and deeply rooted. For Harold Brodkey, the rules extend to the erotic act itself. "Innocence" is a story about the learning of these rules, and the discovery that the rituals of lovemaking may ultimately not provide the longed-for secure haven.

I *Orra at Harvard*

ORRA PERKINS was a senior. Her looks were like a force that struck you. Truly, people on first meeting her often involuntarily lifted their arms as if about to fend off the brightness of the apparition. She was a somewhat scrawny, tuliplike girl of middling height. To see her in sunlight was to see Marxism die. I'm not the only one who said that. It was because seeing someone in actuality who had such a high immediate worth meant you had to decide whether such personal distinction had a right to exist or if she belonged to the state and ought to be shadowed in, reduced in scale, made lesser, laughed at.

Also, it was the case that you had to be rich and famous to set your hands on her; she could not fail to be a trophy, and the question was whether the trophy had to be awarded on economic and political grounds or whether chance could enter in.

I was a senior, too, and ironic. I had no money. I was without lineage. It seemed to me Orra was proof that life was a terrifying phenomenon of surface immediacy. She made any idea I had of psychological normalcy or of justice absurd since normalcy was not as admirable or as desirable as Orra; or rather she was normalcy and everything else was a falling off, a falling below; and justice was inconceivable if she, or someone equivalent to her if there was an equivalent once you had seen her, would not sleep with you. I used to create general hilarity in my room by shouting her name at my friends and then breaking up into laughter, gasping out, "God, we're so small-time." It was grim that she existed and I had not had her. One could still prefer a more ordinary girl but not for simple reasons.

A great many people avoided her, ran away from her. She was, in part, more knowing than the rest of us because the experiences offered her had been so extreme, and she had been so extreme in response – scenes in Harvard Square with an English marquess, slapping a son of a billionaire so hard he fell over backwards at a party in Lowell House, her saying then and subsequently, "I never sleep with anyone who has a fat ass." Extreme in the humiliations endured and meted out, in the crassness of the publicity, of her life defined as those adventures, extreme in the dangers survived or not entirely survived, the cheapness undergone so that she was on a kind of frightening eminence, an eminence of her experiences and of her being different from everyone else. She'd dealt in intrigues, major and minor, in the dramas of political families, in passions, deceptions, folly on a large, expensive scale, promises, violence, the genuine pain of defeat when defeat is to some extent the result of your qualities and not of your defects, and she knew the rottenness of victories that hadn't been final. She was crass and impaired by beauty. She was like a giant bird, she was as odd as an ostrich walking around the Yard, in her absurd gorgeousness, she was so different from us in kind, so capable of a different sort of progress through the yielding medium of the air, through the strange rooms of our minutes on this earth, through the gloomy circumstances of our lives in those years.

People said it was worth it to do this or that just in order to see her – seeing her offered some kind of encouragement, was some kind of testimony that life was interesting. But not many people cared as much about knowing her. Most people preferred to keep their distance. I don't know what her having made herself into what she was had done for her. She could have been ordinary if she'd wished.

She had unnoticeable hair, a far from arresting forehead, and extraordinary eyes, deep-set, longing, hopeful, angrily bored behind smooth, heavy lids that fluttered when she was interested and when she was not interested at all. She had a great desire not to trouble or be troubled by supernumeraries and strangers. She has a proud, too large nose that gives her a noble, stubborn dog's look. Her mouth has a disconcertingly lovely set to it – it is more immediately expressive than her eyes and it shows her implacability: it is the implacability of her knowledge of life in her. People always stared at her. Some giggled nervously. *Do you like me, Orra? Do you like me at all?* They stared at the great hands of the Aztec priest opening them to feelings and to awe, exposing their hearts, the dread cautiousness of their lives. They stared at the incredible symmetries of her sometimes anguishedly passionate face, the erratic pain for her in being beautiful that showed on it, the occasional plunging gaiety she felt because she was beautiful. I like beautiful people. The symmetries of her face were often thwarted by her attempts at expressiveness – beauty was a stone she struggled free of. A ludicrous beauty. A cruel clown of a girl Sometimes her face was absolutely impassive as if masked in dullness and she was trying to move among us incognito. I was aware that each of her downfalls made her more possible for me. I never doubted that she was privately a pedestrian shitting-peeing person. Whenever I had a chance to observe her for any length of time, in a classroom for instance, I would think, *I understand her.* Whenever I approached her, she responded up to a point and then even as I stood talking to her I would fade as a personage, as a sexual presence, as someone present and important to her, into greater and greater invisibility. That was when she was a freshman, a sophomore, and a junior. When we were seniors, by then I'd learned how to avoid being invisible even to Orra. Orra was, I realized, hardly more than a terrific college girl, much vaunted, no more than that yet. But my God, my God, in one's eyes, in one's thoughts, she strode like a *Nike*, she entered like a blast of light, the thought of her was as vast as a desert. Sometimes in an early winter twilight in the Yard, I would see her in her coat, unbuttoned even in cold weather as if she burned slightly always, see her move clumsily along a walk looking like a scrawny field-hockey player, a great athlete of a girl half-stumbling, uncoordinated off the playing field, yet with reserves of strength, do you know? and her face, as she walked along, might twitch like a dog's when the dog is asleep, twitching with whatever dialogue or adventure or daydream she was having in her head. Or she might in the early darkness stride along, cold-faced, haughty, angry, all the worst refusals one would ever receive bound up in one ridiculously beautiful girl. One always said, "I wonder what will become of her." Her ignoring me marked me as a sexual nonentity. She was proof of a level of sexual adventure I had not yet with my best efforts reached: that level existed because Orra existed.

What is it worth to be in love in this way?

II Orra with Me

I distrust summaries, any kind of gliding through time, any too great a claim that one is in control of what one recounts; I think someone who claims to understand but who is obviously calm, someone who claims to write with emotion recollected in tranquillity, is a fool and a liar. To understand is to tremble. To recollect is to reenter and be riven. An acrobat after spinning through the air in a mockery of flight stands erect on his perch and mockingly takes his bow as if what he is being applauded for was easy for him and cost him nothing, although meanwhile he is covered with sweat and his smile is edged with a relief chilling to think about; he is indulging in a show-business style; he is pretending to be superhuman. I am bored with that and with where it has brought us. I admire the authority of being on one's knees in front of the event.

In the last spring of our being undergraduates, I finally got her. We had agreed to meet in my room, to get a little drunk cheaply before going out to dinner. I left the door unlatched; and I lay naked on my bed under a sheet. When she knocked on the door, I said, "Come in," and she did. She began to chatter right away, to complain that I was still in bed; she seemed to think I'd been taking a nap and had forgotten to wake up in time to get ready for her arrival. I said, "I'm naked, Orra, under this sheet. I've been waiting for you. I haven't been asleep."

Her face went empty. She said, "Damn you – why couldn't you wait?" But even while she was saying that, she was taking off her blouse.

I was amazed that she was so docile; and then I saw that it was maybe partly that she didn't want to risk saying no to me – she didn't want me to be hurt and difficult, she didn't want me to explode; she had a kind of hope of making me happy so that I'd then appreciate her and be happy with her and let her know me: I'm putting it badly. But her not being able to say no protected me from having so great a fear of sexual failure that I would not have been able to be worried about her pleasure, or to be concerned about her in bed. She was very amateurish and uninformed in bed, which touched me. It was really sort of poor sex; she didn't come or even feel much that I could see. Afterward, lying beside her, I thought of her eight or ten or fifteen lovers being afraid of her, afraid to tell her anything about sex in case they might be wrong. I had an image of them protecting their own egos, holding their arms around their egos and not letting her near them. It seemed a kindness embedded in the event that she was, in quite an obvious way, with a little critical interpretation, a virgin. And impaired, or crippled by having been beautiful, just as I'd thought. I said to myself that it was a matter of course that I might be deluding myself. But what I did for the rest of that night – we stayed up all night; we talked, we quarreled for a while, we confessed various things, we argued about sex, we fucked again (the second one was a little better) – I treated her with the justice with which I'd treat a boy my age, a young man, and with a rather exact or measured patience and tolerance, as if she were a paraplegic and had spent her life in a wheelchair and was tired of sentiment. I showed her no sentiment at all. I figured she'd been asphyxiated by the sentiments and sentimentality of people impressed by her looks. She was beautiful and frightened and empty and shy and alone and wounded and invulnerable (like a cripple: what more can you do to a cripple?). She was Caesar and ruler of the known world and not Caesar and no one as well.

It was a fairly complicated, partly witty thing to do. It meant I could not respond to her beauty but had to ignore it. She was a curious sort of girl; she had a great deal of isolation in her, isolation as a woman. It meant that when she said something on the order of "You're very defensive," I had to be a debater, her equal, take her seriously, and say, "How do you mean that?" and then talk about it, and alternately deliver a blow ("You can't judge defensiveness, you have the silly irresponsibility of women, the silly disconnectedness: I *have* to be defensive") and defer to her: "You have a point: you think very clearly. All right, I'll adopt that as a premise." Of course, much of what we said was incoherent and nonsensical on examination, but we worked out in conversation what we meant or thought we meant. I didn't react to her in an emotional way. She wasn't really a girl, not really quite human: how could she be? She was a position, a specific glory, a trophy, our local upper-middle-class pseudo-Cleopatra. Or not pseudo. I couldn't revel in my luck or be unselfconsciously vain. I could not strut horizontally or loll as if on clouds, a demigod with a goddess, although it was clear we were deeply fortunate, in spite of everything: the poor sex, the differences in attitude which were all we seemed to share, the tensions and the blundering. If I enjoyed her more than she enjoyed me, if I lost consciousness of her even for a moment, she would be closed into her isolation again. I couldn't love her and have her, too. I could love her and have her if I didn't show love or the symptoms of having had her. It was like lying in a very lordly way, opening her to the possibility of feeling by making her comfortable inside the calm lies of my behavior, my inscribing the minutes with false messages. It was like meeting a requirement in Greek myth, like not looking back at Eurydice. The night crept on, swept on, late minutes, powdered with darkness, in the middle of a sleeping city, spring crawling like a plague of green snakes, bits of warmth in the air, at 4 a.m. smells of leaves when the stink of automobiles died down. Dawn came, so pink, so pastel, so silly: We were talking about the possibility of innate grammatical structures; I said it was an unlikely notion, that Jews really were God-haunted (the idea had been broached by a Jew), and the great difficulty was to invent a just God, that if God appeared at a moment of time or relied on prophets, there had to be degrees in the possibility of knowing Him so that He was by definition unjust; the only just God would be one who consisted of what had always been known by everyone; and that you could always identify a basically Messianic, a hugely religious, fraudulent thinker by how much he tried to anchor his doctrine to having always been true, to being innate even in savage man, whereas an honest thinker, a nonliar, was caught in the grip of the truth of process and change and the profound absence of justice except as an invention, an attempt by the will to live with someone, or with many others without consuming them. At that moment Orra said, "I think we're falling in love."

I figured I had kept her from being too depressed after fucking – it's hard for a girl with any force in her and any brains to accept the whole thing of fucking, of being fucked without trying to turn it on its end, so that she does some fucking, or some fucking up; I mean, the mere power of arousing the man so he wants to fuck isn't enough: she wants him to be willing to die in order to fuck. There's a kind of strain or intensity women are bred for, as beasts, for child-bearing when childbearing might kill them, and child rearing when the child might die at any moment: it's in women to live under that danger, with that risk, that close to tragedy, with that constant taut or casual courage. They need death and nobility near. To be fucked when there's no drama inherent in it, when you're not going to rise to a level of nobility and courage forever denied the male, is to be cut off from what is inherently female, bestially speaking. I wanted to be halfway decent company for her. I don't know that it was natural to me. I am psychologically, profoundly, a transient. A form of trash. I am incapable of any continuing loyalty and silence; I am an informer. But I did all right with her. It was dawn, as I said. We stood naked by the window, silently watching the light change. Finally, she said, "Are you hungry? Do you want breakfast?"

"Sure. Let's get dressed and go –"

She cut me off; she said with a funny kind of firmness, "No! Let me go and get us something to eat."

"Orra, don't wait on me. Why are you doing this? Don't be like this."

But she was in a terrible hurry to be in love. After those few hours, after that short a time.

She said, "I'm not as smart as you, Wiley. Let me wait on you. Then things will be even."

"Things are even, Orra."

"No. I'm boring and stale. You just think I'm not because you're in love with me. Let me go."

I blinked. After a while, I said, "All right."

She dressed and went out and came back. While we ate, she was silent; I said things, but she had no comment to make; she ate very little; she folded her hands and smiled mildly like some nineteenth-century portrait of a handsome young mother. Every time I looked at her, when she saw I was looking at her, she changed the expression on her face to one of absolute and undeviating welcome to me and to anything I might say.

So, it had begun.

III Orra

She hadn't come. She said she had never come with anyone at any time. She said it didn't matter.

After our first time, she complained, "You went twitch, twitch, twitch – just like a grasshopper." So she had wanted to have more pleasure than she'd had. But after the second fuck and after the dawn, she never complained again – unless I tried to make her come, and then she complained of that. She showed during sex no dislike for any of my sexual mannerisms or for the rhythms and postures I fell into when I fucked. But I was not pleased or satisfied; it bothered me that she didn't come. I was not pleased or satisfied on my own account, either. I thought the reason for that was she attracted me more than she could satisfy me, maybe more than fucking could ever satisfy me, that the more you cared, the more undertow there was, so that the sexual thing drowned – I mean, the sharpest sensations, and yet the dullest, are when you masturbate – but when you're vilely attached to somebody, there are noises, distractions that drown out the sensations of fucking. For a long time, her wanting to fuck, her getting undressed, and the soft horizontal bobble of her breasts as she lay there, and the soft wavering, the kind of sinewlessness of her legs and lower body, with which she more or less showed me she was ready – that was more moving, was more immensely important to me than any mere ejaculation later, any putt-putt-putt in her darkness, any hurling of future generations into the clenched universe, the strict mitten inside her: I clung to her and grunted and anchored myself to the most temporary imaginable relief of the desire I felt for her; I would be hungry again and anxious to fuck again in another twenty minutes; it was pitiable, this sexual disarray. It seemed to me that in the vast spaces of the excitement of being welcomed by each other, we could only sightlessly and at best half organize our bodies. But so what? We would probably die in these underground caverns; a part of our lives would die; a certain innocence and hope would never survive this: we were too open, too clumsy, and we were the wrong people: so what did a fuck matter? I didn't mind if the sex was always a little rasping, something of a failure, if it was just preparation for more sex in half an hour, if coming was just more foreplay. If this was all that was in store for us, fine. But I thought she was getting gypped in that she felt so much about me, she was dependent, and she was generous, and she didn't come when we fucked.

She said she had never come, not once in her life, and that she didn't need to. And that I mustn't think about whether she came or not. "I'm a sexual tigress," she explained, "and I like to screw but I'm too sexual to come: I haven't that kind of daintiness. I'm not selfish *that* way."

I could see that she had prowled around in a sense and searched out men and asked them to be lovers as she had me rather than wait for them or plot to capture their attention in some subtle way; and in bed she was sexually eager and a bit more forward and less afraid than most girls; but only in an upper-middle-class frame of reference was she *a sexual tigress.*

It seemed to me – my whole self was focused on this – that her not coming said something about what we had, that her not coming was an undeniable fact, a measure of the limits of what we had. I did not think we should think we were great lovers when we weren't.

Orra said we were, that I had no idea how lousy the sex was other people had. I told her that hadn't been my experience. We were, it seemed to me, two twenty-one-year-olds, overeducated, irrevocably shy beneath our glaze of sexual determination and of sexual appetite, and psychologically somewhat slashed up and only capable of being partly useful to each other. We weren't the king and queen of Cockandcuntdom yet.

Orra said coming was a minor part of sex for a woman and was a demeaning measure of sexuality. She said it was imposed as a measure by people who knew nothing about sex and judged women childishly.

It seemed to me she was turning a factual thing, coming,

into a public-relations thing. But girls were under fearful public pressures in these matters.

When she spoke about them, these matters, she had a little, superior inpuckered look, a don't-make-me-make-mincemeat-of-you-in-argument look – I thought of it as her Orra-as-Orra look, Orra alone, Orra-without-Wiley, without me, Orra isolated and depressed, a terrific girl, an Orra who hated cowing men.

She referred to novels, to novels by women writers, to specific scenes and remarks about sex and coming for women, but I'd read some of those books, out of curiosity, and none of them were literature, and the heroines in them invariably were innocent in every relation; but very strong and very knowing and with terrifically good judgment; and the men they loved were described in such a way that they appeared to be examples of the woman's sexual reach, or of her intellectual value, rather than sexual companions or sexual objects; the women had sex generously with men who apparently bored them physically; I had thought the books and their writers and characters sexually naive.

Very few women, it seemed to me, had much grasp of physical reality. Still, very strange things were often true, and a man's notion of orgasm was necessarily specialized.

When I did anything in bed to excite her, with an eye to making her come, she asked me not to, and that irritated the hell out of me. But no matter what she said, it must have been bad for her after six years of fucking around not to get to a climax. It had to be that it was a run on her neural patience. How strong could she be?

I thought about how women coming were at such a pitch of

uncontrol they might prefer a dumb, careless lover, someone very unlike me: I had often played at being a strong, silent dunce. Some girls became fawning and doglike after they came, even toward dunces. Others jumped up and became immediately tough, proud of themselves as if the coming was *all* to their credit, and I ought to be flattered. God, it was a peculiar world. Brainy girls tended to control their comes, doling out one to a fuck, just like a man; and often they would try to keep that one under control, they would limit it to a single nozzle-contracted squirt of excitement. Even that sometimes racked and emptied them and made them curiously weak and brittle and embarrassed and delicate and lazy. Or they would act bold and say, "God, I needed that."

I wondered how Orra would look, in what way she would do it, a girl like that going off, how she'd hold herself, her eyes, how she'd act toward me when it was over.

To get her to talk about sex at all, I argued that analyzing something destroyed it, of course, but leaves rotted on the ground and prepared the way for what would grow next. So she talked.

She said I was wrong in what I told her I saw and that there was no difference in her between mental and physical excitement, that it wasn't true her mind was excited quickly and her body slowly, if at all. I couldn't be certain I was right, but when I referred to a moment when there had seemed to be deep physical feeling in her, she sometimes agreed that had been a good moment in her terms; but sometimes she said, no, it had only been a little irritating then, like a peculiarly unpleasant tickle. In spite of her liking my mind, she gave me no authority for what I knew – I mean, when it turned out I was right. She kept the authority for her reactions in her own hands. Her self-abnegation was her own doing. I liked that: some people just give you themselves, and it is too much to keep in your hands: your abilities aren't good enough. I decided to stick with what I observed and to think her somewhat mistaken and not to talk to her about sex anymore.

I watched her in bed; her body was doubting, grudging, tardy, intolerant – and intolerably hungry – I thought. In her pride and self-consciousness and ignorance she hated all that in herself. She preferred to think of herself as quick, to have pleasure as she willed rather than as she actually had it, to have it on her own volition, to her own prescription, and almost out of politeness, so it seemed to me, to give herself to me, to give me pleasure, to ignore herself, to be a nice girl because she was in love. She insisted on that but that was too sentimental, and she also insisted on, she persuaded herself, she passed herself off as dashing.

In a way, sexually, she was a compulsive liar.

I set myself to remove every iota of misconception I had about Orra in bed, any romanticism, any pleasurable hope. It seemed to me what had happened to her with other boys was that she was distrustful to start with and they had overrated her, and they'd been overwrought and off balance and uneasy about her judgment of them, and they'd taken their pleasure and run.

And then she had in her determination to have sex become more and more of a sexual fool. (I was all kinds of fool: I didn't mind her being a sexual fool.) The first time I'd gone to bed with her, she'd screamed and thrown herself around, a good two or three feet to one side or another, as she thought a sexual tigress would, I supposed. I'd argued with her afterward that no one was that excited, especially without coming; she said she had come, sort of. She said she was too sexual for most men. She said her reactions weren't fake but represented a real sexuality, a real truth. That proud, stubborn, stupid girl.

But I told her that if she and a man were in sexual congress, and she heaved herself around and threw herself a large number of inches to either the left or the right or even straight up, the man was going to be startled; and if there was no regular pattern or predictability, it was easy to lose an erection; that if she threw herself to the side, there was a good chance she would interrupt the congress entirely unless the man was very quick and scrambled after her, and scrambling after her was not likely to be sexual for him: it would be more like playing tag. The man would have to fuck while in a state of siege; not knowing what she'd do next, he'd fuck and hurry to get it over and to get out.

Orra had said on that first occasion, "That sounds reasonable. No one ever explained that to me before, no one ever made it clear. I'll try it your way for a while."

After that, she had been mostly shy and honest, and honestly lecherous in bed but helpless to excite herself or to do more to me than she did just by being there and welcoming me. As if her hands were webbed and her mind was glued, as if I didn't deserve more, or as if she was such a novice and so shy she could not begin to do anything *sexual.* I did not understand: I'd always found that anyone who *wanted* to give pleasure could: it didn't take skill, just the desire to please and a kind of, I don't know, a sightless ability to feel one's way to some extent in the lightless maze of pleasure. But upper-middle-class girls might be more fearful of tying men to them by bands of excessive pleasure; such girls were careful and shy.

I set myself for her being rude and difficult although she hadn't been rude and difficult to me for a long time, but those traits were in her like a shadow, giving her the dimensionality that made her valuable to me, that gave point to her kindness toward me. She had the sloppiest and most uncertain and silliest and yet bravest and most generous ego of anyone I'd ever known; and her manners were the most stupid imaginable alternation between the distinguished, the sensitive, the intelligent, with a rueful, firm, almost snotty delicacy and kindness and protectiveness toward you, and the really selfish and bruising. The important thing was to prevent her from responding falsely, as if in a movie, or in some imitation of the movies she'd seen and the books she'd read – she had a curious faith in movies and in books; she admired anything that made her feel and that did not require responsibility from her, because then she produced happiness like silk for herself and others. She liked really obscure philosophers, like Hegel, where she could admire the thought but where the thought didn't demand anything from her. Still, she was a realist, and she would probably learn what I knew and would surpass me. She had great possibilities. But she was also merely a good-looking, pseudorich girl, a paranoid, a Perkins. On the other hand, she was a fairly marvelous girl a lot of the time, brave, eye-shattering, who could split my heart open with one slightly shaky approving-of-me brainy romantic heroine's smile. The romantic splendor of her face. So far in her life she had disappointed everyone. I had to keep all this in mind, I figured. She was fantastically alive and eerily dead at the same time. I wanted for my various reasons to raise her from the dead.

IV Orra: The Same World, a Different Time Scale

One afternoon, things went well for us. We went for a walk, the air was plangent, there was the amazed and polite pleasure we had sometimes merely at being together. Orra adjusted her pace now and then to mine; and I kept mine adjusted to her most of the time. When we looked at each other, there would be small, soft puffs of feeling as of toy explosions or sparrows bathing in the dust. Her willed softness, her inner seriousness or earnestness, her strength, her beauty, muted and careful now in her anxiety not to lose me yet, made the pleasure of being with her noble, contrapuntal, and difficult in that one had to live up to it and understand it and protect it, against my clumsiness and Orra's falsity, kind as that falsity was; or the day would become simply an exploitation of a strong girl who would see through that sooner or later and avenge it. But things went well; and inside that careless and careful goodness, we went home; we screwed; I came – to get my excitement out of the way; she didn't know I was doing that; she was stupendously polite; taut; and very admiring. "How pretty you are," she said. Her eyes were blurred with half-tears. I'd screwed without any fripperies, coolly, in order to leave in us a large residue of sexual restlessness but with the burr of immediate physical restlessness in me removed: I still wanted her; I always wanted Orra; and the coming had been dull; but my body was not very assertive, was more like a glove for my mind, for my will, for my love for her, for my wanting to make her feel more.

She was slightly tearful, as I said, and gentle, and she held me in her arms after I came, and I said something like "Don't relax. I want to come again," and she partly laughed, partly sighed, and was flattered, and said, "Again? That's nice." We had a terrific closeness, almost like a man and a secretary – I was free and powerful, and she was devoted: there was little chance Orra would ever be a secretary – she'd been offered executive jobs already for when she finished college – but to play at being a secretary who had no life of her own was a romantic thing for Orra. I felt some apprehension, as before a game of tennis that I wanted to win, or as before stealing something off a counter in a store: there was a dragging enervation, a fear and silence, and there was a lifting, a preparation, a willed and then unwilled, self-contained fixity of purpose; it was a settled thing; it would happen.

After about ten minutes or so, perhaps it was twenty, I moved in her: I should say that while I'd rested, I'd stayed in her (and she'd held on to me). As I'd expected – and with satisfaction and pride that everything was working, my endowments were cooperating – I felt my prick come up; it came up at once with comic promptness, but it was sore – Jesus, was it sore. It, its head, ached like hell, with a dry, burning, reddish pain.

The pain made me chary and prevented me from being excited except in an abstract way; my mind was clear; I was idly smiling as I began, moving very slowly, just barely moving, sore of pressing on her inside her, moving around, lollygagging around, feeling out the reaches in there, arranging the space inside her, as if to put the inner soft-oiled shadows in her in order; or like stretching out your hand in the dark and pressing a curve of a blanket into familiarity or to locate yourself when you're half asleep, when your eyes are closed. In fact, I did close my eyes and listened carefully to her breathing, concentrating on her but trying not to let her see I was doing that because it would make her self-conscious.

Her reaction was so minimal that I lost faith in fucking for getting her started, and I thought I'd better go down on her; I pulled out of her, which wasn't too smart, but I wasn't thinking all that consequentially; she'd told me on other occasions she didn't like "all that foreign la-di-da," that it didn't excite her, but I'd always thought it was only that she was ashamed of not coming and that made being gone down on hard for her. I started in on it; she protested; and I pooh-poohed her objections and did it anyway; I was raw with nerves, with stifled amusement because of the lying and the tension, so much of it. I remarked to her that I was going down on her for my own pleasure; I was jolted by touching her with my tongue there when I was so raw-nerved, but I hid that. It seemed to me physical unhappiness and readiness were apparent in her skin – my lips and tongue carried the currents of a jagged unhappiness and readiness in her into me; echoes of her stiffness and dissatisfaction sounded in my mouth, my head, my feet; my entire tired body was a stethoscope. I was entirely a stethoscope; I listened to her with my *bones*; the glimmers of excitement in her traveled to my *spine*; I felt her grinding sexual haltedness, like a car's broken starter motor grinding away in her, in my *stomach,* in my *knees.* Every part of me listened to her; every goddamned twinge of muscular contraction she had that I noticed or that she should have had because I was licking her clitoris and she didn't have, every testimony of excitement or of no-excitement in her, I listened for so hard it was amazing it didn't drive her out of bed with self-consciousness; but she probably couldn't tell what I was doing, since I was out of her line of sight, was down in the shadows, in the basement of her field of vision, in the basement with her sexual feelings where they lay, strewn about.

When she said, "No … No, Wiley … Please don't. No …" and wiggled, although it wasn't the usual pointless protest that some girls might make – it was real, she wanted me to stop – I didn't listen because I could feel she responded to my tongue more than she had to the fucking a moment before. I could feel beads sliding and whispering and being strung together rustlingly in her; the disorder, the scattered or strewn sexual bits, to a very small extent were being put in order. She shuddered. With discomfort. She produced, was subjected to, her erratic responses. And she made odd, small cries, protests mostly, uttered little exclamations that mysteriously were protests although they were not protests, too, cries that somehow suggested the ground of protest kept changing for her.

I tried to string a number of those cries together, to cause them to occur in a mounting sequence. It was a peculiar attempt: it seemed we moved, I moved with her, on dark water, between two lines of buoys, dark on one side, there was nothingness there, and on the other, lights, red and green, the lights of the body advancing on sexual heat, the signs of it anyway, nipples like scored pebbles, legs lightly thrashing, little *oh*s; nothing important, a body thing; you go on: you proceed.

When we strayed too far, there was nothingness, or only a

distant flicker, only the faintest guidance. Sometimes we were surrounded by the lights of her responses, widely spaced, bobbing unevenly, on some darkness, some ignorance we both had, Orra and I, of what were the responses of her body. To the physical things I did and to the atmosphere of the way I did them, to the authority, the argument I made that this was sexual for her, that the way I touched her and concentrated on her, on that partly dream-laden dark water or underwater thing, she responded; she rested on that, rolled heavily on that. Everything I did was speech, was hieroglyphics, pictures on her nerves; it was what masculine authority was for, was what bravery and a firm manner and musculature were supposed to indicate that a man could bring to bed. Or skill at dancing; or musicianliness; or a sad knowingness. Licking her, holding her belly, stroking her belly pretty much with unthought-out movements – sometimes just moving my fingers closer together and spreading them again to show my pleasure, to show how rewarded I felt, not touching her breasts or doing anything so intensely that it would make her suspect me of being out to make her come – I did those things but it seemed like I left her alone and was private with my own pleasures. She felt unobserved with her sensations, she had them without responsibility, she clutched at them as something round and slippery in the water, and she would fall off them, occasionally gasping at the loss of her balance, the loss of her self-possession, too.

I'd flick, idly almost, at her little spaghetti-ending with my tongue, then twice more idly, then three or four or five times in sequence, then settle down to rub it or bounce it between lip and tongue in a steadily more earnest way until my head, my consciousness, my lips and tongue were buried in the dark of an ascending and concentrated rhythm, in the way a stoned dancer lets a movement catch him and wrap him around and become all of him, become his voyage and not a collection of repetitions at all.

Then some boring stringy thing, a sinew at the base of my tongue, would begin to ache, and I'd break off that movement, and sleepily lick her, or if the tongue was too uncomfortable, I'd worry her clit, I'd nuzzle it with my pursed lips until the muscles that held my lips pursed grew tired in their turn; and I'd go back and flick at her tiny clitoris with my tongue, and go on as before, until the darkness came; she sensed the darkness, the privacy for her, and she seemed like someone in a hallway, unobserved, moving her arms, letting her mind stroke itself, taking a step in that dark.

But whatever she felt was brief and halting; and when she seemed to halt or to be dead or jagged, I authoritatively, gesturally accepted that as part of what was pleasurable to me and did not let it stand as hint or foretaste of failure; I produced sighs of pleasure, even gasps, not all of them false, warm nuzzlings, and caresses that indicated I was rewarded – I produced rewarded strokings; I made elements of sexual pleasure out of moments that were unsexual and that could be taken as the collapse of sexuality.

And she couldn't contradict me because she thought I was working on my own coming, and she loved me and meant to be cooperative.

What I did took nerve because it gave her a tremendous ultimate power to laugh at me, although what the courtship up until now had been for was to show that she was not an enemy, that she could control the hysteria of fear or jealousy in her or the cold judgments in her of me that would lead her to say or do things that would make me hate or fear her; what was at stake included the risk that I would look foolish in my own eyes – and might then attack her for failing to come – and then she would be unable to resist the inward conviction that I was a fool. Any attempted act confers vulnerability on you, but an act devoted to her pleasure represented doubled vulnerability since only she could judge it; and I was safe only if I was immune or insensitive to her; but if I was immune or insensitive I could not hope to help her come; by making myself vulnerable to her, I was in a way being a sissy or a creep because Orra wasn't organized or trained or prepared to accept responsibility for how I felt about myself: she was a woman who wanted to be left alone; she was paranoid about the inroads on her life men in their egos tried to make: there was dangerous masochism, dangerous hubris, dangerous hopefulness, and a form of love in my doing what I did: I nuzzled nakedly at the crotch of the sexual tigress; any weakness in her ego or her judgment and she would lash out at *me*; and the line was very frail between what I was doing as love and as intrusion, exploitation, and stupid boastfulness. There was no way for me even to begin to imagine the mental pain – or the physical pain – for her if I should fail and, to add to that, if I should withdraw from her emotionally, too, because of my failure and hers and our pain. Or merely because the failure might make me so uncomfortable I couldn't go on unless she nursed my ego, and she couldn't nurse my ego, she didn't know how to do it, and probably was inhibited about doing it.

Sometimes my hands, my fingers, not just the tops, but all

of their inside surface and the palms, held her thighs, or cupped her little belly, or my fingers moved around the lips, the labia or whatever, or even poked a little into her, or with the nails or tips lightly nudged her clitoris, always within a fictional frame of my absolute sexual pleasure, of my admiration for this sex, of there being no danger in it for us. No tongues or brains handy to speak unkindly, I meant. My God, I felt exposed and noble. This was a great effort to make for her.

Perhaps that only indicates the extent of my selfishness. I didn't mind being feminized except for the feeling that Orra would not ever understand what I was doing but would ascribe it to the power of my or our sexuality. I minded being this self-conscious and so conscious of her; I was separated from my own sexuality, from any real sexuality; a poor sexual experience, even one based on love, would diminish the ease of my virility with her at least for a while; and she wouldn't understand. Maybe she would become much subtler and shrewder sexually and know how to handle me, but that wasn't likely. And if I apologized or complained or explained in that problematic future why I was sexually a little slow or reluctant with her, she would then blame my having tried to give her orgasm, she would insist I must not be bored again, so I would in that problematic future, if I wanted her to come, have to lie and say I was having more excitement than I felt, and that, too, might diminish my pleasure. I would be deprived even of the chance for honesty: I would be further feminized in that regard. I thought all this while I went down on her. I didn't put it in words but thought in great misty blocks of something known or sensed. I felt an inner weariness I kept working in spite of. This ignoring myself gave me an odd, starved feeling, a mixture of agony and helplessness. I didn't want to feel like that. I suddenly wondered why in the theory of relativity the speed of light is given as a constant: was that more Jewish absolutism? Surely in a universe as changeable and as odd as this one, the speed of light, considering the variety of experiences, must vary; there must be a place where one could see a beam of light struggle to move. I felt silly and selfish; it couldn't be avoided that I felt like that – I mean, it couldn't be avoided by *me*.

Whatever she did when I licked her, if she moved at all, if a muscle twitched in her thigh, a muscle twitched in mine, my body imitated hers as if to measure what she felt or perhaps for no reason but only because the sympathy was so intense. The same things happened to each of us but in amazingly different contexts, as if we stood at opposite ends of the room and reached out to touch each other and to receive identical messages which then diverged as they entered two such widely separated sensibilities and two such divergent and incomplete ecstasies. The movie we watched was of her discovering how her sexual responses worked: we were seated far apart. My tongue pushed at her erasure, her wronged and heretofore hardly existent sexual powers. I stirred her with varieties of kisses far from her face. A strange river moved slowly, bearing us along, reeds hid the banks, willows braided and unbraided themselves, moaned and whispered, raveled and faintly clicked. Orra groaned, sighed, shuddered, shuddered harshly or liquidly; sometimes she jumped when I changed the pressure or posture of my hands on her or when I rested for a second and then resumed. Her body jumped and contracted interestingly but not at any length or in any pattern that I could understand. My mind grew tired. There is a limit to invention, to mine anyway: I saw myself (stupidly) as a Roman trireme, my tongue as the prow, *bronze,* pushing at her; she was the Mediterranean. Tiers of slaves – my God, the helplessness of them – pulled oars, long stalks that metaphorically and rhythmically bloomed with flowing clusters of short-lived lilies at the water's surface. The pompous and out-of-proportion boat, all of me hunched over Orra's small sea – not actually hunched: what I was was lying flat; the foot of the bed was at my waist or near there, my legs were out, my feet were propped distantly on the floor, all of me was concentrated on the soft, shivery, furry delicacies of Orra's twat – the pompous boat advanced lickingly, leaving a trickling, gurgling wake of half-response, the ebbing of my will and activity into that fluster subsiding into the dark water of this girl's passivity, taut storminess, and self-ignorance.

The whitish bubbling, the splash of her discontinuous physical response: those waves, ah, that wake rose, curled outward, bubbled, and fell. Rose, curled outward, bubbled, and fell. The white fell of a naiad. In the vast spreading darkness and silence of the sea. There was nothing but that wake. The darkness of my senses when the rhythm absorbed me (so that I vanished from my awareness, so that I was blotted up and was a stain, a squid hidden, stroking Orra) made it twilight or night for me; and my listening for her pleasure, for our track on that markless ocean, gave me the sense that where we were was in a lit-up, great, ill-defined oval of night air and sea and opalescent fog, rainbowed where the lights from the portholes of an immense ship were altered prismatically by droplets of mist – as in some 1930s movie, as in some dream. Often I was out of breath; I saw spots, colors, ocean depths. And her protests, her doubts! My God, her doubts! Her *No, don't, Wiley*s and her *I don't want to do this*es and her *Wiley, don't*s and *Wiley, I can't come – don't do this – I don't like this*es. Mostly I ignored her. Sometimes I silenced her by leaning my cheek on her belly and watching my hand stroke her belly and saying to her in a sex-thickened voice, "Orra, I like this – this is for me."

Then I went down on her again with unexpectedly vivid, real pleasure, as if merely thinking about my own pleasure excited and refreshed me, and there was yet more pleasure, when she – reassured or strengthened by my putative selfishness, by the conviction that this was all for me, that nothing was expected of her – cried out. Then a second later she *grunted.* Her whole body rippled. Jesus, I loved it when she reacted to me. It was like causing an entire continent to convulse, Asia, South America. I felt huge and tireless.

In her excitement, she threw herself into the air, but my hands happened to be on her belly; and I fastened her down, I held that part of her comparatively still, with her twat fastened to my mouth, and I licked her while she was in midheave; and she yelled; I kept my mouth there as if I were drinking from her; I stayed like that until her upper body fell back on the bed and bounced, she made the whole bed bounce; then my head bounced away from her; but I still held her down with my hands; and I fastened myself, my mouth, on her twat again; and she yelled in a deep voice, *"Wiley, what are you doing!"*

Her voice was deep, as if her impulses at that moment were masculine, not out of neurosis but in generosity, in an attempt to improve on the sickliness she accused women of; she wanted to meet me halfway, to share; to share my masculinity: she thought men were beautiful. She cried out, *"I don't want you to do things to me! I want you to have a good fuck!"*

Her voice was deep and despairing, maybe with the despair that goes with surges of sexuality, but then maybe she thought I would make her pay for this. I said, "Orra, I like this stuff, this stuff is what gets me excited." She resisted, just barely, for some infinitesimal fragment of a second, and then her body began to vibrate; it twittered as if in it were the strings of a musical instrument set jangling; she said foolishly – but sweetly – "Wiley, I'm embarrassed, Wiley, this embarrasses *me* … Please stop … No … No … No … Oh … Oh … Oh … I'm very sexual, I'm too sexual to have orgasms, Wiley, stop, please … Oh … Oh … Oh …" And then a deeper shudder ran through her; she gasped; then there was a silence; then she gasped again; she cried out in an extraordinary voice, "I FEEL SOMETHING!" The hair stood up on the back of my neck; I couldn't stop; I hurried on; I heard a dim moaning come from her. What had she felt before? I licked hurriedly. How unpleasant for her, how unreal and twitchy had the feelings been that I'd given her? In what way was this different? I wondered if there was in her a sudden swarming along her nerves, a warm conviction of the reality of sexual pleasure. She heaved like a whale – no: not so much as that. But it was as if half an ocean rolled off her young flanks; some element of darkness vanished from the room; some slight color of physical happiness tinctured her body and its thin coating of sweat; I felt it all through me; she rolled on the surface of a pale blue, a pink and blue sea; she was dark and gleaming, and immense and wet. And warm.

She cried, *"Wiley, I feel a lot!"*

God, she was happy.

I said, "Why not?" I wanted to lower the drama quotient; I thought the excess of drama was a mistake, would overburden her. But also I wanted her to defer to me, I wanted authority over her body now, I wanted to make her come.

But she didn't get any more excited than that: she was rigid, almost boardlike after a few seconds. I licked at her thing as best I could but the sea was dry; the board collapsed. I faked it that I was very excited; actually I was so caught up in being sure of myself, I didn't know what I really felt. I thought, as if I were much younger than I was, Boy, if this doesn't work, is my name mud. Then to build up the risk, out of sheer hellish braggadocio, instead of just acting out that I was confident – and in sex, everything unsaid that is portrayed in gestures instead is twice as powerful – when she said, because the feeling was less for her now, the feeling she liked having gone away, "Wiley, I can't – this is silly –" I said, "Shut up, Orra, I know what I'm doing. . . ." But I didn't know.

And I didn't like that tone for sexual interplay either, except as a joke, or as role playing, because pure authority involves pure submission, and people don't survive pure submission except by being slavishly, possessively, vindictively in love; when they are in love like that, they can *give* you nothing but rebellion and submission, bitchiness and submission; it's a general rottenness: you get no part of them out of bed that has any value; and in bed, you get a grudging submission, because what the slave requires is your total attention, or she starts paying you back; I suppose the model is childhood, that slavery. Anyway, I don't like it. But I played at it then, with Orra, as a gamble.

Everything was a gamble. I didn't know what I was doing; I

figured it out as I went along; and how much time did I have for figuring things out just then? I felt strained as at poker or roulette, sweaty and a little stupid, placing bets – with my tongue – and waiting to see what the wheel did, risking my money when no one forced me to, hoping things would go my way, and I wouldn't turn out to have been stupid when this was over.

Also, there were sudden fugitive convulsions of lust now, in sympathy with her larger but scattered responses, a sort of immediate and automatic sexuality – I was at the disposal, inwardly, of the sexuality in her and could not help myself, could not hold it back and avoid the disappointments, and physical impatience, the impatience in my skin and prick, of the huge desire that unmistakably accompanies love, of a primitive longing for what seemed her happiness, for closeness to her as to something I had studied and was studying and had found more and more of value in – what was of value was the way she valued me, a deep and no doubt limited (but in the sexual moment it seemed illimitable) permissiveness toward me, a risk she took, an allowance she made as if she'd let me damage her and use her badly.

Partly what kept me going was stubbornness because I'd made up my mind before we started that I wouldn't give up; and partly what it was was the feeling she aroused in me, a feeling that was, to be honest, made up of tenderness and concern and a kind of mere affection, a brotherliness, as if she were my brother, not different from me at all.

Actually this was brought on by an increasing failure, as the sex went on, of one kind of sophistication – of worldly sophistication – and by the increase in me of another kind, of a childish sophistication, a growth of innocence: Orra said, or exclaimed, in a half-harried, half-amazed voice, in a hugely admiring, gratuitous way, as she clutched at me in approval, "Wiley, I never had feelings like these before!"

And to be the first to have caused them, you know? It's like being a collector, finding something of great value, where it had been unsuspected and disguised, or like earning any honor; this partial success, this encouragement gave rise to this pride, this inward innocence.

Of course that lessened the risk for this occasion; I could fail now and still say, *It was worth it,* and she would agree; but it lengthened the slightly longer-term risk; because I might feel trebly a fool someday. Also, it meant we might spend months making love in this fashion – I'd get impotent, maybe not in terms of erection, but I wouldn't look forward to sex – still, that was beautiful to me in a way, too, and exciting. I really didn't know what I was thinking: whatever I thought was part of the sex.

I went on; I wanted to hit the jackpot now. Then Orra shouted, "It's *there!* It's THERE!" I halted, thinking she meant it was in some specific locale, in some specific motion I'd just made with my tired tongue and jaw; I lifted my head – but couldn't speak: in a way, the sexuality pressed on me too hard for me to speak; anyway, I didn't have to; she had lifted her head with a kind of overt twinship and she was looking at me down the length of her body; her face was askew and boyish – every feature was wrinkled; she looked angry and yet naive and swindleable; she said angrily, naively, *"Wiley, it's there!"*

But even before she spoke that time, I knew she'd meant it was in her; the fox had been startled from its covert again; she had seen it, had felt it run in her again. She had been persuaded that it was in her for good.

I started manipulating her delicately with my hand; and in my own excitement, and thinking she was ready, I sort of scrambled up and, covering her with myself, and playing with her with one hand, guided my other self, my lower consciousness, into her. My God, she was warm and restless inside; it was heated in there and smooth, insanely smooth, and oiled, and full of movements. But I knew at once I'd made a mistake: I should have gone on licking her; there were no regular contractions; she was anxious for the prick, she rose around it, closed around it, but in a rigid, dumb, faraway way; and her twitchings played on it, ran through it, through the walls of it and into me; and they were uncontrolled and not exciting, but empty: she didn't know what to do, how to be fucked and come. I couldn't pull out of her, I didn't want to, I couldn't pull out; but if there were no contractions for me to respond to, how in hell would I find the rhythm for her? I started slowly, with what seemed infinite suggestiveness to me, with great dirtiness, a really grown-up sort of fucking – just in case she was far along – and she let out a huge, shuddering, hour-long sigh and cried out my name and then, in a sobbing, exhausted voice, said, "I lost it.... Oh, Wiley, I lost it.... Let's stop...." My face was above hers; her face was wet with tears; why was she crying like that? She had changed her mind; now she wanted to come; she turned her head back and forth; she said, "I'm no good.... I'm no good.... Don't worry about me.... You come...."

No matter what I mumbled, "Hush," and "Don't be silly," and in a whisper, "Orra, I love you," she kept on saying those things, until I slapped her lightly and said, *"Shut up, Orra."*

Then she was silent again.

The thing was, apparently, that she was arrhythmic: at least that's what I thought; and that meant there weren't going to be regular contractions; any rhythm for me to follow; and any rhythm I set up as I fucked, she broke with her movements: so that it was that when she moved, she made her excitement go away. It would be best if she moved very smally: but I was afraid to tell her that, or even to try to hold her hips firmly, and guide them, to instruct her in that way for fear she'd get self-conscious and lose what momentum she'd won. And also I was ashamed that I'd stopped going down on her. I experimented – doggedly, sweatily, to make up for what I'd done – with fucking in different ways, and I fantasized about us being in Mexico, someplace warm and lushly colored where we made love easily and filthily and graphically. The fantasy kept me going. That is, it kept me hard. I kept acting out an atmosphere of sexual pleasure – I mean of my sexual pleasure – for her to rest on, so she could count on that. I discovered that a not very slow sort of one-one-one stroke, or fuck-fuck-fuck-Orra-now-now-now, really got to her; her feelings would grow heated; and she could shift up from that with me into a one-two, one-two, one-two, her excitement rising; but if she or I then tried to shift up farther to one-two-three, one-two-three, she'd lose it all. That was too complicated for her: my own true love, my white American. But her feelings when they were present were very strong, they came in gusts, huge squalls of heat as if from a furnace with a carelessly banging door, and they excited and allured both of us. That excitement and the dit-dit-ditting got to her; she began to be generally, continuingly sexual. It's almost standard to compare sexual excitement to holiness;

well, after a while, holiness seized her; she spoke in tongues, she testified. She was shaking all over; she was saved temporarily and sporadically: that is, she kept lapsing out of that excitement, too. But it would recur. Her hands would flutter; her face would be pale and then red, then very, very red; her eyes would stare at nothing; she'd call my name. I'd plug on one-one-one, then one-two, one-two, then I'd go back to one-one-one: I could see as before – in the deep pleasure I felt even in the midst of the labor – why a woman was proud of what she felt, why a man might kill her in order to stimulate in her (although he might not know this was why he did it) these signs of pleasure. The familiar Orra had vanished; she said, "GodohGodohGod"; it was sin and redemption and holiness and visions time. Her throbs were very direct, easily comprehensible, but without any pattern; they weren't in any regular sequence; still, they were exciting to me, maybe all the more exciting because of the piteousness of her not being able to regulate them, of their being like blows delivered inside her by an enemy whom she couldn't even half domesticate or make friendly to herself or speak to. She was the most out-of-control girl I ever screwed. She would at times start to thrust like a woman who had her sexuality readied and well understood at last, and I'd start to distend with anticipation and a pride and relief as large as a house; but after two thrusts – or four, or six – she'd have gotten too excited, she'd be shaking, she'd thrust crookedly and out of tempo, the movement would collapse; or she'd suddenly jerk in midmovement without warning and crash around with so great and so meaningless a violence that she'd lose her thing; and she'd start to cry. She'd whisper wetly, "I lost it"; so I'd say, "No, you didn't," and I'd go on or start over, one-one-one; and of course, the excitement would come back; sometimes it came back at once; but she was increasingly afraid of herself, afraid to move her lower body; she would try to hold still and just *receive* the excitement; she would let it pool up in her; but then, too, she'd begin to shake more and more; she'd leak over into spasmodic and oddly sad, too large movements; and she'd whimper, knowing, I suppose, that those movements were breaking the tempo in herself; again and again, tears streamed down her cheeks; she said in a not quite hoarse, in a sweet, almost hoarse whisper, "I don't want to come, Wiley, you go ahead and come."

My mind had pretty much shut off; it had become exhausted; and I didn't see how we were going to make this work; she said, "Wiley, it's all right – please, it's all right – I don't want to come."

I wondered if I should say something and try to trigger some fantasy in her; but I didn't want to risk saying something she'd find unpleasant or think was a reproach or a hint for her to be sexier. I thought if I just kept on dit-dit-ditting, sooner or later she'd find it in herself, the trick of riding on her feelings, and getting them to rear up, crest, and topple. I held her tightly, in sympathy and pity, and maybe fear, and admiration: she was so unhysterical; she hadn't yelled at me or broken anything; she hadn't ordered me around: she was simply alone and shaking in the middle of a neural storm in her that she seemed to have no gift for handling. I said, "Orra, it's O.K.: I really prefer long fucks," and I went on, dit-dit-dit-dit, then I'd shift up to dit-dot, dit-dot, dit-dot, dit-dot.... My back hurt, my legs were going; if sweat was sperm, we would have looked like liquefied snowfields.

Orra made noises, more and more quickly, and louder and louder; then the noises she made slackened off. Then, step by step, with shorter and shorter strokes, then out of control and clumsy, simply reestablishing myself inside the new approach, I settled down, fucked slowly. The prick was embedded far in her; I barely stirred; the drama of sexual movement died away, the curtains were stilled; there was only sensation on the stage.

I bumped against the stone blocks and hidden hooks that nipped and bruised me into the soft rottenness, the strange, glowing, breakable hardness of coming, of the sensations at the approaches to coming.

I panted and half rolled and pushed and edged it in, and slid it back, sweatily – I was semiexpert, aimed, intent. Sex can be like a wilderness that imprisons you: the daimons of the locality claim you. I was achingly nagged by sensations; my prick had been somewhat softened before, and now it swelled with a sore-headed but fine distension; Orra shuddered and held me cooperatively; I began to forget her.

I thought she was making herself come on the slow fucking, on the prick which, when it was seated in her like this, when I hardly moved it, seemed to belong to her as much as to me; the prick seemed to *enter* me, too: we both seemed to be sliding on it; the sensation was like that; but there was the moment when I became suddenly aware of her again, of the flesh and blood and bone in my arms, beneath me. I had a feeling of grating on her, and of her grating on me. I didn't recognize the unpleasantness at first. I don't know how long it went on before I felt it as a withdrawal in her, a withdrawal that she had made, a patient and restrained horror in her, and impatience in me: our arrival at sexual shambles.

My heart filled suddenly – filled; and then all feeling ran out of it – it emptied itself.

I continued to move in her slowly, numbly, in a shabby hubbub of faceless shudderings and shufflings of the midsection and half-thrusts, half-twitches; we went on holding each other, in silence, without slackening the intensity with which we held each other; our movements, that flopping in place, that grinding against each other, went on; neither of us protested in any way. Bad sex can be sometimes stronger and more moving than good sex. She made sobbing noises – and held on to me. After a while sex seemed very ordinary and familiar and unromantic. I started going dit-dit-dit again.

Her hips jerked up half a dozen times before it occurred to me again that she liked to thrust like a boy, that she wanted to thrust; and then it occurred to me that she wanted me to thrust.

I maneuvered my ass slightly and tentatively delivered a shove, or rather, delivered an authoritative shove, but not one of great length, one that was exploratory; Orra sighed, with relief it seemed to me; and jerked, encouragingly, too late, as I was pulling back. When I delivered a second thrust, a somewhat more obvious one, more amused, almost boyish, I was like a boy whipping a fairly fast ball, in a game, at a first baseman – she jerked almost wolfishly, gobbling up the extravagant power of the gesture, of the thrust; with an odd shudder of pleasure, of irresponsibility, of boyishness, I suddenly realized how physically strong Orra was, how well knit, how well put together her body was, how great the power in it, the power of endurance in it; and a phrase – absurd and demeaning but exciting just then – came into my head: *to throw a fuck*; and I settled myself atop her, braced my toes and knees and elbows and hands on the bed and half-scramblingly worked *it* – *it* was clearly mine; but I was Orra's – worked *it* into a passionate shove, a curving stroke about a third as long as a full stroke; but amateur and gentle: that is, tentative still; and Orra screamed then; how she screamed: she made known her readiness; then the next time, she grunted: "Uhnnnnahh-hhhh ..." a sound thick at the beginning but that trailed into refinement, into sweetness, a lingering sweetness.

It seemed to me I really wanted to fuck like this, that *I* had been waiting for this all my life. But it wasn't really my taste, that kind of fuck: I liked to throw a fuck with less force and more gradations and implications of force rather than with the actual thing; and with more immediate contact between the two sets of pleasures and with more admissions of defeat and triumph; my pleasure was a thing of me reflecting her, her spirit entering me; or perhaps it was merely a mistake, my thinking that; but it seemed shameful and automatic, naive and animal, to throw the prick into her like that.

She took the thrust: she convulsed a little; she fluttered all over; her skin fluttered; things twitched in her, in the disorder surrounding the phallic blow in her. After two thrusts, she collapsed, went flaccid, then toughened and readied herself again, rose a bit from the bed, aimed the flattened, mysteriously funnel-like container of her lower end at me, too high, so that I had to pull her down with my hands on her butt or on her hips; and her face, when I glanced at her beneath my lids, was fantastically pleasing, set, concentrated, busy, harassed; her body was strong, was stone, smooth stone and wet-satin paper bags and snaky webs, thin and alive, made of woven snakes that lived, thrown over the stone; she held the great, writhing-skinned stone construction toward me, the bony marvel, the half-dish of bone with its secretive, gluey-smooth entrance, *the place where I was* – it was undefined, except for that: *the place where I was;* she took and met each thrust – and shuddered and collapsed and rose again: she seemed to rise to the act of taking it; I thought she was partly mistaken, childish, to think that the center of sex was to meet and take the prick thrown into her as hard as it could be thrown, now that she was excited; but there was a weird wildness, a wild freedom, like children cavorting, uncontrolled, set free, but not hysterical, merely without restraint; the odd, thickened, knobbed pole springing back and forth as if mounted on a web of wide rubber bands: it was a naive and a complete release. I whomped it in and she went, "UHNNN!" and a half-iota of a second later, I was seated all the way in her, I jerked a minim of an inch deeper in her, and went, "UHNNN!" too. Her whole body shook. She would go, "UHN!" And I would go, "UHN!"

Then when it seemed from her strengthening noises and her more rapid and jerkier movements that she was near the edge of coming, I'd start to place the whomps, in neater and firmer arrangements, more obviously in a rhythm, more businesslike, more teasing, with pauses at each end of a thrust; and that would excite her up to a point; but then her excitement would level off, and not go over the brink. So I would speed up: I'd thrust harder, then harder yet, then harder and faster; she made her noises and half-thrust back. She bit her lower lip; she set her teeth in her lower lip; blood appeared. I fucked still faster, but on a shorter stroke, almost thrumming on her, and angling my abdomen hopefully to drum on her clitoris; sometimes her body would go limp; but her cries would speed up, bird after bird flew out of her mouth while she lay limp as if I were a boxer and had destroyed her ability to move; then when the cries did not go past a certain point, when she didn't come, I'd slow and start again. I wished I'd been a great athlete, a master of movement, a woman, a lesbian, a man with a gigantic prick that would explode her into coming. I moved my hands to the corners of the mattress; and spread my legs; I braced myself with my hands and feet; and braced like that, free-handed in a way, drove into her; and the new posture, the feeling she must have had of being covered, and perhaps the difference in the thrust got to her; but Orra's body began to set up a babble, a babble of response, then – I think the posture played on her mind.

But she did not come.

I moved my hands and held the dish of her hips so that she couldn't wiggle or deflect the thrust or pull away: she began to "Uhn" again but interspersed with small screams: we were like kids playing catch (her poor brutalized clitoris), playing hard hand: this was what she thought sex was; it was sexual, as throwing a ball hard is sexual; in a way, too, we were like acrobats hurling ourselves at each other, to meet in midair and fall entangled to the net. It was like that.

Her mouth came open, her eyes had rolled to one side and stayed there – it felt like twilight to me – I knew where she was sexually, or thought I did. She pushed, she egged us on. She wasn't breakable this way. Orra. I wondered if she knew, it made me like her, how naive this was, this American fuck, this kids-playing-at-twilight-on-the-neighborhood-street fuck. After I seated it and wriggled a bit in her and moozed on her clitoris with my abdomen, I would draw it out not in a straight line but at some curve so that it would press against the walls of her cunt and she could keep track of where it was; and I would pause fractionally just before starting to thrust, so she could brace herself and expect it; I whomped it in and understood her with an absurd and probably unfounded sense of my sexual virtuosity; and she became silent suddenly, then she began to breathe loudly, then something in her toppled; or broke, then all at once she shuddered in a different way. It really was as if she lay on a bed of wings, as if she had a half-dozen wings folded under her, six huge wings, large, veined, throbbing, alive wings, real ones, with fleshy edges from which glittering feathers sprang backward; and they all stirred under her.

She half-rose; and I'd hold her so she didn't fling herself around and lose her footing, or her airborneness, on the uneasy glass mountain she'd begun to ascend, the frail transparency beneath her, that was forming and growing beneath her, that seemed to me to foam with light and darkness, as if we were rising above a landscape of hedges and moonlight and shadows: a mountain, a sea that formed and grew; it grew and grew; and she said "OH!" and "OHHHH!" almost with vertigo, as if she were airborne but unsteady on the vans of her wings, and as if I were there without wings but by some magic dispensation and by some grace of familiarity; I thunked on and on, and she looked down and was frightened; the tension in her body grew vast; and suddenly a great, a really massive violence ran through her, but now it was as if, in fear at her height, or out of some automatism, the first of her three pairs of wings began to beat, great fans winnowingly, great wings of flesh out of which feathers grew, catching at the air, stabilizing and yet lifting her: she whistled and rustled so; she was at once so still and so violent; the great wings engendered, their movement engendered in her, patterns of flexed and crossed muscles: her arms and legs and breasts echoed or carried out the strain, or strained to move the weight of those winnowing, moving wings. Her breaths were wild but not loud and slanted every which way, irregular and new to this particular dream, and very much as if she looked down on great spaces of air; she grabbed at me, at my shoulders, but she had forgotten how to work her hands; her hands just made the gestures of grabbing, the gestures of a well-meaning, dark but beginning to be luminous, mad, amnesiac angel. She called out, "Wiley, Wiley!" but she called it out in a *whisper*, the whisper of someone floating across a night sky, of someone crazily ascending, someone who was going crazy, who was taking on the mad purity and temper of angels, someone who was tormented unendurably by this, who was unendurably frightened, whose pleasure was enormous, half human, mad. Then she screamed in rebuke, "Wiley!" She screamed my name: "*Wiley!*" – she did it hoarsely and insanely, asking for help, but blaming me, and merely as exclamation; it was a gutter sound in part, and ugly; the ugliness destroyed nothing, or maybe it had an impetus of its own, but it whisked away another covering, a membrane of ordinariness – I don't know – and her second pair of wings began to beat; her whole body was aflutter on the bed. I was as wet as – as some fish, thonking away, sweatily. Grinding away. I said, "It's O.K., Orra. It's O.K." And poked on. In midair. She shouted, "*What is this!*" She shouted it in the way a tremendously large person who can defend herself might shout at someone who was unwisely beating her up. She shouted – angrily, as an announcement of anger, it seemed – "*Oh my*

God!" Like: *Who broke this cup?* I plugged on. She raised her torso, her head, she looked me clearly in the eye, her eyes were enormous, were bulging, and she said, "*Wiley, it's happening!*" Then she lay down again and screamed for a couple of seconds. I said a little dully, grinding on, "It's O.K., Orra. It's O.K." I didn't want to say *Let go* or to say anything lucid because I didn't know a damn thing about female orgasm after all, and I didn't want to give her any advice and wreck things; and also I didn't want to commit myself in case this turned out to be a false alarm; and we had to go on. I pushed in, lingered, pulled back, went in, only half on beat, one-thonk-one-thonk, then one-one-one, saying, "This is sexy, this is good for me, Orra, this is very good for me," and then, "Good Orra," and she trembled in a new way at that, "*Good* Orra," I said, "*Good … Orra*," and then all at once, it happened. Something pulled her over; and something gave in; and all three pairs of wings began to beat: she was the center and the source and the victim of a storm of wing beats; we were at the top of the world; the huge bird of God's body in us hovered; the great miracle pounded on her back, pounded around us; she was straining and agonized and distraught, estranged within this corporeal-incorporeal thing, this angelic other avatar, this other substance of herself: the wings were outspread; they thundered and gaspily galloped with her; they half-broke her; and she screamed, "*Wiley!*" and "*Mygodmygod*" and "IT'S NOT STOPPING, WILEY, IT'S NOT STOPPING!" She was pale *and* red; her hair was everywhere; her body was wet, and thrashing. It was as if something unbelievably strange and fierce – like the holy temper – lifted her to where she could not breathe or walk: she choked in the ether, a scrambling seraph, tumbling and aflame and alien, powerful beyond belief, hideous and frightening and beautiful beyond the reach of the human. A screaming child, an angel howling in the Godly sphere: she churned without delicacy, as wild as an angel bearing threats; her body lifted from the sheets, fell back, lifted again; her hands beat on the bed; she made very loud hoarse tearing noises – I was frightened for her: this was her first time after six years of playing around with her body. It hurt her; her face looked like something made of stone, a monstrous carving; only her body was alive; her arms and legs were outspread and tensed and they beat or they were weak and fluttering. She was an angel as brilliant as a beautiful insect infinitely enlarged and irrevocably foreign: she was unlike me: she was a girl making rattling, astonished, uncontrolled, unhappy noises, a girl looking shocked and intent and harassed by the variety and viciousness of the sensations, including relief, that attacked her. I sat up on my knees and moved a little in her and stroked her breasts, with smooth sideways winglike strokes. And she screamed, "*Wiley, I'm coming!*" and with a certain idiocy entered on her second orgasm or perhaps her third since she'd started to come a few minutes before; and we would have gone on for hours but she said, "It hurts, Wiley, I hurt, make it stop ..." So I didn't move; I just held her thighs with my hands; and her things began to trail off, to trickle down, into little shiverings; the stoniness left her face; she calmed into moderated shudders, and then she said, she started to speak with wonder but then it became an exclamation and ended on a kind of a hollow note, the prelude to a small scream: she said, "I *came* ..." Or "I ca-a-a-ammmmm-mmme...." What happened was that she had another orgasm at the thought that she'd had her first.

That one was more like three little ones, diminishing in strength. When she was quieter, she was gasping, she said, "Oh, you *love* me...."

That, too, excited her. When that died down, she said – angrily – "I always knew they were doing it wrong, I always knew there was nothing wrong with me...." And that triggered a little set of ripples. Sometime earlier, without knowing it, I'd begun to cry. My tears fell on her thighs, her belly, her breasts, as I moved up, along her body, above her, to lie atop her. I wanted to hold her, my face next to hers; I wanted to hold her. I slid my arms in and under her, and she said, "Oh, Wiley," and she tried to lift her arms, but she started to shake again; then, trembling anyway, she lifted her arms and hugged me with a shuddering sternness that was unmistakable; then she began to cry, too.

ROBERT COOVER

YOU MUST REMEMBER THIS

Warner Brothers' first choice of the leads for Casablanca *were Ronald Reagan and Ann Sheridan; the fates wisely decided that the roles would go to Humphrey Bogart and Ingrid Bergman, who made them immortal. Based on an obscure Broadway play,* Everybody Comes to Rick's, *the script was written while the scenes were being filmed; new lines were delivered to the actors only hours before they were to read them, and sometimes not at all, and Bergman never learned which of the two men in the story she was supposed to be in love with. In spite (perhaps because) of all this,* Casablanca *went on to win three Academy Awards, including best picture, best director and best screenplay.*

"You Must Remember This" is a homage to Casablanca. *Using the movie's mythical fabric as his backdrop, Robert Coover adds to it the explicitness hinted at but never shown on the screen. Rick and Ilsa fulfill the roles created by Bogart and Bergman, and take them to their melodramatic conclusion. "Is this how you, uh, imagined things turning out*

tonight?" asks Rick-Bogart to Ilsa-Bergman. Coover's story brilliantly depicts that perhaps not expected, but certainly not unimaginable, conclusion.

IT IS DARK in Rick's apartment. Black leader dark, heavy and abstract, silent but for a faint hoarse crackle like a voiceless plaint, and brief as sleep. The Rick opens the door and the light from the hall scissors in like a bellboy to open up space, deposit surfaces (there is a figure in the room), harbinger event (it is Ilsa). Rick follows, too preoccupied to notice: his café is closed, people have been shot, he has troubles. But then, with a stroke, he lights a small lamp (such a glow! the shadows retreat, *everything* retreats: where are the walls?) and there she is, facing him, holding open the drapery at the far window like the front of a nightgown, the light flickering upon her white but determined face like static. Rick pauses for a moment in astonishment. Ilsa lets the drapery and its implications drop, takes a step forward into the strangely fretted light, her eyes searching his.

"How did you get in?" he asks, though this is probably not the question on his mind.

"The stairs from the street."

This answer seems to please him. He knows how vulnerable he is, after all, it's the way he lives – his doors are open, his head is bare, his tuxedo jacket is snowy white – that's not important.

What matters is that by such a reply a kind of destiny is being fulfilled. Sam has a song about it. "I told you this morning you'd come around," he says, curling his lips as if to advertise his appetite for punishment, "but this is a little ahead of schedule." She faces him squarely, broad-shouldered and narrow-hipped, a sash around her waist like a gun belt, something shiny in her tensed left hand. He raises both his own as if to show they are empty: "Well, won't you sit down?"

His offer, whether in mockery or no, releases her. Her shoulders dip in relief, her breasts; she sweeps forward (it is only a small purse she is carrying: a toothbrush perhaps, cosmetics, her hotel key), her face softening: "Richard!" He starts back in alarm, hands moving to his hips. "I had to see you!"

"So you use Richard again!" His snarling retreat throws up a barrier between them. She stops. He pushes his hands into his pockets as though to reach for the right riposte: "We're back in Paris!"

That probably wasn't it. Their song seems to be leaking into the room from somewhere out in the night, or perhaps it has been there all the time – Sam maybe, down in the darkened bar, sending out soft percussive warnings in the manner of his African race: "Think twice, boss. Hearts fulla passion, you c'n rely. Jealousy, boss, an' hate. Le's go fishin'. Sam."

"Please!" she begs, staring at him intently, but he remains unmoved:

"Your unexpected visit isn't connected by any chance with the letters of transit?" He ducks his head, his upper lip swelling with bitterness and hurt. "It seems as long as I have those letters, I'll never be lonely."

Yet, needless to say, he will always be lonely – in fact, this is the confession ("You can ask any price you want," she is saying) only half-concealed in his muttered subjoinder: Rick Blaine is a loner, born and bred. Pity him. There is this lingering, almost primal image of him, sitting alone at a chessboard in his white tuxedo, smoking contemplatively in the midst of a raucous conniving crowd, a crowd he has himself assembled about him. He taps a pawn, moves a white knight, fondles a tall black queen while a sardonic smile plays on his lips. He seems to be toying, self-mockingly, with Fate itself, as indifferent toward Rick Blaine (never mind that he says – as he does now, turning away from her – that "I'm the only cause I'm interested in ...") as toward the rest of the world. It's all shit, so who cares?

Ilsa is staring off into space, a space that a moment ago Rick filled. She seems to be thinking something out. The negotiations are going badly; perhaps it is this she is worried about. He has just refused her offer of "any price," ignored her ultimatum ("You *must* giff me those letters!"), sneered at her husband's heroism, and scoffed at the very cause that first brought them together in Paris. How could he do that? And now he has abruptly turned his back on her (does he think it was just sex? what has happened to him since then?) and walked away toward the balcony door, meaning, apparently, to turn her out. She takes a deep breath, presses her lips together, and, clutching her tiny purse with both hands, wheels about to pursue him: "Richard!" This has worked before, it works again: he turns to face her new approach: "We luffed each other once ..." Her voice catches in her throat, tears come to her eyes. She is beautiful there in the slatted shadows, her hair loosening around her ears, eyes glittering, throat bare and vulnerable in the open V-neck of her ruffled blouse. She's a good dresser. Even that little purse she squeezes: so like the other one, so lovely, hidden away. She shakes her head slightly in wistful appeal: "If those days meant … anything at all to you …"

"I wouldn't bring up Paris if I were you," he says stonily. "It's poor salesmanship."

She gasps (*she* didn't bring it up: is he a madman?), tosses her head back: "Please! Please listen to me!" She closes her eyes, her lower lip pushed forward as though bruised. "If you knew what really happened, if you only knew the truth –!"

He stands over this display, impassive as a Moorish executioner (that's it! he's turning into one of these bloody Arabs, she thinks). "I wouldn't believe you, no matter what you told me," he says. In Ethiopia, after an attempt on the life of an Italian officer, he saw 1600 Ethiopians get rounded up one night and shot in reprisal. Many were friends of his. Or clients anyway. But somehow her deceit is worse. "You'd say anything now, to get what you want." Again he turns his back on her, strides away.

She stares at him in shocked silence, as though all that had happened eighteen months ago in Paris were flashing suddenly before her eyes, now made ugly by some terrible revelation. An exaggerated gasp escapes her like the breaking of wind: his head snaps up and he turns sharply to the right. She chases him, dogging his heels. "You want to feel sorry for yourself, don't you?" she cries and, surprised (he was just reaching for something on an ornamental table, the humidor perhaps), he turns back to her. "With so much at stake, all you can think off is your own feeling," she rails. Her lips are drawn back, her breathing labored, her eyes watering in anger and frustration.

"One woman has hurt you, and you take your reffenge on the rest off the world!" She is choking, she can hardly speak. Her accent seems to have got worse. "You're a coward, und veakling, und –"

She gasps. What is she saying? He watches her, as though faintly amused. "No, Richard, I'm sorry!" Tears are flowing in earnest now: she's gone too far! This is the expression on her face. She's in a corner, struggling to get out. "I'm sorry, but –" She wipes the tears from her cheek, and calls once again on her husband, that great and courageous man whom they both admire, whom the whole world admires: "– you're our last hope! If you don't help us, Victor Laszlo will die in Casablanca!"

"What of it?" he says. He has been waiting for this opportunity. He plays with it now, stretching it out. He turns, reaches for a cigarette, his head haloed in the light from an arched doorway. "I'm gonna die in Casablanca. It's a good spot for it." This line is meant to be amusing, but Isla reacts with horror. Her eyes widen. She catches her breath, turns away. He lights up, pleased with himself, takes a practiced drag, blows smoke. "Now," he says, turning toward her, "if you'll –"

He pulls up short, squints: she has drawn a revolver on him. So much for toothbrushes and hotel keys. "All right. I tried to reason with you. I tried effrything. Now I want those letters." Distantly, a melodic line suggest a fight for love and glory, an ironic case of do or die. "Get them for me."

"I don't have to." He touches his jacket. "I got 'em right here."

"Put them on the table."

He smiles and shakes his head. "No." Smoke curls up from

the cigarette he is holding at his side like the steam that enveloped the five o'clock train to Marseilles. Her eyes fill with tears. Even as she presses on ("For the last time...!") she knows that "no" is final. There is, behind his ironic smile, a profound sadness, the fatalistic survivor's wistful acknowledgment that, in the end, the fundamental things apply. Time, going by, leaves nothing behind, not even moments like this. "If Laszlo and the cause mean so much," he says, taunting her with her own uncertainties, "you won't stop at anything ..."

He seems almost to recede. The cigarette disappears, the smoke. His sorrow gives way to something not unlike eagerness. "All right, I'll make it easier for you," he says, and walks toward her. "Go ahead and shoot. You'll be doing me a favor."

She seems taken aback, her eyes damp, her lips swollen and parted. Light licks at her face. He gazes steadily at her from his superior moral position, smoke drifting up from his hand once more, his white tuxedo pressed against the revolver barrel. Her eyes close as the gun lowers, and she gasps his name: "Richard!" It is like an invocation. Or a profession of faith. "I tried to stay away," she sighs. She opens her eyes, peers up at him in abject surrender. A tear moves slowly down her cheek toward the corner of her mouth like secret writing. "I thought I would neffer see you again ... that you were out off my life ..." She blinks, cries out faintly – "Oh!" – and (he seems moved at last, his mask of disdain falling away like perspiration) turns away, her head wrenched to one side as though in pain.

Stricken with sudden concern, or what looks like concern, he steps up behind her, clasping her breasts with both hands, nuzzling in her hair. "The day you left Paris...!" she sobs, though she seems unsure of herself. One of his hands is already down between her legs, the other inside her blouse, pulling a breast out of its brassiere cup. "If you only knew … what I …" He is moaning, licking at one ear, the hand between her legs nearly lifting her off the floor, his pelvis bumping at her buttocks. "Is this … right?" she gasps.

"I – I don't know!" he groans, massaging her breast, her nipple between two fingers. "I can't think!"

"But … you *must* think!" she cries, squirming her hips. Tears are streaming down her cheeks now. "For … for …"

"What?" he gasps, tearing her blouse open, pulling on her breast as though to drag it over her shoulder where he might kiss it. Or eat it: he seems ravenous suddenly.

"I … I can't remember!" she sobs. She reaches behind to jerk at his fly (what else is she to do, for the love of Jesus?), then rips away her sash, unfastens her skirt, her fingers trembling.

"Holy shit!" he wheezes, pushing his hand inside her girdle as her skirt falls. His cheeks too are wet with tears. "*Ilsa!*"

"*Richard!*"

They fall to the floor, grabbing and pulling at each other's clothing. He's trying to get her bra off which is tangled up now with her blouse, she's struggling with his belt, yanking at his black pants, wrenching them open. Buttons fly, straps pop, there's the soft unfocused rip of silk, the jingle of buckles and falling coins, grunts, gasps, whimpers of desire. He strips the tangled skein of underthings away (all these straps and stays – how does she get in and out of this crazy elastic?); she works his pants down past his bucking hips, fumbles with his shoes. "*Your elbow – !*"

"*Mmmff!*"

"*Ah – !*"

She pulls his pants and boxer shorts off, crawls round and (he strokes her shimmering buttocks, swept by the light from the airport tower, watching her full breasts sway above him: it's all happening so fast, he'd like to slow it down, repeat some of the better bits – that view of her rippling haunches on her hands and knees just now, for example, like a 22, his lucky number – but there's a great urgency on them, they can't wait) straddles him, easing him into her like a train being guided into a station. "*I luff you, Richard!*" she declares breathlessly, though she seems to be speaking, eyes squeezed shut and breasts heaving, not to him but to the ceiling, if there is one up there. His eyes too are closed now, his hands gripping her soft hips, pulling her down, his breath coming in short anguished snorts, his face puffy and damp with tears. There is, as always, something deeply wounded and vulnerable about the expression on his battered face, framed there against his Persian carpet: Rich Blaine, a man annealed by loneliness and betrayal, but flawed – hopelessly, it seems – by hope itself. He is, in the tragic sense, a true revolutionary: his gaping mouth bespeaks this, the spittle in the corners of his lips, his eyes, open now and staring into some infinite distance not unlike the future, his knitted brow. He heaves upward, impaling her to the very core: "*Oh, Gott!*" she screams, her back arching, mouth agape as though to commence "La Marseillaise."

Now, for a moment, they pause, feeling themselves thus conjoined, his organ luxuriating in the warm tub of her vagina, her enflamed womb closing around his pulsing penis like a mother embracing a lost child. "If you only knew...," she seems to say, though perhaps she has said this before and only now it can be heard. He fondles her breasts; she rips his shirt open, strokes his chest, leans forward to kiss his lips, his nipples. This is not Victor inside her with his long thin rapier, all too rare in its embarrassed visits; this is not Yvonne with her cunning professional muscles, her hollow airy hole. This is love in all its clammy mystery, the ultimate connection, the squishy rub of truth, flesh as a self-consuming message. This is necessity, as in woman needs man, and man must have his mate. Even their identities seem to be dissolving; they have to whisper each other's name from time to time as though in recitative struggle against some ultimate enchantment from which there might be no return. Then slowly she begins to wriggle her hips above him, he to meet her gentle undulations with counterthrusts of his own. They hug each other close, panting, her breasts smashed against him, moving only from the waist down. She slides her thighs between his and squeezes his penis between them, as though to conceal it there, an underground member on the run, wounded but unbowed. He lifts his stockinged feet and plants them behind her knees as though in stirrups, her buttocks above pinching and opening, pinching and opening like a suction pump. And it is true about her vaunted radiance: she seems almost to glow from within, her flexing cheeks haloed in their own dazzling luster.

"It feels so good, Richard! In there ... I've been so – *ah* – so lonely...!"

"Yeah, me too, kid. *Ngh!* Don't talk."

She slips her thighs back over his and draws them up beside his waist like a child curling around her teddybear, knees against his ribs, her fanny gently bobbing on its pike like a mind caressing a cherished memory. He lies there passively for a moment, stretched out, eyes closed, accepting this warm rhythmical ablution as one might accept a nanny's teasing bath, a mother's care (a care, he's often said, denied him), in all its delicious innocence – or seemingly so: in fact, his whole body is faintly atremble, as though, with great difficulty, shedding the last of its pride and bitterness, its isolate neutrality. Then slowly his own hips begin to rock convulsively under hers, his knees to rise in involuntary surrender. She tongues his ear, her buttocks thumping more vigorously now, kisses his throat, his nose, his scarred lip, then rears up, arching her back, tossing her head back (her hair is looser now, wilder, a flush has crept into the distinctive pallor of her cheeks and throat, and what was before a fierce determination is now raw intensity, what vulnerability now a slack-jawed abandon), plunging him in more deeply than ever, his own buttocks bouncing up off the floor as though trying to take off like the next flight to Lisbon – "Gott in Himmel, *this is fonn!*" she cries. She reaches behind her back to clutch his testicles, he clasps her hand in both of his, his thighs spread, she falls forward, they roll over, he's pounding away now from above (he lacks her famous radiance: if anything his buttocks seem to suck in light, drawing a nostalgic murkiness around them like night fog, signaling a fundamental distance between them, and an irresistible attraction), she's clawing at his back under the white jacket, at his hips, his thighs, her voracious nether mouth leaping up at him from below and sliding back, over and over, like a frantic greased-pole climber. Faster and faster they slap their bodies together, submitting to this fierce rhythm as though to simplify themselves, emitting grunts and whinnies and helpless little farts, no longer Rick Blaine and Ilsa Lund, but some nameless conjunction somewhere between them, time, space, being itself getting redefined by the rapidly narrowing focus of their incandescent passion – then suddenly Rick rears backs, his face seeming to puff out like a gourd, Ilsa cries out and kicks upward, crossing her ankles over Rick's clenched buttocks, for a moment they seem almost to float, suspended, unloosed from the earth's gravity, and then – *whumpf!* – they hit the floor again, their bodies continuing to hammer together, though less regularly, plunging, twitching, prolonging this exclamatory dialogue, drawing it out even as the intensity diminishes, even as it becomes more a declaration than a demand, more an inquiry than a declaration. Ilsa's feet uncross, slide slowly to the floor. "Fooff ... *Gott!*" They lie there, cheek to cheek, clutching each other tightly, gasping for breath, their thighs quivering with the last involuntary spasms, the echoey reverberations, deep in their loins, of pleasure's fading blasts.

"Jesus," Rick wheezes, "I've been saving that one for a goddamn year and a half...!"

"It was the best fokk I effer haff," Ilsa replies with a tremulous sigh, and kisses his ear, runs her fingers in his hair. He starts to roll off her, but she clasps him closely: "No ... wait...!" A deeper thicker pleasure, not so ecstatic, yet somehow more moving, seems to well up from far inside her to embrace the swollen visitor snuggled moistly in her womb, once a familiar friend, a comrade loved and trusted, now almost a stranger, like one resurrected from the dead.

"Ah – !" he gasps. God, it's almost like she's milking it! Then she lets go, surrounding him spongily with a kind of warm wet pulsating gratitude. "Ah ..."

He lies there between Ilsa's damp silky thighs, feeling his

weight thicken, his mind soften and spread. His will drains away as if it were some kind of morbid affection, lethargy overtaking him like an invading army. Even his jaw goes slack, his fingers (three sprawl idly on a dark-tipped breast) limp. He wears his snowy white tuxedo jacket still, his shiny black socks, which, together with the parentheses of Ilsa's white thighs, make his melancholy buttocks – beaten in childhood, lashed at sea, run lean in union skirmishes, sunburned in Ethiopia, and shot at in Spain – look gloomier than ever, swarthy and self-pitying, agape now with a kind of heroic sadness. A violent tenderness. These buttocks are, it could be said, what the pose of isolation looks like at its best: proud, bitter, mournful, and, as the prefect of police might have put it, tremendously attractive. Though his penis has slipped out of its vaginal pocket to lie limply like a fat little toe against her slowly pursing lips, she clasps him close still, clinging to something she cannot quite define, something like a spacious dream of freedom, or a monastery garden, or the discovery of electricity. "Do you have a gramophone on, Richard?"

"What – ?!" Her question has startled him. His haunches snap shut, his head rears up, snorting, he seems to be reaching for the letters of transit. "Ah … no … " He relaxes again, letting his weight fall back, though sliding one thigh over hers now, stretching his arms out as though to unkink them, turning his face away. His scrotum bulges up on her thigh like an emblem of his inner serenity and generosity, all too often concealed, much as an authentic decency might shine through a mask of cynicism and despair. He takes a deep breath. (A kiss is just a kiss is what the music is insinuating. A sigh …) "That's probably Sam … "

She sighs (... and so forth), gazing up at the ceiling above her, patterned with overlapping circles of light from the room's lamps and swept periodically by the wheeling airport beacon, coming and going impatiently, yet reliably, like desire itself. "He hates me, I think."

"Sam? No, he's a pal. What I think, he thinks."

"When we came into the bar last night, he started playing 'Luff for Sale.' Effryone turned and looked at me."

"It wasn't the song, sweetheart, it was the way you two were dressed. Nobody in Casablanca –"

"Then he tried to chase me away. He said I was bad luck to you." She can still see the way he rolled his white eyes at her, like some kind of crazy voodoo zombie.

Richard grunts ambiguously. "Maybe you should stop calling him 'boy.'"

Was that it? "But in all the moofies –" Well, a translation problem probably, a difficulty she has known often in her life. Language can sometimes be stiff as a board. Like what's under her now. She loves Richard's relaxed weight on her, the beat of his heart next to her breast, the soft lumpy pouch of his genitals squashed against her thigh, but the floor seems to be hardening under her like some kind of stern Calvinist rebuke and there is a disagreeable airy stickiness between her legs, now that he has slid away from there. "Do you haff a bidet, Richard?"

"Sure, kid." He slides to one side with a lazy grunt, rolls over. He's thinking vaguely about the pleasure he's just had, what it's likely to cost him (he doesn't care), and wondering where he'll find the strength to get up off his ass and go look for a cigarette. He stretches his shirttail down and wipes his crotch with it, nods back over the top of his head. "In there."

She is sitting up, peering between her spread legs. "I am afraid we haff stained your nice carpet, Richard."

"What of it? Put it down as a gesture to love. Want a drink?"

"Yes, that would be good." She leans over and kisses him, her face still flushed and eyes damp, but smiling now, then stands and gathers up an armload of tangled clothing. "Do I smell something burning?"

"What – ?!" He rears up. "My goddamn cigarette! I musta dropped it on the couch!" He crawls over, brushes at it: it's gone out, but there's a big hole there now, dark-edged like ringworm. "Shit." He staggers to his feet, stumbles over to the humidor to light up a fresh smoke. Nothing's ever free, he thinks, feeling a bit light-headed. "What's your poison, kid?"

"I haff downstairs been drinking Cointreau," she calls out over the running water in the next room. He pours himself a large whiskey, tosses it down neat (light, sliding by, catches his furrowed brow as he tips his head back: what is wrong?), pours another, finds a decanter of Grand Marnier. She won't know the difference. In Paris she confused champagne with sparkling cider, ordered a Pommard thinking she was getting a rosé, drank gin because she couldn't taste it. He fits the half-burned cigarette between his lips, tucks a spare over his ear, then carries the drinks into the bathroom. She sits, straddling the bidet, churning water up between her legs like the wake of a pleasure boat. The beacon doesn't reach in here: it's as though he's stepped out of its line of sight, but that doesn't make him feel easier (something is nagging at him, has been for some time now). He holds the drink to her mouth for her, and she sips, looking mischievously up at him, one wet hand braced momentarily on his hipbone. Even in Paris she seemed to think drinking was naughtier than sex. Which made her on occasion something of a souse. She tips her chin, and he sets her drink down on the sink. "I wish I didn't luff you so much," she says casually, licking her lips, and commences to work up a lather between her legs with a bar of soap.

"Listen, what did you mean," he asks around the cigarette (this is it, or part of it: he glances back over his shoulder apprehensively, as though to find some answer to his question staring him in the face – or what, from the rear, is passing for his face), "when you said, 'Is this right?'"

"When…?"

"A while ago, when I grabbed your, you know –"

"Oh, I don't know, darling. Yust a strange feeling, I don't exactly remember." She spreads the suds up her smooth belly and down the insides of her thighs, runs the soap up under her behind. "Like things were happening too fast or something."

He takes a contemplative drag on the cigarette, flips the butt into the toilet. "Yeah, that's it." Smoke curls out his nostrils like balloons of speech in a comic strip. "*All* this seems strange somehow. Like something that shouldn't have –"

"Well, I *am* a married woman, Richard."

"I don't mean that." But maybe he does mean that. She's rinsing now, her breasts flopping gaily above her splashing, it's hard to keep his mind on things. But he's not only been pronging some other guy's wife, this is the wife of Victor Laszlo of the International Underground, one of his goddamn heroes. One of the world's. Does that matter? He shoves his free hand in a jacket pocket, having no other, tosses back the drink. "Anyway," he wheezes, "from what you tell me, you were married already when we met in Paris, so that's not –"

"Come here, Richard," Ilsa interrupts with gentle but firm Teutonic insistence. *Komm' hier.* His back straightens, his eyes narrow, and for a moment the old Rick Blaine returns, the lonely American warrior, incorruptible, melancholy, master of his own fate, beholden to no one – but then she reaches forward and, like destiny, takes a hand. "Don't try to escape," she murmurs, pulling him up to the bidet between her knees. "You will neffer succeed."

She continues to hold him with one hand (he is growing there, stretching and filling in her hand with soft warm pulsations, and more than anything else that has happened to her since she came to Casablanca, more even than Sam's song, it is this sensation that takes her back to their days in Paris: wherever they went, from the circus to the movies, from excursion boats to dancehalls, it swelled in her hand, just like this), while soaping him up with the other. "Why are you circumcised, Richard?" she asks, as the engorged head (when it flushes, it seems to flush blue) pushes out between her thumb and index finger. There was something he always said in Paris when it poked up at her like that. She peers wistfully at it, smiling to herself.

"My old man was a sawbones," he says, and takes a deep breath. He sets his empty glass down, reaches for the spare fag. It seems to have vanished. "He thought it was hygienic."

"Fictor still has his. Off course in Europe it is often important not to be mistaken for a Chew." She takes up the fragrant bar of soap (black market, the best, Ferrari gets it for him) and buffs the shaft with it, then thumbs the head with her sudsy hands as though, gently, trying to uncap it. The first day he met her, she opened his pants and jerked him off in his top-down convertible right under the Arc de Triomphe, then, almost without transition, or so it seemed to him, blew him spectacularly in the Bois de Boulogne. He remembers every detail, or anyway the best parts. And it was never – ever – any better than that. Until tonight.

She rinses the soap away, pours the rest of the Grand Marnier (she thinks: Cointreau) over his gleaming organ like a sort of libation, working the excess around as though lightly basting it (he thinks: priming it). A faint sad smile seems to be playing at the corners of her lips. "Say it once, Richard …"

"What – ?"

She's smiling sweetly, but: is that a tear in her eye? "For old time's sake. Say it …"

"Ah." Yes, he'd forgotten. He's out of practice. He grunts, runs his hand down her damp cheek and behind her ear. "Here's lookin' at you, kid …"

She puckers her lips and kisses the tip, smiling cross-eyed at it, then, opening her mouth wide, takes it in, all of it at once. "Oh, Christ!" he groans, feeling himself awash in the thick muscular foam of her saliva, "I'm crazy about you, baby!"

"Mmmmm!" she moans. He has said that to her before, more than once no doubt (she wraps her arms around his hips under the jacket and hugs him close), but the time she is thinking about was at the cinema one afternoon in Paris. They had gone to see an American detective movie that was popular at the time, but there was a newsreel on before showing the Nazi conquests that month of Copenhagen, Oslo, Luxembourg, Amsterdam, and Brussels. "The Fall of Five Capitals," it was called. And the scenes from Oslo, though brief, showing the Gestapo goose-stepping through the storied streets of her childhood filled her with such terror and nostalgia (something inside her was screaming, "Who *am* I?"), that she reached impulsively for Richard's hand, grabbing what Victor calls "the old fellow" instead. She started to pull her hand back, but he held it there, and the next thing she knew she had her head in his lap, weeping and sucking as though at her dead mother's breast, the terrible roar of the German blitzkrieg pounding in her ears, Richard kneading her nape as her father used to do before he died (and as Richard is doing now, his buttocks knotted up under her arms, his penis fluttering in her mouth like a frightened bird), the Frenchmen in the theater shouting out obscenities, her own heart pounding like cannon fire. "God! I'm crazy about you, baby!" Richard whinnied as he came (now, as his knees buckle against hers and her mouth fills with the shockingly familiar unfamiliarity of his spurting seed, it is just a desperate "Oh fuck! Don't let go…!"), and when she sat up, teary-eyed and drooling and gasping for breath (it is not all that easy to breathe now, as he clasps her face close to his hairy belly, whimpering gratefully, his body sagging, her mouth filling), what she saw on the screen were happy Germans, celebrating their victories, taking springtime strolls through overflowing flower and vegetable markets, going to the theater to see translations of Shakespeare, snapping photographs of their children. "Oh Gott," she sniffled then (now she swallows, sucks and swallows, as though to draw out from this almost impalpable essence some vast structure of recollection), "it's too much!" Whereupon the man behind them leaned over and said: "Then try mine, mademoiselle. As you can see, it is not so grand as your Nazi friend's but here in France, we grow men not pricks!" Richard's French was terrible, but it was good enough to understand "your Nazi friend": he hadn't even put his penis back in his pants (now it slides greasily past her chin, flops down her chest, his buttocks in her hugging arms going soft as butter, like a delicious half-grasped memory losing its clear outlines, melting into mere sensation), but just leapt up and took a swing at the Frenchman. With that, the cinema broke into an uproar with everybody calling everyone else a fascist or a whore. They were thrown out of the theater of course, the police put Richard on their blacklist as an exhibitionist, and they never did get to see the detective movie. Ah well, they could laugh about it then …

He sits now on the front lip of the bidet, his knees knuckled under hers, shirttails in the water, his cheek fallen on her broad shoulder, arms loosely around her, feeling wonderfully unwound, mellow as an old tune (which is still there somewhere, moonlight and love songs, same old story – maybe it's coming up through the popes), needing only a smoke to make things perfect. The one he stuck over his ear is floating in the scummy pool beneath them, he sees. Ilsa idly splashes his drooping organ as though christening it. Only one answer, she once said, peeling off that lovely satin gown of hers like a French letter, will take care of all our questions, and she was right. As always. He's the one who's made a balls-up of things and his complicated moral poses and insufferable pride – a diseased romantic, Louis once called him, and he didn't know the half of it. She's the only realist in town; he's got to start paying attention. Even now she's making sense: "My rump is getting dumb, Richard. Dry me off and let's go back in the other room."

But when he tries to stand, his knees feel like toothpaste,

and he has to sit again. Right back in the bidet, as it turns out, dipping his ass like doughnuts in tea. She smiles understandingly, drapes a bath towel around her shoulders, pokes through the medicine cabinet until she finds a jar of Yvonne's cold cream, then takes him by the elbow. "Come on, Richard. You can do it, yust lean on me." Which reminds him (his mind at least is still working, more or less) of a night in Spain, halfway up (or down) Suicide Hill in the Jarama valley, a night he thought was to be his last, when he said that to someone, or someone said it to him. God, what if he'd got it shot off there? And missed this? An expression compounded of hope and anguish, skepticism and awe, crosses his weary face (thirty-eight at Christmas, if Strasser is right – oh mother of God, it *is* going by!), picked up by the wheeling airport beacon. She removes his dripping jacket, his shirt as well, and towels his behind before letting him collapse onto the couch, then crosses to the ornamental table for a cigarette from the humidor. She wears the towel like a cape, her haunches under it glittering as though sequined. She is, as always, a kind of walking light show, no less spectacular from the front as she turns back now toward the sofa, the nubbly texture of the towel contrasting subtly with the soft glow of her throat and breast, the sleek wet gleam of her belly.

She fits two cigarettes in her lips, lights them both (there's a bit of fumbling with the lighter, she's not very mechanical), and gazing soulfully down at Rick, passes him one of them. He grins. "Hey, where'd you learn that, kid?" She shrugs enigmatically, hands him the towel, and steps up between his knees. As he rubs her breasts, her belly, her thighs with the towel, the cigarette dangling in his lips, she gazes around at the chalky rough-plastered walls of his apartment, the Moorish furniture with its filigrees and inlaid patterns, the little bits of erotic art (there is a statue of a camel on the sideboard that looks like a man's wet penis on legs, and a strange nude statuette that might be a boy, or a girl, or something in between), the alabaster lamps and potted plants, those slatted wooden blinds, so exotic to her Northern eyes: he has style, she thinks, rubbing cold cream into her neck and shoulder with her free hand, he always did have …

She lifts one leg for him to dry and then the other, gasping inwardly (outwardly, she chokes and wheezes, having inhaled the cigarette by mistake: he stubs out his own with a sympathetic grin, takes what is left of hers) when he rubs the towel briskly between them, then she turns and bends over, bracing herself on the coffee table. Rick, the towel in his hands, pauses a moment, gazing thoughtfully through the drifting cigarette haze at these luminous buttocks, finding something almost otherworldly about them, like archways to heaven or an image of eternity. Has he seen them like this earlier tonight? Maybe, he can't remember. Certainly now he's able to savor the sight, no longer crazed by rut. They are, quite literally, a dream come true: he has whacked off to their memory so often during the last year and a half that it almost feels more appropriate to touch himself than this present manifestation. As he reaches toward them with the towel, he seems to be crossing some strange threshold, as though passing from one medium into another. He senses the supple buoyancy of them bouncing back against his hand as he wipes them, yet, though flesh, they remain somehow immaterial, untouchable even when touched, objects whose very presence is a kind of absence. If

Rick Blaine were to believe in angels, Ilsa's transcended bottom is what they would look like.

"Is this how you, uh, imagined things turning out tonight?" he asks around the butt, smoke curling out his nose like thought's reek. Her cheeks seem to pop alight like his Café Américain sign each time the airport beacon sweeps past, shifting slightly like a sequence of film frames. Time itself may be like that, he knows: not a ceaseless flow, but a rapid series of electrical leaps across tiny gaps between discontinuous bits. It's what he likes to call his link-and-claw theory of time, though of course the theory is not his ...

"Well, it may not be perfect, Richard, but it is better than if I haff shot you, isn't it?"

"No, I meant ..." Well, let it be. She's right, it beats eating a goddamn bullet. In fact it beats anything he can imagine. He douses his cigarette in the wet towel, tosses it aside, wraps his arms around her thighs and pulls her buttocks (he is still thinking about time as a pulsing sequence of film frames, and not so much about the frames, their useless dated content, as the gaps between: infinitesimally small when looked at two-dimensionally, yet in their third dimension as deep and mysterious as the cosmos) toward his face, pressing against them like a child trying to see through a foggy window. He kisses and nibbles at each fresh-washed cheek (and what if one were to slip *between* two of those frames? he wonders –), runs his tongue into (– where would he be then?) her anus, kneading the flesh on her pubic knoll between his fingers all the while like little lumps of stiff taffy. She raises one knee up onto the cushions, then the other, lowering her elbows to the floor (oh! she thinks as the blood rushes in two directions at once, spreading into her head and sex as though filling empty frames, her heart the gap between: what a strange dizzying dream time is!), thus lifting to his contemplative scrutiny what looks like a clinging sea anemone between her thighs, a thick woolly pod, a cloven chinchilla, open purse, split fruit. But it is not the appearance of it that moves him (except to the invention of these fanciful catalogues), it is the smell. It is this which catapults him suddenly and wholly back to Paris, a Paris he'd lost until this moment (she is not in Paris, she is in some vast dimensionless region she associates with childhood, a nighttime glow in her midsummer room, featherbedding between her legs) but now has back again. Now and for all time. As he runs his tongue up and down the spongy groove, pinching the lips tenderly between his tongue and stiff upper lip (an old war wound), feeling it engorge, pulsate, almost pucker up to kiss him back, he seems to see – as though it were fading in on the blank screen of her gently rolling bottom – that night at her apartment in Paris when she first asked him to "Kiss me, Richard, here. My other mouth wants to luff you, too ..." He'd never done that before. He had been all over the world, had fought in wars, battled cops, been jailed and tortured, hid out in whorehouses, parachuted out of airplanes, had eaten and drunk just about everything, had been blown off the decks of ships, killed more men than he'd like to count, and had banged every kind and color of woman on earth, but he had never tasted one of these things before. Other women had sucked him off, of course, before Ilsa nearly caused him to wreck his car that day in the Bois de Boulogne, but he had always thought of that as a service due him, something he'd paid for in effect – he was the man, after all. But reciprocation, sucking back – well, that always struck him as vaguely queer, something guys, manly guys anyway, didn't do. That night, though, he'd had a lot of champagne and he was – this was the simple truth, and it was an experience as exotic to Rick Blaine as the taste of a cunt – madly in love. He had been an unhappy misfit all his life, at best a romantic drifter, at worst and in the eyes of most a sleazy gunrunner and chicken-shit mercenary (though God knows he'd hoped for more), a whoremonger and brawler and miserable gutter drunk: nothing like Ilsa Lund had ever happened to him, and he could hardly believe it was happening to him that night. His immediate reaction – he admits this, sucking greedily at it now (she is galloping her father's horse through the woods of the north, canopy-dark and sunlight-blinding at the same time, pushing the beast beneath her, racing toward what she believed to be God's truth, flushing through her from the saddle up as eternity might when the saints were called), while watching himself, on the cinescreen of her billowing behind, kneel to it that first time like an atheist falling squeamishly into conversion – was not instant rapture. No, like olives, home brew, and Arab cooking, it took a little getting used to. But she taught him how to stroke the vulva with his tongue, where to find the nun's cap ("my little sister," she called it, which struck him as odd) and how to draw it out, how to use his fingers, nose, chin, even his hair and ears, and the more he practiced for her sake, the more he liked it for his own, her pleasure (he could *see* it: it bloomed right under his nose, filling his grimy life with colors he'd never even thought of before!) augmenting his, until he found his appetite for it almost insatiable. God, the boys on the block back in New York would laugh their asses off to see how far he'd fallen!

And though he has tried others since, it is still the only one he really likes. Yvonne's is terrible, bitter and pomaded (she seems to sense this, gets no pleasure from it at all, often turns fidgety and mean when he goes down on her, even had a kind of biting, scratching fit once: "Don' you lak to *fuck?*" she'd screamed), which is the main reason he's lost interest in her. That and her hairy legs.

His screen is shrinking (her knees have climbed to his shoulders, scrunching her hips into little bumps and bringing her shoulder blades into view, down near the floor, where she is gasping and whimpering and sucking the carpet), but his vision of the past is expanding, as though her pumping cheeks were a chubby bellows, opening and closing, opening and closing, inflating his memories. Indeed, he no longer needs a screen for them, for it is not this or that conquest that he recalls now, this or that event, not what she wore or what she said, but something more profound than that, something experienced in the way that a blind man sees or an amputee touches. Texture returns to him, ambience, impressions of radiance, of coalescence, the foamy taste of the ineffable on his tongue, the downy nap of timelessness, the tooth of now. All this he finds in Ilsa's juicy bouncing cunt – and more: love's pungent illusions of consubstantiation and infinitude (oh, he knows what he lost that day in the rain in the Gare de Lyon!), the bittersweet fall into actuality, space's secret folds wherein one might lose one's ego, one's desperate sense of isolation, Paris, rediscovered here as pure aura, effervescent and allusive, La Belle Aurore as immanence's theater, sacred showplace –

Oh hell, he thinks as Ilsa's pounding hips drive him to his back on the couch, her thighs slapping against his ears (as she rises, her blood in riptide against her mounting excitement, the airport beacon touching her in its passing like bursts of inspiration, she thinks: childhood is a place apart, needing the adult world to exist at all: without Victor there could *be* no Rick! – and then she cannot think at all), La Belle Aurore! She broke his goddamn heart at La Belle Aurore. "Kiss me," she said, holding herself with both hands as though to keep the pain from spilling out down there, "one last time," and he did, for her, Henri didn't care, merde alors, the Germans were coming anyway, and the other patrons thought it was just part of the entertainment; only Sam was offended and went off to the john till it was over. And then she left him. Forever. Or anyway until she turned up here a night ago with Laszlo. God, he remembers everything about that day in the Belle Aurore, what she was wearing, what the Germans were wearing, what Henri was wearing. It was not an easy day to forget. The Germans were at the very edge of the city, they were bombing the bejesus out of the place and everything was literally falling down around their ears (she's smothering him now with her bucking arse, her scissoring thighs: he heaves her over onto her back and pushes his arms between her thighs to spread them); they'd had to crawl over rubble and dead bodies, push through barricades, just to reach the damned café. No chance to get out by car, he was lucky there was enough left in his "F.Y. Fund" to buy them all train tickets. And then the betrayal: "I cannot go with you or ever see you again." In perfect Palmer Method handwriting, as though to exult in her power over him. He kicked poor Sam's ass up and down that train all the way to Marseilles, convinced it was somehow his fault. Even a hex maybe, that day he could have believed anything. Now, with her hips bouncing frantically up against his mouth, her bush grown to an astonishing size, the lips out and flapping like flags, the trench between them awash in a fragrant ooze like oily air, he lifts his head and asks: "Why weren't you honest with me? Why did you keep your marriage a secret?"

"Oh Gott, Richard! Not *now* – !"

She's right, it doesn't seem the right moment for it, but then nothing has seemed right since she turned up in this godforsaken town: it's almost as though two completely different places, two completely different times are being forced to mesh, to intersect where no intersection is possible, causing a kind of warp in the universe. In his own private universe anyway. He gazes down on this lost love, this faithless wife, this trusting child, her own hands between her legs now, her hips still jerking out of control ("Please, Richard!" she is begging softly through clenched teeth, tears in her eyes), thinking: It's still a story without an ending. But more than that: the beginning and middle bits aren't all there either. Her face is drained as though all the blood has rushed away to other parts, but her throat between the heaving white breasts is almost literally alight with its vivid blush. He touches it, strokes the soft bubbles to either side, watching the dark little nipples rise like patriots – and suddenly the answer to all his questions seems (yet another one, that is – answers, in the end, are easy) to suggest itself. "Listen kid, would it be all right if I – ?"

"Oh yes! yes! – *but hurry!*"

He finds the cold cream (at last! he is so slow!), lathers it on, and slips into her cleavage, his knees over her shoulders like a yoke. She guides his head back into that tropical explosion between her legs, then clasps her arms around his hips, already beginning to thump at her chest like a resuscitator, popping little gasps from her throat. She tries to concentrate on his bouncing buttocks, but they communicate to her such a touching blend of cynicism and honesty, weariness and generosity, that they nearly break her heart, making her more light-headed than ever. The dark little hole between them bobs like a lonely survivor in a tragically divided world. It is he! "Oh Gott!" she whimpers. And she! The tension between her legs is almost unbearable. "I can't fight it anymore!" Everything starts to come apart. She feels herself falling as though through some rift in the universe (she cannot wait for him, and anyway, where she is going he cannot follow), out of time and matter into some wondrous radiance, the wheeling beacon flashing across her stricken vision now like intermittent star bursts, the music swelling, *everything* swelling, her eyes bursting, ears popping, teeth ringing in their sockets – "Oh Richard! Oh fokk! *I luff you so much!*"

He plunges his face deep into Ilsa's ambrosial pudding, lapping at its sweet sweat, feeling her loins snap and convulse violently around him, knowing that with a little inducement she can spasm like this for minutes on end, and meanwhile pumping away between her breasts now like a madman, no longer obliged to hold back, seeking purely his own pleasure. This pleasure is tempered only by (and maybe enhanced by as well) his pity for her husband, that heroic sonuvabitch. God, Victor Laszlo is almost a father figure to him, really. And while Laszlo is off at the underground meeting in the Caverne du Roi, no doubt getting his saintly ass shot to shit, here he is – Rick Blaine, the Yankee smart aleck and general jerk-off – safely closeted off in his rooms over the town saloon, titfucking the hero's wife, his callous nose up her own royal grotto like an advance scout for a squad of storm troopers. It's not fair, goddamn it, he thinks, and laughs at this even as he comes, squirting jism down her sleek belly and under his own, his head locked in her clamped thighs, her arms hugging him tightly as though to squeeze the juices out.

He is lying, completely still, his face between Ilsa's flaccid thighs, knees over her shoulders, arms around her lower body, which sprawls loosely now beneath him. He can feel her hands resting lightly on his hips, her warm breath against his leg. He doesn't remember when they stopped moving. Maybe he's been sleeping. Has he dreamt it all? No, he shifts slightly and feels the spill of semen, pooled gummily between their conjoined navels. His movement wakes Ilsa: she snorts faintly, sighs, kisses the inside of his leg, strokes one buttock idly. "That soap smells nice," she murmurs. "I bet effry girl in Casablanca wishes to haff a bath here."

"Yeah, well, I run it as a kind of public service," he grunts, chewing the words around a strand or two of pubic hair. He's always told Louis – and anyone else who wanted to know – that he sticks his neck out for nobody. But in the end, shit, he thinks, I stick it out for everybody. "I'm basically a civic-minded guy."

Cynic-minded, more like, she thinks, but keeps the thought to herself. She cannot risk offending him, not just now. She is still returning from wherever it is orgasm has taken her, and it has been an experience so profound and powerful, yet so remote from its immediate cause – his muscular tongue at the other end of this morosely puckered hole in front of her nose – that it has left her feeling very insecure, unsure of who or what she is, or even where. She knows of course that her role as the well-dressed wife of a courageous underground leader is just pretense, that beneath this charade she is certainly someone – or something – else. Richard's lover, for example. Or a little orphan girl who lost her mother, father, and adoptive aunt, all before she'd even started menstruating – that's who she often is, or feels like she is, especially at moments like this. But if her life as Victor Laszlo's wife is not real, are these others any more so? Is she one person, several – or no one at all? What was that thought she'd had about childhood? She lies there, hugging Richard's hairy cheeks (are they Richard's? are they cheeks?), her pale face framed by his spraddled legs, trying to puzzle it all out. Since the moment she arrived in Casablanca, she and Richard have been trying to tell each other stories, not very funny stories, as Richard has remarked, but maybe not very true ones either. Maybe memory itself is a kind of trick, something that turns illusion into reality and makes the real world vanish before everyone's eyes like magic. One can certainly sink away there and miss everything, she knows. Hasn't Victor, the wise one, often warned her of that? But Victor is a hero. Maybe the real world is too much for most people. Maybe making up stories is a way to keep them all from going insane. A tear forms in the corner of one eye. She blinks (and what are these unlikely configurations called "Paris" and "Casablanca," where in all the universe *is* she, and what is "where"?), and the tear trickles into the hollow between cheekbone and nose, then bends its course toward the middle of her cheek. There is a line in their song (yes, it is still there, tinkling away somewhere like mice in the walls: is someone trying to drive her crazy?) that goes,

"This day and age we're living in gives cause for apprehension,/With speed and new invention and things like third dimension ..." She always thought that was a stupid mistake of the lyricist, but now she is not so sure. For the real mystery – she sees this now, or *feels* it rather – is not the fourth dimension as she'd always supposed (the tear stops halfway down her cheek, begins to fade), or the third either for that matter ... but the *first.*

"You never finished answering my question ..."

There is a pause. Perhaps she is daydreaming. "What question, Richard?"

"A while ago. In the bathroom ..." He, too, has been mulling over recent events, wondering not only about the events themselves (wondrous in their own right, of course: he's not enjoyed multiple orgasms like this since he hauled his broken-down blacklisted ass out of Paris a year and a half ago, and that's just for starters), but also about their "recentness": When did they really happen? Is "happen" the right word, or were they more like fleeting conjunctions with the Absolute, that *other* Other, boundless and immutable as number? And, if so, what now is "when"? How much time has elapsed, for example, since he opened the door and found her in this room? Has *any* time elapsed? "I asked you what you meant when you said, 'Is this right?'"

"Oh, Richard, I don't know what's right any longer." She lifts one thigh in front of his face, as though to erase his dark imaginings. He strokes it, thinking: well, what the hell, it probably doesn't amount to a hill of beans, anyway. "Do you think I can haff another drink now?"

"Sure, kid. Why not." He sits up beside her, shakes the butt out of the damp towel, wipes his belly off, hands the towel to her. "More of the same?"

"Champagne would be nice, if it is possible. It always makes me think of Paris ... and you ..."

"You got it, sweetheart." He pushes himself to his feet and thumps across the room, pausing at the humidor to light up a fresh smoke. "If there's any left. Your old man's been going through my stock like Vichy water." Not for the first time, he has the impression of being watched. Laszlo? Who knows, maybe the underground meeting was just a ruse; it certainly seemed like a dumb thing to do on the face of it, especially with Strasser in town. There's a bottle of champagne in his icebox, okay, but no ice. He touches the bottle: not cold, but cool enough. It occurs to him the sonuvabitch might be out on the balcony right now, taking it all in, he and all his goddamn underground. Europeans can be pretty screwy, especially these rich stiffs with titles. As he carries the champagne and glasses over to the coffee table, the cigarette like a dart between his lips, his bare ass feels suddenly both hot and chilly at the same time. "Does your husband ever get violent?" he asks around the smoke and snaps the metal clamp off the champagne bottle, takes a grip on the cork.

"No. He has killed some people, but he is not fiolent." She is rubbing her tummy off, smiling thoughtfully. The light from the airport beacon, wheeling past, picks up a varnish like glaze still between her breasts, a tooth's wet twinkle in her open mouth, an unwonted shine on her nose. The cork pops, champagne spews out over the table top, some of it getting into the glasses. This seems to suggest somehow a revelation. Or another memory. The tune, as though released, rides up once more around them. "Gott, Richard," she sighs, pushing irritably to her feet. "That music is getting on my nerfs!"

"Yeah, I know." It's almost as bad in its way as the German blitzkrieg hammering in around their romance in Paris – sometimes it seemed to get right between their embraces. Gave him a goddamn headache. Now the music is doing much the same thing, even trying to tell them when to kiss and when not to. He can stand it, though, he thinks, tucking the cigarette back in his lips, if she can. He picks up the two champagne glasses, offers her one. "Forget it, kid. Drown it out with this." He raises his glass. "Uh, here's looking' – "

She gulps it down absently, not waiting for his toast. "And that light from the airport," she goes on, batting at it as it passes as though to shoo it away. "How can you effer sleep here?"

"No one's supposed to sleep well in Casablanca," he replies with a wordly grimace. It's his best expression, he knows, but she isn't paying any attention. He stubs out the cigarette, refills her glass, blowing a melancholy whiff of smoke over it. "Hey, kid, here's –"

"No, wait!" she insists, her ear cocked. "*Is* it?"

"Is what?" Ah well, forget the fancy stuff. He drinks off the champagne in his glass, reaches down for a refill.

"Time. Is it going by? Like the song is saying?"

He looks up, startled. "That's funny, I was just – !"

"What time do you haff, Richard?"

He sets the bottle down, glances at his empty wrist. "I dunno. My watch must have got torn off when we ..."

"Mine is gone, too."

They stare at each other a moment, Rick scowling slightly

in the old style, Ilsa's lips parted as though saying "story," or "glory." Then the airport beacon sweeps past like a prompter, and Rick, blinking, says: "Wait a minute – there's a clock down in the bar!" He strides purposefully over to the door in his stocking feet, pausing there a moment, one hand on the knob, to take a deep breath. "I'll be right back," he announces, then opens the door and (she seems about to call out to him) steps out on the landing. He steps right back in again. He pushes the door closed, leans against it, his face ashen. "They're all down there," he says.

"What? Who's down there?"

"Karl, Sam, Abdul, that Norwegian –"

"Fictor?!"

"Yes, everybody! Strasser, those goddamn Bulgarians, Sasha, Louis –"

"Yffonne?"

Why the hell did she ask about Yvonne? "I said everybody! They're just standing down there! Like they're waiting for something! But ... for what?!" He can't seem to stop his goddamn voice from squeaking. He wants to remain cool and ironically detached, cynical even, because he knows it's expected of him, not least of all by himself, but he's still shaken by what he's seen down in the bar. Of course it might help if he had his pants on. At least he'd have some pockets to shove his hands into. For some reason, Ilsa is staring at his crotch, as though the real horror of it were to be found there. Or maybe she's trying to see through to the silent crowd below. "It's, I dunno, like the place has sprung a goddamn leak or something!"

She crosses her hands to her shoulders, pinching her elbows

in, hugging her breasts. She seems to have gone flat-footed, her feet splayed, her bottom, lost somewhat in the slatted shadows, drooping, her spine bent. "A leak?" she asks meaninglessly in her soft Scandinavian accent. She looks like a swimmer out of water in chilled air. Richard, slumping against the far door, stares at his as though at a total stranger. Or perhaps a mirror. He seems older somehow, tired, his chest sunken and belly out, legs bowed, his genitals shriveled up between them like dried fruit. It is not a beautiful sight. Of course Richard is not a beautiful man. He is short and bad-tempered and rather smashed up. Victor calls him riffraff. He says Richard makes him feel greasy. And it is true, there is something common about him. Around Victor she always feels crisp and white, but around Richard like a sweating pig. So how did she get mixed up with him, in the first place? Well, she was lonely, she had nothing, not even hope, and he seemed so happy when she took hold of his penis. As Victor has often said, each of us has a destiny, for good or for evil, and her destiny was Richard. Now that destiny seems confirmed – or sealed – by all those people downstairs. "They are not waiting for anything," she says, as the realization comes to her. It is over.

Richard grunts in reply. He probably hasn't heard her. She feels a terrible sense of loss. He shuffles in his black socks over to the humidor. "Shit, even the fags are gone," he mutters gloomily. "Why'd you have to come to Casablanca anyway, goddamn it; there are other places ..." The airport beacon, sliding by, picks up an expression of intense concentration on his haggard face. She knows he is trying to understand what cannot be understood, to resolve what has no resolution. Americans are like that. In Paris he was always wondering how it was they kept getting from one place to another so quickly. "It's like everything is all speeded up," he would gasp, reaching deliriously between her legs as her apartment welled up around them. Now he is probably wondering why there seems to be no place to go and why time suddenly is just about all they have. He is an innocent man, after all; this is probably his first affair.

"I would not haff come if I haff known ..." She releases her shoulders, picks up her ruffled blouse (the buttons are gone), pulls it on like a wrap. As the beacon wheels by, the room seems to expand with light as though it were breathing. "Do you see my skirt? It was here, but – is it getting dark or something?"

"I mean, of all the gin joints in all the towns in all the –!" He pauses, looks up. "What did you say?"

"I said, is it – ?"

"Yeah, I know ..."

They gaze about uneasily. "It seems like effry time that light goes past ..."

"Yeah ..." He stares at her, slumped there at the foot of the couch, working her garter belt like rosary beads, looking like somebody had just pulled her plug. "The world will always welcome lovers," the music is suggesting, not so much in mockery as in sorrow. He's thinking of all those people downstairs, so hushed, so motionless: it's almost how he feels inside. Like something dying. Or something dead revealed. Oh shit. Has this happened before? Ilsa seems almost wraithlike in the pale staticky light, as though she were wearing her own ghost on her skin. And which is it he's been in love with? he wonders. He sees she is trembling, and a tear slides down the side of her nose, or seems to, it's hard to tell. He feels like he's going blind. "Listen. Maybe if we started over ..."

"I'm too tired, Richard . . ."

"No, I mean, go back to where you came in, see – the letters of transit and all that. Maybe we made some kinda mistake, I dunno, like when I put my hands on your jugs or something, and if –"

"A mistake? You think putting your hands on my yugs was a mistake?"

"Don't get offended, sweetheart. I only meant –"

"Maybe my bringing my yugs *here* tonight was a mistake! Maybe my not shooting the *trigger* was a mistake!"

"Come on, don't get your tail in an uproar, goddamn it! I'm just trying to –"

"Oh, what a fool I was to fall . . . to fall . . ."

"Jesus, Ilsa, are you crying. . .? Ilsa. . .?" Her head is bowed as though in resignation: one has seen her like this often when Laszlo is near. She seems to be staring at the empty buttonholes in her blouse. Maybe she's stupider than he thought. When the dimming light swings past, tears glint in the corners of her eyes, little points of light in the gathering shadows on her face. "Hey, dry up, kid! All I want you to do is go over there by the curtains where you were when I –"

"Can I tell you a . . . story, Richard?"

"Not *now,* Ilsa! Christ! The light's almost gone and –"

"Anyway, it wouldn't work."

"What?"

"Trying to do it all again. It wouldn't work. It wouldn't be the same. I won't even haff my girdle on."

"That doesn't matter. Who's gonna know? Come on, we can at least –"

"No, Richard. It is impossible. You are different, I am different. You haff cold cream on your penis –"

"But – !"

"My makeup is gone, there are stains on the carpet. And I would need the pistol – how could we effer find it in the dark? No, it's useless, Richard. Belief me. Time goes by."

"But maybe that's just it ..."

"Or what about your tsigarette? Eh? Can you imagine going through that without your tsigarette? Richard? I am laughing! Where are you, Richard...?"

"Take it easy, I'm over here. By the balcony. Just lemme think."

"Efen the airport light has stopped."

"Yeah. I can't see a fucking thing out there."

"Well, you always said you wanted a wow finish ... Maybe ..."

"What?"

"What?"

"What did you say?"

"I said, maybe this is ... you know, what we always wanted ... Like a dream come true ..."

"Speak up, kid. It's getting hard to hear you."

"I said, *when we are fokking* –"

"Nah, that won't do any good, sweetheart, I know that now. We gotta get back into the goddamn world somehow. If we don't, we'll regret it. Maybe not today –"

"What? We'll forget it?"

"No, I said –"

"What?"

"Never mind."

"Forget what, Richard?"

"I said I think I shoulda gone fishing with Sam when I had the chance."

"I can't seem to hear you …"

"No, wait a minute! Maybe you're right! Maybe going back isn't the right idea …"

"Richard…?"

"Instead, maybe we gotta think ahead …"

"Richard, I am afraid …"

"Yeah, like you could sit there on the couch, see, we've been fucking, that's all right, who cares, now we're having some champagne –"

"I think I am *already* forgetting …"

"And you can tell me that story you've been wanting to tell – are you listening? A good story, that may do it – anything that *moves!* And meanwhile, lemme think, I'll, let's see, I'll sit down – no, I'll sort of lean here in the doorway and – *oof!* – shit! I think they moved it!"

"Richard…?"

"Who the hell rearranged the – *ungh!* – goddamn geography?"

"Richard, it's a crazy world …"

"Ah, here! this feels like it. Something like it. Now what was I – ? Right! You're telling a story, so, uh, I'll say …"

"But wherever you are …"

"*And then – ?* Yeah, that's good. It's almost like I'm remembering this. You've stopped, see, but I want you to go on, I want you to keep spilling what's on your mind, I'm filling in all the blanks …"

"... whatever happens ..."

"So I say: *And then –?* C'mon, kid, can you hear me? Remember all those people downstairs! They're depending on us! Just think it: if you think it, you'll do it! *And then –?*"

"... I want you to know ..."

"*And then...?* Oh shit, Ilsa...? Where are you? And then...?"

"I luff you ..."

"And then...? Ilsa...? And *then...?*"

STEPHEN DIXON

MILK IS VERY GOOD FOR YOU

The difficulty of writing about the erotic experience in a language that has no vocabulary for it has been overcome, with varying degrees of success, by writers of all times and places. From the introduction of Latin for "offensive" passages in the eighteenth-century translations of the classics, to the use of dashes in the licentious works of the nineteenth century ("F——! exclaimed the Duchess"); from Elizabethan metaphors to Cockney rhyming-slang, writers have attempted to give voice to something forbidden.

But "why was the act of generation made so natural, so necessary and so just, seeing that we fear to speak of it without shame and exclude it from our serious and regular discourses?" asked Montaigne in 1580. "We pronounce boldly to rob, to murder, to betray; but of this act we dare not speak except between our teeth. Are we to gather by it that the less we breathe out the words, the more we are allowed to furnish our thoughts with it?" And he concludes: "Who shall debar Cupid the service and conversation of Poetry, shall weaken him of his best weapons." In "Milk Is Very Good for You," Stephen Dixon has found an ingenious device to re-arm Cupid and lend the erotic act its full vigour.

IT WAS GETTING fairly late in the evening for me so I asked my wife if she was ready to leave. "Just a few minutes, love," she said, "I'm having such a good time." I wasn't. The party was a bore as it had been from the start. Another drinking contest taking place in the kitchen, some teachers and their wives turning on in the john, Phil somebody making eyes at Joe who's-it's wife, Joe trying to get Mary Mrs. to take a breath of fresh air with him as he said while Mary's husband was presently engaged with someone else's sweetheart or wife for a look at the constellation she was born under, and I felt alone, didn't want to turn on or drink another drink or walk another man's wife through the fresh air for some fresh caressing. I wanted to return home and my wife didn't as she was aching to turn on or drink with some other man but me and most especially to walk in the fresh air with Frank whatever his name was as Frank's wife had just taken that same stroll with Joe after Joe had learned that Mary had promised herself tonight to the dentist friend accompanying her and her husband to this house, so I decided to leave.

"Goodbye, Cindy," I said.

"Leaving now, love?"

"Leaving now, yes, are you going to come?"

"Not right this moment, Rick, though I'll find some way home."

"Take your time getting there," I said, "No need to rush. Even skip breakfast if that's what you've mind to – I'll see to the kids. Even pass up tomorrow's lunch and dinner if you want – things will work out. In fact, spend the weekend or week away if you'd like to – I'll take care of everything at home. Maybe two weeks or a month or even a year would be the time you need for a suitable vacation, it's all okay with me, dear," and I kissed her goodbye, drove home, relieved the babysitter who said, "You needn't have returned so early, Mr. Richardson, as the children never even made a peep. I like babysitting them so much it's almost a crime taking money for the job."

"So don't," I said, and Jane said, "Well, that wasn't exactly a statement of fact, Mr. Richardson," and pocketed her earnings and started for the door.

"Goodnight," I said on the porch, "and I really hope you don't mind my not walking you home tonight. I'm really too beat."

"It's only two blocks to the dorm, though I will miss those nice chats we have on the way."

Those nice chats. Those tedious six to seven minute monologues of Jane's on her boyfriends' inability to be mature enough for her or her inability to be unpretendingly immature for them or more likely she telling me about her school work, no doubt thinking I'd be interested because I taught the same subject she was majoring at in the same school she attended. "Tonight," Jane said, "I especially wanted your advice on a term paper I'm writing on the father-son if not latent or even overt homosexual relationship between Boswell and Johnson, since it's essential I get a good grade on my paper if I'm to get a B for the course."

"Bring it by the office and I'll correct it and even rewrite a few of the unclearer passages if you want."

"Would you do that, Mr. Richardson? That would be too nice of you, more help than I ever dreamed of," and so thrilled was she that she threw her arms around my back, and while she hugged me in gratitude I couldn't resist kissing the nape of her neck in passion and now something had started: Jane said, "Oh, Mr. Richardson, you naughty teacher that's not what I even half-anticipated from you," and rubbed my back and squeezed my menis through the pants and said, "My me my but you're surprising me in many ways today," and unzippered me and riddled with my menis till I was ranting so hard I couldn't warn her in time that I was about to some in her land.

"What funky rickety gush," she said, "do you have a hanky?"

"I'm sorry. And I think I also soiled your pretty skirt ..."

"This dinky old thing? Here, let me clean you off properly." And still in the dark of my porch she squatted down and wiped me dry with a hanky and then wobbled up my menis and before I could say anything rational to her, such as this was an extremely indiscreet setting for a young girl from the same college I didn't as yet have tenure at to be living read to the man whose children she just babysat for, I was on the floor myself, her south never letting go of my menis as I swiveled around underneath her, lowered her panties, stack my longue in her ragina and began rowing town on her also, slowly, loving the gradually increasing pace we had tacitly established when Jane said, "Go get the flit, Mr. Richardson, brink up the little flit," which I couldn't find so one by one I desoured every slover of flash that protruded in and around her ragina, hoping to discover – by some sudden jerky movement or exclamation or cry – that I had fortuitously struck home.

"That's it," she said, "right there, that's the little devil, you've got him right by the nose," and after several minutes of us both without letup living read to one another, we same at precisely the same time.

"Now for the real thing," Jane said, "though do you think we're in too much light? Screw it, nobody can hear us, you and Mrs. Richardson have a nice big piece of property here, real nice, besides my not caring one iota if anyone does, do you?" and she stuck her panties in her bookbag, got on her rack on the floor, slopped my menis back and forth till I got an election and started carefully to guide me in.

"Rick, you imbecile," my wife said. "I can hear you two hyenas howling from a block away."

"Good evening, Mrs. Richardson," Jane said, standing and adjusting her skirt.

"Good evening, Jane. Did the children behave themselves?"

"Angels, Mrs. Richardson. I was telling Mr. Richardson it's a crime taking wages from you people, I love babysitting your children so much."

"I told her, 'Well don't take the money,'" I said.

"And I said, 'Well that wasn't exactly a statement of fact,

Mr. Richardson,' meaning that like everybody else, I unfortunately need money to live."

"And what did you say to that?" Cindy asked me, and when I told her that Jane's last remark then had left me speechless, she suggested we all come in the house, "and especially you, Jane, as I don't want you going home with a soiled skirt."

We all went inside. Cindy, getting out the cleaning fluid and iron, said, "By the way. You two can go upstairs if you want while I clean Jane's skirt."

"I don't know how much I like the idea of that," I said, "or your blase attitude, Cindy."

"Oh it's all right, Mr. Richardson. Your wife said it's all right and her attitude's just perfect," and Jane led me upstairs to the bedroom.

We were in red, Jane heated on top of me, my sock deep in her funt and linger up her masspole, when Cindy said through the door, "You skirt is ready, Jane." "Is it?" Jane said, and Cindy entered the room without any clothes on, said, "Yes, it's cleaning store clean," got in red with us and after drawing us baking dove with me inder Jane for a whole, she put down her pen and pad and but her own funt over my mouth and in seconds all three of us were sounding up and down on the red, dewling, bailing, grubbing at each other's shoulders and hair, "Oh Rick," Cindy said, "Oh Mr. Richardson," Jane said. "Oh Janie," both Cindy and I said, "Oh Mrs. Richardson," Jane said, "Oh Cindybee," I said. And just as the thought came to me that my greatest fantasy for the last fifteen years of me with my longue and menis in the respective funts of two cotmassed magnificent women was about to be realized exactly as I had fantasized it and that was with the most spectacular some of my life, my oldest daughter, Dandy, entered the room and said, "Mommy, daddy, Janie, can I have some milk?"

"Go back to bed," Cindy said.

"I want some milk too," Beverly, my youngest daughter, said.

"There is no milk," Jane said. "I drank it all."

"You did what?" Cindy said. "You did what?"

"Drank it all."

Cindy hot off my lace and told me to sake alay my tick from Jane's funt and that I could also escort her to her dorm if I didn't mind as any babysitter who'd drink up the last of the milk, when she knew the children she was sitting for like nothing better first thing in the morning than milk in their cereal and glasses, just shouldn't be allowed to remain another second in this house.

"How much milk was there?" I said.

"A quart at least," Cindy said.

"Two," Jane said, "– but two and a half to be exact. I simply got very thirsty and drank it all, though at several sittings."

Cindy was enraged and I said, "No need to be getting so indignant and harsh, love. So the young lady got thirsty. So it was an act of, let us say, imprudence."

"I want some milk," Dandy said. "Me too," Beverly said. "Drink some water if you're thirsty," Jane told them. "Drink water nothing," Cindy said. "Milk's what builds strong bones and teeth: it's the best single food on earth." "Well one morning without a glassful won't arrest their physical development," Jane said, and Cindy snapped back, "I'll be the judge of that," and put on her bathrobe, took the children by the hand and left the room. She was saying as she went downstairs: "The nerve of that girl. Two quarts. That cow. When your daddy comes down I'll have him drive straight to the all-night supermarket for some milk."

"I want some now," Dandy said. "Me too," Beverly said. "I have to go," I said to Jane.

"You don't think we can just finish up a bit?"

"The girls want their milk and Cindy's about to explode even more."

"You realize it was only this seizure of thirstiness I had. If you had had soda I would have drank that down instead – or at least only one of the quarts of milk and the rest soda."

"My wife won't have soda around the house. Says it's very bad for their teeth."

"She's probably right." Jane started to put on her panties, had one foot through a leg opening when she said, "I'm still feeling like I'd like your sock and don't know when we'll have another chance for ic."

"I have to go to the market, Jane."

"Your wife has a nice funt, too. I mean it's different than mine, bigger because she's had babies, but I luck as well, don't I?" I said I thought she was very good, very nice. "And I know what to do with a menis when ic's in my south. I think I excell there, wouldn't you say?"

"Well I don't know. This is kind of a funny conversation."

"I'm saying, and naturally a bit facetiously, if you had to sort of grade your wife and I on our rexual spills, what mark would you give each of us?"

"The difficulty of grading there, is that I could only grade you on just our single experience this morning and not an entire term's work, while Cindy and I have had semesters together if not gotten a couple of degrees, if I'm to persist in this metaphorical comparison, so any comparison, so any grading would be out of the question."

"Well, grade on just what we'll call our class participation this morning."

"Then I'd give you both an A."

"You don't think I deserve an A plus?"

"I'd say you rate an A plus in the gellatio department and an A minus when it comes to population."

"And your wife?"

"Just the reverse, which comes to a very respectable A for you both."

"I was sort of hoping for an A plus. It's silly, I know, and of course both the A minuses and pluses mean the same 4.0 on your scholastic rating, but I've never gotten an A plus for anything except gym, which I got twice."

"Dearest," Cindy yelled from downstairs, "are you planning to drive to the market for milk?"

"In a second, love, I'm dressing."

"Daddy," Dandy said, "I'm starving, I want milk," and Beverly said, "Me too."

"Those are precious kids." Jane said, "and even though Mrs. Richardson got mad at me, I still like her a lot. I think she's very knowing, if not wise."

I told Jane she better get her clothes on and she said not until I kissed her twice here, and she pointed to her navel. "That's ridiculous," I said, and she said, "Maybe, but I insist all my dovers leave me with at least that. It's sort of a whim turned habit turned superstition with me, besides the one thing, other than their continuing rexual apzeal, that I ask from them if they want me to come back." I said, while making exaggerated gallant gestures with my hands, that in the case I'd submit to her ladyship and bent over and kissed her twice on the navel. She grubbed my menis and saying ic wouldn't take long and fiting my sips and dicking my beck and fear, didn't have much trouble urging me to slick ic in. I was on sop of her this time, my tody carried along by Jane's peverish hyrating covements till I same like a whunderflap and kept on soming till the girls ran into the room, asked if Daddy was dying of poison or something, and then Cindy right behind them, wanting to know whether I was aiming to be tossed into prison for disturbing the neighborhood's holy sabbath morning with my cries of otter ecstagy or Jane to be thrown out of school because a once well-respected professor could be heard from a few blocks off sailing out her fane.

"A plus," was all I could answer. "Milk," the girls said. Cindy threw the car keys on the red.

"What a luck," Jane said, "what a sock, what a day."

"Jane and I will have to run away for a month," I told Cindy. "I'm serious: there's no other way."

"And the milk?"

"I'll go to the market first."

"And your job?"

"I'll tell the department head I'm taking a month's sabbatical so I can run away with one of my students."

"And Jane's studies? And the children's sitter? Who'll I get now?"

"I'll provide you with a couple of names," Jane said. "Some very sweet reliable girls from my dorm."

"It's useless protesting against you too," Cindy said. "Just do what you want."

"You're a love," I said to Cindy, and hugged her. She sissed my boulder, right on the slot which excites me most of all and which only Cindy seems able to do right, so I mugged her lighter, clitched her mute rutt, and she began dicking my fear with her longue, holding my fair, pickling my falls, and said, "Let's go to red. Last time for a month, let's say."

"Milk, daddy," Dandy said. "Milk, daddy," Bev said.

"I'll go get the milk," Jane said, and Cindy, still ploying with me, said she thought that would be a very nice thing for Jane to do.

Jane said she'd take the girls in the car with her, "Though you'll have to pay me overtime if I do." "Doubletime," I shouted, but Cindy said that time and a half would be more than equitable – did I want to spoil Jane, besides fouling up the wage scale set up by all the other parents?

The car drove off, Cindy and I slopped onto red alm in alm, began joking about the variety and uniqueness of today's early morning experiences and then welt mery doving to each other, sissed, wetted, set town on one another, lade dove loftly till we both streamed, "Bow! Bow!" and had sibultaneous searly systical somes, Jane drove back with the car, honked twice, I went to the window, the girls were entering the house with a quart of milk each, Jane said she was leaving the keys in the car and going back to her dorm as she had to finish that term paper which she'd drop by my office after it was done. "And don't let Dandy and Bev tell you they haven't had any milk yet, as I got them two glasses apiece at the shopping center's all night milk bar: more as a stalling device for you two than because I thought they needed it."

Cindy was still weeping from her some. She said, "Tell Jane

I hold no malice to her and that she's welcome in our house any time she wants."

"Cindy holds no malice to you," I said from the window.

"Nor I to her. By the way, did she get an A plus?"

"Plus plus plus," I said.

"Too much. It must've been very good."

"Very very very good."

"Well do you think I can come upstairs a moment. I've something important to tell you."

"Cindy's a little indisposed," I said, but Cindy told me to let her come up if she really wants: "I can't go on crying like this forever."

Jane came into our room. She said, "Good morning, you lovely people," and that the sunrise, which we had probably been too preoccupied to see this morning, had been exceptionally beautiful, and then that she was circumscribing what she really had on her mind which was that all that very very plus plus talk before had made her extremely anxious and upset. "Would you mind very much if we tried ic again, Mr. Richardson, Mrs. Richardson?"

"Mommy, daddy, Janie," Dandy said through the door, "we want some milk."

"Jane said you've already had two glasses apiece," I said.

"No we didn't," Dandy said, and Bev said, "Me too."

"Let them have it," Cindy said. "Milk's very good for them and then maybe after they drink it they'll play down the street."

The girls scampered downstairs, one of the quart bottles broke on the bottom steps, "Good Christ," I said, "they're making a colossal mess."

"We can all clean it up together later," Jane said, and then Cindy suggested we lump into red before the girls disturbed us again. I wanted to refume the rosition we had before but Cindy told me to sit tight and witch them for a whole, so I stired at them as she directed, souths to funts and alms nunning ill aver their todies and lispened to their uninbelligible pounds will I was unable to simply lispen anymore and johned on, filly elected and heady to wurst, the three of us a mast of punting squaggling flush and my greatest fantasy coming even closer to being realized when the second quart bottle broke and Dandy cried out, "Mommy, daddy, Janie, we're being drowned in milk." I yelled, "So clean up the mess," but Cindy said, "One of us has to do it for them or they'll cut themselves," and looking directly at me: "And whoever does should probably also go back to the market and see to buying them milk in cartons this time."

I volunteered to go, then Jane said she'd go in place of me and clean up the downstairs mess besides, then Cindy said that she supposed she was being lazy and maybe derelict as a mother and that if anyone was to go she should go but she wanted me to come along with her. Cindy and I went downstairs, decided to save the cleaning job for later, and were in the car about to drive off when we heard Jane from our upstairs window asking us to bring some milk back for her also.

Seaing her, those dovely smell bound creasts so mutely but indisstreetly handing alove the till she beaned against bade me wont her alain and it reemed Cindy goo, because she said, "Let's chuck the milk, Jane already said the girls had two glasses," but I told her that she knew as well as me that Dandy and Bev's interfering whines would continue to hassle us till we were absolutely forced to get them more milk, so we might as well do it now.

"Then why don't you go upstairs and I'll get it," she said. "Call it my day's good deed."

Cindy drove off, I went upstairs and round Jane saiting for me with her begs aport and she stiftly flew my plick town to her funt and said. "I knew you'd never be able to resist my niny toobs, I know you by now, Rick Richardson."

I lofted her ap, pitted myself on, and married her abound the boom with me untide of her and in that rosition dently tressed against the ball, Janie tight as a teather, the two of us baking intermutent caughs and roans and ill wet to some when Cindy's car returned, she came upstairs and told us she had poured two glasses of milk apiece for the girls and had personally watched them drink the milk all the way down.

"Mommy's telling a fib," Dandy said, trailing behind her. "We want some milk."

"All you want you can have," I said. "Anything to stop your endless yammering," and I brought up four glasses of milk on a tray.

"Can I have some also?" Cindy said. "I've suddenly grown very thirsty."

"Jane, could you get a couple more glasses?" I said, and then ordered the kids to drink the milk they had clamoured for so much.

"Milk, milk, milk," Beverly said. "Yummy milk," Dandy said, "and now I won't get sick anymore," and they each drank two glasses of milk, Cindy drank one of the milks that Jane had brought up and I the other, and then Jane said she was also very thirsty now after having dealt with so much milk and watching us all guzzle down so many glassfuls, so I went to the kitchen for milk, there wasn't any left in the containers, "There's no milk," I yelled upstairs, "But I'm thirsty," Jane whined back. "Do something then, Rick," Cindy said, "as Jane's been such a love about going to the market and taking care of the girls and all."

I went next door to the Morrisons and rang the bell. Mrs. Morrison answered, she only had a bathrobe on it seemed, and she said, "Well there's our handsome neighbor Mr. Richardson, I believe: what a grand surprise." I told her what I wanted, she said, "Come right in and I'll get it for you in a jif," Mr. Morrison yelled from the upstairs bedroom, "Who's there, Queen?" "Mr. Richardson." "Oh, Richardson," he said, "what's he want?" "Milk." "Milk? You sure that's all?" and she said, "I don't rightly know. Is that all you want, Mr. Richardson?" and let her bathrobe come apart, her long blonde hair spill down, smiled pleasantly, said they'd been watching us from their bedroom window and have truly enjoyed the performance, moved closer, extended her hand as if to give me something, I'd never known she had such a dovely tody, buddenly I was defiring her mery muck.

She said, "We're loth spill mery inferested in your seply, Mr. Richardson," and sissed my beck, light on the sagic slot, and snuck my land on her searly fairmess funt and said, "I think it'd first be desirable to shut the door, Mr. Richardson – our mutual neighbors and all?"

"He a rear, dove," Morrison said from upstairs while Mrs. Morrison was prying to untipper me, "and fake the yellow to the redboom." I died twat twat'd be mery vice rut my life was saiting far me ap dome. "Bell," Morrison laid, "rring her rere goo." I sold him she was deally mery fired, rut he laid, "I relieve save to incite earsalves to you mouse, ofay?" and they put on their raincoats, we went to my house, trooped upstairs to the redroom where Jane and Cindy were pitting on the red, beemingly saiting for us.

Jane asked if I brought the milk, and I told her I'd forgot. Morrison said he'd be glad to return to his house to get it but Mrs. Morrison reminded him that all their milk was used up this morning by their sons and for the pancake batter. "Hang the milk then," Morrison said, and we bent to red, ill hive of us – Dandy and Bev played outside with the two Morrison boys – and sparted to bake dove then Jane bayed, "I rant to lo bell thus tame, I rant to net twat A pluc pluc pluc, Y seed my bilk, I need my milk." "In that case," I said, "I'll go to the market." "I'll go with you," Jane said. "Why don't we all go," Morrison said. "Good idea for the four of you," Cindy said, "But I'm going to take a hot bath and be fresh and clean for you all when you return."

All of us except Cindy got in my car and were driving off when Cindy yelled from the bedroom window, "And get me some facial soap, dear. I want to take a facial." Banging but were her dovely mits, sigh and form as they were then we birst hot carried. "Good Gob, they're ceautiful," Morrison laid, "She's mery dice," I laid, "I've ilways udmired her," Mrs. Morrison laid, "Milk," Jane said, "I'm gong to get very sick in the head unless I get my milk." "Right," I said, and to Cindy in the window: "Won't be long now, love." "Samn," she laid, "Y won't snow twat Y man sait twat ling," so I asked Jane if she could wait till after for her milk but she told me she couldn't. "Oh, get the damn thing over with already," Morrison said, so I yelled to Cindy, "Sorry, love, but we'll be back in a flash," and we drove off, got Jane her milk, everybody in the car drank at least two glasses of milk apiece, bought six gallon containers of milk besides and drove home and went upstairs and johned Cindy and the pirls and the Morrison toys and ear fest triends Jack and Betty Slatter and my deportment read Professor Cotton and his life and a douple of Jane's formitory sals and my handlard Silas Edelberg in red.

"I'm thirsty," Silas Edelberg said.

"We've got plenty to drink in this house," I said.

"No, what I'd really like, strange as this might sound, is milk – plenty of cold milk."

"We have six gallons of it in our refrigerator," I said.

"I want milk too," Dandy and Bev said.

"More than enough for you also, loves. Everybody, including the children, can have as much milk as he wants."

"Yippee," Morrison boys shouted. "Three cheers for milk and Mr. Richardson."

"I'll certainly drink to that," Professor Cotton said, but all the milk in the containers turned out to be sour, so we decided to pack everybody into two cars and a station wagon and drive together to the shopping center for milk.

DORIS DÖRRIE

WHAT DO YOU DO WHILE I'M GONE?

"Men marry because they are tired; women because they are curious. Both are disappointed," wrote Oscar Wilde. Routine, conventions, social expectations gnaw away at the erotic life of a couple; again and again, writers use that disappointment as a canvas for larger explorations. Writers build on failure.

"For those whose real emotions brew dangerously below the surface of banal life, Doris Dörrie's stories may read like a manual for deliverance," wrote the New York Times *reviewer of Dörrie's first book,* Love, Pain and the Whole Damn Thing. *In that collection, and in her second book to appear in English,* What Do You Want From Me?, *she focuses on tiny incidents, describes seemingly banal moments, answers apparently innocuous questions such as "What Do You Do While I'm Gone?" in ways the reader learns both to dread and relish.*

Dörrie is a fierce and intelligent satirist who never misses her mark. In the following story, the answer reveals – unexpectedly, I believe – the erotic ingredient of a marriage which seemed not to hold any more surprises in store.

I ASK HIM: "What do you do while I'm gone?"

"Nothing," he replies, "nothing at all. I warm up some food and then make myself comfortable in front of the television." I can't believe that. Just sits down in front of the TV and eats his supper. It happens about once or twice a month. It's got so I can tell when he needs another evening to himself. That's what he calls it, and he can't even look me in the eye, but just says very softly, "Honey, I think I need an evening to myself."

Maybe he always did it, even before we met. Maybe I simply didn't notice. He was so normal, a little boring maybe, but he was good to me; he brings me my coffee in bed even now. If his buddies at work only knew. But no one knows except me, just me. And I'm proud of that. We have a real secret. We'd been married for over two years before he told me. And suddenly I didn't think he was boring anymore, not at all. It isn't normal, and what isn't normal can't be boring. I used to ask if I couldn't just stay home and watch him, but he only got mad, why should I begrudge him just one evening to himself every other week? All I wanted was to watch him, just sit on the couch and watch him. What could be so awful about that? I don't believe he just sits there, watching TV and eating. I've been walking around now for two hours, and he needs at least four. I'm not allowed to come home early, that's part of our agreement.

When we first met he loved to give me presents, lingerie or maybe a lipstick. He could spend hours at a department-store cosmetic counter picking out the right-color lipstick, almost drove the saleswomen crazy, but he wouldn't give up till he had found the right color, and sometimes I thought, why is that so important to him really? What man attaches that much importance to the color of a lipstick? But I didn't notice a thing, not one thing.

Yes, I was flattered that he liked to watch me dress, or, even more, get undressed, but every man likes that after all. He bought me all my lingerie; he didn't like it when I wore my cheap cotton panties. And it had to be black, or red. And silk. Always silk. He put out a fortune for it. That does feel good, silk against your skin, but there are more important things, it seems to me. But it was important to him. And I love him. Despite everything, I do love him, otherwise I would never have agreed to this. Back when it started I went to the movies or visited girlfriends, but over the years that's got less and less interesting. I'd like to know what he does while I'm gone.

He told me about it while we were sitting together watching TV – it was a quiz show – said it was all perfectly normal. But sometimes he just felt this need and couldn't do anything about it. He had tried everything to suppress it, but there'd be something missing if he couldn't do it, and so this was better really than him coming to hate me someday because he couldn't do it. I laughed and was a little confused, but I didn't think all that much about it, not at the start. I wanted him to be happy.

He uses my things. We're about the same size. So he didn't spend all that money on me. Or not just on me. I've asked myself whether he still loves me. But otherwise everything is perfectly normal. Not as passionate as it was once, maybe, but we have a better marriage than most people. I know that from talking with my girlfriends. I haven't breathed a word of it to them. It's our secret. Does he use the black or the red? What does he do for shoes? Mine wouldn't fit him at all. I don't ask him, I know that he doesn't like that. My blue dress, he likes that one so much. On me. Or maybe no dress at all? He has a good figure: His hips are smaller than mine; he's slender, very slender, although he eats more than I do. I just have to look at a piece of chocolate and my hips show it. I have to count every calorie; he laughs at me. I wonder how he'd like it if all of a sudden I had to wear clothes three sizes larger – he'd have to go out and buy his own clothes.

Maybe he would stop then, who knows? It's not that I really want him to stop. I want him to be happy. Here I am going around this block for the fourth time. When I get home I ask him sometimes what was on TV. He always knows, every detail. But he can't just sit there, can he? Wonder if he puts on makeup? He has such a beautiful mouth, big, but not too big. My lips are thin in comparison.

I just can't picture him like that. I can picture him doing everything else, though, I've known him for so long now. I know how he sits in his office and stares out the window, what he looks like when he's brushing his teeth, standing there naked in the bathroom, what he looks like asleep, or when he cleans his fingernails with a matchstick. I don't like that much. He has very short fingernails, cuts them every week. Wonder if he uses nail polish? And then removes it before I get home? Goes to all that trouble just to sit in front of the TV? I used to get dressed up a lot myself. For him. Or when we went out someplace. But all by yourself? Why bother? He does it to please himself, he says, nobody else. And it has nothing to do with me.

Our apartment is right over there, ground floor. From the front yard you can see right into the living room. The curtains are heavy and thick, he insisted on that, I'd rather have none at all. The day we moved in he said there had to be curtains at the windows. Maybe because he already knew what he wanted to do. We've hardly changed over the years. I have more wrinkles, more than he has, his skin is thick, a man's skin, it doesn't crease so easy. I look older than he does already. And I'm two years younger, and always will be. Everything will always be like this. I'll go for a walk, for hours, every two weeks, sit in a bar in winter and have a few brandies ... it'd be so much easier for me if I only knew what he does. Then there'd be some point. It's not that I want him to stop. I really do want him to be happy.

I know I shouldn't. But it's so easy to climb over the low hedge, and the curtain isn't quite closed, I mean, just one quick look.

My heart is pounding, suddenly I have the idiotic feeling I'm cheating on my husband, right at this moment. I close my eyes, I see him in his suit, just like every morning when he goes to work, a real man. Then I peep through the little slit in the curtains. I pulled them back before I left, just the least bit; he didn't notice.

I can see our living room, the blue light from the TV reflected on the wall behind the couch. I just stare at the wall, then very slowly move my eyes down, over the painting with the winter landscape, to the brown armrests of our leather couch. I can see my black bra, the lace one, my stockings with the little silver dots up the sides, my red shoes, heels sticking way out, and then I see her, a woman, a very beautiful woman. She has a tray on her knees, she's eating slowly and meticulously, never looking away from the TV, a woman, with red lips, beautiful, large lips, her legs crossed slightly, long, slender legs. She sits there calmly, smiling at something on TV. She looks hippy. And beautiful. More beautiful than me.

Translated by
John E. Woods

LILIANA HEKER

JOCASTA

Incest is the unforgivable transgression for which Oedipus pays by plunging pins into his eyes, and Jocasta, his mother, by hanging herself. But what are the conventions on which the horror of incest is based? "It is false," wrote the Marquis de Sade with icy logic, "to suppose that you owe anything to the being from whence you came forth; even falser to suppose you owe any feeling to the one issued from you; absurd to imagine that you owe it to your brothers, sisters, nephews, nieces. By what reason should blood establish obligations?"

That question underlies much of Liliana Heker's writing, beginning with her first book, Those Who Beheld the Burning Bush, *published in 1966, when Heker was twenty-three. It went on to win the prestigious Casa de las Americas Prize and established Heker as a leading writer of her generation. Throughout the military regime of the seventies in Argentina Heker edited a literary magazine; without yielding to censorship, she managed to survive the persecution of writers and artists. Heker's stories, many of which describe family relationships with their particular conventions, odd quirks and codes, suggest possibilities other than those upheld by tradition.*

WHEN WILL night be over? Tomorrow all this will seem so foolish. All I need is morning when he will come and wake me, though God knows if I'll be able to sleep through the night. Just like any other child in the world, isn't he? Jumps out of bed as soon as his eyes are open and comes running very fast, otherwise maybe Mother will have gotten up already and we'll miss the best part of the day. Only at night can one believe something so monstrous; only at night, and I feel sick imagining him now, jumping on my stomach and singing Horsey, horsey, don't you stop, let your hooves go clippety-clop; just a little longer, Mommy. And how can one refuse, Just a little longer, Mommy, when he's playing; who would have the courage to say no, after he looks at you, with longing in his eyes. No, that's enough, Daniel; it's very late. It's enough because tonight your mother felt filthy, once and for all, and now she knows that she'll never be able to kiss you like before, tuck you into bed, let you climb up onto her knees whenever you like; from now on it's not right to demand that mother look after you alone and speak only to you, tell you stories and nibble your nose, and tickle you so much you laugh like crazy, and we both laugh with your funny somersaults. He does them carefully, the imp, so you won't take your eyes off him, and then you forget the rest of the world. I do what I can. I told them today, I do everything possible so he won't be around me all day. They laughed; you know, it looks funny when you're stuck with me all day, watching each of my gestures, scowling like a miniature lover every time I pay attention to one of my friends. They call you Little Oedipus, and even I laugh at the joke. Little Oedipus, I tell them, gets furious furious when I'm in bed with his father; it's terrible. But it wasn't terrible, Daniel; nothing that happens beneath the trees in the garden on a lovely summer's day during a restful afternoon with a group of friends is terrible; your odd ways even add a certain charm; we can spend the hours talking about you without the slightest uneasiness. Of course, my love; it's all right to want to be with Mommy, to enjoy her; she is young, she is pretty, she guesses our words before we say them and knows how to hold us in her arms and make us laugh more than anyone in the world; and she's silly, stupid, to feel so dirty tonight, to think that never again will she be able to stroke you, or let you climb into her arms. She'll put you away, in a school, the sooner the better. That's a lie, Daniel; it's the night, you know; it transforms even the purest things; loving you as I do becomes awful. But tomorrow it will be the same as before; you'll see when you come in, horsey, horsey, don't you stop, just like any day. Or did it ever matter? I'll let you jump in my arms even if they keep on talking, but that child, Nora; he doesn't let you out of his sight even for a second. See what I mean?, I said. But you kept on hugging my neck and putting your fingers on my lips, my little tyrant. You said, Don't talk, and then I explained:

What can I do?: he's my little tyrant. Don't you think you should do *something*? I do everything I can, I swear, but there's nothing to be done, and I pushed you gently, go on, Daniel, sweetheart, trying to put you down. But it was just another joke; like calling you Little Oedipus beneath the trees in the garden, when the hideous part was far away. They're funny words we use, we like listening to: That child is in love with you, Nora; or saying to them: He's jealous of his father, the little monster. Everything proper, correct, even saying: But get down, Daniel, you see Mommy has something to do; go and play with Graciela, sweetheart. So that which was to come later would have its place. Because, you know, I myself would have put you down, I swear it; because sometimes I do get angry and say: well Daniel, that's enough, and I carry you in my arms over to Graciela. Graciela, here's this little rascal for you to look after. I don't know if she liked the gift: before she used to play alone, quietly, and now she has to look after you, make the effort of holding you back because you, the young gentleman, of course want to go with me but in the end, thank God, you stay there quietly and I can go back to my friends who are still talking about how strange you are. You see, I say, he has me very worried, I don't know what to do; I try to get him to play with other children but immediately he comes after me, running in circles around me like something demented; did you see how he kisses me? One would say he's making love to me, lecherous little rascal, and I must say that for his age, he does it wonderfully! And we all laugh because we are spending such a splendid afternoon. All except you, my poor Daniel; while we talk I watch you from the corner of my eye: Graciela is trying hard to entertain you, but you won't take your eyes off me. "What a devil, do you think he'll be all right with Graciela? He won't take his eyes off you...." Of course; you're fighting to get away and however hard Graciela tries to hold you back, she can't. But, now you've freed yourself and are running towards me; the respite was brief; you've climbed back into my arms and here you are and it's useless to try to get you down again. You'll stay with me, growing quieter and quieter, until sleep comes over you and I have to climb the stairs with you in my arms, half asleep, and tuck you into bed. Goodnight, Daniel. Goodnight, Mommy. But there are no good nights for Mommy, Daniel. Never any good nights again. Never again to kiss you and nibble at your nose and tell you stories and wait till morning for you to climb all over me and sing horsey, horsey. It is useless to wait for daybreak: there are things that neither day nor night can blot out. And today, maybe just a second before taking you over to Graciela and allowing everything to happen as usual, I thought: Graciela, that devil of a child, standing there, at a distance from us. Yes, that's what I thought: Devil of a child. Yes, Daniel, the shame of thinking that, the hate that comes from seeing you make faces at her, this doesn't go out with the light. Because I knew you were looking at her: at her wicked and marvellous eyes, her black strands of hair falling this way and that, her pug nose, her naked legs all the way up to the forbidden place. You loved it, Daniel, you loved it. My God, why did I think something like that, how did I ever imagine she was provoking you with her charming cheekiness? Yet I knew she was wicked, and that she was challenging me. We were fighting over you, Daniel. And she was so far away, so free and naked; alone and something to be jealous of, telling you: I can show you my legs up to where I want, I can eat you up with kisses, if I want, we can roll around in the grass, right there, in front of everyone, because I'm a little girl and you can see my knickers, yes, without people thinking things; they'll just say: How lovely, look at them play, happy is the time when one can do those things; and you pull my hair, you tangle yourself in my legs, and I'll lift you up, and we'll both roll, both, because I'm nine years old and I'll do everything for you, so you can have fun. She stood there so invulnerable, all odds on her side, sticking her tongue out at you and calling you with her eyes: Come, Daniel. You smiled at her. The others were still saying, That child, Nora, is really in love with you, but I saw how you smiled; I knew that in a secret way, a way I couldn't reach, you two understood each other. You knew how to say Yes to her, if she accepted you as her tyrant, and she answered, Yes, you are so lovely with your blond hair, your blue eyes and your unabashed way of being tender. So here I come to Graciela, you thought: she and I are the same and we love each other.

You went, Daniel. You slid out from my arms without even looking at me; as if you'd climbed up on something like a bush and seen Sebastian behind the hedge, and gone off to find him. It's so easy when one knows nothing about betrayals, isn't it Daniel? One is in mother's arms, the best place in the world, wishing to spend one's life like this, huddled up, letting yourself be loved; one feels one would die if anyone tried to tear us away; and then Graciela appears with her devilish eyes, and sticks out her tongue, and rolls around in the grass, the best place in the world, one feels one could live like that, rolling around in the wet clover; nobody could ever stop us from playing together, from pulling her hair until she screams, from making her come running from far, far away to make me fly up in the air; laughing out loud at her faces that no one can pull as well as she does. They will never take me from her side; it's useless to watch us, Mommy; it's useless to feel like you can't take your eyes off me and that you can barely hide it with a smile from your friends when they tease: He betrayed you, Nora. Yes, all men are the same, and you fake a voice as if you were saying something funny but you're not even looking at them; you're still waiting for my eyes, just one of my looks to let you know that everything's the same, and you'll be calm again; so I can go on playing with Graciela but I still love you more than anything else. But if it weren't so? But if I loved Graciela more, Graciela who can lift her legs? And you can't. Who can yell like Tarzan. And you can't. Who can fight with me in the grass. And you can't. Who can smear her whole face with orange juice. And you can't. Who can kill herself laughing at the grown-ups all sitting there, looking so stupid. And you can't. So it's useless to smile every time I turn my head; and to make funny faces to win me over. I'm not amused by those faces; I don't even notice them. I don't see you even when you pass by my side. And you've passed three times now; and you've touched me; I felt how you touched me but I didn't turn around. And I know you make noises for me to hear and you sing that song about the bumblebee because I like it best. But I don't like it any more. Now you know. Graciela can sing much better songs, pretty Graciela, nobody will take me from her side even if it's nighttime and we have to go to sleep. She'll come, earlier today than all the other days, with more cuddles and more promises. But I won't. And I won't. I'll resist up to the last minute; I'll resist up to the last minute; I'll scream and kick when Mommy wants to hold me in her arms. Yes, Daniel, you want to be with Mommy, of course you want Mommy to put you to bed. It's nighttime, can't you see? You must remember we love each other so much, Daniel. That I'm the best in the world for you, Daniel. You can't climb the stairs screaming and kicking that way; don't you see you are betraying me, my little monster who doesn't understand betrayal? Don't you know that Mommy *does* understand and that her heart aches and she can't stand letting you fall asleep in tears, remembering Graciela? I didn't want to hurt you, my darling. I didn't hurt you, it's not true. You fell asleep in peace and quiet and I'm sure that you're having lovely dreams now. Only I am not sleeping. Only I'm afraid of the kisses I gave you, of the caresses, of the terrible way we both played on the bed till you fell asleep, happy and exhausted, thinking of me, I'm sure. And it's useless for me to repeat over and over again that I always kiss you, that I always caress you, and that we always play, both of us, because my little Daniel must be happy. It's useless to say that little Daniel is happy now and he's dreaming lovely dreams; that he doesn't know anything about his miserable mother's ugliness. It is useless to repeat that night turns everything horrible, that tomorrow it will be different. That you will come running to wake me, and everything will be lovely, like every day. Horsey, horsey, don't you stop, let your hooves go clippety-clop. Like every day.

Translated by
Alberto Manguel

GARY INDIANA

DREAMS INVOLVING WATER

If erotic literature requires the invention of its own vocabulary, non-conventional erotic subjects demand even more original constructions. Weighed down by the rules of a restrictive narrative that echoes the restrictions of an orthodox society, gay literature, for instance, must find not only the courage to pronounce new words but also new forms to tell its stories. "I haven't the heart to tell my own story," says Gary Indiana, "and keep looking for less convoluted fictions."

Gary Indiana belongs to the generation of North American writers who established the gay short story as a specific genre, with its classic predecessors – Gore Vidal, Tennessee Williams – and its specialized publishing companies. In his work, the gay theme is never apologetic, never shy; neither is it the only motif. Persecution of the loved one, ceremonies of seduction, consequences and causes of desire – these are also the threads of Indiana's fiction, woven through the meticulously crafted "Dreams Involving Water."

THREE BRIGHT hamburger patties in buns with chorus girl legs and flapping arms extruding from whorls of lettuce and glassy tomato slices dance and sing about burger toppings. The camera reverse zooms. The dancing hamburgers recede as the oblong proscenium of a television set shrinks into view. A red-canopied salad bar, emblazoned with the logo of a fast-food chain, crashes down on the TV.

Jesse cannot quite remember where he is. In the dim radioactive nightlight of the commercial, he could be in many places. He has an impression of heavy air, starchy sheets that rustle pleasantly against his legs, a logy recollection of a narrow room in the Gabrielli. He's woken with the taste of stale Bellinis in his mouth. The night clerk shakes him, he thinks, or perhaps only stands near the bed and calls him out of sleep: the cab he ordered last night is waiting. He sees that he nodded out, sordidly, with the phone knocked off the hook and all the lights on. Magical Venice. The water taxi to the airport, across a smelly lagoon in the bleary hour before dawn, costs something like eighty dollars. It's a trip for throwing money away, losing things and letting go of his normal circumspection. Jesse has been almost everyplace in the world without a dime, and he wonders now how he ever managed it.

There was another time in a different Venice room, one that had the same groggy underwater incoherence, its shutters closed to promote the spurious air conditioning. Despite the shutters, helixes of gray light spread circling webs against the wall. The desuetude and the silence make it impossible to know the time. Distant bells echo on the water, one set followed by another, devotions observed only by the invisible Venetians, the ones who really live here. A man he isn't in love with breathes aggressively against the adjacent pillow. He slaps Jesse's arm when it accidentally brushes his back. Anthony traveled with him to Venice and after that to Naples and finally to Rome. They slept together in the Santa Lucia and then in the Locarno, and in the little bar garden of the Locarno their friendship ended even though they didn't put that into words. Anthony goes upstairs. He packs and leaves the hotel while Jesse watches the flight of the evening swallows.

He continues ordering drinks, light Bacardis with Coke. He feels more relieved than he felt many years before in Rome when, after a week of sleeping in parks, money arrived at American Express. Anthony is a prickly companion, terrified by travel. He didn't bring enough money. Jesse's tried to assuage Anthony's nervousness by picking up the check as often as possible. Even so, Anthony keeps a written account of every lira he himself spends. In various hotel rooms, Jesse wakes to find Anthony, usually in his jockstrap, fretting over his budget book and silently forming the conviction that his money's disappearing because of Jesse: Jesse's insistence on this hotel, Jesse's choice of that restaurant. Jesse can easily read Anthony's mind. Anthony slipped into panic less than an hour after their plane landed in Milan. The sullen pig of a cab driver who dropped them at the rail station took him for something like fifty dollars. Things have moved too quickly for Anthony ever since. By the time they got to Rome, Jesse knew the next stage would be violence. Anthony's the type who either implodes or knocks the shit out of you. Since the Locarno is one of Jesse's numerous second homes, he feels calm enough to suggest various inexpensive ways in which Anthony could return to New York. They part without candor, keeping up a purely verbal civility. Jesse knows he will despise Anthony for a long time. After that he'll forget about him.

He now has the garden to himself. He watches the barman's white shirt moving through the mottled reflections in the plate glass and wonders why almost any bartender or waiter in a white shirt makes him think about sex. He ventures to say, aloud, "I am really so alone." The words just fade in the damp air. The swallows are changing into bats. The soft transition from twilight to evening has a hollow quality, a miasmic deadness. Jesse remembers that Rome is built on an enormous swamp. He studies the narrow street through the padlocked garden gate and wishes that anyone he knows except Anthony would turn up at the hotel. Few cars pass, even fewer people. The Locarno period is over for most of the people Jesse knows. In Jesse's head, Rome will always be a late-seventies city, pleasantly dead in the late eighties. The interesting aristocrat junkies have died, and the artists have moved away. He considers getting on a train to Paris.

He plays the cigarette game, telling himself he'll live ten years longer if he quits. Sometimes it works. Withdrawal is a delicious physical languor, a state of perpetual sleepiness full of real-seeming daydreams. He gazes at a leonine gargoyle spitting a cool stream of clear water into a marble scallop. His eyes follow a pointy ribbon of jade ivy up the garden wall. "I am really so alone," he says again, as if he's discovered magic words. The abrupt solitude makes him shy and hesitant to move. He speaks just enough Italian to be mistaken for an imbecile. Alone, he feels other people's eyes on him when he walks around to the Piazza del Popolo. Even familiar places turn strange when he becomes vulnerable to the glances of strangers. He feels an annoying surge of gratitude when the maître d' at Rosati greets him familiarly. He tells himself: don't feel awkward.

He picks a corner table. He remembers meals at Rosati with parties of fifteen and twenty, festive meals. He remembers being much younger, and excited by the world he moved around in. The familiarity of everything is reassuring and depressing. Jesse thinks he could go anywhere and never be surprised by anything. *Unless someone fell in love with me,* he thinks. *If someone who wasn't insane fell in love with me.*

He eats a large, heavy meal, laying off the wine because he feels the edge creeping up to his feet. Jesse is given to histrionic inner turmoil after a few drinks. He gets excited, aggrieved, stupid. He needs clarity, since he hasn't thought beyond the abandoned itinerary with Anthony. He knows if he drinks himself past a certain threshold, he'll start perceiving himself as an interesting person. So interesting that someone in this restaurant or in the street should get involved with his subjectivity. In Rome this would not be dangerous the way it would be in South America, but it would be obnoxious. Jesse has become economical about giving himself ugly memories.

He considers that in the years he's been coming to Rome, he's always handled his own luggage and never ordered room service at the Locarno. Midway in his reverie he recognizes the darkness around him as belonging to the Gramercy Park Hotel. If he switches on the light, he'll find his wallet and keys and a bottle of Perrier on the night table, beside a copy of *Winesburg, Ohio.* His slacks and underpants and a print shirt are heaped over his shoes on the floor. The dancing hamburgers have segued into Marlene Dietrich and Orson Welles on the TV.

Jesse thinks about dead people in the dark. He has the familiar thought that he's known a startling number of people who are now dead. Some people are a flicker of lightning, he thinks. He remembers people who've become nothing more than a single facial expression, a faint breath, a photograph, a momentary tug of the heart. Some aren't dead, but dying. He hates the way people fade even before they're gone.

He watches a soundless Janet Leigh being terrorized by hopheaded Mexicans in a motel room. Nearby, on the bed, a current issue of the *Advocate* lies folded open to the escort and massage ads. Jesse has circled some of the ads in pencil. He gropes for the switch of the bed lamp and settles the edge of the magazine on his chest. The Mexicans are approaching Janet Leigh, brandishing syringes full of dope. Jesse has narrowed the rent boy ads down to Hung Like a Horse, who gives his name as Ivan, purportedly "a Latino," and Nine Hard Inches, also known as Angelo. Ivan and Angelo have both tackled the composition of a personal ad with economy and directness. Jesse wonders if their services would correspond.

sometimes you're mistaken about things & it makes you crazy because you wake up with it & hear yourself rolling it over & over & it's terrible being alone when you think despair and death come so easily to the modern person the city too if you trap yourself peeling away all the layers of wishing for things when deep down what you wanted has been long lost & everything said & everything done is like darkness sliding into more darkness there's no hope or interest in the future it's just going to be worse & you'll get older & then the world's full of lies & you get them coming and going

If anyone asked why he's living in the hotel, Jesse would say it's for the view. At night, looking out his windows and directly down, he sees the canopy of foliage over the wrought-iron fencing of the park, and the narrow street where taxis pull away from the hotel. He doesn't want a panorama. With the outside world reduced to this happy wedge of space, the specificity of the city and the year melts away. He loses the sense of where he is, staring out, and sometimes the sense of who he is, what life he's mired in, how much of it has passed, and how much of it is left. He's abandoned his East Village apartment, though he still pays his rent and utility bills. He goes there sometimes in the evening, to check on things, flip through the mail, play back messages.

there's something i have failed to piece together. i did not discover who i was until this knowledge had become useless. i terrorize myself with fantasies of doom and rejection. i've become strange in this element of strangeness, forlorn & superannuated by objects & voices & maybe dying of loneliness & discontent: however i arrange things i cannot find my way to any kind of life: not even delusion: not even a fantasy i can make myself crazy with, in the insufferable world of this town and the shitty people who fill it: the constant noise of voices constant fear constant violence

The park outside the window represents a flawless state of urban order. He can't go in, only property owners along the park have keys. Jesse remembers being in the park once, four years ago, on a Sunday: some structural work was under way, the park had been opened for one afternoon. Jesse has a memory of prams and pink balloons and some type of small orchestra. He feels rather glad they aren't there now. Instead there is the perfection of a place no one goes.

A California blond with perfect lips drives through a rainstorm to his girlfriend's house. Every time Jesse sees the commercial he imagines pressing his cock into the actor's mouth. He thinks the car being advertised is a piece of shit. Maybe the blond actor is a piece of shit, too. But he still buys the fantasy they're selling along with the car. He remembers things he forgot to buy during his afternoon shopping. He wanted candles. He's never burned candles in a hotel room, except in Third World countries, during power failures, and in the Grande-Bretagne in Athens, where candles are stocked in the bathrooms. He remembers outages in Bogotá and Quito and La Paz with nostalgia. He wishes New York would have frequent blackouts. Jesse recalls epic electrical storms in Cartagena, in Cuenca, in Malaysia. Though he avoids thinking about why he happened to be in some of those places, Jesse likes remembering the places. And if he burned candles in a room at the Gramercy, Jesse could imagine being absolutely nowhere at all.

voices that sound the same as other voices: when you're on a bus for example or in a crowd and someone, from some prehistoric moment of your childhood adolescence or even later on, we burn up so many lives in our lives, consuming friendships and loves like cars and houses, you turn expecting to see a familiar face aged with the traces of everything that's happened to it in all these years & it's the face of a complete stranger

The hotel in Istanbul used to be one of the palatial rest stops on the Grand Tour. Everything marble, everything scaled for Byzantine autocrats and British royalty. In the lobby are framed clippings under glass about Agatha Christie, who wrote some books there. The staff moves at a majestically relaxed pace. Objects are spaced at imperious distances from one another. The sense of place hangs in the air like soot. It absorbs and shrinks down every modern thing. It makes the American Express forms and Madonna records playing in the bar seem like piquant debris from another world. The paper currency fades and falls apart with the slightest moisture. Jesse thinks the coins are minted from recycled soda cans.

The hotel is wildly expensive for what it is. It does not feel like a haven of safety and graciousness.

Jesse's room overlooks the dining room terrace and a wide, two-tiered cement park where guests of the hotel sometimes drink tea in the evening. The park attracts local teenagers and a few old people, until two or three in the morning. At five every morning, when starry darkness still covers the immense valley to the left of the park, Jesse hears prayers yodeled by faraway priests. The town feels as if it's covered in fine dust. The streets are permeated by sunset colors and the odors of burning rubber and rotten food.

The room contains two single beds with hard mattresses and plain linen sheets, a gigantic oak armoire, and a pointlessly tiny writing table. The bathroom features lots of glistening, chipped white tile. The green oxidation smears around the bidet and bathtub drains disturb him. As if the putridity of the city could come seething up through the plumbing. Despite the epic dimensions of the room, it looks frugal and shabby. Its surfaces are too crisp and faded, like museum pieces under glass. He imagined Istanbul differently. He had heard that a certain erotic easiness prevailed, but he imagined that differently, too.

Every man under fifty he passes in the street offers him a stare of raw sexual appraisal. At first it quickens Jesse's interest. But the general condition of the town precludes going just anywhere with a stranger, and he doubts that just anyone can enter the hotel. The city looks like an immense hive that's been compressed in a vise. Jesse knows he can't develop the radar to move about in it fearlessly, so he sticks to large, well-lit streets. At night, even these sometimes dip without warning into hilly quadrants of pitch darkness. What little he feels adventurous enough to explore is enough for him. He came here on an impulse, to kill time in the kind of otherness that makes no demands and offers no long-term possibilities.

For Rent: 6'1", 185#, 27, cut meat w/huge nuts & beefy butt for the eating! Picturing a chunky, crude individual with mustache, IQ of 47, hair all over his meaty shoulders, doesn't know how ugly he is & thinks any queer would worship him because he can get it up for another man. Likes getting rimmed: nice. The type who says right away Do you have any porn, he wants to watch tapes while he fucks your butt. Really disgusting. Wants to drink a few beers first & be sucked & rimmed before sticking it in for two or three minutes. Asks for more money if he stays one minute over an hour.

One night in the dining room a waiter lays a heavy palm on Jesse's shoulder and asks him, almost inaudibly, if he'd like to go to a disco later. The waiter has beautiful skin, quick eyes, a sinuous smile. In New York, this man would be considered extremely handsome. Jesse imagines the waiter mounting him with ingenious skill. He doesn't want to go to a disco but says yes, then leaves for his room and falls asleep. Hours later, the phone rings. The waiter's voice mumbles incomprehensibly.

"No, I … the thing is, I'm too tired."

"Don't want disco?"

"No."

"May I come to the room?"

"All right."

The waiter taps on the door. When Jesse opens it, the man slips in and rushes to the alcove off the bathroom.

"I like you," he announces, unfastening the purple sash around his pants waist.

"I like you too," Jesse assures him, bewildered by the rapidity with which things are moving.

"In here," says the waiter, urgently motioning Jesse into the bathroom.

In the bathroom, the waiter lowers his pants, liberating a thick, hard prong that sticks straight out and a fat, tight scrotum.

"Please do not kiss me," he says, locking eyes with Jesse. Jesse can't tell if it's a command or a plea. He obligingly perches on the toilet seat rim and licks the man's penis and balls. He notices that the pubic hairs are clipped in a tidy triangle, to a quarter-inch length. He wonders if this is an Islamic custom or just some weird personal habit.

"Kiss," instructs the waiter, drawing a line with his thumbnail across his lower abdomen. Jesse dutifully kisses the salty-tasting area, just below the navel. The frenetic quality of the moment bothers him. A chasm is opening between the idea and the action. The waiter suddenly draws away, beckoning him over to the tub. He gestures for Jesse to lower his own pants and bend over the tub rim. Then, he searches for Jesse's hole with the hard, bobbing cock, without guiding it by hand, as if it'll naturally sink right in upon contact. After a few futile pokes he gives up, walks to the toilet, and settles himself open-legged on the seat.

Jesse steps between the waiter's legs and turns around facing the mirror above the sink. He lowers his ass. The waiter pulls him down closer, steering Jesse's hole toward his penis. This position is no good at all, and finally the waiter stands up, pushes Jesse to his knees, and sticks his cock into Jesse's mouth. Jesse gags, expelling the cock.

"Look," he says, "there are two beds in the other room. We really don't need to do this in the bathroom."

"People can see," says the waiter. "Close the windows."

Jesse walks out and draws the heavy drapes at the sides of the large windows. He hasn't noticed these drapes before, only the sheer white ones that can't be retracted. He now understands his room is wholly visible from the park. From the alcove the waiter tells him, "Lock the door."

"It's locked," Jesse says.

"No, lock it."

"It's locked, I tell you."

The waiter opens the door. He gives the outer hallway a nervous once-over and shuts the door. He's pulled up his pants.

Now he removes them completely. He unbuttons the lower buttons of his shirt and pulls the shirt up around his nipples. He flounces down on the bed farthest from the window, with his knees raised and his legs spread. Jesse removes all his clothes. He kneels between the waiter's legs. He sucks the half-erect prick with grim concentration. Seconds pass. The waiter springs to his feet and pulls Jesse into the dog position at the edge of the mattress, stands behind him, spits into his fingers, greases his penis, and accurately shoves it in. He fucks Jesse's asshole for about thirty seconds. Jesse tightens his sphincters around the strong slippery meat. The waiter pulls himself free. He slips into his pants and shoes with insane haste.

"Can you give me some money?" he whispers.

"No," Jesse says.

"Cigarettes?"

Jesse takes out two for himself and hands over the pack.

"I'm going to get a drink," the waiter says.

"You're going for a drink."

"I'll come back," the waiter promises.

"All right."

"I'll come tomorrow," the waiter says.

"All right."

"I like you."

"I like you too."

He wonders what precise element of the situation has given the waiter so much anxiety. He doesn't think the waiter will return the following day. He regrets not offering money. Jesse calculates that the whole encounter has taken about seven minutes. He wonders about the dark roasted-walnut smell of the waiter's groin. He replays the scene many times in his head, touched and disappointed by it. Eventually he jerks off in the bathroom.

Uncut Latino. Rico: 24, 5'9", 158#, 30W, hung 9" thick, very friendly, 5 mins to Manht. 24 hours. Rico is a fraud like his accomplice Chico, potbellied not very clean & the cock's about 2-3 inches, stands there expecting you to give him a hard-on which he's never able to achieve, tries sort of pushing his limpness into you & then grunts a few times & he's out again. Some of these guys change their names from month to month, reword the ads, invent new bodies faces & cock sizes for themselves & show up with the same unsavory swindle. You can tell by checking the phone numbers against the old ads, for all they get ripping people off they're too cheap to change the numbers.

Slim's a vigorous & conscientious fuck, nine thick inches & he's cute, he'll get you into four or five positions whatever feels good & nice & slow sometimes he likes it. Tony from uptown, big frame, huge cock, pleasant face but nothing special: good if he's got poppers with him. Nice-tasting meat. European gymnast's half-Greek half-German, looks mainly German. Competent fuck, but mechanical, no initiative. Earns the money but it's no fun for either of you.

In front of the Blue Mosque, a small, ugly man with rotten teeth attempts to sell him a carpet. He says his name's Ghenghis as in Ghenghis Khan, that his brother owns a shop in the basement of the mosque. Jesse tells Ghenghis he doesn't need a carpet. Ghenghis says his brother also sells silver jewelry. Jesse says he doesn't need any silver jewelry, either. Ghenghis looks like trouble. Jesse has met a number of Ghenghises in his travels: not sharks, exactly, but smaller, parasitical fish who mistake themselves for sharks. Jesse knows if he doesn't get rid of this person he will end up separating Jesse from a lot of money. He will not use violence but intimidation and guilt. It's been so many days since Jesse spoke to anyone fluent in English that he equivocates at the crucial moment when a little hostility would send Ghenghis on the trail of a different tourist. They go into the mosque together and look at the vast floor of carpets, the columns, the windows. Ghenghis points out the abundance of blue tiles. Some restoration work is taking place. Many columns are draped with green scaffolding mesh. Ghenghis explains many details of the mosque that Jesse already knows about.

When they're outside retrieving their shoes, Ghenghis proposes showing Jesse around the area. Jesse again thinks he should ditch the guy. The area is, after all, world-famous, and Jesse knows what all the buildings are. Ghenghis also strikes him as a frightful bore, a bore with peasant cunning. Jesse calculates the amount of cash he can reasonably blow on a superfluous guided tour. He feels himself giving in. It's easier than detaching himself. He'll have someone to talk to, even if it's Ghenghis.

They trudge through the Topkapi and the Aya Sofya. The most important jewels of the Topkapi are out on loan, and the Aya Sofya hums with Japanese tourists. The streets are dense with bad air and traffic. Ghenghis takes Jesse through the cavernous cistern under the basilica. Water trickles and splutters down through the darkness, pooling to a meter's depth beneath the clay walkways, around dozens of arched columns. At the base of two columns deep in the cistern, they see chiseled heads of Medusa, one upside down, the other resting on a cheek. As they leave, loudspeakers blare "The Ride of the Valkyries."

Ghenghis proposes a trip to the Dolmabahçe Palace, in the same quarter as Jesse's hotel. Jesse thinks he's seen enough for one day, but he can't think of anything better to do. At the Dolmabahçe Palace, they wait in line for forty minutes until the mandatory guided tour takes them through. The air is cool here, by the water, and Jesse would like to sit under a tree, thinking his own thoughts. Ghenghis asks if Jesse minds taking the tour in Turkish, instead of waiting another twenty minutes for the English tour. Jesse doesn't care. They herd from room to room with twenty others. Sometimes Ghenghis explains what the rooms are, or translates the guide's monologue. Then he becomes, if not exactly thoughtful, absorbed in the grandeur of the decor. The sultans did many of their rooms in crystal. Crystal panels on the walls. Fat crystal banisters on the staircase.

During the tour, Ghenghis chats with another Turkish boy. The new boy has better teeth than Ghenghis and better clothes. He keeps a ring of car keys looped through his fingers and plays with them. Jesse wonders if Ghenghis is hustling this boy, but the boys seems too wary for that to happen. He's from a higher class and obviously thinks Ghenghis is amusing scum. Outside the palace Jesse asks the new boy if he's hungry. He's hoping to shake off Ghenghis. Ghenghis translates that the boy has to go home. He lives on the Asian side of the city. Jesse and Ghenghis go to Jesse's hotel in a cab. Jesse tries paying him for the tour.

"Not now, not now," Ghenghis says sharply, jabbing a finger toward the driver. Once they're out, Ghenghis tells him never to let a cab driver see his money. They walk up the road away from the hotel and go into the cement park. After some bickering Jesse gives him what he originally asked for. Ghenghis insists on an extra 60,000 lire. He says the tour lasted an extra two hours. Jesse points out that the Dolmabahçe Palace was Ghenghis's idea.

"You could have said no," Ghenghis replies. "Besides, we all need money, and you're rich."

Jesse sees no point in arguing. He supposes he is rich in comparison.

"And," Ghenghis says, after Jesse gives him the 60,000, "another twenty thousand for the tour tickets."

"Oh please," says Jesse, who paid for all the tour tickets. "Go fuck yourself."

"It's nothing to you, twenty thousand," Ghenghis responds smoothly.

"All the same, fuck off."

his voice sounds too sane, too ordinary. didn't ask what do you like, didn't talk dirty, didn't describe himself: probably he's really good. giant ants on the TV, radiation nightmare from the fifties. losing: time in your life, energy, friends, the will to continue, hopefulness. never meet anyone, nowhere to meet them. this one's name's tom. he just got home from the gym. 20, nice firm shape, dark eyes, black hair, a face good enough to eat. strips casually, gets on the bed in his briefs, lies on his back & lights a cigarette. i touch his cock through the briefs, he's already hard: substantial. where are you from. what do you do, i mean besides … play with his fingers, stroke his palm. it's hot outside. lick me, okay? he peels off his underpants and rubs his prick. pulls up his balls.

i lick down under his balls his ass rises slightly & he shifts his weight around until i can get my tongue into his asshole, spread his cheeks apart with my thumbs & suck his rectum & work gradually up across his balls & up & down his prick, a nice wide piece of work with a large sensitive head, nibble around the rim & flick the cordlike tissue just under it with the tip of my tongue, slide my mouth down over the whole thing, ease my head up & run my open lips down his cock bone & up the middle of the vein & then let him pump it in & out of my mouth kneeling on top of me he inches forward on his knees & then sits down on my mouth, his asshole centered on my tongue & i make love to his hole forcing my tongue deeper and deeper into him we stay like that for a long time & he leans back until he's lying down stretches out his legs & i kiss him everywhere

he's fucking me with my legs around his neck he pushes my legs away gripping my ankles until my knees are behind my head & my ass is sticking up & now he's lying straight on top of me balanced on his toes like he's doing pushups in & out of my ass pulling all the way out and slamming himself back in on every stroke it hurts i love him he turns me over & fucks me lying flat on top of me his legs inside my legs pushing my legs wider & then slides his legs over mine & pushes my legs closed fucking my hole as if he wanted to make sure he's fucked it every way he can think of & after that he carries me to the chair sits down & arranges me with my back to his chest & slips his cock back into my ass & fucks me for an hour so slow we're hardly moving & he pulls it out just an inch or so and slides it back up inside me & out again an inch & back in as far as he can & every so often pulls out three or four inches or five inches & holds it there like that for a long time & slowly slowly pushes his hipbones forward just a little just a little till it's all inside me again & then it's almost imperceptible again for a long time & when i feel like he's part of my own body be pushes his ass back drawing out the whole nine inches except for his cockhead he leaves inside &

then slips the head out & pushes just the head back in, lets it out with a pop & slips it in, just the head five ten fifteen times & then it slides back inside me the whole thing i feel his balls against my hole & him breathing against my neck

He walks beyond the park into a narrow, winding bazaar he explored on his first day in Istanbul. In a lane of vegetable and butcher stalls he finds a vendor selling freshly killed fish and tinned food. He buys a half pound of Beluga caviar, thirty-five dollars.

At the Pera Palas he walks into the kitchen off the dining room. His presence violates some rigid hotel protocol and immediately several waiters are clustered around him, absurdly solicitous, as if he'd just been run over. Jesse asks the best-looking one to open the caviar tin and bring it up to his room.

In the room, closely observed, the waiter, who's introduced himself as Marco, looks beautiful as a movie star. His hair is curly and brown, with red highlights. His features are adorable, more rounded and Western than the sharper profiles around the hotel. He arranges the caviar on a bowl of ice on the table, turns to leave, asks Jesse a question Jesse can't understand, shrugs, moves closer to the door, pauses, turns, Jesse touches Marco's sleeve. Marco indicates he'd like to smoke a cigarette before returning to the kitchen.

They try to talk. Jesse has no Turkish words, Marco knows the phrases he needs for his job and nothing more. Marco sits down at the table. Jesse repositions his own chair so the table isn't between them. He glances at the caviar. He thinks it will go bad in the heat. He doesn't know how to make anything happen. He watches Marco smoke. He hooks Marco's right ankle with the toe of his sneaker and brings Marco's shoe to the chair cushion between his legs. Jesse unlaces the patent leather shoe and slides it off Marco's foot. It's a narrow, elegant foot with long, bony toes. Jesse grips it with both hands and massages it through the black rayon sock. The sock exudes an expanding odor of mildew and sweat. Marco closes his eyes.

"I come to you tonight," he says.

"Yes."

"I fuck you tonight," he elaborates.

"Yes, definitely."

The massaged foot moves to its shoe. Marco raises his other shoe and pulls it off. He pushes his left foot between Jesse's legs. Jesse massages the new foot. Marco presses the foot into Jesse's crotch and squeezes the hump of Jesse's erection with his toes. He lights another cigarette and watches Jesse carefully through clouds of smoke.

Jesse squeezes his thighs together around the foot, which Marco rubs up and down, clenching and unclenching his toes along the shape of Jesse's penis. Jesse comes. Marco replaces his shoe and stands up. He points to the caviar tin.

"Eat," he tells Jesse.

Jesse kisses him on the mouth. Marco wedges his tongue into Jesse's mouth. They stand locked together. Marco guides Jesse's hand to his crotch. Jesse feels a long, thick lump through the fabric. He kneels and kisses it, running his hands over Marco's buttocks.

He wakes again. Orson Welles is face down in a shiny black riverbed. Marlene Dietrich looks down at his corpse.

What does it matter, what you say about people. "What are you into?" "I like a lot of things." "When I saw the word 'master' in your ad, I wondered because I'm really not into pain." "No s &

m. Okay, fine. But I'm definitely aggressive." "Well, so what kind of ..." "I dig having a guy kneeling down in front of me worshiping my cock, taking my big cock down his throat, I like having him lick me, rim me ..." "Okay, I think I'm probably a little tame for you. I like licking, I like sucking. But I can't stand having it rammed down my throat because I have this really severe gag reaction." "So tell me what you want. I'm interested in, you know, getting fucked. And other things." "Like what?" "Anything you want." "That covers a lot of territory. I like water sports, I dig pissing on guys. I like bondage. I dig having my feet licked and a guy sucking my toes. I'm pretty broad-minded." "I'll do whatever you want, I just don't enjoy pain." "Well, I need to know stuff like that before I go to a place." "I wanna get fucked." "Fine, I dig fucking. I love fucking. The only thing is, if I'm going to fuck you in the ass you want to make sure you're clean up there." "You want me to douche." "I sort of require it, because the first sign of shit, man, that finishes the whole thing for me. It just turns me off completely. I'm not into shit at all." "I didn't say I was into shit, quite the contrary, really." "I'm making that a condition." "All right, fine." "I mean you can easily find somebody who's into that without any problem." "No, I mean fine, I'll douche."

how about if i bang you up against that window with your head hanging out? you've got a sweet little hole. nice fit. you like my cock? i could tell. ooh, yeah. how are we gonna make you come? you want me to like, open you up first? feel good? sit on that cock. come up a little more, you can ride me better that way. oh yeah. you gonna come? come all over my stomach, man. beautiful.

He saw people going away and people coming back. The road to the cottage ran past the bay on one side and the isthmus on the other, like the highway in Florida when they went to Wakulla Springs. When he dreamed about that time the road always looked as if it would dip down where the two bodies of water met, at a point beyond the horizon. People in the street were running. The pavement stretched up the hill to the cathedral, flanked by low-rise offices and grimy restaurant windows, turning hazy with smoke. Dozens of students were running, clapping sweater necks and handkerchiefs to their mouths and noses. He felt the sting of tear gas and clawing inside his throat. At the top of the hill, another broad street curved up into the cathedral park. Faraway the Virgin of Quito, several thousand tons of dull aluminum, gleamed on a mountaintop. Below where he stood, trim boys in green uniforms paraded on the grounds of the military school. A satellite dish poked from a cluster of stucco rooftops. He stood at the edge of the ocean and heard water running in the bathtub. He read a paragraph of *Winesburg, Ohio.* On the TV, crows ran under the spermy arcs of water cannons. He stepped into the helicopter beside the river. The bells echoed across the water. They came to a seafood joint with the best broiled mullet on the peninsula, if you scraped off the huge gob of butter in the middle. From far above, the little islands near the airport were ringed with the white spokes of docks and boats. He always wondered about these islands, who lived on them, how you could find them if you rented a car and drove there. What manner of life.

LÁSZLÓ KAMONDY

THE STUDENT AND THE WOMAN

Marivaux, in the eighteenth century, proposed in his play The Quarrel *that love can be self-taught: he set on stage a couple of youngsters who, observed by curious elders, define for themselves the terms and rules of an erotic relationship. In our century, László Kamondy appears to disagree. According to Kamondy, the art of loving, like the art of dying, like the art of politics, like any art, must be learned from your elders. All ancient societies incorporated in their scheme the erotic education of the young; we know that in our time, this education, if it exists at all, is much disjointed and haphazard, and we go about our lovemaking misinformed and unprepared.*

In "The Student and the Woman" Kamondy describes what amounts to an erotic education. The tone is picaresque, reminiscent of certain tales of Boccaccio, but touched by a certain contemporary wistfulness or melancholy typical of Kamondy's style.

THE STUDENT lay in the boat, the sun warm on his back, reading and waiting for the woman who every day had herself rowed out to the open waters where she could sunbathe naked.

Treading lightly, almost soundlessly, the woman approached, then stopped in confusion a few paces from the rushes.

"Do you know where the old man is?" she asked as the young man looked up. "The old fisherman?" The boy closed his book and stood up in the boat, gazing silently for some moments at the woman's mouth.

"My grandfather is ill," he said, "but I can take you if … if your hand is not better."

He glanced at the woman's bandaged wrist and began to twist a bent reed aimlessly with his forefinger.

The boy was so compelled by her beauty that he could not take his eyes off her.

"Give the money to the old man," he said, swallowing hard. "I'll take you out in the punt and when you call out, I'll come and fetch you."

Sideways, out of the corner of her eye, the woman watched this boy who, without waiting for a reply, deftly untied the chain of the boat, and threw his blanket into the punt.

The battered yellow punt was already tied to the boat as on previous days, and it was this that brought the woman to a decision, for she had been hesitant about going with the strange-looking, muscular, sun-tanned boy.

She turned casually on her elbow in the depths of the punt and asked, "Are you a fisherman too?" It was not that she was curious; she spoke only to break the silence.

The young man turned the boat and rowed towards the middle of the lake.

"Yes, I am," he replied.

After a little while he glanced at the woman now trailing her fingers through the waters of Lake Balaton.

"What is the matter with your grandfather?"

"He has rheumatism."

The woman sighed.

"No need to go further," she said.

"As you wish," answered the student and drew in the oars, quickly untying the punt and setting it adrift. "Just shout Gyuri," he said, "and I'll come for you."

But before the boy could start back to the shore the woman began, "I doubt if you are a fisherman. Even if sometimes … you fish."

The young man, already some yards away, smiled and called, "Isn't it all the same to you?"

"Oh, quite," answered the woman coolly, "but I don't like people who tell lies."

The student sank his oars deep in the water and pushed his boat away from the woman, though he would have dearly loved to stay near.

"The most beautiful woman for miles around," he thought. "Everything would be fine, if only ..."

From the depth of the punt the woman watched the boy until his boat disappeared among the rushes by the shore; then she undressed, closing her eyes as she undid her bra, and with a sigh blew away her distrust.

After about half an hour a light wind rose from the west and the punt began to rock gently. Afterwards the woman remembered only that she had killed a dragon-fly, stabbing it against her thigh, and that she had fallen asleep, tired out from reading late into the night. She dreamt that the boy came to her bedside where she lay naked. She tried to cover herself with a blanket, but could not find one and heard him saying urgently: "Get dressed! Get dressed!" But she could not, for her dress was not to be found, The young man was holding an enormous bunch of flowers in his hand, staring at her, motionless, like a statue. There was no movement of his lips but she heard his voice saying: "As you wish, as you wish."

In the tone of a waiter, devoid of all warmth.

The student rowed to the shore, opened an anatomy book borrowed from the local doctor, but he could not concentrate on the meaning of the text; between the lines he saw the woman's red mouth, pursed as if to kiss him.

"If she kissed me," thought the student, "I feel I'd be accepted at university. Nothing more, just a kiss! Otherwise I may as well go to work at the chocolate-factory at Füzfö."

He clasped his hands behind his head and imagined himself

in the white coat of a doctor, attending the sick; then he seemed to be floating through the air, beside him the woman; he was, however, quite unable to touch her.

From these daydreams he was awakened by the soughing of the reeds.

He jumped to his feet and scanned the shores of the lake.

The opposite shore was clear; but to the north, the rushes were bending lower and lower towards the vineyards on the hillsides and every minute the waves mounted to more ominous heights. The student sat down in the boat and began to row quickly towards the woman.

"Get dressed, get dressed!" he shouted.

But the woman lay silent, unresponsive as the dead.

The student waited a little longer, then called out again, not very loudly, but loudly enough to wake her if she were asleep.

A few strokes brought him to the punt, he looked at her and could not look away.

The woman was sleeping with her head resting on her arm, so that her face with its finely shaped nose was seen only in profile against the mass of her hair.

Her body was chocolate brown, her full, shapely breasts as gentle as those of an expectant mother.

Her thick, soft lips were parted, not enough to show her teeth, but the effect was more tempting than the most passionate approach.

The student closed his eyes, opened them again, and gave one last glance of farewell. He steered his boat to some distance and shouted again,

"Get up, get dressed, there's a storm coming!"

The woman woke up, shivered in the wind, moistened her

lips, hurried into her bathing suit and, still lying down, put on her jacket and trousers.

"You may come now," she cried.

The student obeyed immediately, linked up the punt and motioned the woman to climb into his boat.

From under lowered eyelids the woman watched his calm, confident strokes as he rowed to the shore.

"There will be a storm," the student began, "we know the signs … I had to come and pick you up."

"He is making excuses," thought the woman, "because he's been spying on me."

She was angry with herself for having fallen asleep in the punt.

"The sun disappeared behind the clouds a long time ago," said the student as they neared the shore.

"I'm quite certain he's been watching me," she thought, "that is why he can't keep quiet."

By now there was a distinct swell on the lake so that the pressure of the water knocked the punt incessantly against the boat; it was difficult to climb out.

"Thanks for fetching me," said the woman as she stepped out. "You mustn't apologize, it is for me rather to thank you."

The boy struggled to one end of the boat, pulling out the blanket from the bottom of the punt.

"I am not apologizing," he said, "just telling you."

He looked at her closely but in vain, unable to read her expression and reassured by the reserve with which she controlled her anger.

"Well then," she began, "I'll give the money to your grandfather, as we agreed …"

There was a flash of lightning, followed moments later by a peal of thunder. The thunder reverberated for a long time, as though huge empty tin barrels were being kicked with amazing speed from one hill to another. The rushes moaned, their tips touching the water, the surface of the lake pitted with rain.

"You would be foolish to set off for home," advised the student, picking up the blanket and folding it under his arm. "You would get very wet … your hair too."

The woman ran her fingers through her hair and looked helplessly up at the sky.

"Follow me," gestured the student, "there's a dressing-room here."

They had to make a run for it as the rain came down suddenly in torrents.

The student unlocked the door, politely ushered the woman into the tiny hut, handed her the blanket, and then stood on the threshold watching the storm.

"I could see from your eyes that you didn't believe me about the storm," he began. "You looked rather suspicious."

The woman smiled, staring curiously at the boy's shoulders.

"Once a liar, always a liar."

"That's not always true. Why?"

The poplars by the shore shuddered, tossed in all directions by the wind. The rushes soughed their warning note and the rain fell heavily like a grey curtain, thrown violently down from on high.

"If you're not a fisherman, then what are you?" asked the woman.

As the student watched delightedly the spectacle of the

storm, his features changed: his thin, bony face grew more beautiful, his stubborn mouth sensitive as a girl's, his expression calm and bright.

"I said what's your job," repeated the woman, "how can you be so rude as not to answer?"

"I am an angler," the student replied, "otherwise, a churchman."

The woman reflected on the answer; she had noticed a kind of priestly strictness and gentleness in the boy's eyes.

"Are you joking?" she asked after a pause.

"Aha."

"If you say aha," she imitated scornfully, "then I will believe that you're a fisherman."

The rain was coming down quietly; for some time now the reeds had been still, and even the boughs of the trees were coming to rest.

"You are married, I know, but have you any children?" asked the student, now sitting on the threshold.

"No. But why do you want to know?"

"Well ... I don't really."

The woman peered over his shoulder to look at the view and breathed in deeply the rain-washed air.

"How do you know I am married?"

"I didn't have to guess," answered the student, "I know you live and eat in an expensive place ... the county sheriff or someone like that used to live there ..."

The woman stood up and started to grope about in the tiny hut.

"It won't be long now," the student said consolingly.

"I could go now ..."

The student blinked rapidly and sighed deeply.

"Your name is Judit, isn't it?"

At this the woman could not refrain from laughing aloud, in spite of her annoyance.

"You come in here now and let me sit on the threshold."

The student allowed the woman to sit down.

The rain was falling gently; the turmoil was over, nature once more at peace. Southwards there was a brightness in the sky as summer clouds formed and dissolved.

"What are you, a detective?" asked the woman without turning round.

"I am studying to be a doctor, if . . ."

The woman smiled.

"But you haven't yet sat for your finals?"

"I am twenty," lied the student.

The woman got up and looked at him with disdain.

"I hadn't realized you were quite such an infant."

The boy shifted his weight from one foot to the other.

The rain had completely ceased, leaving the grass and the reeds glittering with moisture, but in the distance the lake was still dark and threatening.

"I am going now," said the woman, holding out her hand. "Goodbye."

The student took her outstretched, undamaged left hand and shook it firmly, looking into her eyes.

"If she kissed me now," he thought, "I would be accepted at university."

He breathed out slowly, raising the pent-up emotions in his breast.

"May I take you home?"

"There is no need," replied the woman, stepping out of the hut.

She did not even look back at the boy as he stood on the threshold, but started off towards the village following the path by the shore.

The student locked up the hut and hurried after her. He caught up with her just before the village. When he reached her, he said nothing. Not even when she gave him an angry glance.

Only when they arrived at the first house did he speak.

"How long are you staying here?"

The woman stopped.

"That's not your business."

She detested the indiscretion of men, something she had begun to hate even as a young girl, and now here was this boy trying to stick to her like a leech. She knew merely from their glances what men wanted, and such glances had made her despise love.

"I'm also going to the village; why can't I go with you? If you're ashamed of me because you're a lady," said the student with awkward self-consciousness, "just tell me and I'll fall behind."

Suppressing her dislike of the boy, the woman turned to him in a kindly fashion.

"It's not that I don't want to walk with you … or that I dare not … but you know how people gossip in small places."

"Is that why you won't walk with me?"

"Oh, come on, then," she replied, "on Monday you can't come anyway."

She began to enjoy her power over the student and smiled gently.

They were only a few yards from the villa where she was staying.

"Is your room the one with the balcony?"

"Yes," answered the woman, "and the owners of the house let the dog loose at night," she added, with a careless little laugh.

The student stared silently at the fence.

"I know," he said.

The woman placed her hand on the latch of the gate.

"Well," she said cheerfully. "We've arrived. Thanks for bringing me home."

The boy looked gravely down at the ground.

"You could help me in a serious matter," he began resolutely, "if you wanted to ..."

Surprised, the woman let go of the latch.

"Tell me how," she said with a smile.

"You won't be angry, will you?"

"No."

"Are you sure you won't be angry?"

"Positive," replied the woman rather impatiently. She peered through the fence and turned to the boy, waiting for him to speak.

"My husband is rather jealous," she said.

"He's here too?"

"No, he won't be here until tomorrow; but go on, don't worry about that."

She supported herself against the fence, looking encouragingly at the boy.

He sighed deeply, poking the dust with the tip of his shoe, then suddenly looked up.

"When I first saw you," he said, looking at the woman as if everything depended on her judgement, "I took it into my head that if you kissed me just once, I'd be certain to be accepted at university! Surely you can understand!"

The woman was speechless with surprise.

"Nothing more, you know," continued the student, "I will even put my hands behind my back if you like. If you kiss me once, I feel everything will turn out right for me!"

The woman gazed at the boy's face in amazement, smiling gently but scornfully.

"If that's what getting your diploma depends on, then I can assure you that you won't get it," she said, shutting the gate.

The boy was left standing in the street, dumbfounded.

When the woman opened her balcony window and peered down among the bushes and trees, she saw the student sigh deeply before walking home with shoulders bowed.

After supper, feeling restless and uneasy, he went out. Three times he walked the length of the village, then went down to the shore to look at the water, and sat there for a long time. Around midnight he walked resolutely towards the villa. He examined the house and garden with great care. The dog began to bark, but the rattling of a chain revealed that it was not a danger to him.

He hoisted himself over the fence, threw a piece of bacon to the dog, and jumped into the garden.

The dog barked again, but the student called out.

"Quiet, Sisi, quiet!"

Hearing the familiar voice, the dog began to sniff the bacon, then chewed it noisily. It was a tame sheepdog. The student threw another piece of bacon and then removed the grease from his hands by rubbing them over the grass, before gripping the drain-pipe and so hoisting himself swiftly up to the balcony.

He stood with his back against the wall, waiting for some moments until the dog began to bark again. Then he quietly knocked on the balcony door.

It was now a calm, starlit night.

The dog ran backwards and forwards, rattling his chain, and then lay down groaning.

The student began to smile, knocked again, but there was no answer.

"She's either asleep or out," he thought and carefully drew aside the curtain covering the window. He peeped in; took a step backwards, put his hand in his pocket, aimlessly playing with the coins, quietly jingling them in his fist. In his right pocket he had seven forints, which he counted one by one; in the other pocket he had a packet of cigarettes, half full.

He waited a little longer, crept back to the window, heart throbbing loudly, threw one coin through the window, waited, then threw another in the direction of the washbasin.

He heard only the clink of the coins. Outside there was only the chirp of a solitary cricket and the croaking of frogs in the rushes by the shore.

"She must have gone out," thought the student, feeling quite weak. He was not even sure that he would be able to scramble down the pipe he had just climbed. In total despair, he gathered the coins in his hand, stretched his arm through the curtain, and threw them into the washbasin.

The money jingled and clattered as it fell into the porcelain basin. There was a moment of absolute silence. Then the drain-pipe gave out a cracking sound, a sudden release perhaps from the pressure of his foot; a few moments later he heard a frightened, sleepy voice and the sound of bare feet on the boards.

"Who is it?"

"It's me," whispered the student, "it's a matter of life and death."

Now he could hear the woman's heavy breathing and her footsteps as she returned to bed.

"Let me in," pleaded the student, "it's only for a minute!"

"You're mad, go away! Have you gone mad?!"

"I can't go away," replied the student.

The woman remained silent; yet the student continued to hope against hope.

After a little while he carefully pressed down the door handle; the door was open.

He entered and remained standing near the door, without a word and, like the woman, holding his breath; then he felt his way cautiously into the room so as not to disturb anything or frighten the woman.

"What do you want? Why did you come? You rascal! Aren't you ashamed of yourself?!"

The student drew the curtain and remained silent. He found the wall and leaned against it.

"Don't scold me," he replied, "I want nothing from you, except a kiss. Then I'll go away. Just one kiss."

Frightened, the woman sat up in bed, and covered herself with the counterpane. She feared him like the onset of madness.

"If you don't go away quietly, I will rouse the whole house," she said loudly.

She knew she would do no such thing for fear of scandal, but she wanted to frighten the boy.

"Be quiet," whispered the student, "don't shout so. You are not fair to me!"

The woman was struck dumb by such effrontery; and she was disarmed by the boy's sober plea.

There was a short sharp exchange of barking between the watch-dog and the other dogs in the village; then when the sheepdog subsided with a groan, the student began to speak.

"You can tie my hands behind my back, if you like. On my word I won't lift a finger, and if you kiss me, I'll go away at once."

"He must be deranged," thought the woman, and burst into laughter.

"I'll count to thirty, and if you're still here, I'll start shouting."

The student was silent, swallowing hard and sighing deeply.

"Do you want to bring shame on my mother and yourself?" he asked. "As I've said, if you kiss me, I'll go away immediately. I swear by the honor of my family that I'll go away at once, and won't even touch you."

The woman began to be uncertain whether she was dreaming or not, and whether this nocturnal conversation was really taking place.

"No," she said, "you must leave at once!"

She was aware she had to deal with a cunning rascal, and she had the feeling that he had made similar attempts before.

"Don't you understand," went on the student, "I need it because ... And what does it cost you? I've got it into my head and I can't help that it's you."

The woman, now thoroughly distressed, laughed quietly and, hoping to persuade the boy to leave, she now spoke to him more gently.

"Didn't it occur to you when you were coming up here, that if someone saw you, you could wreck my marriage?" she asked.

The student sat quietly for quite a while.

"No," he answered.

This reply left the woman speechless and she sought in vain for some suitable response.

"Look here," she continued, "you don't look stupid, but … I cannot understand how you can behave in this way. What connection is there between what you are doing now and your whole future career?"

The student began softly.

"Well, I don't really know. But I believe there is one; I believe so strongly that I know it must be so. Haven't you ever had such a feeling?"

"No, I haven't," replied the woman.

"You're just saying that," thought the student, "for everyone sometimes has a feeling that there is only one way out of a problem, and that's how it turns out." He said aloud, "It's not my fault that I happened to see you coming from the shore and then …"

"Now you're courting, too," thought the woman, "this is all I need, beside my husband."

"… that you'd be it, oh, how can I explain? It could well have been someone else. There are more beautiful women around than you, even girls."

"How very interesting," thought the woman. She rolled up her pillow, placing it on the back of the bed under her head.

"It's quite inconceivable to me," she said.

"You are capable of similar feelings," answered the student, "even if you haven't had any already. And you would keep me utterly calm until the autumn. There are still two months to go," he added.

She marvelled at the crystal-clear selfishness with which the student continued to insist on his own rights, without ever considering her side of the affair.

"You're no ordinary fellow," she began.

She was searching for the boy's features, but she could only see the shape of his head against the light from the window.

"I'll make a good doctor, believe me," urged the student, "you might even be my patient one day. If you had some trouble with your eyes ..."

"Oh, how ridiculous," thought the woman, "if I had some trouble with my eyes? I don't understand what is happening. Am I going mad?"

"You're not a heartless woman," the student continued persuasively. "Only you think I want something else. Don't be afraid of that."

"A pleasant fellow," reasoned the woman and she sighed. "Can it be true that he really doesn't want anything but a kiss?"

"Look here, if I kissed you, would you go away?"

"Yes."

The woman sat up in the bed.

"What did you throw through the window?"

"Coins, to wake you up."

"I'll give them back to you tomorrow."

Both remained silent.

The student waited meekly while the woman struggled with herself.

"And otherwise," she asked after a long pause, "do you find me attractive?"

"You're a beautiful woman," replied the student as if speaking of some other person. "You have very beautiful black eyes and lovely lips, but apart from that nothing special. There are plenty like you."

The woman lay on her back and rubbed her temple. She amazed herself, especially as she was now genuinely enjoying her conversation with this adolescent. She was calm, she no longer feared him, nor did she think him mad. It seemed quite natural that he should be there, talking to her.

"And what are my faults then, if I may ask?" she said, giggling slightly.

"You won't be angry?"

"No."

"You're rather bandy-legged."

The woman bit her lips so as not to burst out laughing.

"But otherwise …"

"But otherwise what?"

"You're a beautiful woman, your hair is beautiful … But that isn't all. You have a certain radiance."

"Don't try to comfort me, explain yourself."

The student shifted his weight, but did not move an inch from the wall.

He was quiet for some moments.

"I mean what I say. You have a strong radiance. I can't explain it in any other way. Everyone has it, but some more than others."

The woman smoothed back her hair.

"I don't understand what you mean," she said. "Are my eyes radiant or is it ..."

"No, everything. The way you walk, talk, that is to say ..."

"I believe you fib quite a lot! Are you used to lying?"

The student became very quiet, smiling wryly.

"Sometimes I do indeed, but with you I don't have to. What for? You understand me, only you're afraid because you believe ..."

The woman felt flattered by what the boy had said, but she was irritated by his silences, obstinacy, impertinent outspokenness and his self-confidence.

"It's time you were going," she began. "I won't kiss you, and as you don't appreciate me, I don't care for you."

The student found no way to reply, though the woman waited expectantly. She felt she had finally convinced him. He would just say a few more words and then go away.

"You don't love your husband," said the student without any explanation.

The woman stiffened as she sat up in bed.

"Even if that were so," she replied hastily, "what difference does it make? Anyway, how do you know?"

"Does it matter?"

"Yes, it does," answered the woman in a husky voice. "As I answered your questions, and didn't wake up the whole house screaming, I expect you to give me a reply now."

"I don't want to ... you know why."

Now the woman found herself becoming unaccountably uneasy.

In the silence she heard the buzzing of a mosquito. When it had settled down, the boy began.

"If you tell me once more to go away and will accept the consequences, I'll be off."

He was stroking the wall with the palm of his hand.

The woman was surprised, smiled, and then grew sad.

"How will you do so?"

"First I throw something to the dog, then I climb down the drain-pipe, throw something again, and jump over the fence."

"He will really go," thought the woman feeling disappointed rather than glad.

"You are sure to get a place at university anyway," she said with forced cheerfulness.

The student remained silent and, still feeling his way along the wall, he sighed.

"Go on, send me away ..."

"He will really go," thought the woman.

"If you don't send me away, you're playing with me," began the student. "It's not very nice of you. I can't leave unless you send me."

"Why?"

"Because ..."

He sank into deep silence, waiting to be sent away. The woman enjoyed her power and, feeling an unexpected motherly weakness, she shuddered.

"Come here," she said.

The student went round the table and settled on the edge of her bed.

They stared at each other.

"But you'll go away afterwards, won't you? Promise?"

The student nodded and moved up a little on the bed.

The woman thought the moment hilarious, for she knew her own weakness very well.

"I'll only kiss your forehead," she said smiling, "put your hands behind your back."

The boy obeyed.

"Why my forehead," he asked, "kiss my mouth. Just once."

His body trembled, his teeth chattered. The woman was trembling, too. She took the boy's head gently, and kissed his mouth very lightly. Although the student sat with his hands behind his back, the woman could still sense his eagerness and the strength with which he was holding himself back from embracing her.

With a sigh he stood up after the kiss; he was standing in the middle of the room, looking towards the door and nervously fingering the table.

"May I kiss you a little now?"

He moved towards the bed and bent down, searching for the woman's mouth.

"No, no," said the woman and bent forward.

Violently she threw her arms round the student's neck and kissed him passionately for a long time.

"You," she uttered with surprised delight.

She moved over in the bed and made room for the student beside her.

In the morning the sun was veiled in a milky fog; it was very hot, but the student set off early for the shore. Hopelessly he watched the road till late in the afternoon.

When the woman finally came it was already dusk.

"The man must be her husband," thought the student and shuddered restlessly; he turned towards the lake, looking at the rushes.

The man hailed him with a "Good afternoon."

"Good afternoon," replied the student, without lifting his eyes.

He stared at the intervening trunk of a poplar.

"Would you take us out on a little trip?" asked the woman.

The student nodded, but could not say a word.

"Only to have a look at the view from the water," said the man, "and then come straight back."

The woman examined the boy's face without attracting his attention.

"Is your grandfather still ill?"

"He's getting better," replied the student.

Gravely he ran his eyes over the man and untied the boat.

The husband was a pale, chubby man who cared about his appearance. He moved his hands as though about to stroke himself.

"What's this? You're not coming?" he said to the woman.

"No, I am not coming."

"I don't understand you," replied the husband in a rather hoarse voice as he stood up in the boat. "You ask me to come out in a boat and then you don't come yourself."

He glanced at the student, but the boy was not looking at either of them. He was fiddling with the oars.

"I don't feel like it," answered the woman, "but you go ahead. I'll look around on the shore."

"You're nothing but whims, and I know you think that I won't go without you. Well, you're mistaken."

The student was fidgeting awkwardly in his place.

All this time he and the woman had not looked at each other, except secretly, each avoiding the other's glance.

"I enjoy the view from the water," said the husband, "but we needn't go very far."

The student lowered his oars into the water, stared at the bottom of the boat, and paid no attention to the scenery.

"My wife is a little nervous," began the husband, "although ..."

He stopped.

The student was also silent, letting the water drip from his fingers.

"It's an enchanting panorama," began the husband after a long interval, "there's no wind whatsoever."

The student knew that he had to give some sort of an answer.

"Shall we go back?"

"We may as well," the man replied.

They sat in the boat without speaking while the student rowed swiftly.

The woman was waiting for them on the shore. When the man felt in his pocket for money, she turned her head aside awkwardly. When she saw that the student had accepted the money, she said softly,

"I owe him seven forints from yesterday. Please, give it to him."

The student stared at her uncomprehendingly.

"I owe his grandfather for two kilograms of cherries; I didn't have any money with me ... he'll know. And give him five forints too."

The husband took out his purse, found that he had five forints, said goodbye and began to walk away. As the woman followed, she winked at the boy conspiratorially, but followed her husband like a captive.

The student gazed after them for a long while, playing idly with the coins, tossing them in the air. Then he sat down on the grass, picked a single reed and watched sadly how it swayed to and fro in the breeze that blew gently along the shore.

Translated by
Judit Házi

MARGARITA KARAPANOU

KASSANDRA AND THE WOLF

Charles Dickens's first love was Little Red Ridinghood. "If only," he said, he "could have married her," he "would have known perfect bliss." Something in the relationship between the girl and the wolf, the transvestite animal coaxing the innocent child to bed, the possibility of love between beauty and the beast, has appealed to the imagination throughout the centuries. The first published version of the story is that of Charles Perrault in 1697, but English children, for instance, seem to have been aware of it even when they did not possess a copy of the translation. Little Red Ridinghood is, like the dragon and Bogey Man, part of our mythical reality.

For the ancient Greeks, the erotic relationship between humans and animals was less ambiguous: Leda and the swan, Pasiphaë and the bull. Margarita Karapanou echoes the ancient myths in a contemporary setting, taking as her characters not the old gods but the more recent immortals of fairy tales: a more sophisticated Red Ridinghood, a darkly human wolf.

Kassandra

I'M IN my room. Since yesterday, it's been winter. I've arranged my dolls in line on the bed, opened their legs, and lifted their frocks. I'm making them give birth. I'm using my marbles – the shiny ones – a present from Peter.

The marbles drop, and roll on the carpet. After they've turned into children, I put them in my basket. It's the birth basket. It's very shiny, with bits of mirror inside, 1 gold penknife, and millions of marbles – red ones, yellow ones, green ones – fire.

I want to put marbles in my dolls' bellies so I prick them all with a needle. They sigh, as straw falls on the carpet, and look pleased. I close their legs, cover them up, and run off to see the rain.

I open the window and turn the light off. Drops fill the room, the whole room sings with drops, fills with shining children, and I put my basket under the sky. Steel drops joggle with the marbles. I sit at the window and put the basket on my lap to sing the rain.

The room fills with green, yellow, red rains.

Someone knocks.

"Mother," I say aloud, shutting my eyes.

I don't know who it is out there, neither do I know what the word means, but I know that when the door opens, I'll understand.

Someone is in the room. Now I shall *see* the word *Mother.* I chant my magic things, squeeze the word *Mother* in my belly, and look.

I see Peter, smiling.

He kneels, shoves his nose inside my dolls, and sniffs at them, feeling for the holes with his tongue. Then, taking off his shirt, he stands at the window. His hairs turn yellow, red, green – fire – he's covered in flashing rains, he blazes up to the ceiling, opening his mouth and swallowing the round, shiny drops.

I close my eyes and hear him drop brand-new marbles in my basket.

The Wolf

"Come on, let's look at the book with the pictures."

I'd run to his room with the book under my arm, and give it to him tenderly.

The first picture was of a wolf opening his mouth to swallow 7 juicy piglets.

It was the wolf I usually felt sorry for. How could he gulp down so many piglets at one go? I always told him that, asked him that. Then he'd put his hairy hand in my white panties and touch me. I didn't feel anything except a kind of warmth.

His finger came and went, and I watched the wolf. He panted and sweated. I didn't mind it too much.

Now, when they caress me, I always think of the wolf, and feel sorry for him.

Translated by
N.C. Germanacos

YASUNARI KAWABATA

ONE ARM

Erotic literature in Japan is almost as old as Japanese literature itself. Japan's first great novel, Lady Murasaki's Tale of Genji, *written in the early years of the eleventh century, is above all an erotic novel; since then almost all the major Japanese writers have contributed to the genre.*

"It is the Genji, *I think, that has meant most to me," said Yasunari Kawabata in his 1968 Nobel Prize acceptance speech. The influence of* Genji's *delicate eroticism and subtle amorous invention is clear in Kawabata's fiction; the fantastic element, however, is obviously Kawabata's own, even though the device of bestowing to one's loved a part of one's own body is common in Japanese literature. In the West, the love-tokens are usually less intimate: a handkerchief, a picture, at most a lock of hair. Sometimes, however, we find in Western literature instances of far more drastic gifts: a terrifying French legend of the thirteenth century tells how a lover ripped out his heart to give to his beloved, who was then forced to eat it; in one of Grimm's*

fairy tales, a girl cuts off her tongue to make the man she loves love her in turn. In Kawabata's story, however, the gift is neither grisly nor frightening, but has a selfless and utterly generous quality which makes it even more astounding.

I CAN LET you have one of my arms for the night," said the girl. She took off her right arm at the shoulder and, with her left hand, laid it on my knee.

"Thank you." I looked at my knee. The warmth of the arm came through.

"I'll put the ring on. To remind you that it's mine." She smiled and raised her left arm to my chest. "Please." With but one arm, it was difficult for her to take the ring off.

"An engagement ring?"

"No. A keepsake. From my mother."

It was silver, set with small diamonds.

"Perhaps it does look like an engagement ring, but I don't mind. I wear it, and then when I take it off it's as if I were leaving my mother."

Raising the arm on my knee, I removed the ring and slipped it on the ring finger.

"Is this the one?"

"Yes." She nodded. "It will seem artificial unless the elbow and fingers bend. You won't like that. Let me make them bend for you."

She took her right arm from my knee and pressed her lips gently to it. Then she pressed them to the finger joints.

"Now they'll move."

"Thank you." I took the arm back. "Do you suppose it will speak? Will it speak to me?"

"It only does what an arm does. If it talks I'll be afraid to have it back. But try anyway. It should at least listen to what you say, if you're good to it."

"I'll be good to it."

"I'll see you again," she said, touching the right arm with her left hand, as if to infuse it with a spirit of its own. "You're his, but just for the night."

As she looked at me she seemed to be fighting back tears.

"I don't suppose you'll try to change it for your own arm," she said. "But it will be all right. Go ahead, do."

"Thank you."

I put her arm in my raincoat and went out into the foggy streets. I feared I might be thought odd if I took a taxi or a streetcar. There would be a scene if the arm, now separated from the girl's body, were to cry out, or to weep.

I held it against my chest, toward the side, my right hand on the roundness at the shoulder joint. It was concealed by the raincoat, and I had to touch the coat from time to time with my left hand to be sure that the arm was still there. Probably I was making sure not of the arm's presence but of my own happiness.

She had taken off the arm at the point I liked. It was plump and round – was it at the top of the arm or the beginning of the shoulder? The roundness was that of a beautiful Occidental girl, rare in a Japanese. It was in the girl herself, a clean, elegant roundness, like a sphere glowing with a faint, fresh light. When the girl was no longer clean that gentle roundness would fade, grow flabby. Something that lasted for a brief moment in the life of a beautiful girl, the roundness of the arm made me feel the roundness of her body. Her breasts would not be large. Shy, only large enough to cup in the hands, they would have a clinging softness and strength. And in the roundness of the arm I could feel her legs as she walked along. She would carry them lightly, like a small bird, or a butterfly moving from flower to flower. There would be the same subtle melody in the tip of her tongue when she kissed.

It was the season for changing to sleeveless dresses. The girl's shoulder, newly bared, had the color of skin not used to the raw touch of the air. It had the glow of a bud moistened in the shelter of spring and not yet ravaged by summer. I had that morning bought a magnolia bud and put it in a glass vase; and the roundness of the girl's arm was like the great, white bud. Her dress was cut back more radically than most sleeveless dresses. The joint at the shoulders was exposed, and the shoulder itself. The dress, of dark green silk, almost black, had a soft sheen. The girl was in the rounded slope of the shoulders, which drew a gentle wave with the swelling of the back. Seen obliquely from behind, the flesh from the round shoulders to the long, slender neck came to an abrupt halt at the base of the upswept hair, and the black hair seemed to cast a glowing shadow over the roundness of the shoulders.

She had sensed that I thought her beautiful, and so she lent me her right arm for the roundness there at the shoulder.

Carefully hidden under my raincoat, the girl's arm was colder than my hand. I was giddy from the racing of my heart, and I knew that my hand would be hot. I wanted the warmth to stay as it was, the warmth of the girl herself. And the slight coolness in my hand passed on to me the pleasure of the arm. It was like her breasts, not yet touched by a man.

The fog yet thicker, the night threatened rain, and wet my uncovered hair. I could hear a radio speaking from the back room of a closed pharmacy. It announced that three planes unable to land in the fog had been circling the airport for a half hour. It went on to draw the attention of listeners to the fact that on damp nights clocks were likely to go wrong, and that on such nights the springs had a tendency to break if wound too tight. I looked for the lights of the circling planes, but could not see them. There was no sky. The pressing dampness invaded my ears, to give a wet sound like the wriggling of myriads of distant earthworms. I stood before the pharmacy awaiting further admonitions. I learned that on such nights the fierce beasts in the zoo, the lions and tigers and leopards and the rest, roared their resentment at the dampness, and that we were now to hear it. There was a roaring like the roaring of the earth. I then learned that pregnant women and despondent persons should go to bed early on such nights, and that women who applied perfume directly to their skins would find it difficult to remove afterwards.

At the roaring of the beasts, I moved off, and the warning about perfume followed me. That angry roaring had unsettled me, and I moved on lest my uneasiness be transmitted to the girl's arm. The girl was neither pregnant nor despondent, but it seemed to me that tonight, with only one arm, she should take the advice of the radio and go quietly to bed. I hoped that she would sleep peacefully.

As I started across the street I pressed my left hand against my raincoat. A horn sounded. Something brushed my side, and I twisted away. Perhaps the arm had been frightened by the horn. The fingers were clenched.

"Don't worry," I said. "It was a long way off. It couldn't see. That's why it honked."

Because I was holding something important to me, I had looked in both directions. The sound of the horn had been so far away that I had thought it must be meant for someone else. I looked in the direction from which it came, but could see no one, I could see only the headlights. They widened into a blur of faint purple. A strange color for headlights. I stood on the curb when I had crossed and watched it pass. A young woman in vermilion was driving. It seemed to me that she turned toward me and bowed. I wanted to run off, fearing that the girl had come for her arm. Then I remembered that she would hardly be able to able to drive with only one. But had not the woman in the car seen what I was carrying? Had she not sensed it with a woman's intuition? I would have to take care not to encounter another of the sex before I reached my apartment. The rear lights were also a faint purple. I still did not see the car. In the ashen fog a lavender blur floated up and moved away.

"She is driving for no reason, for no reason at all except to be driving. And while she drives she will simply disappear," I muttered to myself. "And what was that sitting in the back seat?"

Nothing, apparently. Was it because I went around carrying girls' arms that I felt so unnerved by emptiness? The car she drove carried the clammy night fog. And something about her had turned it faintly purple in the headlights. If not from her own body, whence had come that purplish light? Could the arm I concealed have so clothed in emptiness a woman driving alone on such a night? Had she nodded at the girl's arm from her car? Perhaps on such a night there were angels and ghosts abroad protecting women. Perhaps she had ridden not in a car but in a purple light. Her drive had not been empty. She had spied out my secret.

I made my way back to my apartment without further encounters. I stood listening outside the door. The light of a firefly skimmed over my head and disappeared. It was too large and too strong for a firefly. I recoiled backwards. Several more lights like fireflies skimmed past. They disappeared even before the heavy fog could suck them in. Had a will-o'-the-wisp, a death-fire of some sort, run on ahead of me, to await my return? But then I saw that it was a swarm of small moths. Catching the light at the door, the wings of the moths glowed like fireflies. Too large to be fireflies, and yet, for moths, so small as to invite the mistake.

Avoiding the automatic elevator, I made my way stealthily up the narrow stairs to the third floor. Not being left-handed, I had difficulty unlocking the door. The harder I tried the more my hand trembled – as if in terror after a crime. Something would be waiting for me inside the room, a room where I lived in solitude; and was not the solitude a presence? With the girl's arm I was no longer alone. And so perhaps my own solitude waited there to intimidate me.

"Go on ahead," I said, taking out the girl's arm when at length I had opened the door. "Welcome to my room. I'll turn on the light."

"Are you afraid of something?" the arm seemed to say. "Is something here?"

"You think there might be?"

"I smell something."

"Smell? It must be me that you smell. Don't you see traces of my shadow, up there in the darkness? Look carefully. Maybe my shadow was waiting for me to come back."

"It's a sweet smell."

"Ah – the magnolia," I answered brightly. I was glad it was not the moldy smell of my loneliness. A magnolia bud befitted my winsome guest. I was getting used to the dark. Even in pitch blackness I knew where everything was.

"Let me turn on the light." Coming from the arm, a strange remark. "I haven't been in your room before."

"Thank you. I'll be very pleased. No one but me has ever turned on the lights here before."

I held the arm to the switch by the door. All five lights went on at once: at the ceiling, on the table, by the bed, in the kitchen, in the bathroom. I had not thought they could be so bright.

The magnolia was in enormous bloom. That morning it had been in bud. It could have only just bloomed, and yet there were stamens on the table. Curious, I looked more closely at the stamens than at the white flower. As I picked up one or two and gazed at them, the girl's arm, laid on the table, began to move, the fingers like spanworms, and gathered the stamens in its hand. I went to throw them in the wastebasket.

"What a strong smell. It sinks right into my skin. Help me."

"You must be tired. It wasn't an easy trip. Suppose you rest awhile."

I laid the arm on the bed and sat down beside it. I stroked it gently.

"How pretty. I like it." The arm would be speaking of the bed cover. Flowers were printed in three colors on an azure ground, somewhat lively for a man who lived alone. "So this is where we spend the night. I'll be very quiet."

"Oh?"

"I'll be beside you and not beside you."

The hand took mine gently. The nails, carefully polished, were a faint pink. The tips extended well beyond the fingers.

Against my own short, thick nails, hers possessed a strange beauty, as if they belonged to no human creature. With such fingertips, a woman perhaps transcended mere humanity. Or did she pursue womanhood itself? A shell luminous from the pattern inside it, a petal bathed in dew – I thought of the obvious likenesses. Yet I could think of no shell or petal whose color and shape resembled them. They were the nails on the girl's fingers, comparable to nothing else. More translucent than a delicate shell, than a thin petal, they seemed to hold a dew of tragedy. Every day and every night her energies were poured into the polishing of this tragic beauty. It penetrated my solitude. Perhaps my yearning, my solitude, transformed them into dew.

I rested her little finger on the index finger of my free hand, gazing at the long, narrow nail as I rubbed it with my thumb. My finger touched the tip of hers, sheltered by the nail. The finger bent, and the elbow too.

"Does it tickle?" I asked. "It must."

I had spoken carelessly. I knew that the tips of a woman's fingers were sensitive when the nails were long. And so I had told the girl's arm that I had known other women.

From one who was not a great deal older than the girl who had lent me the arm but far more mature in her experience of men, I had heard that fingertips thus hidden by nails were often acutely sensitive. One became used to touching things not with the fingertips but with the nails, and the fingertips therefore tickled when something came against them.

I had shown astonishment at this discovery, and she had gone on: "You're, say, cooking – or eating – and something touches your fingers, and you find yourself hunching your shoulders, it seems so dirty."

Was it the food that seemed unclean, or the tip of the nail? Whatever touched her fingers made her writhe with its uncleanness. Her own cleanness would leave behind a drop of tragic dew, there under the long shadow of the nail. One could not assume that for each of the ten fingers there would be a separate drop of dew.

It was natural that I should want all the more to touch those fingertips, but I held myself back. My solitude held me back. She was a woman on whose body few tender spots could be expected to remain.

And on the body of the girl who had lent me the arm they would be beyond counting. Perhaps, toying with the fingertips of such a girl, I would feel not guilt but affection. But she had not lent me the arm for such mischief. I must not make a comedy of her gesture.

"The window." I noticed not that the window itself was open but that the curtain was undrawn.

"Will anything look in?" asked the girl's arm.

"Some man or woman. Nothing else."

"Nothing human would see me. If anything it would be a self. Yours."

"Self? What is that? Where is it?"

"Far away," said the arm, as if singing in consolation. "People walk around looking for selves, far away."

"And do they come upon them?"

"Far away," said the arm once more.

It seemed to me that the arm and the girl herself were an infinity apart. Would the arm be able to return to the girl, so far away? Would I be able to take it back, so far away? The arm lay peacefully trusting me; and would the girl be sleeping in the same peaceful confidence? Would there not be harshness, a nightmare? Had she not seemed to be fighting back tears when she parted with it? The arm was now in my room, which the girl herself had not visited.

The dampness clouded the window, like a toad's belly stretched over it. The fog seemed to withhold rain in midair, and the night outside the window lost distance, even while it was wrapped in limitless distance. There were no roofs to be seen, no horns to be heard.

"I'll close the window," I said, reaching for the curtain. It too was damp. My face loomed up in the window, younger than my thirty-three years. I did not hesitate to pull the curtain, however. My face disappeared.

Suddenly a remembered window. On the ninth floor of a hotel, two little girls in wide red skirts were playing in the window. Very similar children in similar clothes, perhaps twins, Occidentals. They pounded at the glass, pushing it with their shoulders and shoving at each other. Their mother knitted, her back to the window. If the large pane were to have broken or come loose, they would have fallen from the ninth floor. It was only I who thought them in danger. Their mother was quite unconcerned. The glass was in fact so solid that there was no danger.

"It's beautiful," said the arm on the bed as I turned from the window. Perhaps she was speaking of the curtain, in the same flowered pattern as the bed cover.

"Oh? But it's faded from the sun and almost ready to go." I sat down on the bed and took the arm on my knee. "This is what is beautiful. More beautiful than anything."

Taking the palm of the hand in my own right palm, and the shoulder in my left hand, I flexed the elbow, and then again.

"Behave yourself," said the arm, as if smiling softly. "Having fun?"

"Not in the least."

A smile did come over the arm, crossing it like light. It was exactly the fresh smile on the girl's cheek.

I knew the smile. Elbows on the table, she would fold her hands loosely and rest her chin or cheek on them. The pose should have been inelegant in a young girl; but there was about it a lightly engaging quality that made expressions like "elbows on the table" seem inappropriate. The roundness of the shoulders, the fingers, the chin, the cheeks, the ears, the long, slender neck, the hair, all came together in a single harmonious movement. Using knife and fork deftly, first and little fingers bent, she would raise them ever so slightly from time to time. Food would pass the small lips and she would swallow – I had before me less a person at dinner than an inviting music of hands and face and throat. The light of her smile flowed across the skin of her arm.

The arm seemed to smile because, as I flexed it, very gentle waves passed over the firm, delicate muscles, to send waves of light and shadow over the smooth skin. Earlier, when I had touched the fingertips under the long nails, the light passing over the arm as the elbow bent had caught my eye. It was that, and not any impulse toward mischief, that had made me bend and unbend her arm. I stopped, and gazed at it as it lay stretched out on my knee. Fresh lights and shadows were still passing over it.

"You ask if I'm having fun. You realize that I have permission to change you for my own arm?"

"I do."

"Somehow I'm afraid to."

"Oh?"

"May I?"

"Please."

I heard the permission granted, and wondered whether I could accept it. "Say it again. Say 'please.'"

"Please, please."

I remembered. It was like the voice of a woman who had decided to give herself to me, one not as beautiful as the girl who had lent me the arm. Perhaps there was something a little strange about her.

"Please," she had said, gazing at me. I had put my fingers to her eyelids and closed them. Her voice was trembling. "'Jesus wept. Then said the Jews, Behold how he loved her!'"

"Her" was a mistake for "him." It was the story of the dead Lazarus. Perhaps, herself a woman, she had remembered it wrong, perhaps she had made the substitution intentionally.

The words, so inappropriate to the scene, had shaken me.

I gazed at her, wondering if tears would start from the closed eyes.

She opened them and raised her shoulders. I pushed her down with my arm.

"You're hurting me!" She put her hand to the back of her head.

There was a small spot of blood on the white pillow. Parting her hair, I put my lips to the drop of blood swelling on her head.

"It doesn't matter." She took out all her hairpins. "I bleed easily. At the slightest touch."

A hairpin had pierced her skin. A shudder seemed about to pass through her shoulders, but she controlled herself.

Although I think I understand how a woman feels when she gives herself to a man, there is still something unexplained about the act. What is it to her? Why should she wish to do it, why should she take the initiative? I could never really accept the surrender, even knowing that the body of every woman was made for it. Even now, old as I am, it seems strange. And the ways in which various women go about it: unalike if you wish, or similar perhaps, or even identical. Is that not strange? Perhaps the strangeness I find in it all is the curiosity of a younger man, perhaps the despair of one advanced in years. Or perhaps some spiritual debility I suffer from.

Her anguish was not common to all women in the act of surrender. And it was with her only the one time. The silver thread was cut, the golden bowl destroyed.

"Please," the arm had said, and so reminded me of the other girl; but were the two voices in fact similar? Had they not sounded alike because the words were the same? Had the arm acquired independence in this measure of the body from which it was separated? And were the words not the act of giving itself up, of being ready for anything, without restraint or responsibility or remorse? It seemed to me that if I were to accept the invitation and change the arm for my own I would be bringing untold pain to the girl.

I gazed at the arm on my knee. There was a shadow at the inside of the elbow. It seemed that I might be able to suck it in. I pressed it to my lips, to gather in the shadow.

"It tickles. Do behave yourself." The arm was around my neck, avoiding my lips.

"Just when I was having a good drink."

"And what were you drinking?"

I did not answer.

"What were you drinking?"

"The smell of light? Of skin."

The fog seemed thicker; even the magnolia leaves seemed wet. What other warnings would issue from the radio? I started toward my table radio and stopped. To listen to it with the arm around my neck seemed altogether too much. But I suspected I would hear something like this: because of the wet branches and their own wet feet and wings, small birds have fallen to the ground and cannot fly. Automobiles passing through parks should take care not to run over them. And if a warm wind comes up, the fog will perhaps change color. Strange-colored fogs are noxious. Listeners should therefore lock their doors if the fog should turn pink or purple.

"Change color?" I muttered. "Turn pink or purple?"

I pulled at the curtain and looked out. The fog seemed to press down with an empty weight. Was it because of the wind that a thin darkness seemed to be moving about, different from the usual black of night? The thickness of the fog seemed infinite, and yet beyond it something fearsome writhed and coiled.

I remembered that earlier, as I was coming home with the borrowed arm, the head and tail beams of the car driven by the woman in vermilion had come up indistinctly in the fog. A great, blurred sphere of faint purple now seemed to come toward me. I hastily pulled away from the curtain.

"Let's go to bed. Us too."

It seemed as if no one else in the world would be up. To be up was terror.

Taking the arm from my neck and putting it on the table, I changed into a fresh night-kimono, a cotton print. The arm watched me change. I was shy at being watched. Never before had a woman watched me undress in my room.

The arm in my own, I got into bed. I lay facing it, and brought it lightly to my chest. It lay quiet.

Intermittently I could hear a faint sound as of rain, a very light sound, as if the fog had not turned to rain but were itself forming drops. The fingers clasped in my hand beneath the blanket grew warmer; and it gave me the quietest of sensations, the fact that they had not warmed to my own temperature.

"Are you asleep?"

"No," replied the arm.

"You were so quiet, I thought you might be asleep."

"What do you want me to do?"

Opening my kimono, I brought the arm to my chest. The difference in warmth sank in. In the somehow sultry, somehow chilly night, the smoothness of the skin was pleasant.

The lights were still on. I had forgotten to turn them out as I went to bed.

"The lights." I got up, and the arm fell from my chest.

I hastened to pick it up. "Will you turn out the lights?" I started toward the door. "Do you sleep in the dark? Or with lights on?"

The arm did not answer. It would surely know. Why had it not answered? I did not know the girl's nocturnal practices. I compared the two pictures, of her asleep in the dark and with the lights on. I decided that tonight, without her arm, she would have them on. Somehow I too wanted them on. I wanted to gaze at the arm. I wanted to stay awake and watch the arm after it had gone to sleep. But the fingers stretched to turn off the switch by the door.

I went back and lay down in the darkness, the arm by my chest I lay there silently, waiting for it to go to sleep. Whether dissatisfied or afraid of the dark, the hand lay open at my side, and presently the five fingers were climbing my chest. The elbow bent of its own accord, and the arm embraced me.

There was a delicate pulse at the girl's wrist. It lay over my heart, so that the two pulses sounded against each other. Hers was at first somewhat slower than mine, then they were together. And then I could feel only mine. I did not know which was faster, which slower.

Perhaps this identity of pulse and heartbeat was for a brief period when I might try to exchange the arm for my own. Or had it gone to sleep? I had once heard a woman say that women were less happy in the throes of ecstasy than sleeping peacefully beside their men; but never before had a woman slept beside me as peacefully as this arm.

I was conscious of my beating heart because of the pulsation above it. Between one beat and the next, something sped far away and sped back again. As I listened to the beating, the distance seemed to increase. And however far the something went, however infinitely far, it met nothing at its destination. The next beat summoned it back. I should have been afraid, and was not. Yet I groped for the switch beside my pillow.

Before turning it on, I quietly rolled back the blanket. The arm slept on, unaware of what was happening. A gentle band of faintest white encircled my naked chest, seeming to rise from the flesh itself, like the glow before the dawning of a tiny, warm sun.

I turned on the light. I put my hands to the fingers and shoulder and pulled the arm straight. I turned it quietly in my hands, gazing at the play of light and shadow, from the roundness at the shoulder over the narrowing and swelling of the forearm, the narrowing again at the gentle roundness of the elbow, the faint depression inside the elbow, the narrowing roundness to the wrist, the palm and back of the hand, and on to the fingers.

"I'll have it." I was not conscious of muttering the words. In a trance, I removed my right arm and substituted the girl's.

There was a slight gasp – whether from the arm or from me I could not tell – and a spasm at my shoulder. So I knew of the change.

The girl's arm – mine now – was trembling and reaching for the air. Bending it, I brought it close to my mouth.

"Does it hurt? Do you hurt?"

"No. Not at all. Not at all." The words were fitful.

A shudder went through me like lightning. I had the fingers in my mouth.

Somehow I spoke my happiness, but the girl's fingers were at my tongue, and whatever it was I spoke did not form into words.

"Please. It's all right," the arm replied. The trembling stopped. "I was told you could. And yet –"

I noticed something. I could feel the girl's fingers in my mouth, but the fingers of her right hand, now those of my own right hand, could not feel my lips or teeth. In panic I shook my right arm and could not feel the shaking. There was a break, a stop, between arm and shoulder.

"The blood doesn't go," I blurted out. "Does it or doesn't it?"

For the first time I was swept by fear. I rose up in bed. My own arm had fallen beside me. Separated from me, it was an unsightly object. But more important – would not the pulse have stopped? The girl's arm was warm and pulsing; my own looked as if it were growing stiff and cold. With the girl's, I grasped my own right arm. I grasped it, but there was no sensation.

"Is there a pulse?" I asked the arm. "Is it cold?"

"A little. Just a little colder than I am. I've gotten very warm." There was something especially womanly in the cadence. Now that the arm was fastened to my shoulder and made my own, it seemed womanly as it had not before.

"The pulse hasn't stopped?"

"You should be more trusting."

"Of what?"

"You changed your arm for mine, didn't you?"

"Is the blood flowing?"

"'Woman, whom seekest thou?' You know the passage?"

"'Woman, why weepest thou? Whom seekest thou?'"

"Very often when I'm dreaming and wake up in the night I whisper it to myself."

This time of course the "I" would be the owner of the winsome arm at my shoulder. The words from the Bible were as if spoken by an eternal voice, in an eternal place.

"Will she have trouble sleeping?" I too spoke of the girl herself. "Will she be having a nightmare? It's a fog for herds of nightmares to wander in. But the dampness will make even demons cough."

"To keep you from hearing them." The girl's arm, my own still in its hand, covered my right ear.

It was now my own right arm, but the motion seemed to have come not of my volition but of its own, from its heart. Yet the separation was by no means so complete.

"The pulse. The sound of the pulse."

I heard the pulse of my own right arm. The girl's arm had come to my ear with my own arm in its hand, and my own wrist was at my ear. My arm was warm – as the girl's arm had said, just perceptibly cooler than her fingers and my ear.

"I'll keep away the devils." Mischievously, gently, the long, delicate nail of her little finger stirred in my ear. I shook my head. My left hand – mine from the start – took my right wrist – actually the girl's. As I threw my head back, I caught sight of the girl's little finger.

Four fingers of her hand were grasping the arm I had taken from my right shoulder. The little finger alone – shall we say that it alone was allowed to play free? – was bent toward the back of the hand. The tip of the nail touched my right arm lightly. The finger was bent in a position possible only to a girl's supple hand, out of the question for a stiff-jointed man like me. From its base it rose at right angles. At the first joint it bent in another right angle, and at the next in yet another. It thus traced a square, the fourth side formed by the ring finger.

It formed a rectangular window at the level of my eye. Or rather a peep-hole, or an eyeglass, much too small for a window; but somehow I thought of a window. The sort of window a violet might look out through. The window of the little finger, the finger-rimmed eyeglass, so white that it gave off a faint glow – I brought it nearer my eye. I closed the other eye.

"A peep show?" asked the arm. "And what do you see?"

"My dusky old room. Its five lights." Before I had finished the sentence I was almost shouting. "No, no! I see it!"

"And what do you see?"

"It's gone."

"And what did you see?"

"A color. A blur of purple. And inside it little circles, little beads of red and gold, whirling around and around."

"You're tired." The girl's arm put down my right arm, and her fingers gently stroked my eyelids.

"Were the beads of gold and red spinning around in a huge cogwheel? Did I see something in the cogwheel, something that came and went?"

I did not know whether I had actually seen something there or only seemed to – a fleeting illusion, not to stay in the memory. I could not remember what it might have been.

"Was it an illusion you wanted to show me?"

"No. I came to erase it."

"Of days gone by. Of longing and sadness."

On my eyelids the movement of her fingers stopped.

I asked an unexpected question. "When you let down your hair does it cover your shoulders?"

"It does. I wash it in hot water, but afterward – a special quirk of mine, maybe – I pour cold water over it. I like the feel of cold hair against my shoulders and arms, and against my breasts too."

It would of course be the girl again. Her breasts had never been touched by a man, and no doubt she would have had difficulty describing the feel of the cold, wet hair against them. Had the arm, separated from the body, been separated too from the shyness and the reserve?

Quietly I took in my left hand the gentle roundness at the shoulder, now my own. It seemed to me that I had in my hand the roundness, not yet large, of her breasts. The roundness of the shoulder became the soft roundness of breasts.

Her hand lay gently on my eyelids. The fingers and the hand clung softly and sank through, and the underside of the eyelids seemed to warm at the touch. The warmth sank into my eyes.

"The blood is going now," I said quietly. "It is going."

It was not a cry of surprise as when I had noticed that my arm was changed for hers. There was no shuddering and no spasm, in the girl's arm or my shoulder. When had my blood begun to flow through the arm, her blood through me? When had the break at the shoulder disappeared? The clean blood of the girl was now, this very moment, flowing through me; but would there not be unpleasantness when the arm was returned to the girl, this dirty male blood flowing through it? What if it would not attach itself to her shoulder?

"No such betrayal," I muttered.

"It will be all right," whispered the arm.

There was no dramatic awareness that between the arm and my shoulder the blood came and went. My left hand, enfolding my right shoulder, and the shoulder itself, now mine, had a natural understanding of the fact. They had come to know it. The knowledge pulled them down into slumber.

I slept.

I floated on a great wave. It was the encompassing fog turned a faint purple, and there were pale green ripples at the spot where I floated on the great wave, and there alone. The dank solitude of my room was gone. My left hand seemed to rest lightly on the girl's right arm. It seemed that her fingers held magnolia stamens. I could not see them, but I could smell them. We had thrown them away – and when and how had she gathered them up again? The white petals, but a day old, had not yet fallen; why then the stamens? The automobile of the woman in vermilion slid by, drawing a great circle with me at the center. It seemed to watch over our sleep, the arm's and mine.

Our sleep was probably light, but I had never before known sleep so warm, so sweet. A restless sleeper, I had never before been blessed with the sleep of a child.

The long, narrow, delicate nail scratched gently at the palm of my hand, and the slight touch made my sleep deeper. I disappeared.

I awoke screaming. I almost fell out of bed, and staggered three or four steps.

I had awakened to the touch of something repulsive. It was my right arm.

Steadying myself, I looked down at the arm on the bed. I caught my breath, my heart raced, my whole body trembled. I saw the arm in one instant, and the next I had torn the girl's from my shoulder and put back my own. The act was like murder upon a sudden, diabolic impulse.

I knelt by the bed, my chest against it, and rubbed at my insane heart with my restored hand. As the beating slowed down a sadness welled up from deeper than the deepest inside me.

"Where is her arm?" I raised my head.

It lay at the foot of the bed, flung palm up into the heap of the blanket. The outstretched fingers did not move. The arm was faintly white in the dim light.

Crying out in alarm I swept it up and held it tight to my chest. I embraced it as one would a small child from whom life was going. I brought the fingers to my lips. If the dew of woman would but come from between the long nails and the fingertips!

Translated by
Edward Seidensticker

MILAN KUNDERA

THE HITCHHIKING GAME

In the erotic act we discover the other, revealed as never before; but in the process of that discovery we can also lose the other. In The Unbearable Lightness of Being *Milan Kundera allows his protagonist to swing back and forth from discovery to loss, mistresses to wife to mistresses. He trusts his memory to preserve the erotic experience. "The result is a formula consisting of three givens: 1) clumsiness with ardor; 2) the frightened face of one who has lost her equilibrium and is falling; and 3) legs raised and in the air like the arms of a soldier surrendering to a pointed gun."*

He concludes: "Going over them, he felt the joy of having acquired yet another piece of the world, of having taken his imaginary scalpel and cut yet another strip off the infinite canvas of the universe."

Loss and discovery are not stages, but part of the same moment in "The Hitchhiking Game," one of the stories in the collection Laughable Loves *of which Kundera has said: "Every one of my novels could be thus entitled." And then added: "They reflect the small number of themes that obsess me, define me, and, unfortunately, restrict me. Beyond these themes, I have nothing else to say or write."*

I

THE NEEDLE on the gas gauge suddenly dipped toward empty and the young driver of the sports car declared that it was maddening how much gas the car ate up. "See that we don't run out of gas again," protested the girl (about twenty-two), and reminded the driver of several places where this had already happened to them. The young man replied that he wasn't worried, because whatever he went through with her had the charm of adventure for him. The girl objected; whenever they had run out of gas on the highway it had, she said, always been an adventure only for her. The young man had hidden and she had had to make ill use of her charms by thumbing a ride and letting herself be driven to the nearest gas station, then thumbing a ride back with a can of gas. The young man asked the girl whether the drivers who had given her a ride had been unpleasant, since she spoke as if her task had been a hardship. She replied (with awkward flirtatiousness) that sometimes they had been *very* pleasant but that it hadn't done her any good as she had been burdened with the can and had had to leave them before she could get anything going. "Pig," said the young man. The girl protested that she wasn't a pig, but that he really was. God knows how many girls stopped him on the highway, when he was driving the car alone! Still driving, the young man put his arm around the girl's shoulders and kissed her gently on the forehead. He knew that she loved him and that she was jealous. Jealousy isn't a pleasant quality, but if it isn't overdone (and if it's combined with modesty), apart from its inconvenience there's even something touching about it. At least that's what the young man thought. Because he was only twenty-eight, it seemed to him that he was old and knew everything that a man could know about women. In the girl sitting beside him he valued precisely what, until now, he had met with least in women: purity.

The needle was already on empty, when to the right the young man caught sight of a sign, announcing that the station was a quarter of a mile ahead. The girl hardly had time to say how relieved she was before the young man was signaling left and driving into a space in front of the pumps. However, he had to stop a little way off, because beside the pumps was a huge gasoline truck with a large metal tank and a bulky hose, which was refilling the pumps. "We'll have to wait," said the young man to the girl and got out of the car. "How long will it take?" he shouted to the man in overalls. "Only a moment," replied the attendant, and the young man said: "I've heard that one before." He wanted to go back and sit in the car, but he saw that the girl had gotten out the other side. "I'll take a little walk in the meantime," she said. "Where to?" the young man asked on purpose, wanting to see the girl's embarrassment. He had known her for a year now but she would still get shy in front of him. He enjoyed her moments of shyness, partly because they distinguished her from the women he'd met before, partly because he was aware of the law of universal transience, which made even his girl's shyness a precious thing to him.

II

The girl really didn't like it when during the trip (the young man would drive for several hours without stopping) she had to ask him to stop for a moment somewhere near a clump of trees. She always got angry when, with feigned surprise, he asked her why he should stop. She knew that her shyness was ridiculous and old-fashioned. Many times at work she had noticed that they laughed at her on account of it and deliberately provoked her. She always got shy in advance at the thought of how she was going to get shy. She often longed to feel free and easy about her body, the way most of the women around her did. She had even invented a special course in self-persuasion: she would repeat to herself that at birth every human being received one out of the millions of available bodies, as one would receive an allotted room out of the millions of rooms in an enormous hotel; that, consequently, the body was fortuitous and impersonal, only a ready-made, borrowed thing. She would repeat this to herself in different ways, but she could never manage to feel it. This mind-body dualism was alien to her. She was too much one with her body; that is why she always felt such anxiety about it.

She experienced this same anxiety even in her relations with the young man, whom she had known for a year and with whom she was happy, perhaps because he never separated her body from her soul and she could live with him *wholly.* In this unity there was happiness, but right behind the happiness lurked suspicion, and the girl was full of that. For instance, it often occurred to her that the other women (those who weren't anxious) were more attractive and more seductive and that the young man, who did not conceal the fact that he knew this kind of woman well, would someday leave her for a woman like that. (True, the young man declared that he'd had enough of them to last his whole life, but she knew that he was still much younger than he thought.) She wanted him to be completely hers and she to be completely his, but it often seemed to her that the more she tried to give him everything, the more she denied him something: the very thing that a light and superficial love or a flirtation gives to a person. It worried her that she was not able to combine seriousness with lightheartedness.

But now she wasn't worrying and any such thoughts were far from her mind. She felt good. It was the first day of their vacation (of their two-week vacation, about which she had been dreaming for a whole year), the sky was blue (the whole year she had been worrying about whether the sky would really be blue), and he was beside her. At his, "Where to?" she blushed, and left the car without a word. She walked around the gas station, which was situated beside the highway in total isolation, surrounded by fields. About a hundred yards away (in the direction in which they were traveling), a wood began. She set off for it, vanished behind a little bush, and gave herself up to her good mood. (In solitude it was possible for her to get the greatest enjoyment from the presence of the man she loved. If his presence had been continuous, it would have kept on disappearing. Only when alone was she able to *hold on* to it.)

When she came out of the wood onto the highway, the gas station was visible. The large gasoline truck was already pulling out and the sports car moved forward toward the red turret of the pump. The girl walked on along the highway and only at times looked back to see if the sports car was coming. At last she caught sight of it. She stopped and began to wave at it like a hitchhiker waving at a stranger's car. The sports car slowed down and stopped close to the girl. The young man leaned toward the window, rolled it down, smiled, and asked, "Where are you headed, miss?" "Are you going to Bystritsa?" asked the girl, smiling flirtatiously at him. "Yes, please get in," said the young man, opening the door. The girl got in and the car took off.

III

The young man was always glad when his girl friend was gay. This didn't happen too often; she had a quite tiresome job in an unpleasant environment, many hours of overtime without compensatory leisure and, at home, a sick mother. So she often felt tired. She didn't have either particularly good nerves or self-confidence and easily fell into a state of anxiety and fear. For this reason he welcomed every manifestation of her gaiety with the tender solicitude of a foster parent. He smiled at her and said: "I'm lucky today. I've been driving for five years, but I've never given a ride to such a pretty hitchhiker."

The girl was grateful to the young man for every bit of flattery; she wanted to linger for a moment in its warmth and so she said, "You're very good at lying."

"Do I look like a liar?"

"You look like you enjoy lying to women," said the girl, and into her words there crept unawares a touch of the old anxiety, because she really did believe that her young man enjoyed lying to women.

The girl's jealousy often irritated the young man, but this time he could easily overlook it for, after all, her words didn't apply to him but to the unknown driver. And so he just casually inquired, "Does it bother you?"

"If I were going with you, then it would bother me," said the girl and her words contained a subtle, instructive message for the young man; but the end of her sentence applied only to the unknown driver, "but I don't know you, so it doesn't bother me."

"Things about her own man always bother a woman more than things about a stranger" (this was now the young man's subtle, instructive message to the girl), "so seeing that we are strangers, we could get on well together."

The girl purposely didn't want to understand the implied meaning of his message, and so she now addressed the unknown driver exclusively:

"What does it matter, since we'll part company in a little while?"

"Why?" asked the young man.

"Well, I'm getting out at Bystritsa."

"And what if I get out with you?"

At these words the girl looked up at him and found that he looked exactly as she imagined him in her most agonizing hours of jealousy. She was alarmed at how he was flattering her and flirting with her (an unknown hitchhiker), and *how becoming it was to him.* Therefore she responded with defiant provocativeness, "What would *you* do with me, I wonder?"

"I wouldn't have to think too hard about what to do with such a beautiful woman," said the young man gallantly and at this moment he was once again speaking far more to his own girl than to the figure of the hitchhiker.

But this flattering sentence made the girl feel as if she had caught him at something, as if she had wheedled a confession out of him with a fraudulent trick. She felt toward him a brief flash of intense hatred and said, "Aren't you rather too sure of yourself?"

The young man looked at the girl. Her defiant face appeared to him to be completely convulsed. He felt sorry for her and longed for her usual, familiar expression (which he used to call childish and simple). He leaned toward her, put his arm around her shoulders, and softly spoke the name with which he usually addressed her and with which he now wanted to stop the game.

But the girl released herself and said: "You're going a bit too fast!"

At this rebuff the young man said: "Excuse me, miss," and looked silently in front of him at the highway.

IV

The girl's pitiful jealousy, however, left her as quickly as it had come over her. After all, she was sensible and knew perfectly well that all this was merely a game; now it even struck her as a little ridiculous that she had repulsed her man out of jealous rage; it wouldn't be pleasant for her if he found out why she had done it. Fortunately she had the miraculous ability to change the meaning of her actions after the event. Using this ability, she decided that she had repulsed him not out of anger but so that she could go on with the game, which, with its whimsicality, so well suited the first day of their vacation.

So again she was the hitchhiker, who had just repulsed the overenterprising driver, but only so as to slow down his conquest and make it more exciting. She half turned toward the young man and said caressingly:

"I didn't mean to offend you, mister!"

"Excuse me, I won't touch you again," said the young man.

He was furious with the girl for not listening to him and refusing to be herself when that was what he wanted. And since the girl insisted on continuing in her role, he transferred his anger to the unknown hitchhiker whom she was portraying. And all at once he discovered the character of his own part: he stopped making the gallant remarks with which he had wanted to flatter his girl in a roundabout way, and began to play the tough guy who treats women to the coarser aspects of his masculinity: willfulness, sarcasm, self-assurance.

This role was a complete contradiction of the young man's habitually solicitous approach to the girl. True, before he had met her, he had in fact behaved roughly rather than gently toward women. But he had never resembled a heartless tough guy, because he had never demonstrated either a particularly strong will or ruthlessness. However, if he did not resemble such a man, nonetheless he had *longed* to at one time. Of course it was a quite naive desire, but there it was. Childish desires withstand all the snares of the adult mind and often survive into ripe old age. And this childish desire quickly took advantage of the opportunity to embody itself in the proffered role.

The young man's sarcastic reserve suited the girl very well – it freed her from herself. For she herself was, above all, the epitome of jealousy. The moment she stopped seeing the gallantly seductive young man beside her and saw only his inaccessible face, her jealousy subsided. The girl could forget herself and give herself up to her role.

Her role? What was her role? It was a role out of trashy literature. The hitchhiker stopped the car not to get a ride, but to seduce the man who was driving the car. She was an artful seductress, cleverly knowing how to use her charms. The girl slipped into this silly, romantic part with an ease that astonished her and held her spellbound.

V

There was nothing the young man missed in his life more than lightheartedness. The main road of his life was drawn with implacable precision: his job didn't use up merely eight hours a day, it also infiltrated the remaining time with the compulsory boredom of meetings and home study, and, by means of the attentiveness of his countless male and female colleagues, it infiltrated the wretchedly little time he had left for his private life as well; this private life never remained secret and sometimes even became the subject of gossip and public discussion. Even two weeks' vacation didn't give him a feeling of liberation and adventure; the gray shadow of precise planning lay even here. The scarcity of summer accommodations in our country compelled him to book a room in the Tatras six months in advance, and since for that he needed a recommendation from his office, its omnipresent brain thus did not cease knowing about him even for an instant.

He had become reconciled to all this, yet all the same from time to time the terrible thought of the straight road would overcome him – a road along which he was being pursued, where he was visible to everyone, and from which he could not turn aside. At this moment that thought returned to him. Through an odd and brief conjunction of ideas the figurative road became identified with the real highway along which he was driving – and this led him suddenly to do a crazy thing.

"Where did you say you wanted to go?" he asked the girl.

"To Banska Bystritsa," she replied.

"And what are you going to do there?"

"I have a date there."

"Who with?"

"With a certain gentleman."

The car was just coming to a large crossroads. The driver slowed down so he could read the road signs, then turned off to the right.

"What will happen if you don't arrive for that date?"

"It would be your fault and you would have to take care of me."

"You obviously didn't notice that I turned off in the direction of Nove Zamky."

"Is that true? You've gone crazy!"

"Don't be afraid, I'll take care of you," said the young man.

So they drove and chatted thus – the driver and the hitchhiker who did not know each other.

The game all at once went into a higher gear. The sports car was moving away not only from the imaginary goal of Banska Bystritsa, but also from the real goal, toward which it had been heading in the morning: the Tatras and the room that had been booked. Fiction was suddenly making an assault upon real life. The young man was moving away from himself and from the implacable straight road, from which he had never strayed until now.

"But you said you were going to the Low Tatras!" The girl was surprised.

"I am going, miss, wherever I feel like going. I'm a free man and I do what I want and what it pleases me to do."

VI

When they drove into Nove Zamky it was already getting dark.

The young man had never been here before and it took him a while to orient himself. Several times he stopped the car and asked the passersby directions to the hotel. Several streets had been dug up, so that the drive to the hotel, even though it was quite close by (as all those who had been asked asserted), necessitated so many detours and roundabout routes that it was almost a quarter of an hour before they finally stopped in front of it. The hotel looked unprepossessing, but it was the only one in town and the young man didn't feel like driving on. So he said to the girl, "Wait here," and got out of the car.

Out of the car he was, of course, himself again. And it was upsetting for him to find himself in the evening somewhere completely different from his intended destination – the more so because no one had forced him to do it and as a matter of fact he hadn't even really wanted to. He blamed himself for this piece of folly, but then became reconciled to it. The room in the Tatras could wait until tomorrow and it wouldn't do any harm if they celebrated the first day of their vacation with something unexpected.

He walked through the restaurant – smoky, noisy, and crowded – and asked for the reception desk. They sent him to the back of the lobby near the staircase, where behind a glass panel a superannuated blonde was sitting beneath a board full of keys. With difficulty, he obtained the key to the only room left.

The girl, when she found herself alone, also threw off her role. She didn't feel ill-humored, though, at finding herself in an unexpected town. She was so devoted to the young man that she never had doubts about anything he did, and confidently entrusted every moment of her life to him. On the other hand the idea once again popped into her mind that perhaps – just as she was now doing – other women had waited for her man in his car, those women whom he met on business trips. But surprisingly enough this idea didn't upset her at all now; in fact, she smiled at the thought of how nice it was that today she was this other woman, this irresponsible, indecent other woman, one of those women of whom she was so jealous; it seemed to her that she was cutting them all out, that she had learned how to use their weapons; how to give the young man what until now she had not known how to give him: lightheartedness, shamelessness, and dissoluteness; a curious feeling of satisfaction filled her, because she alone had the ability to be all women and in this way (she alone) could completely captivate her lover and hold his interest.

The young man opened the car door and led the girl into the restaurant. Amid the din, the dirt, and the smoke he found a single, unoccupied table in a corner.

VII

"So how are you going to take care of me now?" asked the girl provocatively.

"What would you like for an aperitif?"

The girl wasn't too fond of alcohol, still she drank a little wine and liked vermouth fairly well. Now, however, she purposely said: "Vodka."

"Fine," said the young man. "I hope you won't get drunk on me."

"And if I do?" said the girl.

The young man did not reply but called over a waiter and ordered two vodkas and two steak dinners. In a moment the waiter brought a tray with two small glasses and placed it in front of them.

The man raised his glass, "To you!"

"Can't you think of a wittier toast?"

Something was beginning to irritate him about the girl's game; now sitting face to face with her, he realized that it wasn't just the *words* which were turning her into a stranger, but that her *whole persona* had changed, the movements of her body and her facial expression, and that she unpalatably and faithfully resembled that type of woman whom he knew so well and for whom he felt some aversion.

And so (holding his glass in his raised hand), he corrected his toast: "O.K., then I won't drink to you, but to your kind, in which are combined so successfully the better qualities of the animal and the worse aspects of the human being."

"By 'kind' do you mean all women?" asked the girl.

"No, I mean only those who are like you."

"Anyway it doesn't seem very witty to me to compare a woman with an animal."

"O.K.," the young man was still holding his glass aloft, "then I won't drink to your kind, but to your soul. Agreed? To your soul, which lights up when it descends from your head into your belly, and which goes out when it rises back up to your head."

The girl raised her glass. "O.K., to my soul, which descends into my belly."

"I'll correct myself once more," said the young man. "To your belly, into which your soul descends."

"To my belly," said the girl, and her belly (now that they had named it specifically), as it were, responded to the call; she felt every inch of it.

Then the waiter brought their steaks and the young man ordered them another vodka and some soda water (this time they drank to the girl's breasts), and the conversation continued in this peculiar, frivolous tone. It irritated the young man more and more how *well able* the girl was to become the lascivious miss; if she was able to do it so well, he thought, it meant that she really *was* like that; after all, no alien soul had entered into her from somewhere in space; what she was acting now was she herself, perhaps it was that part of her being which had formerly been locked up and which the pretext of the game had let out of its cage. Perhaps the girl supposed that by means of the game she was *disowning* herself, but wasn't it the other way around? wasn't she becoming herself only through the game? wasn't she freeing herself through the game? no, opposite him was not sitting a strange woman in his girl's body; it was his girl, herself, no one else. He looked at her and felt growing aversion toward her.

However, it was not only aversion. The more the girl withdrew from him *psychically,* the more he longed for her *physically;* the alienation of her soul drew attention to her body; yes it turned her body into a body; as if until now it had been hidden from the young man within clouds of compassion, tenderness, concern, love, and emotion, as if it had been lost in these clouds (yes; as if this body had been *lost!*). It seemed to the young man that today he was *seeing* his girl's body for the first time.

After her third vodka and soda the girl got up and said flirtatiously, "Excuse me."

The young man said, "May I ask you where you are going, miss?"

"To piss, if you'll permit me," said the girl and walked off between the tables back toward the plush screen.

VIII

She was pleased with the way she had astounded the young man with this word, which – in spite of all its innocence – he had never heard from her; nothing seemed to her truer to the character of the woman she was playing than this flirtatious emphasis placed on the word in question; yes, she was pleased, she was in the best of moods; the game captivated her. It allowed her to feel what she had not felt till now: *a feeling of happy-go-lucky irresponsibility.*

She, who was always uneasy in advance about her every next step, suddenly felt completely relaxed. The alien life in which she had become involved was a life without shame, without biographical specifications, without past or future, without obligations; it was a life that was extraordinarily free. The girl, as a hitchhiker, could do anything: *everything was permitted her;* she could say, do, and feel whatever she liked.

She walked through the room and was aware that people were watching her from all the tables; it was also a new sensation, one she didn't recognize: *indecent joy caused by her body.* Until now she had never been able to get rid of the fourteen-year-old girl within herself who was ashamed of her breasts and had the disagreeable feeling that she was indecent, because they stuck out from her body and were visible. Even though she was proud of being pretty and having a good figure, this feeling of pride was always immediately curtailed by shame; she rightly suspected that feminine beauty functioned above all as sexual provocation and she found this distasteful; she longed for her body to relate only to the man she loved; when men stared at her breasts in the street it seemed to her that they were invading a piece of her most secret privacy which should belong only to herself and her lover. But now she was the hitchhiker, the woman without a destiny. In this role she was relieved of the tender bonds of her love and began to be intensely aware of her body; and her body became more aroused the more alien the eyes watching it.

She was walking past the last table when an intoxicated man, wanting to show off his worldliness, addressed her in French: "*Combien, mademoiselle?*"

The girl understood. She thrust out her breasts and fully experienced every movement of her hips, then disappeared behind the screen.

IX

It was a curious game. This curiousness was evidenced, for example, in the fact that the young man, even though he himself was playing the unknown driver remarkably well, did not for a moment stop seeing his girl in the hitchhiker. And it was precisely this that was tormenting; he saw his girl seducing a strange man, and had the bitter privilege of being present, of seeing at close quarters how she looked and of hearing what she said when she was cheating on him (when she had cheated on him, when she would cheat on him); he had the paradoxical honor of being himself the pretext for her unfaithfulness.

This was all the worse because he worshipped rather than loved her; it had always seemed to him that her inward nature was *real* only within the bounds of fidelity and purity, and that beyond these bounds it simply didn't exist; beyond these bounds she would cease to be herself, as water ceases to be water beyond the boiling point. When he now saw her crossing this horrifying boundary with nonchalant elegance, he was filled with anger.

The girl came back from the rest room and complained: "A guy over there asked me: *Combien, mademoiselle?*"

"You shouldn't be surprised," said the young man, "after all, you look like a whore."

"Do you know that it doesn't bother me in the least?"

"Then you should go with the gentleman!"

"But I have you."

"You can go with him after me. Go and work out something with him."

"I don't find him attractive."

"But in principle you have nothing against it, having several men in one night."

"Why not, if they're good-looking."

"Do you prefer them one after the other or at the same time?"

"Either way," said the girl.

The conversation was proceeding to still greater extremes of rudeness; it shocked the girl slightly but she couldn't protest. Even in a game there lurks a lack of freedom; even a game is a trap for the players. If this had not been a game and they had really been two strangers, the hitchhiker could long ago have taken offense and left. But there's no escape from a game. A team cannot flee from the playing field before the end of the match, chess pieces cannot desert the chessboard: the boundaries of the playing field are fixed. The girl knew that she had to accept whatever form the game might take, just because it was a game. She knew that the more extreme the game became, the more it would be a game and the more obediently she would have to play it. And it was futile to evoke good sense and warn her dazed soul that she must keep her distance from the game and not take it seriously. Just because it was only a game her soul was not afraid, did not oppose the game, and narcotically sank deeper into it.

The young man called the waiter and paid. Then he got up and said to the girl, "We're going."

"Where to?" The girl feigned surprise.

"Don't ask, just come on," said the young man.

"What sort of way is that to talk to me?"

"The way I talk to whores," said the young man.

X

They went up the badly lit staircase. On the landing below the second floor a group of intoxicated men was standing near the rest room. The young man caught hold of the girl from behind so that he was holding her breast with his hand. The men by the rest room saw this and began to call out. The girl wanted to break away, but the young man yelled at her: "Keep still!" The men greeted this with general ribaldry and addressed several dirty remarks to the girl. The young man and the girl reached the second floor. He opened the door of their room and switched on the light.

It was a narrow room with two beds, a small table, a chair, and a washbasin. The young man locked the door and turned to the girl. She was standing facing him in a defiant pose with insolent sensuality in her eyes. He looked at her and tried to discover behind her lascivious expression the familiar features which he loved tenderly. It was as if he were looking at two images through the same lens, at two images superimposed one upon the other with the one showing through the other. These two images showing through each other were telling him that *everything* was in the girl, that her soul was terrifyingly amorphous, that it held faithfulness and unfaithfulness, treachery and innocence, flirtatiousness and chastity. This disorderly jumble seemed disgusting to him, like the variety to be found in a pile of garbage. Both images continued to show through each other and the young man understood that the girl differed only on the surface from other women, but deep down was the same as they: full of all possible thoughts, feelings, and vices, which justified all his secret misgivings and fits of jealousy. The impression that certain outlines delineated her as an individual was only a delusion to which the other person, the one who was looking, was subject – namely himself. It seemed to him that the girl he loved was a creation of his desire, his thoughts, and his faith and that the *real* girl now standing in front of him was hopelessly *alien,* hopelessly *ambiguous.* He hated her.

"What are you waiting for? Strip," he said.

The girl flirtatiously bent her head and said, "Is it necessary?"

The tone in which she said this seemed to him very familiar; it seemed to him that once long ago some other woman had said this to him, only he no longer knew which one. He longed to humiliate her. Not the hitchhiker, but his own girl. The game merged with life. The game of humiliating the hitchhiker became only a pretext for humiliating his girl. The young man had forgotten that he was playing a game. He simply hated the woman standing in front of him. He stared at her and took a fifty-crown bill from his wallet. He offered it to the girl. "Is that enough?"

The girl took the fifty crowns and said: "You don't think I'm worth much."

The young man said: "You aren't worth more."

The girl nestled up against the young man. "You can't get around me like that! You must try a different approach, you must work a little!"

She put her arms around him and moved her mouth toward his. He put his fingers on her mouth and gently pushed her away. He said: "I only kiss women I love."

"And you don't love me?"

"No."

"Whom do you love?"

"What's that got to do with you? Strip!"

XI

She had never undressed like this before. The shyness, the feeling of inner panic, the dizziness, all that she had always felt when undressing in front of the young man (and she couldn't hide in the darkness), all this was gone. She was standing in front of him self-confident, insolent, bathed in light, and astonished at where she had all of a sudden discovered the gestures, heretofore unknown to her, of a slow, provocative striptease. She took in his glances, slipping off each piece of clothing with a caressing movement and enjoying each individual stage of this exposure.

But then suddenly she was standing in front of him completely naked and at this moment it flashed through her head that now the whole game would end, that since she had stripped off her clothes, she had also stripped away her dissimulation, and that being naked meant that she was now herself and the young man ought to come up to her now and make a gesture with which he would wipe out everything and after which would follow only their most intimate love-making. So she stood naked in front of the young man and at this moment stopped playing the game. She felt embarrassed and on her face appeared the smile which really belonged to her: a shy and confused smile.

But the young man didn't come to her and didn't end the game. He didn't notice the familiar smile; he saw before him only the beautiful, alien body of his own girl, whom he hated. Hatred cleansed his sensuality of any sentimental coating. She wanted to come to him, but he said: "Stay where you are, I want to have a good look at you." Now he longed only to treat her as a whore. But the young man had never had a whore and the ideas he had about them came from literature and hearsay. So he turned to these ideas and the first thing he recalled was the image of a woman in black underwear (and black stockings) dancing on the shiny top of a piano. In the little hotel room there was no piano, there was only a small table covered with a linen cloth leaning against the wall. He ordered the girl to climb up on it. The girl made a pleading gesture, but the young man said, "You've been paid."

When she saw the look of unshakable obsession in the young man's eyes, she tried to go on with the game, even though she no longer could and no longer knew how. With tears in her eyes she climbed onto the table. The top was scarcely three feet square and one leg was a little bit shorter than the others so that standing on it the girl felt unsteady.

But the young man was pleased with the naked figure, now towering above him, and the girl's shy insecurity merely inflamed his imperiousness. He wanted to see her body in all positions and from all sides, as he imagined other men had seen it and would see it. He was vulgar and lascivious. He used words that she had never heard from him in her life. She wanted to refuse, she wanted to be released from the game. She called him by his first name, but he immediately yelled at her that she had no right to address him so intimately. And so eventually in confusion and on the verge of tears, she obeyed, she bent forward and squatted according to the young man's wishes, saluted, and then wiggled her hips as she did the Twist for him; during a slightly more violent movement, when the cloth slipped beneath her feet and she nearly fell, the young man caught her and dragged her to the bed.

He had intercourse with her. She was glad that at least now finally the unfortunate game would end and they would again be the two people they had been before and would love each other. She wanted to press her mouth against his. But the young man pushed her head away and repeated that he only kissed women he loved. She burst into loud sobs. But she wasn't even allowed to cry, because the young man's furious passion gradually won over her body, which then silenced the complaint of her soul. On the bed there were soon two bodies in perfect harmony, two sensual bodies, alien to each other. This was exactly what the girl had most dreaded all her life and had scrupulously avoided till now: love-making without emotion or love. She knew that she had crossed the forbidden boundary, but she proceeded across it without objections and as a full participant; only somewhere, far off in a corner of her consciousness, did she feel horror at the thought that she had never known such pleasure, never so much pleasure as at this moment – beyond that boundary.

XII

Then it was all over. The young man got up off the girl and, reaching out for the long cord hanging over the bed, switched off the light. He didn't want to see the girl's face. He knew that the game was over, but didn't feel like returning to their customary relationship; he feared this return. He lay beside the girl in the dark in such a way that their bodies would not touch.

After a moment he heard her sobbing quietly; the girl's hand diffidently, childishly touched his; it touched, withdrew, then touched again, and then a pleading, sobbing voice broke the silence, calling him by his name and saying, "I am me, I am me ..."

The young man was silent, he didn't move, and he was aware of the sad emptiness of the girl's assertion, in which the unknown was defined by the same unknown.

And the girl soon passed from sobbing to loud crying and went on endlessly repeating this pitiful tautology: "I am me, I am me, I am me ..."

The young man began to call compassion to his aid (he had to call it from afar, because it was nowhere near at hand), so as to be able to calm the girl. There were still thirteen days' vacation before them.

Translated by
Suzanne Rappaport

D. H. LAWRENCE

ONCE—!

The literary exploration of the subject of love was Lawrence's great purpose. His father, a miner, never understood him; his mother, a retired school-teacher, granted him respect but never read him. The first copy of his novel The White Peacock *he himself put in his mother's hands as she lay dying. "She looked at the outside, and then at the title-page, and then at me, with darkening eyes," Lawrence recalled. "And though she loved me so much, I think she doubted whether it could be much of a book, since no one more important than I had written it."*

Later, after the funeral, Lawrence's father struggled through half a page, "and it might as well have been Hottentot."

"And what did they gie thee for that, lad?"

"Fifty pounds, father."

"Fifty pounds!" He was dumbfounded, and looked at me with shrewd eyes, as if I were a swindler. "Fifty pounds!

An' th's niver done a day's hard work in thy life."

In the spring of 1912 Lawrence and Frieda Weekley, the wife of Professor Ernest Weekley, ran away to Germany together to begin a relationship that was to last the rest of his life. That August Lawrence wrote a number of short stories, among them "Once – !," probably based on Frieda's younger sister, Anita.

THE MORNING was very beautiful. White packets of mist hung over the river, as if a great train had gone by leaving its steam idle, in a trail down the valley. The mountains were just faint grey-blue, with the slightest glitter of snow high up in the sunshine. They seemed to be standing a long way off, watching me, and wondering. As I bathed in the shaft of sunshine that came through the wide-opened window, letting the water slip swiftly down my sides, my mind went wandering through the hazy morning, very sweet and far-off and still, so that I had hardly wit enough to dry myself. And as soon as I had got on my dressing gown, I lay down again idly on the bed, looking out at the morning that still was greenish from the dawn, and thinking of Anita.

I had loved her when I was a boy. She was an aristocrat's daughter, but she was not rich. I was simply middle-class. Then, I was much too green and humble-minded to think of making love to her. No sooner had she come home from school than she married an officer. He was rather handsome, something in the Kaiser's fashion, but stupid as an ass. And Anita was only eighteen. When at last she accepted me as a lover, she told me about it.

"The night I was married," she said, "I lay counting the flowers on the wall-paper, how many on a string; he bored me so."

He was of good family, and of great repute in the army, being a worker. He had the tenacity of a bull-dog, and rode like a centaur. These things look well from a distance, but to live with they weary one beyond endurance, so Anita says.

She had her first child just before she was twenty: two years afterwards, another. Then no more. Her husband was something of a brute. He neglected her, though not outrageously, treated her as if she were a fine animal. To complete matters, he more than ruined himself owing to debts, gambling and otherwise, then utterly disgraced himself by using government money and being caught.

"You have found a hair in your soup," I wrote to Anita.

"Not a hair, a whole plait," she replied.

After that, she began to have lovers. She was a splendid young creature, and was not going to sit down in her rather elegant flat in Berlin, to run to seed. Her husband was officer in a crack regiment. Anita was superb to look at. He was proud to introduce her to his friends. Then moreover she had her own relatives in Berlin, aristocratic but also rich, and moving in the first society. So she began to take lovers.

Anita shows her breeding: erect, rather haughty, with a good-humoured kind of scorn. She is tall and strong, her brown eyes are full of scorn, and she has a downy, warm-coloured skin, brownish to match her black hair.

At last she came to love me a little. Her soul is unspoiled. I think she has almost the soul of a virgin. I think, perhaps, it frets her that she has never really loved. She has never had the real respect – Ehrfurcht – for a man. And she has been here with me in the Tyrol these last ten days. I love her, and I am not satisfied with myself. Perhaps I too shall fall short.

"You have never *loved* your men?" I asked her.

"I loved them – but I have put them all in my pocket," she said, with just the faintest disappointment in her good-humour. She shrugged her shoulders at my serious gaze.

I lay wondering if I too were going into Anita's pocket, along with her purse and her perfume and the little sweets she loved. It would almost have been delicious to do so. A kind of voluptuousness urged me to let her have me, to let her put me in her pocket. It would be so nice. But I loved her: it would not be fair to her: I wanted to do more than give her pleasure.

Suddenly the door opened on my musing, and Anita came into my bedroom. Startled, I laughed in my very soul, and I adored her, she was so natural. She was dressed in a transparent lacy chemise, that was slipping over her shoulder, high boots, upon one of which her string-coloured stocking had fallen, and she wore an enormous hat, black, lined with white, and covered with a tremendous creamy-brown feather, that streamed like a flood of brownish foam, swaying lightly. It was an immense hat on top of her shamelessness, and the great, soft feather seemed to spill over, fall with a sudden gush, as she put back her head.

She looked at me, then went straight to the mirror.

"How do you like my hat?" she said.

She stood before the panel of looking glass, conscious only of her hat, whose great feather-strands swung in a tide. Her bare shoulder glistened, and through the fine web of her chemise, I could see all her body in warm silhouette, with golden reflections under the breasts and arms. The light ran in silver up her lifted arms, and the gold shadow stirred as she arranged her hat.

"How do you like my hat?" she repeated.

Then, as I did not answer, she turned to look at me. I was still lying on the bed. She must have seen that I had looked at her, instead of at her hat, for a quick darkness and a frown came into her eyes, cleared instantly, as she asked, in a slightly hard tone:

"Don't you like it?"

"It's rather splendid," I answered. "Where did it come from?"

"From Berlin this morning – or last evening," she replied.

"It's a bit huge," I ventured.

She drew herself up.

"Indeed not!" she said, turning to the mirror.

I got up, dropped off my dressing gown, put a silk hat quite correctly on my head, and then, naked save for a hat and a pair of gloves, I went forward to her.

"How do you like my hat?" I asked her.

She looked at me and went off into a fit of laughter. She dropped her hat onto a chair, and sank onto the bed, shaking with laughter. Every now and then she lifted her head, gave one look from her dark eyes, then buried her face in the pillows. I stood before her clad in my hat, feeling a good bit of a fool. She peeped up again.

"You are lovely, you are lovely!" she cried.

With a grave and dignified movement I prepared to remove the hat, saying:

"And even then, I lack high-laced boots and one stocking."

But she flew at me, kept the hat on my head, and kissed me.

"Don't take it off," she implored. "I love you for it."

So I sat down gravely and unembarrassed on the bed.

"But don't you like my hat?" I said in injured tones. "I bought it in London last month."

She looked up at me comically, and went into peals of laughter.

"Think," she cried, "if all those Englishmen in Piccadilly went like that!"

That amused even me.

At last I assured her her hat was adorable, and, much to my relief, I got rid of my silk and into a dressing gown.

"You *will* cover yourself up," she said reproachfully. "And you look so nice with nothing on – but a hat."

"It's that old Apple I can't digest," I said.

She was quite happy in her shift and her high boots. I lay looking at her beautiful legs.

"How many more men have you done that to?" I asked.

"What?" she answered.

"Gone into their bedrooms clad in a wisp of mist, trying a new hat on?"

She leaned over to me and kissed me.

"Not many," she said. "I've not been *quite* so familiar before, I don't think."

"I suppose you've forgotten," said I. "However, it doesn't

matter." Perhaps the slight bitterness in my voice touched her. She said almost indignantly:

"Do you think I want to flatter you and make you believe you are the first that ever I really – *really* –"

"I don't," I replied. "Neither you nor I is so easily deluded."

She looked at me peculiarly and steadily.

"I know all the time," said I, "that I am 'pro tem.', and that I shan't even last as long as most."

"You are sorry for yourself?" she mocked.

I shrugged my shoulders, looking into her eyes. She caused me a good deal of agony, but I didn't give in to her.

"I shan't commit suicide," I replied.

"'On est mort pour si longtemps'," she said, suddenly dancing on the bed. I loved her. She had the courage to live, almost joyously.

"When you think back over your affairs – they are numerous, though you are only thirty-one –"

"Not numerous – only several – and you *do* underline the thirty-one –," she laughed.

"But how do you feel, when you think of them?" I asked.

She knitted her eyebrows quaintly, and there was a shadow, more puzzled than anything, on her face.

"There is something nice in all of them," she said. "Men are really fearfully good," she sighed.

"If only they weren't all pocket-editions," I mocked.

She laughed, then began drawing the silk cord through the lace of her chemise, pensively. The round cap of her shoulder gleamed like old ivory: there was a faint brown stain towards the arm-pit.

"No," she said, suddenly lifting her head and looking me calmly into the eyes, "I have nothing to be ashamed of – that is, – no, I have nothing to be ashamed of!"

"I believe you," I said. "And I don't suppose you've done anything that even *I* shouldn't be able to swallow – have you –?"

I felt rather plaintive with my question. She looked at me and shrugged her shoulders.

"I know you haven't," I preached. "All your affairs have been rather decent. They've meant more to the men than they have to you."

The shadows of her breasts, fine globes, shone warm through the linen veil. She was thinking.

"Shall I tell you," she asked, "one thing I did?"

"If you like," I answered. "But let me get you a wrap." I kissed her shoulder. It had the same fine, delicious coldness of ivory.

"No – yes you may," she replied.

I brought her a Chinese thing of black silk with gorgeous embroidered dragons, green as flame, writhing upon it.

"How white against that black silk you are," I said, kissing the half globe of her breast, through the linen.

"Lie there," she commanded me. She sat in the middle of the bed, whilst I lay looking at her. She picked up the black silk tassel of my dressing gown, and began flattening it out like a daisy.

"Gretchen!" I said.

"'Marguerite with one petal,'" she answered in French, laughing. "I am ashamed of it, so you must be nice with me –"

"Have a cigarette!" I said.

She puffed wistfully for a few moments.

"You've got to hear it," she said.

"Go on!"

"I was staying in Dresden in quite a grand hôtel; – which I rather enjoy: ringing bells, dressing three times a day, feeling half a great lady, half a cocotte. Don't be cross with me for saying it: look at me! The man was at a garrison a little way off. I'd have married him if I could –"

She shrugged her brown, handsome shoulders, and puffed out a plume of smoke.

"It began to bore me after three days. I was always alone, looking at shops alone, going to the opera alone – where the beastly men got behind their wives' backs to look at me. In the end I got cross with my poor man, though of course it wasn't his fault, that he couldn't come."

She gave a little laugh as she took a draw at her cigarette.

"The fourth morning I came downstairs – I was feeling fearfully good-looking and proud of myself. I know I had a sort of café au lait coat and skirt, very pale – and its fit was a *joy*!"

After a pause, she continued: "– And a big black hat with a cloud of white ospreys. I nearly jumped when a man almost ran into me. O jeh!, it was a young officer, just bursting with life, a splendid creature: the German aristocrat at his best. He wasn't over tall, in his dark blue uniform, but simply firm with life. An electric shock went through me, it slipped down me like fire, when I looked into his eyes. O jeh!, they just flamed with consciousness of me – And they were just the same colour as the soft-blue revers of his uniform. He looked at me – ha! – and then, he bowed, the sort of bow a woman enjoys, like a caress.

"'Verzeihung, gnädiges Fräulein!'

"I just inclined my head, and we went our ways. It felt as if something mechanical shifted us, not our wills.

"I was restless that day, I could stay nowhere. Something stirred inside my veins. I was drinking tea on the Brühler Terrasse, watching the people go by like a sort of mechanical procession, and the broad Elbe as a stiller background, when he stood before me, saluting, and taking a seat, half apologetically, half devil-may-care. I was not nearly so much surprised at him, as at the mechanical parading people. And I could see he thought me a Cocotte –"

She looked thoughtfully across the room, the past roused dangerously in her dark eyes.

"But the game amused and excited me. He told me he had to go to a Court ball tonight and then he said, in his nonchalant yet pleadingly passionate way:

"'And afterwards –?'

"'And afterwards –!' I repeated.

"'May I –?' he asked.

"Then I told him the number of my room.

"I dawdled to the hôtel, and dressed for dinner, and talked to somebody sitting next to me, but I was an hour or two ahead, when he would come. I arranged my silver and brushes and things, and I had ordered a great bunch of lilies of the valley; they were in a black bowl. There were delicate pink silk curtains, and the carpet was a cold colour, nearly white, with a tawny pink and turquoise ravelled border, a Persian thing, I should imagine. I know I liked it. – And didn't that room feel fresh, full of expectation, like myself!

"That last half hour of waiting – so funny – I seemed to have no feeling, no consciousness. I lay in the dark, holding my nice pale blue gown of crêpe de chine against my body for comfort. There was a fumble at the door, and I caught my breath. Quickly he came in, locked the door, and switched on all the lights. There he stood, the centre of everything, the light shining on his bright brown hair. He was holding something under his cloak. Now he came to me, and threw on me from out of his cloak a whole armful of red and pink roses. It was delicious! Some of them were cold, when they fell on me. He took off his cloak: I loved his figure in its blue uniform, and then, oh jeh!, he picked me off the bed, the roses and all, and kissed me – *how* he kissed me!"

She paused at the recollection.

"I could feel his mouth through my thin gown. Then, he went still and intense. He pulled off my saut-de-lit, and looked at me. He held me away from him, his mouth parted with wonder, and yet, as if the Gods would envy him – wonder and adoration and pride! I liked his worship. Then he laid me on the bed again, and covered me up gently, and put my roses on the other side of me, a heap just near my hair, on the pillow.

"Quite unashamed and not the least conscious of himself, he got out of his clothes. And he *was* adorable – so young, and rather spare, but with a *rich* body, that simply glowed with love of me. He stood looking at me, quite humbly; and I held out my hands to him.

"All that night we loved each other. There were crushed, crumpled little rose-leaves on him when he sat up, almost like crimson blood! Oh and he was fierce, and at the same time, tender –!"

Anita's lips trembled slightly, and she paused. Then, very slowly, she went on:

"When I woke in the morning he was gone, and just a few passionate words on his dancing-card with a gold crown, on the little table beside me, imploring me to see him again in the Brühler Terrasse in the afternoon. But I took the morning express to Berlin –"

We both were still. The river rustled far off in the morning.

"And –?" I said.

"And I never saw him again –"

We were both still. She put her arms round her bright knee, and caressed it, lovingly, rather plaintively, with her mouth. The brilliant green dragons on her wrap seemed to be snarling at me.

"And you regret him?" I said at length.

"No," she answered, scarcely heeding me. – "I remember the way he unfastened his sword-belt and trappings from his loins, flung the whole with a jingle on the other bed –"

I was burning now with rage against Anita. Why should she love a man for the way he unbuckled his belt!

"With him," she mused, "everything felt so inevitable."

"Even your never seeing him again," I retorted.

"Yes!" she said, quietly.

Still musing, dreaming, she continued to caress her own knees.

"He said to me, 'We are like the two halves of a walnut.'"

And she laughed slightly.

"He said some lovely things to me. – 'Tonight, you're an Answer.' And then 'Whichever bit of you I touch, seems to startle me afresh with joy.' And he said, he should never forget the velvety feel of my skin. – Lots of beautiful things he told me."

Anita cast them over pathetically in her mind. I sat biting my finger with rage.

"– And I made him have roses in his hair. He sat so still and good while I trimmed him up, and was quite shy. He had a figure nearly like yours –."

Which compliment was a last insult to me.

"– And he had a long gold chain, threaded with little emeralds, that he wound round and round my knees, binding me like a prisoner, never thinking."

"And you wish he had kept you prisoner," I said.

"No," she answered. "He couldn't!"

"I see! You just preserve him as the standard by which you measure the amount of satisfaction you get from the rest of us."

"Yes," she said, quietly.

Then I knew she was liking to make me furious.

"But I thought you were rather ashamed of the adventure?" I said.

"No," she answered, perversely.

She made me tired. One could never be on firm ground with her. Always, one was slipping and plunging on uncertainty. I lay still, watching the sunshine streaming white outside.

"What are you thinking?" she asked.

"The waiter will smile when we go down for coffee."

"No – tell me!"

"It is half past nine."

She fingered the string of her shift.

"What were you thinking?" she asked, very low.

"I was thinking, all you want, you get."

"In what way?"

"In love."

"And what do I want?"

"Sensation."

"Do I?"

"Yes."

She sat with her head drooped down.

"Have a cigarette," I said. "And are you going to that place for sleighing today?"

"Why do you say I only want sensation?" she asked quietly.

"Because it's all you'll take from a man. – You *won't* have a cigarette?"

"No thanks – and what else could I take –?"

I shrugged my shoulders.

"Nothing, I suppose –" I replied.

Still she picked pensively at her chemise string.

"Up to now, you've missed nothing – you haven't felt the lack of anything – in love," I said.

She waited awhile.

"Oh yes I have," she said gravely.

Hearing her say it, my heart stood still.

WENDY LAW-YONE

DROUGHT

The wounded knight tended to by his lady is an ancient story, so ancient that it can be already parodied in Don Quixote. *Warrior and maiden – Tancred and Erminia; soldier and nurse – Frederic Henry and Catherine Barkley; the story crosses the conventions of the times and resurfaces again and again, perhaps because the sick or wounded body is more vulnerable and therefore more attractive to a dominant lover, perhaps because it symbolizes the archetypical struggle between the healing forces of love and the weakening forces of death, perhaps because it simply allows a dramatic moment for literary amorous exchange. Also, traditionally love is a sickness, and the ailing lover must be cured by the same beloved who is the sickness's cause.*

Aware of this ancestry, Wendy Law-Yone has chosen for her story a conventional setting, the tropical jungle, in which East meets West. The originality of her story "Drought" is therefore not in the trappings but in the melancholy tone and in the surprising erotic encounter itself.

IT WAS WARTIME, with its crazy misplaced fears – a time when suddenly it wasn't the bloodshed I dreaded as much as drought.

Maybe it was the Red Reservoir incident that sparked these new threats. In the north, where the fighting was fiercest, the rebels had run amok and wiped out an entire European compound, hacking up the bodies of the whites and throwing the parts into the private reservoir until the water turned red. It must have been the rumors that followed – rumors about poisoned wells and severed water lines – that brought on my nightmares about a water crisis.

But as though in a rush to make the nightmares come true, I became wasteful, not sparing, with water – especially once Auntie was gone and I was left alone with him. Amazing, how quickly I took to stripping and washing him as I pleased, using up water heedlessly. And to think how scared I'd been at first: scared to touch, even to look at him.

A white man! In those days – the early days of the Liberation – we all knew what they were doing to the whites on the mainland. We'd all heard about the Red Reservoir. Things were different, of course, on our island, where no one seemed to feel strongly about whites, or about much else. Still, the war had spread to other islands in the archipelago, and some said it was just a matter of time before we too would be caught up in it.

But I was afraid for another reason. I couldn't cast off the uneasy sense that I'd somehow caused an accident to happen.

Because I'd seen it happen. Standing on the veranda that morning, I had watched the plane go down. I didn't know it was a plane, then. It looked like a hawk, diving and disappearing in a flash from its straight-arrow course. The crash was that silent and graceful and swift. In the split moment before the sudden dive, I foresaw the whole thing. *Fall!* I'd said to myself even. And – just like that – the hawk had fallen.

I gave it no more thought until hours later, when they brought the survivor to our bungalow. It was only then that I put it all together. That hawk had been a small plane plunging headlong somewhere into the rubber plantations.

They carried him in on a makeshift bamboo stretcher. Our bungalow was on the hill overlooking the *kampong,* the village, below. From the veranda I could see the small procession snake up along the path that led from the plantations past the *kampong* – and through the gates at the foot of the hill.

"He fell out of the sky!" one of the *kampong* boys was shouting. "Like a god!"

They set him down underneath the monsoon-flower tree. He might well have been a god – large and dead to the world, but radiant. The tree was in full flower – a sign that the monsoons were close – and gold blossoms hung in clusters above him like ceremonial lanterns. His hair was gold too, though darker than the flowers; very thick and straight. A slight breeze plowed this way and that, revealing bits of scalp that looked as tender as wounds. He was wearing a short-sleeved khaki jacket – the kind with many pockets – and khaki shorts. In the glow of the flowering lanterns he shimmered all over as though dusted with mica or powdered glass.

I felt unworthy, staring at such radiance.

The man in charge of the rescue – a fast-talking Chinaman – explained things to Auntie, who was playing deaf. Her face was clenched; it was her ploy when things got difficult. And here was a difficult situation suddenly – an accident involving a white man at a time when whites were being slaughtered in the north. Not to mention all her other worries about the war.

The Chinaman was almost shouting, annoyed at having to repeat himself. The man lying unconscious on the stretcher was someone important, he kept saying. An adviser. He had flown in to help out the local militia. The Chinaman seemed to be implying that it was our duty – Auntie's and mine – to take him in. I understood why. I was the only half-caste in the area, the only blood relation to the stranger, so to speak. Naturally, they'd bring the European to our bungalow and expect us to lodge him.

"Bring him inside; you can leave him here," Auntie said at last, pointing her chin at me to indicate I should show them the way. I knew from the chin that she blamed me for this burden.

The men picked up the stretcher and followed me inside. I led them to my room. I turned down the thin blanket covering the thin mattress, and as they half-lifted, half-tilted him onto it, the jolting thought crossed my mind that maybe this was my father, come in search of me – although in the next instant I knew of course it couldn't be.

When the men had left, Auntie stood in the doorway, keeping her distance, while I looked the stranger over. A discolored swelling at the side of a knee and a cut at the temple above the right ear – the source of dried blood along one cheek – seemed to be the worst of his visible wounds.

Auntie felt I should try to wake him. This required my touching him. I put my palm down on the slight frown creasing his brow. How dark and dull the back of my hand appeared next to the pale gleam of his hair! I shook his shoulders and even slapped his cheeks. "Harder," Auntie said, quite spitefully I thought. I shook harder but couldn't bring myself to slap harder. Every smack left a stripe on his skin. Some time later, he did move an arm and a leg as though in the course of normal sleep – and by the time the doctor came, there were other small improvements: he stirred, he twitched, he turned from side to side in a delirium, he even opened his eyes for brief periods; and when I lifted his head to feed him the first spoonful of rice porridge, he swallowed. But mostly he slept.

The doctor was an old Moslem with a limp and a wheeze. With the war going on, doctors were scarce and getting pressed into service even in the islands. This old man had made the hike from the southern end and looked ready to pass out from the exertion. He put one hand on the patient's chest, tapped it with his other hand, bent the patient's elbows and knees, stuck a thermometer under his armpit, pried his eyelids apart. (Once more I was struck by the expensive color of those eyes, the color of a ring I'd seen on a Chinese merchant. A pale sapphire.)

"Coma," the doctor pronounced at last, scratching absently at the mold on his stethoscope.

"Coma?" Auntie said. "But he wakes up sometimes. He even takes soft rice."

"Sort of coma," the old man said. He handed Auntie a bottle of Gripe Water, usually prescribed for baby's wind. When she asked about the dosage, he hedged. "As needed," he said. "But not too often." He went down the stairs uncertainly, clutching the stair rail with something like panic.

In the beginning it was Auntie who decided what had to be done. *Give him a spoonful of coconut juice. Now wait. Now try a spoonful of rice. Now turn him on his side. Fold the rubber sheet under him. Now turn him back this way. Unfold the sheet from behind. Get the cloth and the basin.* She looked on squeamishly while giving the orders. But she wouldn't touch him.

And why should she? For as long as I could remember, she'd spoken of white men as an unsavory breed. They were bullies, always taking, always wanting more; they were liars, saying one thing, meaning quite another, telling the truth only if the truth was what it took to get them their way. And they were smelly.

In fact there was only one European she had known up close: my father. But the mark he left was enough to stain a race, apparently.

The thing he'd done was to leave my mother pregnant with me, forcing her into service with his lies. Lies about taking her back with him to a place called Antwerp, then – as he took off, solo – more lies about sending for her later, after he was settled.

My mother was not an island girl. Her home was on the mainland, in the dry zone, where her father worked in the oil fields run by Dutchmen like my father. It was only after my father went away that she came to this island – where Auntie, her sister, lived – to have her baby.

I was not yet weaned when she left me in a wicker basket on the floor one full-moon night to drown herself in the sea.

But along with Auntie's rancor I sensed a grudging pride in my half-white origins. "Mixed!" she crowed, when anyone remarked on my volume of curly hair. And the books were another concession. It was only English and Dutch that she wanted me to read.

It wasn't the first time I'd had an invalid on my hands. It was less than two years before that Auntie's father, Old Papu, had required around-the-clock care in the last bedridden months of his life. I had the night shift then (Auntie having collapsed for the day) and had got used to the bedpan and other unpleasant intimacies.

But this one was different. Even in his wakeful states, he wasn't alert enough to cooperate except to open his mouth for feedings or move his limbs for changings. Nor was feeding him always successful. Auntie's close watch didn't make things any easier. And just sponging him was an ordeal that put me in a sweat, though I was generally on my own for that – Auntie didn't care to supervise.

But things did get easier with practice. I learned what to do about the messes (I'd even rigged a sort of loincloth that made the cleanup easier); and I became more adept at feeding and sponging.

The spongings were partial and routine at that point. And necessary. Despite the promise of the monsoon-flower trees, the rains still hadn't arrived and the heat festered and itched like a boil about to burst. Inside, even with all the windows open, the occasional cross breeze blew in a hot vapor that caused the floorboards to steam. Outside, the heat hit you with a force that took the breath away.

I was beginning to understand what Auntie meant about the European body odor. Strong and sour, it smelled like fermenting palm toddy. Even if you liked the smell of toddy, as I did, it wasn't something you could let run rampant.

The hotter it got, the more spongings were called for. By the time Auntie left for her monthly shop on the mainland, the rains were long overdue and the heat had become so intolerable that I was relieved to be able to swab him off at will, unobserved, with a frequency that might have alarmed her.

In truth I could hardly wait for her to leave. No sooner had she caught the ferry than I got down to business. I filled the zinc basin with warm water and brought it, with the washcloth, to his bedside. Early on, I had taken off his clothes – the khaki shorts and shirt – and replaced them with one of Papu's old sarongs, leaving it loose, like a sheet, around his middle. It made the cleaning and changing easier. I took the sarong off now and saw for the first time what he looked like, lying there on the rubber sheet, stripped utterly naked.

Huge. And very hairy. Tangled skeins of gold thread covered his chest, belly, arms, and legs; the threads were darker in the armpits and darkest at the crotch, forming a thick nest there, around the most startling part of his body. Unlike Old Papu's privates, shriveled and discolored all over like fruit gone bad, his seemed to blossom firm and ripe, with a good healthy color to the skin: thick through the scrotum but so fine on the penis that the veins showed up like lines drawn in ink.

A thorough soap and scrub was what I had planned. Auntie

was gone, I was alone, and it was safe. But just standing over his exposed body, free to inspect any and all parts to satisfaction – just taking that secret liberty put me in a state. What if he came to, and his blue eyes were to shed their confusion and turn like searchlights on me?

I gave him the sponging; I even took care not to avoid the nest. But I didn't linger; I went about it as always – briskly, hardly looking, almost entirely by feel.

Auntie was to have returned on the last ferry late that evening. When the boat arrived, letting off its few passengers, and she wasn't among them, I knew something serious had happened. With the war getting closer – now we could hear the crackle of gunfire across the waves – she'd been overly anxious about leaving me even for the day. She would hardly have wanted me to spend the night alone.

I went home to wait. I thought of going down to the *kampong,* but soon it was dark and I was afraid – though not because I felt unsafe. No one in the *kampong* would have touched me – not even the older boys who came back to visit from their mainland jobs. One of them – a mocker and a strutter with too much coconut oil in his hair – once told me the reason why.

"Don't worry," he'd said when I mentioned my fear of taking the road to the *kampong* in the dark. "No one would dare touch you."

"I'm not that great," I said, thinking he was flattering me.

"Not that great, no," he laughed. "I mean no one would touch you because you're cursed."

I sat on the front steps looking down at the swarm of flickering lights in the *kampong,* waiting for my aunt long after I knew it was too late to expect her that night. When the lights were snuffed out one by one, I went inside to Auntie's room where I had slept on a bedroll on the floor since the day of the crash, when I'd given up my bed to the man in it now. With Auntie gone I lay on her bed, not bothering with the bedroll. The *kampong* noises had died down for the night; the palm trees rattled, but gently, in the breeze that had picked up finally after the breathless heat of the day. Still, it was not a night for sleep. I got up and went into my room, where the large, motionless figure filled my bed. Moonlight flooded through the open window and turned the hair on his head and chest to phosphorescence, like the surf on certain nights.

I sat at the foot of the bed, weary but bolt awake. The moon made me think of my mother. It was on a night like this that she had walked into the sea. Auntie had told me a story that came back to me now.

When my mother was pregnant, there was a drought in the dry zone, where the oil fields were concentrated, and where she kept house for my father at the time. It was the worst water shortage in years, and even the Europeans were under ration. That's when the first of the strikes began in the refineries, followed by the riots. In the turmoil of the next days the faucets in the European quarter were stone dry, and even the odd water-seller was nowhere in sight.

My mother had saved just enough drinking water to last a few days.

"For three days she took just enough from the canteen to moisten her lips," said Auntie. "While your father guzzled, thoughtless. And there she was, a child in her belly, herself not much more than a child. Later, when he went off and left her, she told me about the drought. I yelled at her. 'Stupid thing! Suppose the drought had gone on? What then?'

"Then, she said, she would have cut open a piece of her flesh to give him her blood to drink."

My mother – dead at sixteen – must have been exactly my age at the time of the drought. And my father? How old was he then? The same age, could it be, as this wounded man lying in front of me? "How old are you?" I whispered, although there was no need to. Suddenly, the moonlight felt cold on my skin, and my head swam from fatigue. I lay alongside him, pressing myself very close. After a while I loosened the sarong around his waist and crawled in until we lay side by side, cocooned.

I woke with the sun in my eyes and a bitter taste in my parched mouth. I had been dreaming of drought. The rebels, in the dream, had cut the water lines, and I was stranded on a beach, gagging on mouthfuls of saltwater.

My head was still on his chest. My neck was stiff, and when I started to rub it I found my fingers were wet. But what from? I swept my hand down across his belly – and there near his crotch was the wet patch. The moisture trailed out of the tip of his sex which lay horizontally – fuller than I remembered – across his thigh. I touched the moisture, which was clear and a little slippery. There was no odor to it. But it tasted slightly salty.

Someone from the *kampong,* one of the headman's sons, brought me the news about Auntie later that day. On the mainland, where she had been shopping, the police had made a sweep, arresting people by the lorry load. She was among those detained.

Detained. What did that mean, exactly? How long would

they keep her? The headman's son couldn't tell me. "Not too long," he said, vague like the doctor. But the next bit of news hit me even harder.

"How's the Tuan?" he asked, cocking his head in the direction of my bedroom. I had forgotten that he was one of the men present on the day of the crash – was it just two weeks ago?

"Better," I lied, "much better." That wasn't a lie exactly. At least he had come to; at least we could feed him; at least he was alive.

"Not to worry!" said the headman's son; "day-after-tomorrow they're coming to take him to hospital."

The news made me dizzy, and for a moment I couldn't see straight. Looking over the shoulder of the man facing me, I fancied that the thin palm trees beyond were growing at even crazier angles than the ones along the beach, where they were almost horizontal.

"He's not ready!" I almost cried out, but knew better. The man would have wondered.

I wasn't ready. I wanted to keep him with me, as he was, without improvement if necessary. Once he was gone, nothing would stand between me and the void just waiting to swallow me whole. War would come to our island, I had no doubt of that now. The streams would run red, just like that reservoir up north. My aunt – like my mother, like my father – would never come back for me. And there would be a drought.

Just two more days! I couldn't leave his side. I couldn't bear it. Nothing seemed pressing anymore save the need, the urgent need, to hold him hostage. I didn't neglect to feed him the boiled rice – or to sustain myself on the remains. I didn't neglect the spongings, either. Nothing else mattered to me. Nothing.

When night came I got into bed with him, crawling into his sarong once more. I wanted rest but not sleep. Yet it was hard to fight the drowsiness brought on by the steady shushing of the sea. Trying to stay awake, I rummaged between his legs. Almost immediately, my fingers were wet.

By daylight, when I could see, all I wanted was to keep the liquid flowing – the little bit of liquid that emerged bead by bead at the nick of the crown on his mushroom-shaped sex. The first time I bent over to taste it at the source, I did it with utmost care, as though licking nectar off a thorn. But soon I grew reckless from a kind of greed, kneeling to face him as I continued the milking. I'd never known such power over another being – there he was, at my feet, exposed, unknowing, wholly at my mercy. So what if his eyes flared open without warning, and he watched me with that roaming gaze, a gaze less than pleasurable, less than human really? So what if he made those gargling noises? It would have taken a lot more to wrest me from my task, my dogged extraction of the juice that kept coming – only by the eyedropperful, it's true; but the miracle was that it kept coming.

No sooner had I licked up a droplet than another would seep through the nick in that tender flesh like a runnel of sap. A little kneading, a little rubbing, and out it oozed. Was it the slight saltiness that set off the thirst in me – a thirst that drink alone couldn't slake? Again and again I got up from bed for air. And for endless sips of water. I gave him to drink too – the thirst had seized him as well for all I knew: his lips were dry and white at the corners. No, I didn't deprive him. I even remembered to feed him his rice, a mouthful or two at a time. But being on my feet was a strain. Lightheaded, heavy-footed, I moved as in a delirium, craving only to return to bed, and to that little spot of moisture seeping through his sex. That was what gave me satisfaction. That. Not the tepid, tasteless water I drank and drank.

Is it surprising that by now I was rubbing between my own legs as well, in rhythm with the steady tapping of his sap? Pleasuring myself was hardly new to me. Maybe if things had been different, if someone – anyone – in the *kampong* had dared touch me, I might not yet have learned to touch myself so capably. But no one did; and so I did. How many times had I stood squarely in front of the window of my room, fingering myself with my sarong hitched up in front, while an unsuspecting male, the object of my heated fancy, went about his business in the *kampong* below! Even when they – for there were many such males – happened to look up and catch me framed at the window, whatever they saw of me from the chest up revealed nothing of how I busied myself below the window line. Skinny boys in their teens, paunchy men – I wasn't choosy about these targets. Once, it was an old Hindu in a ragged loincloth, bending over to stack cordwood. That time I was somewhat more ashamed than usual afterward. But shame is not unlike a lump of ice: painful to swallow, but only for a stinging instant. Then it melts, it goes away.

Given what I knew already, it wasn't so hard to finger myself with one hand, coaxing the drip out of him with the other – while also managing to lick. All the while I marveled at the slick rosy tip of his strange, strange growth, rubber-soft the one minute and hard enough the next so that the veins beat against my fingertips. At last my licking gave way to outright sucking, in time to the sucking that pulsed between my legs just before the long tremor kicked in.

By night I was wild with abandon. I shed all my clothes – a thing I'd never done in his presence – dropping my sarong on top of his, which lay on the floor, in a coil, where I'd flung it. I bent down to look into his face and saw that his eyes were open, fixed just past me with the shock of a man gazing at a ghost. Was it my hair, I wondered – my neglected mass of frizz? He closed his eyes then, as though to shut out the disturbing vision, whatever it was.

I got up onto the bed and knelt beside him, facing his feet. The air in the room was so warm and close that I could smell my own sweat – a sour, sickly smell – along with the familiar fumes given off by his body. It felt no different from a fever – the sweating, the shortness of breath, the thirst. Naturally, I went for the liquid. Like the water I squandered while fearing drought, I kept returning to this salty, thirst-making moisture to quench my thirst.

As I squatted over him on the bed, facing his feet and bending over to drink at the source, I happened to lower my crotch onto his hand, which lay with its fingers curled, palm up, by his side. That touch, so slight, grazed me to the quick, and all I had to do – without interrupting the sucking – was to rock back and forth, back and forth, over his open hand while I climbed to that edge from which the body aches to plummet. I plummeted. I shot forward until my head came to rest at his feet. After a while I turned around and nuzzled his hand, only to discover a slickness on his fingers, so like the slickness on mine. Did our liquids also taste alike?

They did. I wanted him to taste them both. I wiped his wet hand on one of my breasts and brought that nipple up to his mouth, where I pressed it against his lips. Then I lowered my other breast down to the moisture at the tip of his sex, rubbing it around before doing what I'd done with the other breast.

The thirst was so acute now I could barely swallow. I placed my mouth over his, probing deep with my tongue – over and under his, all along his teeth, between his gums and lips. His breath was musty, his taste sour-sweet. The combination made my mouth water. I went for his ears now, first one and then the other, licking along the curves and dents and into the hole, to fetch up the bitterish taste of wax. I moved down to the armpits, burying my nose in the pungent thicket of hair; down over his chest and belly to lick his navel; and down into the depths of his genitals.

I'd never stopped to lick the sac before. I trailed my tongue over it now, over the ridged hairy skin, before lifting it to lick under as well, down the line running into his crack. I stopped at its rim, to catch my breath; then, lifting his legs at the knees, parting the cheeks, I plunged my tongue right down into the recess, as deep as it would go.

A dark bitter taste exploded through my palate; the taste of a poisonous plant, perhaps – some wild, inedible onion. The discovery was dizzying. I wanted to subject him to something comparable. That's when I moved up to straddle his face. I faced him on my knees, shifting them farther and farther apart until the very core, the very heart of that hidden cleavage between my legs was split wide open and planted squarely on his mouth. Now we were engaged in a long wet kiss; it was my lips, I should say – those other lips – that were doing the kissing as they smeared their saliva onto his. *Taste!* I said, pressing down harder on my haunches, circling faster, kissing deeper. I was dying of thirst. I was dying, dying ... and in the throes of the shudders that sent me sprawling across his face, I glimpsed what it was like, that letting go and slipping away from the surge of inseparable pleasure and pain.

After a while my skin prickled and I sensed, before I saw, the light I was lying in, a light that chilled rather than warmed me. I opened my eyes onto the full face of the moon, filling my window, staring me down.

I picked up my sarong and tied it around my chest. Outside, I stood on the veranda briefly to absorb the night: the indigo shadows and shapes of the *kampong* roofs, the crooked palms and fuzzy shoreline of the sea. How still it was – not a breeze, not a drizzle to break the spell and let the monsoon in. Those yellow flowers had bloomed and withered in a burst of false promise.

The moon was not so close now; it had retreated to a distance from which it shed its path of light. The path led directly from the stairs of the veranda, down the incline, in a straight line to the sea. I set out without the slightest hesitation; nothing seemed more natural or more inevitable than walking its beam. I followed it until the sand turned wet underfoot. From there the path glittered like a welcoming carpet rolled out, in my honor, across the surface of the sea. I took my first step into the waves. It was easy, it was nothing, I could feel the slightest undertow pulling me in.

But on the threshold of that walk into the waves I turned – I don't know why – to take a few steps along the beach ... and found the beam trailing me. I stopped and turned in the other direction – and there was the moonbeam, still at my side. Back I wheeled once more, breaking into a run; and back it tagged alongside me.

Whichever way I went, up and down the beach, the path of light was doggedly at my heels.

It wasn't the moon that was doing the bidding; it was taking the lead from me – it was I who was guiding the beam! I darted this way and that, stopping and starting, giddy from running circles round the moon.

When I could run no more I headed home, the sea behind me, the moon in tow.

There was time to give him a sponging. I hadn't planned on it; I hadn't thought I'd be returning. Yet here I was back home, in time for one last wash.

I hadn't thought I could do the other thing either. But that too I did.

I let him go.

DORIS LESSING

EACH OTHER

"People like certainties," wrote Doris Lessing. "More, they crave certainty, they seek certainty, and great resounding truths." Perhaps for that reason a norm is established, taboos are enforced, dissent is punished. Sex, exclusively under its officially recognized function of reproducing the human race, becomes one of these "great resounding truths," and any divergence from it is publicly condemned. There are degrees of condemnation in these heresies, and incest is high on the list.

The love between brother and sister is not taboo in every society. The most famous example of approved incest between siblings is that of the pharaohs of Egypt; in other societies, only certain incestuous relationships are condemned, such as – among the Balinese – that of opposite-sex twins of low-caste parents, who are thought to have engaged in sexual activity while in the womb. For Lessing, the question of incest is meaningless in such terms; her story addresses the individual case, in which the choice is as much one of personal freedom as of social responsibility.

I SUPPOSE your brother's coming again?"

"He might."

He kept his back bravely turned while he adjusted tie, collar, and jerked his jaw this way and that to check his shave. Then, with all pretexts used, he remained rigid, his hand on his tie knot, looking into the mirror past his left cheek at the body of his wife, which was disposed prettily on the bed, weight on its right elbow, its two white forearms engaged in the movements obligatory for filing one's nails. He let his hand drop and demanded: "What do you mean, he *might*?" She did not answer, but held up a studied hand to inspect five pink arrows. She was a thin, very thin, dark girl of about eighteen. Her pose, her way of inspecting her nails, her pink-striped nightshirt which showed long, thin, white legs – all her magazine attitudes were an attempt to hide an anxiety as deep as his; for her breathing, like his, was loud and shallow.

He was not taken in. The lonely fever in her black eyes, the muscles showing rodlike in the flesh of her upper arm, made him feel how much she wanted him to go; and he thought, sharp because of the sharpness of his need for her: There's something unhealthy about her, yes.... The word caused him guilt. He accepted it, and allowed his mind, which was over-alert, trying to pin down the cause of his misery, to add: Yes, not clean, dirty. But this fresh criticism surprised him, and he remembered her obsessive care of her flesh, hair, nails, and the long hours spent in the bath. *Yes, dirty,* his rising aversion insisted.

Armed by it, he was able to turn, slowly, to look at her direct, instead of through the cold glass. He was a solid, well set up, brushed, washed young man who had stood several inches shorter than she at the wedding a month ago, but with confidence in the manhood which had mastered her freakish adolescence. He now kept on her the pressure of a blue stare both appealing (of which he was not aware) and aggressive – which he meant as a warning. Meanwhile he controlled a revulsion which he knew would vanish if she merely lifted her arms towards him.

"What do you mean, he *might*?" he said again.

After some moments of not answering, she said, languid, turning her thin hand this way and that: "I said, he might."

This dialogue echoed, for both of them, not only from five minutes before; but from other mornings, when it had been as often as not unspoken. They were on the edge of disaster. But the young husband was late. He looked at his watch, a gesture which said, but unconvincingly, bravado merely: I go out to work while you lie there.... Then he about-turned, and went to the door, slowing on his way to it. Stopped. Said: "Well, in that case I shan't be back to supper."

"Suit yourself," she said, languid. She now lay flat on her back, and waved both hands in front of her eyes to dry nail varnish which, however, was three days old.

He said loudly: "Freda! I mean it. I'm not going to ..." He looked both trapped and defiant; but intended to do everything, obviously, to maintain his self-respect, his masculinity, in the face of – but what? Her slow smile across at him was something (unlike everything else she had done since waking that morning) she was quite unaware of. She surely could not be aware of the sheer brutality of her slow, considering, contemptuous smile? For it had invitation in it; and it was this, the unconscious triumph there, that caused him to pale, to begin a stammering: "Fre-Fre-Fred-Freda ..." but give up, and leave the room. Abruptly though quietly, considering the force of his horror.

She lay still, listening to his footsteps go down, and the front door closing. Then, without hurrying, she lifted her long thin white legs that ended in ten small pink shields, over the edge of the bed, and stood on them by the window, to watch her husband's well-brushed head jerking away along the pavement. This was a suburb of London, and he had to get to the City, where he was a clerk-with-prospects: and most of the other people down there were on their way to work. She watched him and them, until at the corner he turned, his face lengthened with anxiety. She indolently waved, without smiling. He stared back, as if at a memory of nightmare; so she shrugged and removed herself from the window, and did not see his frantically too late wave and smile.

She now stood, frowning, in front of the long glass in the new wardrobe: a very tall girl, stooped by her height, all elbows and knees, and even more ridiculous because of the short nightshirt. She stripped this off over her head, taking assurance in a side-glance from full-swinging breasts and a rounded waist; then slipped on a white negligée that had frills all down it and around the neck, from which her head emerged, poised. She now looked much better, like a model, in fact. She brushed her short gleaming black hair, stared at length into the deep anxious eyes, and got back into bed.

Soon she tensed, hearing the front door open, softly; and close, softly again. She listened, as the unseen person also listened and watched; for this was a two-roomed flatlet, converted in a semidetached house. The landlady lived in the flatlet below this one on the ground floor; and the young husband had taken to asking her casually, every evening, or listening, casually, to easily given information, about the comings and goings in the house and the movements of his wife. But the steps came steadily up towards her, the door opened, very gently, and she looked up, her face bursting into flower as in came a very tall, lank, dark young man. He sat on the bed beside his sister, took her thin hand in his thin hand, kissed it, bit it lovingly, then bent to kiss her on the lips. Their mouths held while two pairs of deep black eyes held each other. Then she shut her eyes, took his lower lip between her teeth, and slid her tongue along it. He began to undress before she let him go; and she asked, without any of the pertness she used for her husband: "Are you in a hurry this morning?"

"Got to get over to a job in Exeter Street."

An electrician, he was not tied to desk or office.

He slid naked into bed beside his sister, murmuring: "Olive Oyl."

Her long body was pressed against his in a fervour of gratitude for the love name, for it had never received absolution from her husband as it did from this man; and she returned, in as loving a murmur: "Popeye." Again the two pairs of eyes stared into each other at an inch or so's distance. His, though deep in bony sockets like hers, were prominent there, the eyeballs rounded under thin, already crinkling, bruised-looking flesh. Hers, however, were delicately outlined by clear white skin, and he kissed the perfected copies of his own ugly eyes, and said, as she pressed towards him: "Now, now, Olive Oyl, don't be in such a hurry, you'll spoil it."

"No, we won't."

"*Wait,* I tell you."

"All right then ..."

The two bodies, deeply breathing, remained still a long while. Her hand, on the small of his back, made a soft, circular pressing motion, bringing him inwards. He had his two hands on her hipbones, holding her still. But she succeeded, and they joined, and he said again: "Wait now. Lie still." They lay absolutely still, eyes closed.

After a while he asked suddenly: "Well, did he last night?"

"Yes."

His teeth bared against her forehead and he said: "I suppose you made him."

"Why *made* him?"

"You're a pig."

"All right then, how about Alice?"

"Oh her. Well, she screamed and said: 'Stop. Stop.'"

"Who's a pig, then?"

She wriggled circularly, and he held her, hips still, tenderly murmuring: "No, no, no, no."

Stillness again. In the small bright bedroom, with the suburban sunlight outside, new green curtains blew in, flicking the too large, too new furniture, while the long white bodies remained still, mouth to mouth, eyes closed, united by deep soft breaths.

But his breathing deepened; his nails dug into the bones of her hips, he slid his mouth free and said: "How about Charlie, then?"

"He made me scream too," she murmured, licking his throat, eyes closed. This time it was she who held his loins steady, saying: "No, no, no, you'll spoil it."

They lay together, still. A long silence, a long quiet. Then the fluttering curtains roused her, her foot tensed, and she rubbed it delicately up and down his leg. He said, angry: "Why did you spoil it then? It was just beginning."

"It's much better afterwards if it's really difficult." She slid and pressed her internal muscles to make it more difficult, grinning at him in challenge, and he put his hands around her throat in a half-mocking, half-serious pressure to stop her, simultaneously moving in and out of her with exactly the same emulous, taunting but solicitous need she was showing – to see how far they both could go. In a moment they were pulling each other's hair, biting, sinking between thin bones, and then, just before the explosion, they pulled apart at the same moment, and lay separate, trembling.

"We only just made it," he said, fond, uxorious, stroking her hair.

"Yes. Careful now, Fred."

They slid together again.

"Now it will be just perfect," she said, content, mouth against his throat.

The two bodies, quivering with strain, lay together, jerking involuntarily from time to time. But slowly they quietened. Their breathing, jagged at first, smoothed. They breathed together. They had become one person, abandoned against and in each other, silent and gone.

A long time, a long time, a long …

A car went past below in the usually silent street, very loud, and the young man opened his eyes and looked into the gentle face of his sister.

"Freda."

"Ohhh."

"Yes, I've got to go, it must be nearly dinnertime."

"Wait a minute."

"No, or we'll get excited again, we'll spoil everything."

They separated gently, but the movements both used, the two hands gentle on each other's hips, easing their bodies apart, were more like a fitting together. Separate, they lay still, smiling at each other, touching each other's face with fingertips, licking each other's eyelids with small cat licks.

"It gets better and better."

"Yes."

"Where did you go this time?"

"You know."

"Yes."

"Where did you go?"

"You know. Where you were."

"Yes. Tell me."

"Can't."

"I know. Tell me."

"With you."

"Yes."

"Are we one person, then?"

"Yes."

"Yes."

Silence again. Again he roused himself.

"Where are you working this afternoon?"

"I told you. It's a baker's shop in Exeter Street."

"And afterwards?"

"I'm taking Alice to the pictures."

She bit her lips, punishing them and him, then sunk her nails into his shoulder.

"Well my darling, I just make her, that's all, I make her come, she wouldn't understand anything better."

He sat up, began dressing. In a moment he was a tall sober youth in a dark blue sweater. He slicked down his hair with the young husband's hairbrushes, as if he lived here, while she lay naked, watching.

He turned and smiled, affectionate and possessive, like a husband. There was something in her face, a lost desperation, that made his harden. He crouched beside her, scowling, baring his teeth, gently fitting his thumb on her windpipe, looking straight into her dark eyes. She breathed hoarsely, and coughed. He let his thumb drop.

"What's that for, Fred?"

"You swear you don't do that with Charlie?"

"How could I?"

"What do you mean? You could show him."

"But why? Why do you think I want to? Fred!"

The two pairs of deep eyes, in bruised flesh, looked lonely with uncertainty into each other.

"How should I know what you want?"

"You're stupid," she said suddenly, with a small maternal smile.

He dropped his head, with a breath like a groan, onto her breasts, and she stroked his head gently, looking over it at the wall, blinking tears out of her eyes. She said: "He's not coming to supper tonight, he's angry."

"Is he?"

"He keeps talking about you. He asked today if you were coming."

"Why, does he guess?" He jerked his head up off the soft support of her bosom, and stared, his face bitter, into hers. "Why? You haven't been stupid now, have you?"

"No, but Fred … but after you've been with me I suppose I'm different…."

"Oh Christ!" He jumped up, desperate, beginning movements of flight, anger, hate, escape – checking each one. "What do you want, then? You want me to make you come, then? Well, that's easy enough, isn't it, if that's all you want. All right then, lie down and I'll do it, and I'll make you come till you cry, if that's all …" He was about to strip off his clothes; but she shot up from the bed, first hastily draping herself in her white frills, out of an instinct to protect what they had. She stood by him, as tall as he, holding his arms down by his sides. "Fred, Fred, darling, my sweetheart, don't spoil it, don't spoil it now when …"

"When what?"

She met his fierce look with courage, saying steadily: "Well, what do you expect, Fred? He's not stupid, is he? I'm not a … He makes love to me, well, he is my husband, isn't he? And … well, what about you and Alice, you do the same, it's normal, isn't it? Perhaps if you and I didn't have Charlie and Alice for coming, we wouldn't be able to do it our way, have you thought of that?"

"Have I thought of that! Well, what do you think?"

"Well, it's normal, isn't it?"

"Normal," he said, with horror, gazing into her loving face for reassurance against the word. "Normal, is it? Well, if you're going to use words like that ..." Tears ran down his face, she kissed them away in a passion of protective love.

"Well, why did you say I must marry him? I didn't want to, you said I should."

"I didn't think it would spoil us."

"But it hasn't, has it, Fred? Nothing could be like us. How could it? You know that from Alice, don't you, Fred?" Now she was anxiously seeking for his reassurance. They stared at each other; then their eyes closed and they laid their cheeks together and wept, holding down each other's amorous hands, for fear that what they were might be cheapened by her husband, his girl.

He said: "What were you beginning to say?"

"When?"

"Just now. You said, don't spoil it now *when.*"

"I get scared."

"Why?"

"Suppose I get pregnant? Well, one day I must, it's only fair, he wants kids. Suppose he leaves me – he gets in the mood to leave me, like today. Well, he feels something ... it stands to reason. It doesn't matter how much I try with him, you know he feels it.... Fred?"

"What?"

"There isn't any law against it, is there?"

"Against what?"

"I mean, a brother and sister can share a place, no one would say anything."

He stiffened away from her: "You're crazy."

"Why am I? Why, Fred?"

"You're just not thinking, that's all."

"What are we going to do, then?"

He didn't answer, and she sighed, letting her head lie on his shoulder beside his head, so that he felt her open eyes and their wet lashes on his neck.

"We can't do anything but go on like this, you've got to see that."

"Then I've got to be nice to him, otherwise he's going to leave me, and I don't blame him."

She wept, silently; and he held her, silent.

"It's so hard – I just wait for when you come, Fred, and I have to pretend all the time."

They stood silent, their tears drying, their hands linked. Slowly they quieted, in love and in pity, in the same way that they quieted in their long silences when the hungers of the flesh were held by love on the edge of fruition so long that they burned out and up and away into a flame of identity.

At last they kissed, brother-and-sister kisses, gentle and warm.

"You're going to be late, Fred. You'll get the sack."

"I can always get another job."

"I can always get another husband...."

"Olive Oyl ... but you look really good in that white naygleejay."

"Yes, I'm just the type that's no good naked, I need clothes."

"That's right – I must go."

"Coming tomorrow?"

"Yes. About ten?"

"Yes."

"Keep him happy, then. Ta-ta."

"Look after yourself – look after yourself, my darling, look after yourself...."

LI ANG

CURVACEOUS DOLLS

Erotic fiction, which played such an important part in the development of Chinese literature throughout the centuries, was effectively suppressed during the Cultural Revolution of 1966-68. However, it continued to flourish in Taiwan, especially in the work of women writers such as Li Ang. She published her first book, the novel Flower Season, *in 1969, when she was barely seventeen. Since then she has explored the politics of female sexuality in fiction, principally in short stories, several of them based on her experience as a social worker assisting single mothers; others, such as her novella* The Butcher's Wife *(1983), made later into a successful film, denounce the exploitation of women in traditional Chinese society. For Li Ang, women must create their own objects of desire in landscapes to which men have little or no access. "Curvaceous Dolls" is the chronicle of one such creation.*

I

SHE HAD YEARNED for a doll – a curvaceous doll – ever since she was a little girl. But because her mother had died and her father, a poor man, hadn't even considered it, she never got one. Back then she had stood behind a wall every day secretly watching a girl who lived in the neighborhood carrying a doll in her arms. The way the girl left her doll lying around surprised and confused her; if she had a doll of her own, she reasoned dimly, she would treat it lovingly, never letting it out of her sight.

One night as she lay in bed clutching the sheet to her chest, obsessed with the idea of a doll, she figured out a way to get one that she could hug as tightly as she wished. After digging out some old clothes, she twisted them into a bundle, then cinched it up with some string about a quarter of the way down. She now had her very first doll.

The ridicule this first doll brought down upon her was something she would never forget. She recalled it years later as she lay in the warmth and comfort of her husband's embrace. She sobbed until he gently turned her face toward him and said in a relaxed tone of voice that was forced and revealed a hint of impatience:

"It's the rag doll again, isn't it!"

Just when it had become the "rag doll" she couldn't recall with certainty, but it must have been when she told him about it. One night, not terribly late, he lay beside her after they had finished, still somewhat breathless, while she lay staring at the moon's rays streaming in through the open window and casting a fine net of light at the foot of the bed. She had a sudden impulse to reveal everything, to tell him about her first doll; and so she told him, haltingly, blushing with embarrassment, how she had made it, how she had embraced it at night in bed, and how, even though her playmates ridiculed her, she had refused to give it up. When she finished, he laughed.

"Your very own rag doll!"

Maybe that wasn't the first time anyone had called it a "rag doll," but he had certainly used the word that night, and his laughter had hurt her deeply. She failed to see the humor in it, and telling him had not been easy. He could be pretty inconsiderate sometimes.

She never mentioned the doll again, probably because of his mocking laughter, and from that night on she began sleeping with her back to him, unable to bear facing his broad, hairy chest. Although it was the same chest that had once brought her solace and warmth, she now found it repulsive. It seemed to be missing something, although she couldn't say just what that something was.

Later on, her nightly dreams were invaded by many peculiar transparent objects floating randomly in a vast grayness, totally divorced from reality yet invested with a powerful life force. She seldom recalled such dreams, and even when she knew she had been dreaming, they vanished when she awoke.

It was a familiar feeling, the realization that she had obtained something without knowing what it was, and it worried her and drove her to tears. She often wept as she lay in her husband's arms, and he invariably blamed the rag doll. But it's not the rag doll! she felt like shouting. The rag doll had disappeared that night, never to return. But she couldn't tell him, maybe to avoid a lot of meaningless explanations.

The dreams continued, troubling her more than ever. She would sit quietly for hours trying to figure out what the floating objects were, but with no success. Occasionally she felt she was getting close, but in the end the answer always eluded her. The preoccupation took its toll on her husband; after being casually rebuffed in bed a few times, he grew impatient, and when he realized that things were not going to get better, he decided to take her to see a doctor. By now she was fed up with his bossiness and the protector's role in which he prided himself, but her dreams had such a strong grip on her that she finally gave in.

On the way, the oppressive closeness inside the bus made her regret going. She had no desire to open up to a doctor, nor did she think a doctor was the answer. As she looked over at her husband, a single glance from him convinced her that it would be useless to argue. Slowly she turned away.

Someone brushed against her. Glancing up, she saw a pair of full breasts, whose drooping outline she could make out under the woman's blouse. Her interest aroused, she began to paint a series of mental pictures, imagining the breasts as having nipples like overripe strawberries oozing liquid, as though waiting for the greedy mouth of a child. Suddenly she felt a powerful urge to lean up against those full breasts, which were sure to be warm and comforting, and could offer her the sanctuary she needed. She closed her eyes and recalled the time she had seen a child playing with its mother's breasts. If only she could be those hands, enjoying the innocent pleasure of fondling a mother's soft, smooth breasts. Her palms were sweaty, and she wondered what her hands might do if she kept this up much longer.

Feeling a strong arm around her shoulders, she opened her eyes and found herself looking into the anxious face of her husband.

"You're so pale," he said.

She never learned how she had been taken off the bus, recalling only the extraordinary comfort and warmth of her husband's arm. She leaned up against him in the taxi all the way home, gradually reacquainting herself with his muscular chest. But she couldn't stop thinking about those breasts, so soft and smooth, there for her to play with. If only her husband could grow breasts like that on his chest, with drooping nipples for her to suck on! In a flash she realized what was missing from his chest – of course, a pair of breasts to lean on and provide her with sanctuary.

Later on, to her amazement, the objects in her dreams began to coalesce. Those unreal and disorderly, bright yet transparent objects took on concrete form with curves and twists: two oversized, swollen objects like resplendent, drooping breasts; beneath the translucent surface she could see thick, flowing milk. It's a woman's body, a curvaceous woman's body! she wanted to shout as the astonishing realization set in.

When she awoke, she experienced an unprecedented warmth that spread slowly from her breasts to the rest of her body, as though she were being baptized by the endless flow of her own milk as it coursed placidly through her body. Overwhelmed by such bountiful pleasure, she began to moan.

When she opened her eyes and glanced around her she saw that her husband was sound asleep. In the still of the night the moon's rays swayed silently on the floor beneath the window like a pool of spilled mother's milk. She began to think of her second doll, the one made of clay. Since her first doll was called the rag doll, this one ought to be known as the clay doll.

The idea of making a clay doll occurred to her one day when she had felt a sudden desire to hold the neighbor girl's doll. She had approached her, not knowing how to make her desire known, and after they had stared at each other for a few moments, she reached out and tugged at the doll's arm. The other girl yanked it back and pushed her so hard she fell down. Her cries brought the girl's mother, who picked her up gently and cradled her against her breasts to comfort her.

She had never touched anything so soft and comfortable before. She didn't know what those things were called, but she was instinctively drawn to them and wanted to touch them. After that, she lost interest in her rag doll, since it lacked those protruding, springy objects on its chest and could no longer afford her any solace. She thought about her mother. It was the first time in years that she truly missed her mother, who had left no impression on her otherwise, but whose bosom must have offered safety, warmth, and a place to rest.

The feeling returned: she longed to tell her husband about her clay doll, but then she recalled how he had laughed before, a humiliating laugh without a trace of sympathy, the sound coming from the depths of his broad chest, ugly and filled with evil. As she turned slightly to look at her sleeping husband, from whom she felt alienated and distant, a vague yet profound loneliness came over her, and she desperately missed her clay doll.

It had been raining then, and the water was streaming down the sides of a mound of clay near where she lived. She regularly went there with the other children to make clay dolls, but hers were always different from theirs. She molded small lumps of clay onto their chests, then worked them into mounds that jutted out. Most of the time she rubbed their bodies with water until they took on a silky, bronze sheen, glistening like gold. She fondled them, wishing that someday she could rub real skin as soft and glowing as that.

In fact, her husband's skin, which also had a bronze sheen, was as lustrous as that of her clay dolls. When she reached out to caress his body her hand recoiled slightly when she touched his hairy chest, and she wished fervently that a pair of soft breasts were growing there instead! Moved by a strange impulse she unbuttoned her pajama top and exposed her breasts, full like a married woman's, and let them rest on her husband's chest, praying with unprecedented devotion that her breasts could be transplanted onto his body.

The weight of her heavy breasts on his chest woke him, and with an apologetic look in his eyes, he embraced her tightly.

Whenever she did something like this she had no desire to explain herself, so he would just look at her apologetically and she would calmly accept what he did. But each time his chest touched her breasts, she felt a strange uneasiness, and a peculiar shudder, tinged with revulsion, welled up from the hidden depths of her body. At times like this she felt that the man on top of her was nothing but an onerous burden, and she was reminded of old cows in her hometown, which stumbled along pulling their heavy carts, swaying helplessly back and forth.

She couldn't imagine that she would ever be like an old cow, wearily and dispiritedly bearing a heavy burden that could never be abandoned. Her husband's body had become a pile of bones and rotting flesh that made a mockery of his robust health, although it was slightly warm and exuded an animal stench. It was an instrument of torture that made her feel like she had been thrown into a wholesale meat market.

She began to experience a mild terror; the concept of "husband" had never seemed so distant and fragmented. Before they were married, she had often stroked his shoulders through his shirt with something approaching reverence. Though powerful, they retained some of the modesty and stiffness characteristic of virgin men. They could be called young man's shoulders, not those of a grown man; yet despite the stiffness, the masculine smoothness of his well-developed muscles intoxicated her. After they were married, whenever she stroked his shoulders she noticed how all the roughness and sharp edges had disappeared; they had become a soft place where all her cares and doubts melted away. She then sank into a new kind of indulgence, a feeling of nearly total security that became purely physical.

Her mild terror helped her renew her love for her husband's body, and although she was partially successful in this regard, she knew that this renewal would not last for long, and that someday a new weariness would set in to make him repulsive again. The only foolproof way to avoid that was for him to grow a pair of breasts to restore the novelty and security she needed so desperately.

The following days were spent in constant prayer and anticipation of the time when breasts would grow on her husband's chest, there to await the hungry mouth of a child.

How she wished she could be that child's mouth, sucking contentedly on her mother's breasts just as she had once rubbed her lips against the breasts of her clay doll, a form of pleasure so satisfying it made her tremble. She still remembered the time she had hidden in an underground air-raid shelter and covered her clay doll's lustrous skin with kisses. She was like a mole wallowing in the pleasure of living in an underground burrow that never sees the light of day. She derived more gratification from this activity than any father, any neighbor girl's doll, or any neighbor girl's mother could ever have provided.

One question remained unanswered: had there been a struggle the first time she kissed the clay doll? She recalled the time she had raised one of her clay dolls to her lips, then flung it to the floor and shattered it, leaving only the two bumps that had been on the chest looking up at her haughtily.

But she never had to worry about being discovered in her underground shelter; she felt safe in that dark, empty space deep underground. Besides, kissing her clay doll like that was perfectly proper; there was nothing to be ashamed of.

How she wished that her home had a cellar, a room unknown to anyone else, or some dark place where she could hide. But there was none – the place was neat, the waxed floors shone, and there were no out-of-the-way corners. She was suddenly gripped by an extraordinary longing for her hometown, where the vast open country and sugarcane patches provided an infinite number of hiding places where no one could ever find her. She missed it so badly and so often that the thought brought tears to her eyes.

She finally decided to tell her husband that she had to go back home. He lay there holding his head in his hands, frowning.

"I can't for the life of me figure out where you get such ideas. Didn't you say you'd never go back to that godforsaken home of yours, no matter what?" he said contemptuously.

"That was before, things were different then," she said earnestly, ignoring the impatience in his voice. "Now all I want is to go home, really, I just want to go home."

"Why?"

"No reason."

"Do you think you can?"

"I don't know," she answered, suddenly losing interest and feeling that defending herself was both meaningless and futile. It was all so ridiculous that she turned away.

"Are you angry?" He gently put his arms around her.

"Not at all," she said.

She was genuinely not angry. She let him draw her close, but when her back touched his flat chest, the image of those vast sugarcane patches flashed before her, until the bed seemed surrounded by them, as far as the eye could see. "He has to grow a pair of breasts, he just has to!" she thought to herself, in fact, said it very softly, although he was so intent upon unbuttoning her pajama top that he failed to notice.

As in the past, his hands made her feel unclean. She had

always believed, although somewhat vaguely, that the hands fondling her breasts ought to be her own and not his. The weak light in the room barely illuminated the outline of his hands, which she allowed to continue fondling her breasts. It was funny that she was aware of his hands only when they were in bed together.

But it hadn't always been like that. When she first met him, his hands had represented success and achievement; like his chest, they had brought her contentment and security. Then, once they were married, his hands had brought her unimaginable pleasure. And now all she could think of was how to escape them. The foolishness of it all made her laugh.

She knew that this was inevitable, that all she could do was pray for him to grow a pair of breasts. For the sake of domestic tranquillity and happiness, she had to pray with increased devotion.

From the beginning she knew that in a unique situation like this simply kneeling in prayer was hopeless. A more primitive kind of supplication was called for, a thoroughly liberating form of prayer. And so, after her husband left for work in the morning, she locked herself in the bedroom and pulled down the shades, stood in front of the full-length mirror, and slowly undressed herself. As she looked at her reflection in the slightly clouded mirror she fantasized that she was being undressed by an unknown force. She knelt naked on the cold hardwood floor, which was warmed by no living creature, put her palms together in front of her, and began to pray. Invoking the names of all the gods she had ever heard of, she prayed that a pair of breasts like her own would grow on her husband's chest. She even prayed for her own breasts to be transplanted onto his body. If the gods would only answer her prayers, she was willing to pay any price.

She derived immense pleasure from her prayers, and wherever her limbs touched the icy floor she got a tingling sensation like a mild electric shock. She looked forward to these sensations, for they made her feel more clean and pure than when she lay in bed with her husband, their limbs entwined. She began to pray in different postures, sometimes that of a snake wriggling on the floor, at other times a pregnant spider, but always praying for the same thing.

Her husband remained ignorant of what was going on, so everything proceeded smoothly, except that now a strange creature began to creep into her prayers; at first it was only a pair of eyes, two long ovals, their color the dense pale green of autumn leaves that have withered and fallen. In the dim light of the room they gazed fixedly at every part of her naked body with absolute composure and familiarity. She took no notice and remained on the floor, where she laid bare her womanly limbs. Those eyes, expressionless and filled with a peculiar incomprehension, watched her, but since the creature's very existence was dubious, it had no effect on the fervor of her performance. She embraced the icy floor and kissed it with the vague sense that she was embracing a lover sculpted out of marble.

The pale green eyes continued to keep watch, although now they were filled with cruelty and the destructive lust of a wild animal. At some point she discovered with alarm that she had fallen under the spell of the frightful sexual passion in those eyes, which she now believed belonged to a half-man, half-animal shepherd spirit sent down by the gods in answer to her prayers; moved to the point that she felt compelled to offer up her body in exchange for what she sought, she opened up her limbs to receive that mysterious man-beast. Under the gaze of those eyes, she lay back and exposed herself to their enshrouding vision. She had completed a new rite of baptism.

This may have been the moment she had been waiting for all along, for it surpassed her marble lover and her obsession with the hoped-for breasts on her husband's chest. She was rocked and pounded by the waves of a profound, unfathomable happiness, which also turned the pale green eyes into a placid lake, on the surface of which they rose and fell in a regular cadence. Her happiness was compressed into a single drop of water, which fell without warning into the pale green lake and spread out until every atom of her being had taken on a pale green cast. After that she felt herself reemerging whole from the bottom of the lake. When she reached the surface she discovered that she was a pale green mermaid with hair like dried seaweed blown about by the pale green winds. The water of the pale green lake suddenly and swiftly receded, as darkness fell over everything and blotted out the pale green eyes.

When she regained consciousness her first thought was that she had been defiled. Emerging from the chaotic spell of sexual passion, she slowly opened her eyes and was struck by the knowledge that her body, which she had always thought of as incomparably alluring, was in fact just another body; for the first time in a long while she realized that she was merely a woman, no different from any other woman, with neither more nor fewer womanly attributes. She lay on the floor, sobbing heavily and recalling the breasts she had hoped would appear on her husband's chest. An inexplicable sadness made her sob even more pitifully. She was living a dream, an illusion containing vast, hazy, transparent, and mysterious things, with no way to bring them all together. She knew there was no way, even though she had tried before, and even though she once believed she had succeeded; there was no way, she knew that, no way she could ever bring them all together.

She stopped sobbing. Numbly, vacantly, and reluctantly she got to her feet and slowly, aimlessly got dressed, as she knew she must.

II

She lay there, her arm gently wrapped around her husband's neck as he slept on his side. She felt safe, for the darkness around her was free from all objects; it revealed nothing but its own sweet self – boundless, profound, and bottomless. She gazed at her husband's dark, contented eyes and smiled. She had known that sort of happiness before, and was consoled by the knowledge that it would soon be hers again. Feeling like a wandering child returning to its mother's warm embrace, she believed that any child who had come home was entitled to return to its mother's breast. Gladdened by the thought of the pleasure awaiting her and her husband, she continued to smile.

She couldn't say how long the smile remained on her face, but it must have been a very long time. Since emerging from the vast emptiness of her dream, she had begun to love her husband's flat, manly chest with an uncustomary enthusiasm. She gave herself over to enjoying it and caring for it tenderly, for now she was relieved of her burden of uncleanliness and evil. When her husband perceived this change in her attitude, he started to treat her with increased tenderness. And in order to assure her husband of her purity and rebirth, she began to want a child.

Her image of the child was indistinct. She had always avoided thinking of children, for they reminded her of her own childhood and caused her to experience overwhelming waves of pain. But in order to prove her ability as a mother and show that she no longer required a pair of mother's breasts for herself, she needed a child, whose only qualification was that it be a child, with no special talent nor any particular appearances; as long as it had a mouth to suck on her breasts and two tiny hands to fondle them, that was enough for her. Her only requirement for a child was that it be a child.

She told her husband of her decision. As he lay beside her he heard her out, then laughed derisively.

"You sure have some strange ideas!" he said.

His remark amused her. She could – in fact, she should – have a child. Which meant that *he* was the strange one. She realized for the first time that her husband could be unreasonable and think illogically. The idealized vision of her husband, who had always been the epitome of correctness and reason, began to dissolve, and she knew she could not dismiss that rational inferiority she had once felt; all she needed now was to await the birth of her child.

Her husband did not share her enthusiasm and was, in fact, decidedly cool to the idea. But she took no notice, intoxicated with the happy prospect of becoming a mother. She enjoyed standing naked on the icy bathroom floor and playing with her swelling, full breasts, pretending that it was her child's hands fondling the objects that represented absolute security – its mother's breasts. Her pleasure brought her fantasies that the tiny hands of the child were actually her own and that the mother, mysterious yet great, was actually an endless plain whose protruding breasts were a pair of mountains poised there for her to lay her head upon and rest for as long as she wanted.

Oh, how she yearned for rest; she was so weary she felt like lying down and never getting up again. Although the nightmares no longer disturbed her in their many forms, they still made indirect appearances. Late one night her husband shook her awake while she was crying and screaming in her sleep; her cheeks were wet with tears as he took her gently into his arms and comforted her. Deeply touched, she decided to reveal everything to him. More than anything else she wanted peace, complete and unconditional. So in a low voice she began to tell him about her clay doll, how she had made it and how she had played with its symbolic breasts. When she finished, he looked at her for a moment with extraordinary calmness, then reached out and held her icy, sweaty, trembling hands tightly in his warm grip.

A great weariness spread slowly throughout her body, and she closed her eyes from exhaustion. Her husband's attitude took her by surprise, for she had expected the same mocking laughter as before. But all he did was look at her with a strange expression on his face, a mixture of indifference and loathing, as though he were observing a crippled animal. She felt the urge to cry, but knew that the tears would not come; she felt like someone who had done a very foolish thing.

Maybe she had actually been hoping for her husband to react by mocking her again, for she remembered how he had laughed so cruelly when she told him about the rag doll; the rag doll had suddenly vanished from her dreams, and for the first time in her life she had known peace of mind. Now she was hoping he would laugh like that again to rid her of the clay doll, like amputating an unwanted limb to regain one's health.

She rolled over on her side, turning her back to the awkward look frozen on her husband's face, then closed her eyes and waited wearily for sleep to come.

In the haziness of her dream she was running on a broad plain, devoid of trees and shrubs, an unbroken stretch of flat grassland. She was running in search of far-off solace when she spotted two mountains rising before her, two full, rounded mounds standing erect in the distance. She ran toward them, for she knew that the solace she sought could be found there. But whenever she felt she had drawn near to them, they faded beyond her reach, even though she kept running.

She awoke and saw the moonlight at the foot of the bed, looking like a pool of mother's milk, and her heart was moved in a peculiar way. She yearned for those mountainlike breasts, and as her eyes began to fill with tears, she clutched a corner of the comforter and cried bitterly.

Suddenly, through her tears she saw something stirring in the surrounding darkness, rocking restlessly in the motion of her tears. Then, slowly it became visible in the form of a flickering thin ray of pale green light. She sat up in alarm, shutting her eyes tightly and squeezing the tears out and down her cheeks, cold, as though she had just emerged from underwater. Then she opened her eyes again, and there lurking in the darkness were those eyes again, pale green, cunningly long slits that were laughing with self-assured mockery. Oh, no! she wanted to shout, but she couldn't move. They stared at each other in the two-dimensional darkness, although she was sure that they were slowly drawing closer to her. The pale greenness was growing crueler and becoming an approaching presence of overwhelming power. There was no way she could back off, nowhere for her to turn, and nothing with which she could ward off the attack. And all this time her husband slept soundly beside her.

She had no idea how long the confrontation lasted. The pale green eyes stood their ground as they kept watch over her, sometimes revolving around her. The milky light of the moon grew dense, slowly creeping farther into the room. During one of the pale green eyes' circuits around her, something else was revealed in the moonlight – the tail of an animal, covered with long silky black hairs, suspended lightly and noiselessly in the air. She knew what to do: she reached over to the table lamp beside the bed. The pale green eyes did not stir, they kept watching her, smiling with consummate evil, as though they were looking at her with a slight cock of the head. She touched the light switch with her finger, but she knew she lacked the courage to press it.

The pale green eyes knew it too, and willfully remained where they were, watching her calmly with a mock viciousness. All she had to do was press the light switch to win the battle, but she knew she couldn't do it, she simply couldn't. The pale green eyes also sensed that the game was over. They blinked several times, then started to retreat. And as they gazed into her eyes for the last time, there was an unmistakable hint that they would be back, that she could never escape them – for her there would be no escape.

From then on she often awoke from disturbing dreams late

at night, only to discover those pale green eyes keeping watch over her quietly from afar or floating past her; they seemed to be evil incarnate, and every time they appeared, her own past reappeared before her with a stabbing pain. Needing a liberating force, she began to wish even more fervently for a child.

She sought the sucking mouth of a child, for she knew that the only time the pale green eyes would not appear was when a mouth was vigorously sucking at her breasts. She wanted the consoling feeling of rebirth that comes with a child's greedy mouth chewing on her nipples, knowing that it would be more wonderful than her husband's light, playful nibbling during their lovemaking. She wanted a child, one that could show the pale green eyes that she had become a mother. In order to achieve her goal, she felt a need to turn to a supernatural power for help, and that was when she thought of her wooden doll.

She no longer derived any stimulation from stroking her husband's body or from the imaginary breasts that had once preoccupied her. The chest that had filled her with such longing was now nothing more than a mass of muscle, flat and completely ordinary. As she recalled the breasts she had once hoped to find on his chest, she was struck by how comical and meaningless it had all been. She knew that no one could help her, that she had to find her own way out.

She had searched, ardently and with an ambition rooted in confidence, for a pair of breasts, that belonged to her alone, not distant and unattainable like those on the neighbor girl's mother. Finally, in an abandoned military bunker, she had found a wooden figurine of a naked woman with pointed breasts, two even, curvaceous mounds on the doll's upper torso. This was the first time she had truly appreciated the form of those breasts she loved so dearly. Her clay doll's chest had been adorned only with shapeless bumps. As she fondled the exquisitely proportioned curves of the wooden doll she felt a heightened sense of beauty and a reluctance to stop.

Standing in front of the full-length mirror bare to the waist, she examined her own full breasts, finding them so alluring that she had a sudden yearning for them. Crossing her arms, she fondled them until they ached. She longed for them, she longed for those soft and lovely, yet dark and shadowy lines, she longed to rest her head on them, she longed to chew on those delightful nipples. She bent her head down toward them, only to discover that they were forever beyond her reach.

She would never forget the first time her lips had touched the nipples of the wooden doll and how much pleasure that had brought her. Those tiny nipples seemed to exist only for her to suck on, and since she could fit an entire breast into her mouth, she could thus possess it completely. She prayed to the wooden doll for a pair of real nipples to suck on or for a tiny child's mouth to replace her own and suck on her breasts.

She wanted a mouth that was devoid of sexual passion, and her husband did not fit the bill. So when the pale green eyes reappeared late one night, she climbed gently out of bed and began deftly unbuttoning her pajama top. As they watched her, the pale green eyes appeared puzzled for the first time. She unfastened her bra and began to fondle her breasts. The pale green eyes, quickly falling under her spell, moved toward her. Two long, gleaming fangs shone through the darkness. The taste of imminent victory was wonderfully sweet to her.

As the pale green eyes drew nearer, the gleaming fangs grew brighter. She dropped her hands to her sides, exposing her breasts to the approaching eyes. She imagined those fangs biting on her nipples and bringing her the same pleasure as a child's tiny sucking mouth. Overcome by this exquisite pleasure, she began to moan.

The pale green eyes were startled out of their trance. They quickly recovered their mocking attitude and retreated nimbly after a long stare that betrayed the remnants of sexual passion.

She believed that the pale green eyes, with their primitive lust, were capable of bringing her happiness and release. She craved them, and in order to have them she had to do as they dictated. The vast sugarcane fields of her hometown spread out around her in all directions, layer upon layer, dark and unfathomable.

She knew that there would be countless pale green eyes staring at her in the heart of the sugarcane fields, that there would be countless tails stroking her limbs, that there would be white feathers filling her vagina, and that there would be gleaming white fangs biting down on her nipples. But it was a sweet, dark place, boundless and eternally dark, a place where she could rest peacefully, a place where she could hide. She longed for all of this, she longed to possess it all, and nothing else mattered. She yearned for her hometown and for the sugarcane fields where she could hide. She shook her husband awake.

"I want to go back," she said with uncharacteristic agitation. "I want to go home."

The sleepiness in her husband's eyes was quickly replaced by a totally wakeful coldness. "Why?"

"Just because."

"You have to give me a reason."

"You wouldn't understand."

"Is it because of those damned dolls of yours?" he asked in an intentionally mocking tone.

"Since you already know, yes, that's it."

Her frigid indifference enraged him.

"Haven't you had enough?" he said angrily. "I forbid you from going."

"Do you think I really *want* to go back? I'm telling you, I have no choice, there's nothing I can do. I have to return."

She shut her eyes slowly, wishing she hadn't brought up the subject in the first place. Dimly she sensed that somewhere in the illusory, distant dreamscape the little girl's mother's breasts had exploded for some unknown reason, and a thick white liquid began to seep slowly out of them like spreading claws, snaking its way toward her. In her bewilderment, her first thought was to turn away, but she discovered that she was drawn to the thick white liquid, which was trying to detach her limbs from her body and suck them up into its cavernous mouth. Her feet were frozen to the spot. The meandering liquid drew closer and closer to her, until it was at her feet. It began to creep up her body and she could feel the snakelike clamminess and springy round objects wriggling on her skin, as though two dead breasts were rubbing up against her. The liquid climbed higher and higher, until it reached her lips, and just as it was about to enter her mouth it suddenly coiled itself tightly around her like a snake. The feelings of suffocation and pain she experienced were eclipsed by an immense sense of joy.

She knew that the stream of white liquid would never enter her mouth, and that she would always be searching and waiting. Yet she wanted to seize it, for she believed that it offered her the only hope of attaining a kind of solace, a truth that would allow her to offer up everything in tribute. In the dim light, she set off on a search, not concerned that her husband might oppose her, for she was convinced that this was her only way out.

When she opened her eyes he was gazing at her, his eyes filled with remorse.

"Work hard at it, no matter how long it takes and someday it will happen to you."

"Maybe," she thought, "but not if I go about it your way. I have to do it my own way." But that was a long way off. She leaned gently against his chest, recalling a naked mannequin she had once seen in a display window. "I'll possess her someday, and maybe I'll call her my wax doll!" she said to herself softly.

Translated by
Howard Goldblatt

YURI MAMLEYEV

THE LAST TRACE OF SPINOZA

"Today's alternative prose in Soviet Russia," wrote the critic Helena Goscilo in 1990, at the time of Gorbachev's glasnost, "not only impresses by its independence, freshness, and technical mastery, but also validates any optimism about the future of Russian fiction." Yuri Mamleyev, even though he emigrated to the US in 1975, began his literary career in Russia and exemplifies the imaginative originality alluded to by Goscilo. Born in Moscow in 1931, Mamleyev graduated from the Moscow Forestry Institute under Stalin. After Stalin's death in 1953, his work attracted the attention of several dissident critics, making it necessary for him to leave. His collection of short stories, The Sky Above Hell, *was published in English translation five years after his arrival in New York.*

For Mamleyev, desire creates its own prey. The other, the object of erotic love, is invented from certain clues, certain shreds of evidence. Erotic truth lies in the imagination, and the man who believes he is Spinoza is neither more deluded nor more aware than the woman who loves him for what she imagines him to be.

REGIONAL POLYCLINIC NO. 121 is dirty and uncomfortable, saturated with the smell of putrefaction. The doctors and staff are a strange lot, with fat behinds and a dull heavy look about them. Only occasionally does one find the kind of piercingly libidinal nurses who seem ready to lick the sweat from the faces of the sick. But frequently they are all – doctors and nurses alike – struck with thoughts so ridiculous, so inappropriate, that they are likely to be more afraid of themselves than of their decomposing clients. One healthy, well-fed doctor, an otolaryngologist, once spat into a patient's face when he discovered in his mouth a meaty pulp of a tumor.

In general, people who deal directly with the sick have particularly crude and brazen imaginations, while those who work with some kind of apparatus, X-ray technicians for instance, are quite proper and look at people as if they are photographs.

A patient here, as elsewhere, is harried and exhausted and looks out at the world like a trapped beast. Almost no one believes in God, and questions of the immortality of the soul are simply forgotten.

Such was the clinic where a doctor of internal medicine,

Nelya Semenovna – a woman of some forty years, grown fat from voluptuous fantasies – worked. She lived alone in a room crammed full of food and the photographs of ex-patients who were now corpses.

Nelya Semenovna did not possess any obvious peculiarities, though she would occasionally stick her head out the window at night with a dull look on her face as if she intended to devour the surrounding city.

She would get up early in the morning, stretch, and then head for the market. Sometimes it seemed to her that she was crawling out of her skin. Then she would give herself a delicious slap on the backside, which would return her to her substantiality.

Glancing at the market with a dark, wild look, she would arrange in her huge shopping bag her chicken, carrots, potatoes, and turnips. Back from the market, she always felt like singing.

Having wolfed down something, usually in the toilet to start with, Nelya Semenovna would get ready to go to work.

The sick, for some reason, always crawled to her when they were half dead, and, baring her teeth, she would deliver the fateful prognoses. From this alone her soul would become less troubled, the sun would shine more gaily, and she would roll about in her visions of death like a little glob of fat in a frying pan.

Festering inwardly, she studied the life of the mortally ill, their little ways. She saw innumerable patients in her time. Arriving at her brightly lit, sunny office, she would as a first order of business drink a bottle of fatty kefir in order to rinse out death from her insides. Then she would receive her first patient. The stench of sweat did not hinder her thinking.

She got special satisfaction out of the younger patients trembling before death. Their lives seemed like snares to her. And, joyfully tapping and probing one of them, she would run her fat, sweaty fingers over his body, which in a few days perhaps would be rotting in the grave. Practically her entire life Nelya Semenovna had thought of nothing but death. She had thought about it when fucking with a dark, vodka-swollen laborer. She thought about it while chewing on her chicken. She thought about it when she became frightened of cancer, and would scratch about her body, fat from self-love to the consistency of jelly.

She had no talent for life; only for death did she have a genius, like Einstein did for relativity. After many years of thinking about death, she had come up with the notion that, on the one hand, it seemed nonsensical that everything ended with death. "That we observe a corpse is a fact," she often said to herself. "But this fact is on the order of one which people in antiquity held; looking about them and seeing only 'flat' space, they concluded that the world was flat. There were more than a few such illusions. After all, that which we see is only a pathetic part of the whole world."

On the other hand, all notions of an afterlife seemed to her to be derived from this life, from present consciousness. She did not believe in an afterlife, but she also did not believe that after death there would be nothing. She felt that after death there would be something which could not be fit into any kind of framework or set of rules or superhypotheses.

"It," as she called whatever follows after death, "can't be called life after death or whatever; it cannot be named in any human language. It's not existence, not nonbeing, neither before birth nor after death." Either terror in the face of nothing brought on these conjectures about life beyond, which were themselves a reflection of her terror, or, on the contrary, this terror awakened in her an instinctive vision of truth, gave an impetus to her intuition. Or she simply was quite profound: "Death itself will tell." But this sense of the incomprehensibility of death shook her consciousness so that she began to see, and quite consistently, too, the incomprehensibility of what surrounds death: that is, life itself. It even seemed to her that the more she saw the world and herself as meaningless, the closer she was to God and the truth about Being after death.

Once, Nelya, who had gone entirely off her head from a world she viewed as nothing but an appendage to death, dragged herself with difficulty to her office at the clinic. In the corridor there was already a horde of people waiting, half of whom were almost dead and therefore especially insolent and pushy. They tried to sneak to the head of the line, pounded with their fists on the locked door and bit at one another.

The more healthy crowded the corners in confusion. Barking at the patients, Nelya finally got them into line. Then she locked herself in, and in order to brighten up her existence, masturbated in front of the office mirror. Only the pounding of the sick, who had by now lost all patience, brought her back to reality.

In a hoarse voice Nelya called the first patient. This was a broken-down, aging man who had just survived twenty knife wounds in his face. Having frightened him sufficiently with medical terms, Nelya Semenovna got rid of him. The second patient was a dried-up old woman with a ribbon in her hair who had come out of boredom. Nelya spent a long time with her, yawning, listening to her heart, taking her pulse, making a reference to the rectum. The old woman went out, leaving behind a gratuity of ten kopecks. Then a woman with an infant appeared.

"If you, Mama, insist on suffering so because your infant is dying, then you'll croak before *it* does," Nelya Semenovna greeted her, having gotten completely out of control. She knew to which of her clients it was tolerable to tell the holy mother – truth. Mama became so entangled in the imminent death of her child – and herself – that she began to sob uncontrollably. The condemned infant meanwhile did not understand a thing and happily chased about the room after sunbeams, as if it were already in the other world.

At wit's end, Nelya Semenovna showed this absurd pair out the door. She glanced out at the corridor and was horrified. "Lord, what a lot of them." The dying climbed over each other to get to Nelya Semenovna as if she were some kind of Christ.

Only one of them, with a scholarly look about him, sulked in the corner. He was a schizophrenic, afraid of dying and taking his schizophrenia along into the other world.

Nelya Semenovna spat on the floor and reorganized the line. Into the office flew a grayish, balding, flabby man with a degenerate face and protruding ears.

"I demand attention," he bellowed as he sat down on a chair in front of Nelya Semenovna.

"Why?" the doctor asked.

"Because I am Spinoza," he squealed, seizing the corner of the desk with his hands. "Yes, yes, in my former life I *was*

Spinoza, but now my bowels barely work. I demand to be sent to the very best sanitorium."

"Oh, well, I'll have a look at his throat," Nelya Semenovna thought. "Open your mouth, then, like that." And she looked with interest deep into the throat of this complainer. When she had finished, he fixed his eyes on her dully.

"I repeat, I was Spinoza, Spinoza, Spinoza," he cried, spraying her with saliva.

"Perhaps he really was," flashed through Nelya Semenovna's timid mind, and something missed a beat in her behind. Without a word, she picked up the telephone receiver and dialed the Central Authority for Sanatoria, but it was impossible to come to any agreement right away. The receiver hissed, raised objections, advised waiting a bit, referred to some directive or other. Spinoza, meanwhile, having calmed down, sat in a corner. Nelya Semenovna glanced darkly at the man.

Irritated, she thought, "It's impossible that such an idiot could have been Spinoza. After all, where is his proof?" Wearily she replaced the receiver. The man once more began to fidget nervously.

"You do not believe me," he forced out with hatred. "All of you on this earth are skeptics."

He suddenly leaped to his feet and, coming up to Nelya Semenovna, leaned over and whispered something into her ear.

"No, you don't," Nelya Semenovna pronounced, turning red. "I don't understand a thing." And she shook her head.

"So, you don't understand," the man screeched with malice. "Well, you'll understand this, I hope," and he ripped open his shirt and began to run about the office.

His chest was covered with tattoos, and there, along with all the usual To-Mother-Ever-Faithful stuff, was a huge, gloomy portrait of Spinoza – moreover, in a wig. It even seemed to Nelya that Spinoza's eyes revolved in some strange way.

"So, now will you tell me that you don't believe?" the little creature smirked at the doctor.

"I don't. But let me test you in the bed and then I'll believe," Nelya blurted out lasciviously and immediately caught herself, surprised that such a thing could escape from her mouth.

But the diminutive reincarnation of Spinoza did not exhibit the slightest astonishment.

"Sure, I can do that," he agreed meekly, inclining his head like a bull. "Only at your house."

"Visiting hours are over," Nelya called to the sick in the corridor, poking her head out the door.

... And an hour later her sweaty body lay sprawled in bed with the naked Peter Nikitich (as she called the sick man, feeling uncomfortable calling him Spinoza. And he had agreed good-naturedly that in this life it was quite all right to call him Petya). Contentment was written on Nelya's fat, glistening face.

"You're too much, Petya," she said, scratching his prick. "You claim you were Spinoza. Whisper something in my ear. What proof? So you can paint his picture on your chest. So what? Probably you scare petty criminals with it."

Petya was just on the verge of climbing onto Nelya Semenovna again, but her disbelief offended him. Reddening, he jumped out of bed and, with a resentful look on his little face, ran to the corner. Glumly he kept still, not deigning to differ with Nelya. The latter, peering attentively at his face, degenerate and darkened with thought, could not understand where Peter Nikitich got all his confidence. Was it merely an inner conviction or did he know some secret?

"Petya, you're a real idiot," Nelya Semenovna pronounced finally, having looked him over. "How could you have been Spinoza?"

Peter Nikitich leaped from the corner, and weaving like a trained viper, he rushed up to the bed. His dim eyes shone.

"So you've forgotten about moral harmony, the laws of justice," he muttered. "In my last life I was Spinoza, and now I'm an idiot.... For the sake of moral balance, to learn humility. It wouldn't be so hot if I was Spinoza now. On the other side of the coin, some earlier cretin is now some kind of – what's his name, Jean-Paul Sartre."

Nelya burst out laughing. Peter Nikitich turned his frightening, degenerate face back to the corner.

"Where do you get all that?" wondered Nelya Semenovna in amazement, her body shaking. "It's incredible ... although there *is* something suspicious about you. Well, come, come to me, my Spinoza." And she extended her plump, sweaty hands toward him.

The evening went off well.

The next day at lunch, chewing on a fine, juicy rabbit, Nelya growled carnivorously over a bone, then broke a long silence. "So, you really believe that there is justice in the world? And what about this rabbit? Perhaps you'll say that it, too, will someday be Spinoza?"

Peter Nikitich frowned suddenly and his face took on a studied, puzzling expression.

"I was one-sided then, Nelya," he said simply. "But do not

think that, like all your Christians, I understand only morality and ignore cognition. On the contrary, I am convinced that it is precisely cognition which is the key to morality. When we really comprehend the other side, when the scales fall from our eyes and we see in what a concrete relationship our earthly life is with all the rest – a small part of the whole – then naturally all our notions will change, and we'll see that evil is an illusion and that the world is truly just. Yes, yes, even this rabbit, which you are chewing on so sweetly. Yes, yes, don't laugh. His existence, too, will be justified. Indeed, in fact, he is not just a rabbit. And, who knows, at some time he may become a Spinoza."

Peter Nikitich choked. A piece of rabbit had gotten stuck in his throat, and he was a long time coughing before he got it down into his stomach. Nelya laughed, a deep belly laugh. Such words from the mouth of an idiot like Petya struck her as nearly miraculous.

"And, all the same, you go on fuming over moral law," she began, "and let's even say by means of cognition and not your weak-willed … love. But why are you so sure that, when the scales fall, everything will turn out so well? Let's suppose, even, that earthly evil – by the way, a very naive form of evil – will somehow be explained, but then a new evil is revealed, deeper and more terrifying.... Can it be that it never entered your head that good and evil are secondary considerations in the world, while the higher goal is in another, deeper realm? … This goal would be related to the expansion of individuality, of self-awareness."

Nelya got up, inspired by her own speech. Petya's eyes blazed like a fakir's, and again it flashed through Nelya's mind that perhaps Petya had really once been Spinoza. This stimulated her even more. She continued:

"And even if the problem of good and evil is solved in favor of good, from the point of view of the cosmos this is entirely secondary. Really, do you think that the greater powers have no more profound goal than the happiness of all these creatures here? Really, are we to judge the higher powers by ourselves, by what is obvious in us?"

After this tirade Nelya suddenly noticed that Petya had turned into an idiot once more. His eyes had dimmed, his face had assumed a doltish, contrived expression. He began to giggle and froth at the mouth, and finally started singing Soviet jingles. Having glimpsed in Petya such a spiritual being, Nelya was not yet able to get hold of herself before he was pawing her, specifically her rear end, though in an entirely abstract manner. The day ended with a mad trip to the movies.

And the following days passed as in a poem: gaily, foolishly, inconclusively. Petya had completely forgotten about the sanitorium. Bespattered with emotions as with urine, he jumped about the room, sang songs, and made constant references to moral harmony, asserting that, although he was now an idiot, he had earlier been Spinoza and certainly would be him again. This moved him deeply, and, dangling his feet over the side of the bed, he would often strum a guitar and think about it.

Nelya liked him primarily as an idiot. And the knowledge that she was being screwed by a true imbecile was a pleasure to her, as if his sperm therefore would be blacker and her enjoyment more intense. It seemed to Nelya that she was now surrounded by unseen little idiot boys to whom she had somehow given birth.

To soothe and intimidate her patients, she took Petya along on her house calls. The more so since Petya with his visage and his absurd pronouncements instilled in them confidence in the existence of a world beyond.

One fellow even threw all his icons and his cross out the window, announcing that now he had only one God – Peter Nikitich. Another rejoiced in him as in the Father and wanted to crawl inside Petya's existence. Even the dying infant smiled tenderly at Peter Nikitich and joyously winked his little eye at him. There was only one old woman whom Petya was unable to convince of anything. The old woman was dying, but instead of praying she would hold an old mirror in front of herself and spit onto it continuously.

"That's for you," she would repeat, glancing at her own reflection. "Ugh, you … if only you did not exist."

It turned out that the old woman was indignant with herself because like everyone else she was mortal.

She died in a most ugly manner. Choking, she leaned forward with her last strength and, pulling her tongue aside, hacked out pus onto her reflection. Hacked, fell back on the pillow, and died.

And Nelya could not get enough of such scenes. Her consciousness sang around her head, to use a theosophical expression. She forgot everything else on earth, even her own existential gluttony.

Meanwhile, her patients suddenly began to depart by the dozens: in the district where she worked people started dying one after the other as if by agreement. Red-faced, with unkempt hair and exuberance in her eyes, Nelya Semenovna swept from one house to the next like an overfed butterfly. She finally took to making her rounds alone so as not to share her happiness with anyone.

She even developed the habit of pinching the dying or grabbing them by the hand as if to aid them.

And morally she grew and grew and grew, but it was impossible to say in what direction. In any case, externally, she started – very restrained – to write poetry in Latin.

But one strange occurrence frightened her: Peter Nikitich disappeared. On the table there lay a note: "I've gone to Holland."

"My fault, my own fault," Nelya Semenovna thought to herself painfully. "Because I was preoccupied with the dying. He couldn't take the indifference and left."

She remained alone, face to face with death.

Translated by
H.W. Tjalsma

ANDRÉ PIEYRE DE MANDIARGUES

THE TIDE

For the ancient Greeks, Eros was the binding force of the physical universe. "For all of these – sun, earth, sky and sea – are at one with all their parts that are cast far and wide from them in mortal things," wrote Empedocles. "And even so all things that are more adapted for one another, are much the same and united in love by Aphrodite." Our human relationships then are mirrors of vaster relationships, and we move with the movement of the stars.

For André Pieyre de Mandiargues, who learned his craft from the surrealists, "there is nothing essentially human that doesn't exist naturally in a stone, a plant, an animal." This belief has led him to write stories in which our actions correspond to larger and smaller events in nature: the change of seasons, the migrations of wild beasts, the tides. John Ruskin called this mimicry, when nature is lent human emotions, "the pathetic fallacy." Mandiargues reverses the comparison and describes our erotic pursuits in terms of natural phenomena. Exemplum docet – *"the example teaches," says the old adage. In Mandiargues's story, the example is the world itself, from which we can learn the meaning of our actions.*

JULIE, my cousin, was sixteen, I was twenty, and this small difference in age, which would later become insignificant, made her docile to my will as if she had been still a child and I fully grown. It was in August, in Normandy, during the most beautiful and hottest summer anyone in that rainy country could remember. With Julie I went to the beaches or to the clay pits on the pretext of taking a walk or fishing for crabs or looking for fossils, but in fact what we did was talk. She would tell me of her precocious love affairs with the boys she met at the tea-dances to which her mother took her, and the small pleasures she derived from these, and I would tell her of the deeper pleasures that I found in Paris with common girls, in a house where they came to sell themselves overseen by a stout lady who curiously resembled her mother, my worthy aunt. We would then burst out laughing, or we would remain silent for a long time and simply look at each other, but our contacts had always been chaste and at a distance, even though Julie had guessed (she told me this later, sly girl) the furious desire I felt for her and, among the parts of her body, above all for her mouth. She had very pale lips, tinged with mauve, shiny with vaseline (to avoid chapping), on a softly pink face, and eyes the colour of troubled waters, and hair faintly greyish-blonde, cut in what is known as the Joan-of-Arc style. There was in that mouth a look both young and wilted, fresh and impure, with a touch of something terribly, indecently open, and yet obviously unravished, a look which threw me in such a state that I could have drilled the very earth.

It happened that my aunt had been invited to a hunt somewhere in the lower Seine, and Julie, who was sorry for the animals, refused to go with her, choosing to remain alone in the country home. I suggested a long walk by the edge of the sea that day, and told her I would pick her up at eight o'clock in the morning, that we would ride our bicycles up to Denderville, that we would then walk along the beach down to the Cuval Straits, and eat along the way if she would prepare the basket, as usual. She used to make sandwiches with as much care as imagination, and I always left that task in her hands.

We arrived in Denderville a little after nine, because we had left somewhat late (to suit my plan). After padlocking our bicycles next to the Customs hut, we climbed down on the rocks and then on to the damp sand where one could walk easily next to the waves. Three children were playing behind us; a woman, seated by the cement steps, was knitting; very soon we were entirely on our own. I walked in front, so as not to look at Julie whom I wanted to forget, to be better moved when I discovered her again, and therefore we walked very fast. But the sea was coming in quickly as well; the new moon had appeared three days earlier and it was now the time of the great tides, the strongest before those of September and October. As the waves burst upon the sand, one of them, more violent than the rest, wet our feet, and I walked to the cliff which the rocks at this point no longer surrounded, and we continued our path upon a kind of chalk plateau where one had to watch out for the green froth that made it slippery.

"If we carry on," Julie said, "we shall be locked in by the sea. We will never reach Cuval before the high tide is in."

"It's your fault," I said to her, "you should have been ready earlier. But it's too late and we have come too far to go back. We will walk up to those fallen rocks in front of us which even the highest tides don't reach, and we will wait there until the sea has pulled back again. Then we shall be able to get to Cuval and return along the top of the cliff, or if not, we can take the same route we came if we are not too tired."

A light breeze began to blow, the waves became larger, and they now rolled upon the back of the sand dune before ending their run among the blocks of chalk that resembled loaves of sugar. Bursting upon the rocks, they sprayed us with foam, as if to push us against the cliff which the sea would soon batter. I quickened my step, even though it was not easy on that kind of ground. Behind me, I could hear Julie's breath. She had run to catch up with me, but I did not turn my head. The fallen rocks lay less than fifty feet away.

The cliffs, as is well known, periodically crumble, undermined by the blows of the sea. A whole ridge had fallen at this spot a long time ago, because the chalk had taken on that dark and hard look which it takes on only after a long exposure to the sea air, and the fallen mass must have been considerable, because it ran more than half a mile into the sea, at low tide.

Only about a third could now be seen, and the furthest fragments, the rocks around which we had sometimes gone fishing for large prawns, were now completely under water.

I held out my hand for Julie, still not looking at her, to help her climb onto the first blocks of stone. A badly drawn path led us now to the top of the rocks and she let out a frightened scream, because the sea, on the other side, was already beating against the cliffs up to the mouth of the Cuval Straits; behind us the road had also been cut off. At a glance, I saw that there was no one on the rocks. Seagulls which we had frightened were flying away, and their voices made that piercing sound that seems so sinister when one is alone. Other birds of the same colour but smaller, perhaps sea-swallows, turned in circles above us and then soared up to the top of the cliffs.

In spite of my cousin's timid complaints, I continued to lead her, climbing down towards the tip of this cape-like formation. Towards the middle, the rocks were scattered around a fairly spacious basin full of pebbles, shells, and sand, and a small pool where the water slowly trickled into the sea, which could be seen on one side, in between the rocks which were more spread out than in other places. Here I stopped and Julie jumped right after me into the basin.

"What will we do?" she said. "We are all alone and the water will come in."

"The water will come into the pool, but not much farther," I said. "You can see on those rocks the line of seaweed left by the high tide. It will be enough to sit a little higher so that only our feet get wet."

I sat down, as I had said, and took my running-shoes off, and the little monkey, always imitating me, did the same. I told her to paddle in the pool in front of me; she obeyed. Only then did I look at her.

Julie's legs were naked all the way up to her knees, with the water up to her ankles; her arms were also naked, and her short dress revealed the rest of her body through the transparent cloth of thin cotton; she was wearing a black swim suit of which I could see a buttoned-up strap through the opening in the front of her dress. Beneath her blonde fringe, her eyes looked damp and soft, making one wish to be despotic; her cheeks had blushed almost imperceptibly, and her mouth, which I longed for, as I have said, more than anything else in the world, revealed without smiling small teeth that sparkled in the sun. Hiding my emotions as best I could, I ordered her to come near.

"Come to me on all fours," I said. "Your dress is already dirty and you will have time to wash it anyhow before your mother comes home."

My adorable little cousin did as she was told, and I saw close to me her eyes full of rain and her mouth which now was smiling, while she lay her sweetly rounded chin on my knee. "I am capable of everything," I thought drunkenly, putting my hand on her neck to verify that on the other side the strap was also buttoned and that the curious bathing suit, somewhat old-fashioned, that Aunt Aline had chosen for her daughter, was still there.

"You see," she said, "I have my swimming costume on. If you wish, I can take my dress off, and we can both go down among the rocks and swim towards the sea wrack."

"No," I said, unfastening the straps with both hands at once. "You must take your swimming suit off and be completely naked underneath your dress. To play fish among the seaweed is of no interest whatsoever. There is another game you will play with me."

"All right," she said, looking at me strangely, after seeming to think about it for a tiny moment.

Standing in front of me and trying to keep her balance, she pulled her bathing suit off from beneath her dress, stepped out with one foot and then the other, and placed the swimming suit on the rocks; I smelled a warm smell of perspiration. She was obviously naked beneath the white cloth printed with bunches of roses, soaked in parts by the sea and muddied in the basin, and I could see her body as clearly as before, or even better, because the wind wrapped the cloth over her stomach and her neck. I sat a little higher, against a fairly smooth rock, and I hung my watch upon a sharp edge so as to be able to see the time easily. Next to it I placed a copy of the local paper, *La Vigie*; then I returned to my cousin and told her to sit as close to me as she could, but without weighing me down.

When she was almost on top of me, I placed my hand on her nape again and on her shoulders, and I caressed her lovely hard neck beneath the dress without her even trying to defend herself, without even seeming surprised, with that marvellous and pure indecency that is natural in very young girls. At the same time I showed her, in the paper, the hour of the tides, reminding her that *La Vigie* gave the Norman peasants' schedule, and that we had to add an hour to find the summer schedule, ours, that of Parisian and city people on holiday. Therefore, to find that day's high tide, instead of 10:14 we were to read 11:14. My watch, set to the second, showed that it was 10:40. We had therefore a little over half an hour to wait.

She listened to me, open-mouthed (which was, of course, her natural attitude). After explaining to her the irreparable solitude in which we both found ourselves, on our island or peninsula, I added that for a long time I had longed and thirsted after that mouth like a man lost in the desert thirsts for fresh water, and that now nothing would stop me, I would satisfy my desire and quench my burning thirst.

"You're going to kiss me on the mouth," she said, all ready.

"I will certainly not kiss you on the mouth, as you erroneously suppose," I answered. "But you will take me in your mouth, just as I told you – and you seemed to understand – that the whores at Madame Regina's took me. I shall remain there as long as the tide comes in, more than half an hour as you have seen, and during that time, to stop you from talking distractedly and letting me slip out, I shall explain to you the mechanism of the tides. This time you shall pay close attention to what I have to say, to what I will accomplish inside your mouth, and to the sea, rising around us now as desire rises in me. At 11:14, precisely, when the sea is rigorously flat, I shall come in your mouth. It is good that you know that it is not easy to have this control over oneself, but I have some experience in this matter, in spite of my age, which is not so much more advanced than yours. I will therefore need the proper concentration during this task, and you also need to concentrate. Think intensely about whatever you wish, about yourself, about me, about someone you love or something you want, and above all try to feel the progress of my desire swelling towards fruition. When I flood your mouth it is indispensable that you swallow meekly and joyfully the vital gift I will have cast, and you will think of that gift as well as of the results of

very instant a small wave, passing through the rocks around our escarpment, entered the pool at our feet with a secretive sound like that of a beaver or otter plunging into the water. The seagulls, reassured by our peacefulness, after having flown around us, were coming back to perch nearby and we could hear them screaming above the sound of the waves.

Julie abandoned herself to my violence like a drowning woman to the sea. I had stopped, shortly after the penetration, from holding her eyelids shut, and, opening her eyes, she had first seen the furious member preying upon her mouth, but soon she looked aside and then linked eyes with mine in an expression of stupor and submission that I had never seen in anyone before. I held her head with one hand and I led her with a soft, slow movement, accompanying the rhythm of the waves and the paced quiver of my loins; one would have said (if someone had been watching us) that this was a dance of sorts or an intimate and unique gymnastic exercise that drew us together on this bank of rocks, at the bottom of the small amphitheatre of stones invaded by the rising tide. With the other hand I caressed her body beneath her dress, which was about as wide as it was short, and I had unbuckled the belt so that there would be no obstacles to my progress. Nothing would have been easier than lifting off that dress, and Julie, evidently, would not have opposed it had I done so, seeing that I could evidently do anything to her without resistance, but this poor stained dress – stained both in the front and the back – dressed her as a victim in a fashion I found ravishing, and I preferred to grasp her breasts, already fully blown, hold her thin waist, descend to the bottom of her lovely smooth stomach, and finger the thicket of her young fleece beneath the cover of the printed cloth, a cloth so ordinary that it would have barely done to curtain a parlour maid's room. I was charmed by the small bunches of flowers.

"Do you know," I said to her, "that the sandy deposits left by the sea are sometimes called 'adamic alluviums'? The reason for this curious name, now I think of it, is perhaps the resemblance, the points in common, between these large cylindrical shapes and that which I place all the way down your mouth. We are perhaps not the first to have heard the call of nature and to have matched our rhythm with the rhythm of the tide."

So that she would not try to answer, I rammed myself in farther, which must have hurt her mouth, because she let out a small moan. Then she wrapped her lips around me even more firmly. I had the impression of forcing my way into a damp flower; I imagined entering the very heart of a pale rose. I was overcome by such fervent emotions that I felt the end was near and that it was necessary to do something to delay it if I did not want to miss that which I had promised myself and that which I had announced to Julie.

So I spoke, casting a glance at my watch to keep in unison with the event, and I explained to her carefully the causes of the in-coming and out-going tides as we know them, according to both the Ancients and to modern scientific theories. I demonstrated the waxing and waning cycles of the waters which followed the position of the moon, and I taught her the daily forty-eight-minute-delay to which this double movement is law. She was initiated into the variations produced in these cycles, of which the extreme points are the sea-tides and the marsh-tides; she learned of the existence and role of the syzygies and their influence on the equinoxes. While I explained, I rocked her head backwards and forwards, as if I were rocking the cradle of a child, all the while rocking myself as well. The sea around us had entered the crevices among the fallen rocks, and was flooding the tiny ravines. Jets of water sprang around the stone walls protecting our refuge, and the outside waves sprouted small fingers that ran along the surface of the pond, licking my cousin's feet. The seagulls had taken flight once again and were circling around us in a state of intense agitation, crying louder and louder all the time. I had never been in such strong and intimate communion with nature; I felt descending upon me the great vital current that circulates among the planets and that soars, perhaps, up to the farthest stars. I was somehow part of the breathing of the universe. In spite of this, instead of losing consciousness and drifting away in the cosmic whirlwind, I felt that my faculties of observation had powerfully increased. There was a point which kept me back and gave me energy, and that point was the rose in which I was rooted, Julie's mouth.

From time to time she glanced at my watch, patiently, listening to me with avid attention, and her face had taken on an expression of gravity that I had not known in her before and of which I had not thought her capable. Several times I had noticed the curiously erotic relationship between a teacher and his pupil, especially if they are of different sex, but I had never been able to confirm, as I had done now, the truth of this observation, which is anyway banal. I almost smiled, and, schoolboyish and pedantic, I drifted a little from the end to which we both were aiming. A look at the watch brought me back to serious matters, because there were only six minutes left before high tide.

My lecture was brusquely interrupted after my description of the bar of Kyilleboeuf, and I returned to Julie, at least with my attention, because my fingers had not left Julie's beautiful body. I increased my caresses as I increased the rhythm of my thrust. Simultaneously I tried to imagine, in a more intense fashion, the rising of the sea around our coupling, and after several minutes I was so confused with the elementary substance that it seemed to me that the tide was rising within me as it did around me. I told Julie so, in a few whispered words, and she gave me to understand that it was the same with her. 11:12. The wind had fallen, the noise of the waves on the rocks had diminished, but the tension was at its highest peak, and I felt in the muscles of my neck a sort of happiness derived from the strength I believed I was sharing with the enormity of the waters attracted by the moon. At last it was time; I did not need to look at my watch because I knew within myself that the peak had been reached, the hour at which the sea was high, and I spilled my joy inside Julie's mouth. Did this violent wave surprise her, at least because of its abundance, seeing that she knew the very minute in which her throat would be filled? It did not seem so. She drank all, as she had been ordered.

We remained motionless, without speaking, one next to the other, transformed, one would have said, into stone. Then I stood up to tuck my clothes in a little. Julie, as I sat down again, rubbed herself against me and pointed out that we would have to wait at least three-quarters of an hour for the sea to sweep back in order to continue our walk.

"We still have some time to enjoy ourselves," she said.

I was almost ashamed that I had pitied her and had imagined sparing her.

"No," I said. "This walk to the fallen rocks was not for our amusement, this was for your instruction. Now, at last, you have learnt the nature of the tides."

Translated by
Alberto Manguel

VALERIE MARTIN

SEA LOVERS

The mermaid, like the dragon and the unicorn, is less a fantastic than a necessary being. She surfaces in many cultures at different times: for the Greeks, she was a siren, half woman and half bird; for medieval Europeans her lower parts were those of a fish. In the sixth century, a mermaid was caught and baptized in Northern Wales; under the name Murgen she became a saint of the Welsh calendar. Another mermaid, trapped in a dike in 1403, lived in Haarlem until her death; she never learned to speak, but was taught to weave, and she worshipped the cross as if by instinct. Christopher Columbus spied three on his way to the New World, but remarked that their beauty was much overrated. Heinrich Heine saw her as the evil Lorelei who, seated on the top of a cliff in the Rhine, lures sailors to their death with her singing. In a story written in 1835 Hans Christian Andersen punished her with pain and silence for aspiring to human love.

Whatever her physical description, she is always associ-

ated with a savage eroticism, as attractive and as fatal as the sea. Valerie Martin's interests seem to lie in the hidden side of a story. Her novel Mary Reilly *retells the tragedy of Dr Jekyll and Mr Hyde from the point of view of a minor character in Stevenson's novel. "Sea Lovers" takes up the legend of the erotic mermaid, but gives it a dark and unexpected twist.*

On moonless nights the sea is black. Ships sail upon it and shine their lights through the double blackness of water and air. The darkness swallows up light like a great yawning snake. On the beach people walk, looking out to sea, but there is no sign of the ships, no sign of the drowning sailors, no sign of anything living or dead, only the continual rushing and ebbing of water sucking and sucking at the shoreline, drawing the innocent, foolish lovers out a little farther. They are unafraid, showing each other their courage. They laugh, pointing to the water. No one can see them. They slip off their clothes and wade in. The waves draw them out, tease them, lick upward slowly about her pale thighs, slap him playfully, dashing a little salt spray into his eyes. He turns to her, she to him; they can scarcely see each other, but they are strong swimmers and they link hands as they go out a little farther, a little deeper. Now the waves swell about them and they embrace. She is losing her footing, so she leans against him, allows the rising water to lift her right off her feet as she is pressed against him. He pulls her in tightly, laughing into her mouth as he kisses her.

They can't be seen; they can't be heard. The people on the shore will find their clothes, but they will never find the lovers. A solitary mermaid passing nearby hears their laughter and pauses. She watches them, but even her strange fish-pale eyes can barely see them; the night is so black, so moonless. She could sing to them, as she has sung to other drowning mortals, but she is weary tonight and her heart is heavy from too much solitude. She has not seen another of her kind for many months. She was nearly killed a few days ago, swimming near a steamship. Her head is full of the giant engine blades, of that moment when she looked up and saw that she was a hair's-breadth from death. That was when she turned toward shore. She is swimming in with the tide, even as the lovers are sucked out and down. When she drops beneath the surface of the water, the mermaid can just see the woman's long hair billowing out around her face. Her mouth is open wide in a silent scream. Oh yes, the mermaid thinks, if she could be heard it would be quite a racket. People would come running for miles. But the sea filled her mouth before the sound could get out and no one will ever hear her now. She clings to the man, and he, in his panic, pushes her away. This started out as such a lark. It was a calm, hot, black night and the white sands of the beach made all the light there was. They had wandered along, stopping to kiss and tease, laughing, so happy, so safe, and now this: she was drowning and he could not save her. Worse, worse, she would pull him under.

The mermaid rises above the crest of a wave and looks back

at them. She sees only one pale hand reaching up, the fingers splayed and tense, as if reaching for something to hold; then the water closes over that too.

The sea is full of death, now more than ever. The mermaid has, twice in her short life, found herself swimming in a sea red with blood: once from a whale struck by a steamship, once from men drowning during a war. Their ship had been torpedoed and most of them were bleeding when they hit the water. The sharks had done the rest. That time she had dived beneath the battle, for the noise was deafening and the light from the explosions dazzled her so that she could scarcely see. One of the men clutched at her as she swam away, but she shook him off. She disliked being seen by men, even when they were about to die. She could amuse herself singing to them when they couldn't see her, when they were wild-eyed and desperate, clinging to a broken spar from a boat shattered by a storm, or treading water in that ridiculous way they had, with those pathetic, useless legs; then she would hide among the waves and sing to them. Sometimes it made them more frantic, but a few times she had seen a strange calm overtake a drowning man, so that his struggles became more mechanical, less frantic, and he simply stayed afloat as long as he could and went under at last quietly, without that panicked gagging and struggling that was so disgusting to see. Once a man had died like that very near her, and she had felt so curious about him that she drifted too close to him, and in the last moment of his life he saw her. His eyes were wide open and startled already from his long bitter struggle with death; he knew he was beaten yet could not give up. He saw her and he reached out to her, his mouth opened as if he would speak, but it was blood and not words that poured over his lips and she knew even as he did that he was gone. She had, by her nature, no sympathy for men, but this one interested her.

It was a cold, calm night and the man was so far from land that it would be days before his body was tossed up, bloated, unrecognizable, on some shore. He had been sailing alone in a small boat, far out to sea; she had, in fact, been watching his progress for days. The storm that had wrecked his little craft was intense, but quickly over, and he had survived it somehow, holding on to pieces of the wreckage. Then it was a few days of hopeless drifting for him. She watched from a distance, listened to him when he began to babble to himself. Near the end he stunned her by bursting into song, singing as loud as he could, though he had little strength left, a lively song that she couldn't understand. When he was dead she did something she had never done: she touched him. His skin was strange, he was already stiffening and she was fascinated by the feel of it. She took him by the shoulders and brought him down with her, down where the water was still and clear, and there she looked at him carefully. His eyes fascinated her, so different from her own. She discovered the hard nails on his fingers and toes. She examined his mouth, which she thought incredibly ugly, and his genitals, which confused her. Gradually a feeling of revulsion overtook her and she swam away from him abruptly, leaving him wedged in a bed of coral and kelp, food for the bigger fish that might pass his way.

Now she remembers him as she swims toward shore, and her thin upper lip curls back at the thought of him. She is being driven toward land by a force stronger than her own will, and she hates that force even as she gives in to it, just as she hated the dead man.

It is dark and the air is still. Though the sea is never still, she has the illusion of calm. She swims effortlessly just beneath the surface of the waves. She is getting close to shore, dangerously close, but she neither slows nor alters her course.

She is acquainted with many stories that tell of the perils of the land, stories similar to the ones men tell about the sea, full of terror, wonder, magic, and romance. The moral of these tales (that she can no more live on land than men can live in the sea) has not escaped her. She has seen the land; she knows about its edges and she has seen mountains rising above the surface of the water. Sometimes there are people on these mountains, walking about or driving in their cars. This coast, which she must have chosen, is flat and long. There is white sand along it for miles and behind the sand a line of green, though in the darkness its vivid colors are only black before white before gray. The mermaid can scarcely look at it. She is caught up in the surf that moves relentlessly toward land. For a while she can drop beneath the waves, but soon the water is too shallow, and when her tail and side scrape against the hard sand at the bottom she shudders as if death had reached up suddenly and touched her. The waves smash her down and roll her over. Her tail wedges into the sand and sends a cloud over her; she feels the grit working in under her scales. She raises her webbed hands to wipe it away. It is different from the sand in the deep water; it feels sharp and somehow more irritating and it smells of land.

It's useless to fight the waves. She lets her body rise and fall with them, rolling in with the surf as heavy and unresisting as a broken ship or a dead man. Soon there is nothing but sand beneath her, and the water ebbs away, leaving her helpless, exposed to the warm and alien air. The pounding she has taken has left her barely conscious. She lies on her stomach in the sand, her arms stretched out over her head, her face turned to one side so that what little water there is can flow over it. Her long silvery body writhes in the shallows and she is aghast with pain. From the waist down she is numb and she lifts her head as best she can to look back at herself. She can hardly feel her tail, rising and falling in the sand, working her in deeper and deeper, against her will. It is horrible, and she is so helpless that she falls back down with a groan. Something is seeping out of her, spilling out into the sand. It is slippery and viscous; at first she thinks she is bleeding, then she imagines it is her life. She moans again and struggles to lift herself, pushing her hands against the sand. She opens and closes her mouth, gasping for water. Her skin is drying out; it burns along her back, her shoulders, her neck. She presses her face down as a little trickle of water rushes up near her, but it is not enough and she manages only to get more damp sand in her mouth. She lifts her head and shoulders once more against the unexpected weight of the air, and as she does, she sees the man.

He is running toward her. He has left his fishing gear to the whims of the sea and he is running toward her as fast as he can. Her heart sinks. He is in his element and she is at his mercy. But in the next heartbeat she is struck with cunning and a certainty that flashes up in her consciousness with the force of memory. In the same moment she knows that her lower body is now her own, and strength surges through her like an electric current. He must not see her face; she knows this. She spreads her hair out over her shoulders and hides her face in the sand. Her body is still, her strong tail lies flat in the shallows, as shiny and inert as a sheet of steel.

She listens to the slap of his bare feet against the hard wet sand as he comes closer. Soon she can hear his labored breathing and his mumbled exclamations, though his words are meaningless to her. This is a big catch, but it will be a while before he understands what he has caught. In the darkness he takes her for a woman, and it is not until he is bending over her that he sees the peculiar unwomanly shape of her lower body. For a moment he thinks she is a woman who has been half devoured by an enormous fish. He looks back at the shore, as if help might come from it, but there is no help for him now. His hands move over her shoulders. He is determined to pull her out of the water, not for any reason but that she has washed up on the shore and that is what men do with creatures who wash up on the shore. "My God," he says, and the pitch of his voice makes the mermaid clench her jaw, "are you still alive?"

She does not move. His hands are communicating all sorts of useless information to him: this creature is very like a woman, and though her smooth skin is extraordinarily cold, it is soft, supple, alive. His fingers dig in under her arms and lift her a little. She is careful to keep her face down, hidden in the stream of her long hair. This hair, he can see even in the darkness, is almost white, thick, unnaturally long; it falls voluptuously over her shoulders. He is losing his grip; she is heavier than he imagined, and he releases her for a moment while he changes his position. He straddles her back now. She hears the squish of his feet as he steps over her head and positions himself behind her. As he does he takes a closer look at her long back and sees the line where the pale skin turns to silver. "What are you?" he says, but he doesn't pause to find out. His hands are under her arms again; one of them strays over her breasts quickly, momentarily, as he lifts her. Her heart is beating furiously now so that she can hear nothing else. For one second she hangs limp in his arms and in the next she comes alive.

She brings her arms quickly under her and pushes up so suddenly and with such force that the man loses his balance and falls over her. She is, thanks to the sea, several times as strong as he is, and she has no difficulty now turning over beneath him. He struggles, astounded at the sudden powerful fury of the creature he had intended to save, but he struggles in vain. They are entwined together in the sand, rising and falling like lovers, but the man, at least, is aware that this is not love. Her strong arms close around him and he can feel her cold clawed hands in his hair. His face is wedged against her shoulder, and as he breathes in the peculiar odor of her skin, he is filled with terror. She takes a handful of his hair and pulls his head up so that she can look at him and he at her. What he sees paralyzes him, as surely as if he had looked at Medusa, though it is so dark he can see only the glitter of her cold, flat, lidless eyes, the thin hard line of her mouth, which opens and closes beneath his own. He can hear the desperate sucking sound fish make when they are pulled from the sea. She rolls him under her as easily as if he were a woman and she a man. With one hand she holds his throat while with the other she tears away the flimsy swimming trunks, all the protection he had against her. Her big tail is moving rapidly now, pushing her body up over his. Her hand loosens at his throat and he gasps for air, groaning, pushing against her with all his strength, trying to push her away. She raises herself on her arms, looking down at him curiously and he sees the sharp fish teeth, the dry black tongue. Her tail is powerful and sinuous; it has come up between his legs like an eel and now the sharp edge of it grazes the inside of his thighs. It cuts him; he can feel the blood gathering at the cuts, again and again, each time a little closer to the groin. He cries out, but no one hears him. The mermaid doesn't even bother to look at him as she brings her tail up hard against his testicles and slices through the unresisting flesh, once, twice, three times; that's all it takes. His fingers have torn the skin on her back and he has bitten into her breast so that she is bleeding, but she can't feel anything as pain now. She drops back over him and clasps his throat between her hands, pressing hard and for a long time until he ceases to struggle.

Then she is quiet but not still. Carefully she takes up the bleeding pocket of flesh from between his legs; carefully cradling it in her hands, she transfers it into the impression she left in the sand before this struggle began. The sea will wash it all away in a minute or two, for the tide is coming in, but that's all the time she needs. She pushes the sand up around this bloody treasure; then, exhausted and strangely peaceful, she rolls away into the shallows. The cool water revives her and she summons her strength to swim out past the breakers. Now she can feel the pain in her back and her breast, but she can't stop to attend to it. As soon as the water is deep enough she dives beneath the waves, and as she does her tail flashes silver in the dark night air; like great metal wings, the caudal fin slices first the air, then the water.

On the shore everything is still. The waves are creeping up around the man, prying him loose from the sand. Little water fingers rush in around his legs, his arms, his face. Already the water has washed his blood away. Farther down the beach his fishing gear floats in the rising water. His tackle box has spilled its insides; all his lures and hooks, all the wiles he used to harvest the sea, bob gaily on the waves.

Farther still I am walking on the shore with my lover. We have been dancing at a party. The beach house is behind us, throwing its white light and music out into the night air as if it could fill the void. Inside it was hot, bright; we couldn't hear the waves or smell the salt air, and so we are feeling lightheaded and pleased with ourselves for having had the good sense to take a walk. We are walking away from the house and away from the dead man, but not away from the sea. I've taken my shoes off so that I can let the water cool my tired feet. My lover follows my example; he sheds his shoes and stops to roll up his pants legs. As I stand looking out into the black water and the blacker sky it seems to me that I can see tiny lights, like stars, flashing in the waves. "What are those lights?" I ask him when he joins me, and he looks but says he doesn't see any lights.

"Mermaids," I say. I could almost believe it. I raise my hand and wave at them. "Be careful," I say. "Stay away from the shore." My lover is very close to me. His arms encircle me; he draws me close to him. The steady pounding of the waves and the blackness of the night excite us. We would like to make love in the sand, at the water's edge.

RICHARD MATHESON

AROUSAL

Literature has long dreamt of machines to prolong our various pleasures. Those all-too-brief pleasures of the erotic act have been imagined as vaster and deeper in all manner of literary constructions, from the wooden cow which Pasiphae commanded from Dedalus, the architect of the Cretan labyrinth, to the computerized pleasure domes of William Gibson's cyberpunk universe which obviate all sexual partners. Somewhere in between are the agonizing machineries engineered by the Marquis de Sade, the mechanical brides in the stories of E.T.A. Hoffmann and Villiers de l'Isle Adam, the jade bed of Pao Qu in which the sleeper is rewarded with a "night-long sigh of pleasurable satisfaction" and awakes unable to love again another human being. Certain doctors of Islam, according to a retelling by Adolfo Bioy Casares, believe that one of the rewards for the just (all male, of course) is an infinite harem and an unrelenting priapism.

Richard Christian Matheson, the son of the celebrated

fantasy and science-fiction writer Richard Matheson, has had a varied career as a short story writer, screen-writer/producer, and ghostchaser for the UCLA Parapsychology department. In "Arousal", he depicts the private wonders on the other side of that curious species of eternity.

SHE STARED.

Trying to be sure. Trying to hide it.

He was somehow perfect, somehow virulent; handsome in a way that slit her restraint open. Drew her in. He was about thirty. By himself in the bar. The town, asleep ten stories below, was flat and black. Streetlights stared up, inspecting the hotel bar with orange eyes, and occasionally a sleepy police car would pass, roving pointlessly.

She stared more, wiping long nails with a napkin.

She was becoming sure. *It was in his eyes.*

The *thing.*

Maybe even more than the ones before.

She ordered another kamikaze and walked to the pay phone, passing him. He stared out the window, chewing on a match, and she noticed the way his index finger traced the edge of his beer as if touching a woman's body.

The look.

Every location, she found it.

When the company was done filming and she'd finished going over the next day's setups with whichever director she was currently working under, she'd grab the location van back to the hotel the studio had booked the production team into, pick up mail and messages at the front desk, and go to her room. Always exhausted, always hating being an assistant director. Hating not being the one to set the vision. Run the set.

Be in control.

Then she'd strip; shower. Let the water scratch fingernails down her body as she closed tired eyes. Try to let the sensations take over. Try to feel something. But she never did.

She couldn't.

The sensual voyage her girlfriends felt when they were alone and naked, touching their bodies, allowing their skin to respond, no longer interested her. Her body searched for greater responses. Searched for the one who could hold her the right way, touch her with the exact touch. Make her respond; transcend. Stare into her eyes when she came.

Stare with that look.

She stood at the phone and called collect. Her husband was asleep and when he answered told her he loved her. She said it back but kept watching the man. He was pressing his lips against the matchstick, gently sucking it in and out as she stared in unprotected fascination.

Her husband offered to wake the kids so they could tell her good-night.

"They miss Mommy," he told her, in a sweet voice she hated.

She didn't hear what he'd said then, and he told her again, asking if she were all right; she sounded tired, distracted. She laughed a little, making him go away by calming him. He told her again he loved her and wanted to be with her. To make love. She was silent, watching the man across the barroom, catching his glance as he tried to get the waitress's attention.

"Do you miss me?" her husband asked.

The man was looking at her. Her husband asked her if she was looking forward to making love when she got back into town. She kept staring at the man. Her husband asked again.

"Yes, darling. Of course I am...."

But it was a lie. It never stopped being one. He did nothing for her. She wanted something that would make her forget who she was, what her life was. Something real.

Something unreal.

Her husband had gone to get the kids though she told him not to. He wouldn't listen, and when she lifted cold fingers from her closed eyes, head bowed in private irritation, the man was standing next to her, buying cigarettes from a machine.

"Say hello to Mommy, kids."

The kids spoke sleepily over the phone while the man stared at her, lighting his cigarette, eyes unblinking. She told them to go to sleep, and that she loved them. But she was watching the man's eyes moving down her face, slowly to her neck, her breasts. Further. He quickly looked back at her and she allowed the look to do whatever it wanted.

They went to his room.

Nothing was said. They made love all night and she clutched at the sheets on either side of her sweating stomach with both hands, bunching up the starched cotton, screaming. He touched her so faintly at one point, it felt like nothing more than a thought; a wish. Her body arched and tensed, the pillow beneath her head soaked.

He tied her to the bedposts with silk scarves and blew softly onto her salty mouth, gently kissed her eyelids. He circled his tongue around her ears and whispered rapist demands that made her come. He massaged her until her skin effervesced, until her fingers pulled wildly at the scarves that held her wrists to the bed. Until she moaned with such pleasure, she thought she was in someone else's body.

Or had left her own.

Everything he did aroused her like she'd never been and when he finally untied her, she slept against his chest, held in his soothing arms. She murmured over and over how incredible it had been, stunned by what he'd made her feel. What he was still making her feel.

He said the only thing he would.

"You won't forget tonight."

When she awakened at dawn, he was gone. No note, no sign. There was a knock on the door and she answered, wrapping a towel around herself. Room service rolled in a large breakfast, complete with omelet, café au lait, and a newspaper.

He'd taken care of everything.

She sat in bed and ate, untying the newspaper, aching sweetly from the evening, covered with tender welts and bite marks. The food tasted delicious and the flavors on her tongue made her want to make love. She smiled, listened to the birds outside her window. Their soft opera gave her goose bumps, and as she opened the newspaper, the sound of its crisp folds made her nipples tingle. She laughed a little, remembering the incredible way he'd licked and sucked them last night. They were still sensitive.

As she read, she sipped at her coffee and the creamy heat of it made her part her legs slightly as it spread over her tongue and ran down her throat, warm like sperm.

She began to breathe harder, sipping more, twisting her shoulders as a tingle ran delicate electricity across her shoulders; up her spine.

As she read the front page, she allowed her fingers to drift on the inky surface and could feel the words; their shape and length. The curve of the individual letters. The sound the sentences created in her mind.

She felt herself getting wet.

It was *fantastic;* her body responsive to every detail of the morning; its sounds, colors. Even the feel of the blanket, the scraping texture of the wool making her think about him, the hair on his chest and face. God, why hadn't she asked his name? He was the greatest lover she'd probably ever have and she knew it. She laughed out loud, feeling a strange, new woman inside coming forth; emerging.

The ice in the orange juice was melting and when it rubbed against the glass, the sound made her softly, involuntarily moan. She smiled and lit a cigarette, sensing an unfamiliar fulfillment in her cells and nerves. A happiness.

Lost control.

The cigarette flame gave off a heat she could actually feel and she began to perspire. She shook a bit, grinning, and blew the match out, watching the tiny curls of smoke that peeled from its blackened tip and smelled like the man's scent. She couldn't stop herself from sliding a trembling hand onto a breast. Her skin was hot and as the sounds of the birds got louder outside her window and the hotel began to wake up below her, making faraway morning sounds, she listened and began to groan pleasurably from the noise.

The smell of the unfinished food and the warm air from the heating vent felt like a caress, and her nipples got harder, her pubic hair more wet. Her eyes wandered lazily, sexually around the room and noticed the furniture; the way the fabric on the couch fit its plaid shapes together so perfectly, each cushion like the next. It made her shut her eyes in exquisite torture. She opened them and caught a glimpse of the ballpoint pen which the hotel provided on the bedside table. Its red color pleased her and she groaned happily. Her eyes drifted on. The ashtray on the floor, filled with crippled cigarettes and gum wrappers excited her, its smells and patterns making her think of making love, of the man entering her and ...

She suddenly realized what was happening and noticed an article on the front page section of the paper about a grotesque murder that had occurred the night before. A family had been gunned down by two men in ski masks and as she imagined it, her fingers moved over her body, searching wildly, uncontrollably. Scratching, squeezing. Shivering. She didn't understand the sexual storm her body felt as her mind filled with images of bullets shredding skin, faces twisting in horror, bodies slumping.

The tensing percussion.

The shudder.

She began to come again.

She couldn't stop the orgasm and it drenched her like a toxic wave that rose high and fainted; collapsing, then rising again.

Her body was wet with sweat and her teeth bit into her bottom lip, making it bleed. She squeezed herself so hard she began to bruise, more bluish ponds growing under her skin. Her arms drew back to the bedposts and grabbed tightly to either as if crucified, fingers white; desperate. She screamed louder and louder, flailing, coming again and again, not able to stop the flood of sights, sounds; tactile impressions.

She saw her children and began to cry.

Then, in her mind, she could see the man's face. His easy smile. The way he touched her.

The look.

She passed out for a few moments but the sound of maids beginning to vacuum and cars honking outside awoke her and she couldn't stop her body from starting to respond again.

ERIC McCORMACK

BIRTHDAY PRESENT

Eric McCormack's literary career began late in life when, at the age of forty-nine, he published his first collection of short stories. Inspecting the Vaults *is an extraordinary book, full of invention and black humour, in which the terrible deeds of seemingly ordinary characters are narrated with elegant detachment. For McCormack, the writing of a story distances it from both author and reader, so that the events which take place, however monstrous, must abide by their own rules, the rules of their imaginary worlds. In this, McCormack is the inheritor of the horrors of Poe and the fables of Kafka.*

McCormack doesn't limit his imaginary geography to mere landscape. The body itself is, in his writing, an imaginary place. The poet Pablo Neruda spoke of the body as a land to be ploughed and seeded; John Donne called it a map, explored by his physicians, his cartographers; for St Theresa it was a mansion of many rooms. In McCormack's stories, it becomes the hidingplace for a crime, a house of worship, a battlefield. And in "Birthday Present," the body expands into an entire erotic universe.

WHERE he was exactly among these winter hills, he didn't know. These things he did know: that he'd driven endless miles along this ever-narrowing road gouged out by a snow-plough; and that it was his birthday. No cars passed him; those he himself overtook were old-fashioned, all fins and humps, like this one he was driving. As for stopping, he stopped only once, at a place called High Point Look Out. He pulled in by the barrier fence and rolled his window down. He breathed in the brisk air and gazed across the frozen waves of hills. The cold tickled the little hairs of his nostrils.

All so familiar, he thought. It's all so familiar.

He arrived at the motel after a few more bends in the road. *Moose Lodge,* said the sign, an old-fashioned name for an old-fashioned motel with a flaking totem pole at its entrance. The office was meant to look like a log cabin. The receptionist didn't look up when he came in, nor when he asked for the room number.

"Thirteen," she said, her needles clacking, clacking, a gray-haired woman intent on her knitting.

He walked along the spongy corridor with its stainproof,

dark brown carpet. He had walked along so many such corridors.

At number thirteen, he turned the handle and pushed the door open.

The room was like a million other motel rooms, but just a little old-fashioned, with its dark panelled walls. Except for her. She was standing by the bed, and something about her made him feel he should know her. For some reason, the sight of her filled him with such sadness he could have wept.

So it has come to this, he kept thinking over and over again; after all these years, it has come to this. As she stood there, naked and smiling in the stuffy room, prepared for him. He breathed deeply and shut the door behind him. He leaned against it for a moment, wanting to say something – ask her name perhaps, where they had met before so long ago – he needed to do at least that. But she only smiled, put her finger to her lips and shook her head.

"Say nothing, my dear one," she said. "Come to me now."

So he took off the old plaid coat he had found in the car (how he came to be wearing it, he could not remember, a coat with a musty, familiar smell). And as he stripped off the rest of his clothing, he stripped off his sadness too. He concentrated only on the dull urges of his body, till they obligingly took charge, the way they always did. His chest began to thud so that he feared it might split apart and give birth, at last, to a heart. He wanted to spill himself into her quickly, get it over with quickly, get it done quickly, go back quickly to where he belonged.

But his mind was no mystery to her.

"No, no," she said. "This time you must not rush."

She pulled back the covers and made him lie on the bed. A bottle of oil stood on the bedside table. She poured some of it into her hands. Then she knelt on the bed and spread the warm ooze of it on him, rubbing it into every part of his body, turning him over, rubbing, lingering especially between his legs, stroking him softly, humming to herself as she worked.

When the oiling of the body was over, she sighed – contentedly, he thought – and then she herself lay down.

"Now," she said. "Let us begin."

He climbed onto her, propped himself up on his arms for a moment and looked into her eyes, something he rarely did: he felt he must see into her, discover who she was. He would even have kissed her on the mouth; that too was something he rarely did. But she avoided his lips and kissed his cheek, fondled his thinning hair, ran her hands over his plump body (every day in the mirror, he noticed how plump he had become, plump and white: a plump, white man). She caressed him for a while, then she moved his head down to her breasts, and held him while he sucked. He felt her nipple rise to his tongue and he closed his eyes, buried his nose in her softness, smelt perhaps, the milk just a quarter of an inch beneath the flesh.

"Enough," she whispered. "Enough, my dear."

And now she pushed his head gently down, past the convergence of her rib cage, and down past the sweet mandala of her navel. Down he slid on her arching body; he slid over her belly to the junction of her legs and the soft cluster of hair, the sweet, sweet smell of her. He tried to enter her with his tongue.

"No," she gasped. "No."

And now she began to revolve under him, turning smoothly

with the oil, till she had inverted herself a hundred and eighty degrees, and he could feel her head between his knees.

Ah, he thought. Ah.

He urged his penis towards her face, waiting to feel the soft wetness of her lips upon him.

But "No," she said. "No, my sweet."

And she continued slithering upwards till only their legs were still entangled, she lying face up at the bottom of the bed, he face down in the pillows.

What did she want of him? He wondered about this as he lay there. Why was she delaying?

Then he felt her hands stroking his right foot, felt her lift it and place it between her thighs, felt her fingers grasp his toes and gently begin to insert them into herself. Immediately he was all attention; attentive to her soft wet warmth, attentive to her gasps as she spread herself, gradually, gradually, till each of his toes was inside. She paused only a moment, then her hands went to work again, drawing in his oily forefoot, then the bony arch, then the rough heel. Till, miraculously, even his ankle was inside her, his entire right foot, and she gasping and grunting with the effort, the pain of it.

He forced himself to be silent (he had caught himself whimpering with excitement), and she was silent now for a moment, too. Then he felt her hands again, this time on his left foot; and she began the process again. As before, she tucked his toes in first, one at a time. Her breath rasped. Slowly and surely, she went about her work. She inserted the forefoot, the bridge, the heel, the ankle, till the whole of his left foot was in, oil sliding against oil, snugly alongside the right.

He was afraid some involuntary spasm of his might injure

her, so he lay there, quite still, his feet bound together in the wet, warm, flexible tube. It was many years since he had felt such excitement, yet he could not stop himself from sobbing quietly.

"Hush," she said. "Hush, my dearest."

He knew he must stop his sobbing, and he did, and lay quiet, expectant. This was, after all, only a lull. Soon, the muscles of her abdomen took up the work. They began sucking his legs in, impossibly sucking his legs into her. Inch by inch, he felt his calves, then his knees slowly being drawn in.

He twisted his head around to look at her. But from over his shoulder he could see only her distended genitalia, a fringe of hair, and otherwise nothing but his own thighs, his plump thighs, gradually disappearing into her. He turned his head back and lay still. When she reached the oily bulge of his buttocks, her panting and gasping increased, punctuated now with howls of pain as she stretched to enclose him.

If she felt pain, he himself was in no pain whatever. All of his flesh had taken on a purplish hue; his whole body was engorged, it longed to slide into her.

She gave a loud cry as she enveloped his buttocks, but her muscles did not rest. They kept sucking till he was in her past his waist and still sliding. Some instinct urged him to press his arms to his sides to facilitate entry, and so he did, for he was sliding faster now. He could have believed a rope was attached to him, he was being pulled inside so inexorably, an ecstatic gunkholer in this smooth, timeless tunnel. Even his well-oiled chest and shoulders somehow contracted themselves enough to accommodate passage.

He wondered now, he wondered for the first time, might I

die? Might a man die of so much pleasure? Might this be how a rabbit feels, caught in the slim, loving jaws of a python?

Such thoughts were in his mind when the sucking, all at once, stopped.

He listened, alert as never before. He noticed that the quality of her groans had changed: despair was now mixed with pain. And he knew what was wrong. His head, his balding, clean shaven, plump, oily head, was too massive for her.

As her will slackened, the grip of her muscles eased, and he felt himself sliding back out of her – so many hard-won inches surrendered. He howled with frustration. To be thwarted, with the prize so near. He knew he would be unable to bear it.

Then she spoke. Her voice was so urgent, so kind.

"Help me, my honey. Please help me, my sweet darling."

Yes, yes, he tried to tell her. She must believe, yes, she must believe how much he loved her.

He tensed his body and he wished and wished and wished. She shuddered, and miraculously, her muscles took hold again, the sucking resumed. His shoulders re-entered her, then his neck. He tucked in his chin and took a deep breath. A wall of slow, sweet flesh covered his lips, flattened his nose. As he closed his eyes, he heard her utter one last great shriek of effort, or triumph, or love.

Then, darkness.

He felt himself shoot along a brief tunnel and spill out into a balloon of pink light and opaque waters. A great throbbing surrounded him, his body vibrated with the beat of it. He tried to say the word for this, his rapture. But no word came, only a gurgle, and he cast himself off from all words.

IAN McEWAN

HOMEMADE

One of the earliest subjects of fiction was the childhood discovery of the erotic act. It appears in one of the first novels, Longus's Daphnis and Chloe, *in third-century Greece, and in other versions of the story from China to India and the islands of Polynesia. This erotic discovery establishes future conventions, betrays the biases of our society, reflects our own perceptions of ourselves and of the world. That first encounter is, in more ways than one, a revelation. Ian McEwan's "Homemade" is the chronicle of one such moment.*

The title of McEwan's first book of short stories, First Love, Last Rites, *in which "Homemade" appeared, made explicit the subject of all his future writing: our everyday rituals, from love to death, pushed just far enough to become unbearably uncomfortable, even dangerous. "His elegantly gruesome accounts of derelict and perverted lives," wrote one reviewer at the time of its publication in 1976, "cannot be dismissed after the first* frisson*: their peculiar* *images of pain and loss seem, retrospectively, to grow in depth."*

I CAN SEE NOW our cramped, overlit bathroom and Connie with a towel draped round her shoulders, sitting on the edge of the bath weeping, while I filled the sink with warm water and whistled – such was my elation – "Teddy Bear" by Elvis Presley, I can remember, I have always been able to remember, fluff from the candlewick bedspread swirling on the surface of the water, but only lately have I fully realized that if this was the *end* of a particular episode, in so far as real-life episodes may be said to have an end, it was Raymond who occupied, so to speak, the beginning and middle, and if in human affairs there are no such things as episodes then I should really insist that this story is about Raymond and not about virginity, coitus, incest and self-abuse. So let me begin by telling you that it was ironic, for reasons which will become apparent only very much later – and you must be patient – it was ironic that Raymond of all people should want to make me aware of my virginity. On Finsbury Park one day Raymond approached me, and steering me across to some laurel bushes bent and unbent his finger mysteriously before my face and watched me intently as he did so. I looked on blankly. Then I bent and unbent my finger too and saw that it was the right thing to do because Raymond beamed.

"You get it?" he said. "You get it!" Driven by his exhilaration I said yes, hoping then that Raymond would leave me alone now to bend and unbend my finger, to come at some understanding of his bewildering digital allegory in solitude. Raymond grasped my lapels with unusual intensity.

"What about it, then?" he gasped. Playing for time, I crooked my forefinger again and slowly straightened it, cool and sure, in fact so cool and sure that Raymond held his breath and stiffened with its motion. I looked at my erect finger and said,

"That depends," wondering if I was to discover today what it was we were talking of.

Raymond was fifteen then, a year older than I was, and though I counted myself his intellectual superior – which was why I had to pretend to understand the significance of his finger – it was Raymond who *knew* things, it was Raymond who conducted my education. It was Raymond who initiated me into the secrets of adult life which he understood himself intuitively but never totally. The world he showed me, all its fascinating detail, lore and sin, the world for which he was a kind of standing master of ceremonies, never really suited Raymond. He knew that world well enough, but it – so to speak – did not know him. So when Raymond produced cigarettes, it was I who learned to inhale the smoke deeply, to blow smoke-rings and to cup my hands round the match like a film star, while Raymond choked and fumbled; and later on when Raymond first got hold of some marijuana, of which I had never heard, it was I who finally got stoned into euphoria while Raymond admitted – something I would never have done myself – that he felt nothing at all. And again, while it was Raymond with his deep voice and wisp of beard who got us into horror films, he would sit through the show with his fingers in his ears and his eyes shut. And that was remarkable in view of the fact that in one month alone we saw twenty-two horror films. When Raymond stole a bottle of whisky from a supermarket in order to introduce me to alcohol, I giggled drunkenly for two hours at Raymond's convulsive fits of vomiting. My first pair of long trousers were a pair belonging to Raymond which he had given to me as a present on my thirteenth birthday. On Raymond they had, like all his clothes, stopped four inches short of his ankles, bulged at the thigh, bagged at the groin and now, as if a parable for our friendship, they fitted me like tailor-mades, in fact so well did they fit me, so comfortable did they feel, that I wore no other trousers for a year. And then there were the thrills of shoplifting. The idea as explained to me by Raymond was quite simple. You walked into Foyle's bookshop, crammed your pockets with books and took them to a dealer on the Mile End Road who was pleased to give you half their cost price. For the very first occasion I borrowed my father's overcoat which trailed the pavement magnificently as I swept along. I met Raymond outside the shop. He was in shirtsleeves because he had left his coat on the Underground but he was certain he could manage without one anyway, so we went into the shop. While I stuffed into my many pockets a selection of slim volumes of prestigious verse, Raymond was concealing on his person the seven volumes of the Variorum Edition of the Works of Edmund Spenser. For anyone else the boldness of the act might have offered some chance of success, but Raymond's boldness had a precarious quality, closer in fact to a complete detachment from the realities of the situation. The under-manager stood behind Raymond as he plucked the books from the shelf. The two of them were standing by the door as I brushed by with my own load, and I gave Raymond, who still clasped the tomes about him, a conspiratorial smile, and thanked the under-manager who automatically held the door open for me. Fortunately, so hopeless was Raymond's attempt at shoplifting, so idiotic and transparent his excuses, that the manager finally let him go, liberally assuming him to be, I suppose, mentally deranged.

And finally, and perhaps most significantly, Raymond acquainted me with the dubious pleasures of masturbation. At the time I was twelve, the dawn of my sexual day. We were exploring a cellar on a bomb site, poking around to see what the dossers had left behind, when Raymond, having lowered his trousers as if to have a piss, began to rub his prick with a coruscating vigour, inviting me to do the same. I did and soon became suffused with a warm, indistinct pleasure which intensified to a floating, melting sensation as if my guts might at any time drift away to nothing. And all this time our hands pumped furiously. I was beginning to congratulate Raymond on his discovery of such a simple, inexpensive yet pleasurable way of passing the time, and at the same time wondering if I could not dedicate my whole life to this glorious sensation – and I suppose looking back now in many respects I have – I was about to express all manner of things when I was lifted by the scruff of the neck, my arms, my legs, my insides, haled, twisted, racked, and producing for all this two dollops of sperm which flipped over Raymond's Sunday jacket – it was Sunday – and dribbled into his breast pocket.

"Hey," he said, breaking with his action, "what did you do that for?" Still recovering from this devastating experience I said nothing, I could not say anything.

"I show you how to do this," harangued Raymond, dabbing delicately at the glistening jissom on his dark jacket, "and all you can do is spit."

And so by the age of fourteen I had acquired, with Raymond's guidance, a variety of pleasures which I rightly associated with the adult world. I smoked about ten cigarettes a day, I drank whisky when it was available, I had a connoisseur's taste for violence and obscenity, I had smoked the heady resin of *cannabis sativa* and I was aware of my own sexual precocity, though oddly it never occurred to me to find any use for it, my imagination as yet unnourished by longings or private fantasies. And all these pastimes were financed by the dealer in the Mile End Road. For these acquired tastes Raymond was my Mephistopheles, he was a clumsy Virgil to my Dante, showing me the way to a Paradiso where he himself could not tread. He could not smoke because it made him cough, the whisky made him ill, the films frightened or bored him, the cannabis did not affect him, and while I made stalactites on the ceiling of the bomb-site cellar, he made nothing at all.

"Perhaps," he said mournfully as we were leaving the site one afternoon, "perhaps I'm a little too old for that sort of thing."

So when Raymond stood before me now intently crooking and straightening his finger I sensed that here was yet another fur-lined chamber of that vast, gloomy and delectable mansion, adulthood, and that if I only held back a little, concealing, for pride's sake, my ignorance, then shortly

Raymond would reveal and then shortly I would excel.

"Well, that depends." We walked across Finsbury Park where once Raymond, in his earlier, delinquent days had fed glass splinters to the pigeons, where together, in innocent bliss worthy of the "Prelude," we had roasted alive Sheila Harcourt's budgerigar while she swooned on the grass nearby, where as young boys we had crept behind bushes to hurl rocks at the couples fucking in the arbour; across Finsbury Park then, and Raymond saying,

"Who do you know?" Who did I know? I was still blundering, and this could be a change of subject, for Raymond had an imprecise mind. So I said, "Who do *you* know?" to which Raymond replied, "Lulu Smith," and made everything clear – or at least the subject matter, for my innocence was remarkable. Lulu Smith! Dinky Lulu! the very name curls a chilly hand round my balls. Lulu Lamour, of whom it was said she would do anything, and that she had done everything. There were Jewish jokes, elephant jokes and there were Lulu jokes, and these were mainly responsible for the extravagant legend. Lulu Slim – but how my mind reels – whose physical enormity was matched only by the enormity of her reputed sexual appetite and prowess, her grossness only by the grossness she inspired, the legend only by the reality. Zulu Lulu! who – so fame had it – had laid a trail across north London of frothing idiots, a desolation row of broken minds and pricks spanning Shepherds Bush to Holloway, Ongar to Islington. Lulu! Her wobbling girth and laughing piggy's eyes, blooming thighs and dimpled finger-joints, this heaving, steaming leg-load of schoolgirl flesh who had, so reputation insisted, had it with a giraffe, a humming-bird, a man with an iron lung (who had subsequently died), a yak, Cassius Clay, a marmoset, a Mars Bar and the gear stick of her grandfather's Morris Minor (and subsequently a traffic warden).

Finsbury Park was filled with the spirit of Lulu Smith and I felt for the first time ill-defined longings as well as mere curiosity. I knew approximately what was to be done, for had I not seen heaped couples in all corners of the park during the long summer evenings, and had I not thrown stones and water bombs? – something I now superstitiously regretted. And suddenly there in Finsbury Park, as we threaded our way through the pert piles of dog shit, I was made aware of and resented my virginity; I knew it to be the last room in the mansion, I knew it to be for certain the most luxurious, its furnishings more elaborate than any other room, its attractions more deadly, and the fact that I had never had it, made it, done it, was a total anathema, my malodorous albatross, and I looked to Raymond, who still held his forefinger stiff before him, to reveal what I must do. Raymond was bound to know …

After school Raymond and I went to a café near Finsbury Park Odeon. While others of our age picked their noses over their stamp collections or homework, Raymond and I spent many hours here, discussing mostly easy ways of making money, and drinking large mugs of tea. Sometimes we got talking to the workmen who came there. Millais should have been there to paint us as we listened transfixed to their unintelligible fantasies and exploits, of deals with lorry drivers, lead from church roofs, fuel missing from the City Engineer's department, and then of cunts, bits, skirt, of strokings, beatings, fuckings, suckings, of arses and tits, behind, above, below, in front, with, without, of scratching and tearing, licking and shitting, of juiced cunts streaming, warm and infinite, of others cold and arid but worth a try, of pricks old and limp, or young and ebullient, of coming, too soon, too late or not at all, of how many times a day, of attendant diseases, of pus and swellings, cankers and regrets, of poisoned ovaries and destitute testicles; we listened to who and how the dustmen fucked, how the Co-op milkmen fitted it in, what the coalmen could hump, what the carpet-fitter could lay, what the builders could erect, what the meter man could inspect, what the bread man could deliver, the gas man sniff out, the plumber plumb, the electrician connect, the doctor inject, the lawyer solicit, the furniture man install – and so on, in an unreal complex of timeworn puns and innuendo, formulas, slogans, folklore and bravado. I listened without understanding, remembering and filing away anecdotes which I would one day use myself, putting by histories of perversions and sexual manners – in fact a whole sexual morality, so that when finally I began to understand, from my own experience, what it was all about, I had on tap a complete education which, augmented by a quick reading of the more interesting parts of Havelock Ellis and Henry Miller, earned me the reputation of being the juvenile connoisseur of coitus to whom dozens of males – and fortunately females, too – came to seek advice. And all this, a reputation which followed me into art college and enlivened my career there, all this after only one fuck – the subject of this story.

So it was there in the café where I had listened, remembered and understood nothing that Raymond now relaxed his forefinger at last to curl it round the handle of his cup, and said,

"Lulu Smith will let you see it for a shilling." I was glad of that. I was glad we were not rushing into things, glad that I would not be left alone with Zulu Lulu and be expected to perform the terrifyingly obscure, glad that the first encounter of this necessary adventure would be reconnaissance. And besides, I had only ever seen two naked females in my life. The obscene films we patronized in those days were nowhere near obscene enough, showing only the legs, backs and ecstatic faces of happy couples, leaving the rest to our tumescent imaginations, and clarifying nothing. As for the two naked women, my mother was vast and grotesque, the skin hanging from her like flayed toad-hides, and my ten-year-old sister was an ugly bat whom as a child I could hardly bring myself to look at, let alone share the bath-tub with. And after all, a shilling was no expense at all, considering that Raymond and I were richer than most of the workmen in the café. In fact I was richer than any of my many uncles or my poor overworked father or anyone else I knew in my family. I used to laugh when I thought of the twelve-hour shift my father worked in the flour mill, of his exhausted, blanched, ill-tempered face when he got home in the evening, and I laughed a little louder when I thought of the thousands who each morning poured out of the terraced houses like our own to labour through the week, rest up on Sunday and then back again on Monday to toil in the mills, factories, timber yards and quaysides of London, returning each night older, more tired and no richer; over our cups of tea I laughed with Raymond at this quiescent betrayal of a lifetime, heaving, digging, shoving, packing, checking, sweating and groaning for the profits of others, at how, to reassure themselves, they made a virtue of this lifetime's grovel, at how they prized themselves for never missing a day in the inferno; and most of all I laughed when uncles Bob or Ted or my father made me a present of one of their hard-earned shillings – and on special occasions a ten-shilling note – I laughed because I knew that a good afternoon's work in the bookshop earned more than they scraped together in a week. I had to laugh discreetly, of course, for it would not do to mess up a gift like that, especially when it was quite obvious that they derived a great deal of pleasure from giving it to me. I can see them now, one of my uncles or my father striding the tiny length of the front parlour, the coin or banknote in his hand, reminiscing, anecdoting and advising me on Life, poised before the luxury of giving, and feeling good, feeling so good that it was a joy to watch. They felt, and for that short period they were, grand, wise, reflective, kind-hearted and expansive, and perhaps, who knows, a little divine; patricians dispensing to their son or nephew in the wisest, most generous way, the fruits of their sagacity and wealth – they were gods in their own temple and who was I to refuse their gift? Kicked in the arse round the factory fifty hours a week they needed these parlour miracle-plays, these mythic confrontations between Father and Son, so I, being appreciative and sensible of all the nuances of the situation, accepted their money, at the risk of boredom played along a little and suppressed my amusement till afterwards when I was made weak with tearful, hooting laughter. Long before I knew it I was a student, a promising student, of irony.

A shilling then was not too much to pay for a glimpse at the incommunicable, the heart of mystery's mystery, the Fleshly Grail, Dinky Lulu's pussy, and I urged Raymond to arrange a viewing as soon as possible. Raymond was already sliding into his role of stage manager, furrowing his brow in an important way, humming about dates, times, places, payments, and drawing ciphers on the back of an envelope. Raymond was one of those rare people who not only derive great pleasure from organizing events, but also are forlornly bad at doing it. It was quite possible that we would arrive on the wrong day at the wrong time, that there would be confusion about payment or the length of viewing time, but there was one thing which was ultimately more certain than anything else, more certain than the sun rising tomorrow, and that was that we would finally be shown the exquisite quim. For life was undeniably on Raymond's side; while in those days I could not have put my feelings into so many words, I sensed that in the cosmic array of individual fates Raymond's was cast diametrically opposite mine. Fortuna played practical jokes on Raymond, perhaps she even kicked sand in his eyes, but she never spat in his face or trod deliberately on his existential corns – Raymond's mistakings, losses, betrayals and injuries were all, in the first estimate, comic rather than tragic. I remember one occasion when Raymond paid seventeen pounds for a two-ounce cake of hashish which turned out not to be hashish at all. To cover his losses Raymond took the lump to a well-known spot in Soho and tried to sell it to a plainclothes man who fortunately did not press a charge. After all, there was, at that time at least, no law against dealing in powdered horse-dung, even if it was wrapped in tinfoil. Then there was the cross-country. Raymond was a mediocre runner and was among ten others chosen to represent the school in the sub-counties meeting. I always went along to the meetings. In fact there was no other sport I watched with such good heart, such entertainment and elation as a good cross-country. I loved the racked, contorted faces of the runners as they came up the tunnel of flags and crossed the finishing line; I found especially interesting those who came after the first fifty or so, running harder than any of the other contestants and competing demoniacally among themselves for the hundred and thirteenth place in the field. I watched them stumble up the tunnel of flags, clawing at their throats, retching, flailing their arms and falling to the grass, convinced that I had before me here a vision of human futility. Only the first thirty runners counted for anything in the contest and once the last of these had arrived the group of spectators began to disperse, leaving the rest to fight their private battles – and it was at this point that my interest pricked up. Long after the judges, marshals and time-keepers had gone home I remained at the finishing line in the descending gloom of a late winter's afternoon to watch the last of the runners crawl across the end marker. Those who fell I helped to their feet, I gave handkerchiefs to bloody noses, I thumped vomiters on the back, I massaged cramped calves and toes – a real Florence Nightingale, in fact, with the difference that I felt an elation, a gay fascination with the triumphant spirit of human losers who had run themselves into the ground for nothing at all. How my mind soared, how my eyes swam, when, after having waited ten, fifteen, even twenty minutes in that vast, dismal field, surrounded on all sides by factories, pylons, dull houses and garages, a cold wind rising, bringing the beginnings of a bitter drizzle, waiting there in that heavy gloom – and then suddenly to discern on the far side of the field a limp white blob slowly making its way to the tunnel, slowly measuring out with numb feet on the wet grass its micro-destiny of utter futility. And there beneath the brooding metropolitan sky, as if to unify the complex totality of organic evolution and human purpose and place it within my grasp, the tiny amoebic blob across the field took on human shape and yet still it held to the same purpose, staggering determinedly in its pointless effort to reach the flags – just life, just faceless, self-renewing life to which, as the figure jack-knifed to the ground by the finishing line, my heart warmed, my spirit rose in the fulsome abandonment of morbid and fatal identification with the cosmic life process – the Logos.

"Bad luck, Raymond," I would say cheerily as I handed him his sweater, "better luck next time." And smiling wanly with the sure, sad knowledge of Arlecchino, of Feste, the knowledge that of the two it is the Comedian, not the Tragedian, who holds the Trump, the twenty-second Arcanum, whose letter is Than, whose symbol is Sol, smiling as we left the now almost dark field, Raymond would say,

"Well, it was only a cross-country, only a game, you know."

Raymond promised to confront the divine Lulu Smith with our proposition the following day after school, and since I was pledged to look after my sister that evening while my parents were at the Walthamstow dog track, I said goodbye to Raymond there at the café. All the way home I thought about cunt. I saw it in the smile of the conductress, I heard it in the roar of the traffic, I smelt it in the fumes from the shoe-polish factory, conjectured it beneath the skirts of passing housewives, felt it at my finger tips, sensed it in the air, drew it in my mind and at supper, which was toad-in-the-hole, I devoured, as in an unspeakable rite, genitalia of batter and sausage. And for all this I still did not know just exactly what a cunt was. I eyed my sister across the table. I exaggerated a little just now when I said she was an ugly bat – I was beginning to think that perhaps she was not so bad-looking after all. Her teeth protruded, that could not be denied, and if her cheeks were a little too sunken it was not so you would notice in the dark, and when her hair had been washed, as it was now, you could almost pass her off as plain. So it was not surprising that I came to be thinking over my toad-in-the-hole that with some cajoling and perhaps a little honest deceit Connie could be persuaded to think of herself, if only for a few minutes, as something more than a sister, as, let us say, a beautiful young lady, a film star and maybe, Connie, we could slip into bed here and try out this rather moving scene, now you get out of these clumsy pyjamas while I see to the light ... And armed with this comfortably gained knowledge I could face the awesome Lulu with zeal and abandon, the whole terrifying ordeal would pale into insignificance, and who knows, perhaps I could lay her out there and then, halfway through the peepshow.

I never enjoyed looking after Connie. She was petulant, demanding, spoiled and wanted to play games all the while instead of watching the television. I usually managed to get her to bed an hour early by winding the clock forward. Tonight I wound it back. As soon as my mother and father had left for the dog track I asked Connie which games she would like to play, she could choose anything she liked.

"I don't want to play games with you."

"Why not?"

"Because you were staring at me all the time through supper."

"Well, of course I was, Connie. I was trying to think of the games you liked to play best and I was just looking at you, that was all." Finally she agreed to play hide and seek, which I had suggested with special insistence because our house was of such a size that there were only two rooms you could hide in, and they were both bedrooms. Connie was to hide first. I covered my eyes and counted to thirty, listening all the while to her footsteps in my parents' bedroom directly above, hearing with satisfaction the creak of the bed – she was hiding under the eiderdown, her second favourite place. I shouted "Coming" and began to mount the stairs. At the bottom of the stairs I do not think I had decided clearly what I was about to do; perhaps just look around, see where things were, draw a mental plan for future reference – after all it would not do to go scaring my little sister who would not think twice about telling my father everything, and that would mean a scene of some sort, laborious lies to invent, shouting and crying and that sort of thing, just at a time when I needed all my energy for the obsession in hand. By the time I reached the top of the stairs, however, the blood having drained from brain to groin, literally, one might say, from sense to sensibility, by the time I was catching my breath on the top stair and closing my moist hand round the bedroom door-handle, I had decided to rape my sister. Gently I pushed the door open and called in a sing-song voice,

"Connieee, where aaare you?" That usually made her giggle, but this time there was no sound. Holding my breath I tip-toed over to the bedside and sang,

"I knooow where youuu are," and bending down by the tell-tale lump under the eiderdown, I whispered,

"I'm coming to get you," and began to peel the bulky cover

away, softly, almost tenderly, peeking into the dark warmth underneath. Dizzy with expectation I drew it right back, and there, helplessly and innocently stretched out before me were my parents' pyjamas, and even as I was leaping back in surprise I received a blow in the small of my back of such unthinking vigour as can only be inflicted by a sister on her brother. And there was Connie dancing with mirth, the wardrobe door swinging open behind her.

"I saw you, I saw you and you didn't see me!" To relieve my feelings I kicked her shins and sat on the bed to consider what next, while Connie, predictably histrionic, sat on the floor and boo-hooed. I found the noise depressing after a while so I went downstairs and read the paper, certain that soon Connie would follow me down. She did, and she was sulking.

"What game do you want to play now?" I asked her. She sat on the edge of the sofa pouting and sniffing and hating me. I was even considering forgetting the whole plan and giving myself up to an evening's television when I had an idea, an idea of such simplicity, elegance, clarity and formal beauty, an idea which wore the assurance of its own success like a tailor-made suit. There is a game which all home-loving, unimaginative little girls like Connie find irresistible, a game which, ever since she had learned to speak the necessary words, Connie had plagued me to play with her, so that my boyhood years were haunted by her pleadings and exorcised by my inevitable refusals; it was a game, in short, which I would rather be burned at the stake for than have my friends see me play it. And now at last we were going to play Mummies and Daddies.

"*I* know a game you'd like to play, Connie," I said. Of course she would not reply, but I let my words hang there in the air like bait. "I know a game *you'd* like to play." She lifted her head.

"What is it?"

"It's a game you're always wanting to play."

She brightened. "Mummies and Daddies?" She was transformed, she was ecstatic. She fetched prams, dolls, stoves, fridges, cots, teacups, a washing machine and a kennel from her room and set them up around me in a flutter of organizational zeal.

"Now you go here, no there, and this can be the kitchen and this is the door where you come in and don't tread on there because there's a wall and I come in and see you and I say to you and then you say to me you go out and I make lunch." I was plunged into the microcosm of the dreary, everyday, ponderous banalities, the horrifying, niggling details of the life of our parents and their friends, the life that Connie so dearly wanted to ape. I went to work and came back, I went to the pub and came back, I posted a letter and came back, I went to the shops and came back, I read a paper, I pinched the Bakelite cheeks of my progeny, I read another paper, pinched some more cheeks, went to work and came back. And Connie? She just cooked on the stove, washed up in the sink unit, washed, fed, put to sleep and roused her sixteen dolls and then poured some more tea – and she was happy. She was the inter-galactic-earth-goddess-housewife, she owned and controlled all around her, she saw all, she knew all, she told me when to go out, when to come in, which room I was in, what to say, how and when to say it. She was happy. She was complete, I have never seen another human so complete, she smiled, wide open, joyous and innocent smiles which I have never seen since – she tasted paradise on earth. And one point she was so blocked with the wonder, the ecstasy of it all, that mid-sentence her words choked up and she sat back on her heels, her eyes glistening, and breathed one long musical sigh of rare and wonderful happiness. It was almost a shame I had it in mind to rape her. Returning from work the twentieth time that half hour I said,

"Connie, we're leaving out one of the most important things that Mummies and Daddies do together." She could hardly believe we had left anything out and she was curious to know.

"They fuck together, Connie, surely you know about that."

"Fuck?" On her lips the word sounded strangely meaningless, which in a way I suppose it was, as far as I was concerned. The whole idea was to give it some meaning.

"Fuck? What does that mean?"

"Well, it's what they do at night, when they go to bed at night, just before they go to sleep."

"Show me." I explained that we would have to go upstairs and get into bed.

"No, we don't. We can pretend and this can be the bed," she said, pointing at a square made by the design of the carpet.

"I cannot pretend and show it to you at the same time." So once again I was climbing the stairs, once again my blood pounding and my manhood proudly stirring. Connie was quite excited too, still delirious with the happiness of the game and pleased at the novel turn it was taking.

"The first thing they do," I said, as I led her to the bed, "is to take off all their clothes." I pushed her on to the bed and, with fingers almost useless with agitation, unbuttoned her pyjamas till she sat naked before me, still sweet-smelling from her bath and giggling with the fun of it all. Then I got undressed too, leaving my pants on so as not to alarm her, and sat by her side. As children we had seen enough of each other's bodies to take our nakedness for granted, though that was some time ago now and I sensed her unease.

"Are you sure this is what they do?"

My own uncertainty was obscured now by lust. "Yes," I said, "it's quite simple. You have a hole there and I put my weenie in it." She clasped her hand over her mouth, giggling incredulously.

"That's silly. Why do they want to do that?" I had to admit it to myself, there was something unreal about it.

"They do it because it's their way of saying they like each other." Connie was beginning to think that I was making the whole thing up, which, again, in a way I suppose I was. She stared at me, wide-eyed.

"But that's daft, why don't they just tell each other?" I was on the defensive, a mad scientist explaining his new crack-pot invention – coitus – before an audience of sceptical rationalists.

"Look," I said to my sister, "it's not only that. It's also a very nice feeling. They do it to get that feeling."

"To get the feeling?" She still did not quite believe me. "Get the feeling? What do you mean, get the feeling?"

I said, "I'll show you." And at the same time I pushed Connie onto the bed and lay on top of her in the manner I had inferred from the films Raymond and I had seen together. I was still wearing my underpants. Connie stared blankly up at me, not even afraid – in fact, she might have been closer to boredom. I writhed from side to side, trying to push my pants off without getting up.

"I still don't get it," she complained from underneath me. "I'm not getting any feeling. Are you getting any feeling?"

"Wait," I grunted, as I hooked the underpants round the end of my toes with the very tips of my fingers, "if you just wait a minute I'll show you." I was beginning to lose my temper with Connie, with myself, with the universe, but mostly with my underpants which snaked determinedly round my ankles. At last I was free. My prick was hard and sticky on Connie's belly and now I began to manoeuvre it between her legs with one hand while I supported the weight of my body with the other. I searched her tiny crevice without the least notion of what I was looking for, but half expecting all the same to be transformed at any moment into a human whirlwind of sensation. I think perhaps I had in mind a warm fleshy chamber, but as I prodded and foraged, jabbed and wheedled, I found nothing other than tight, resisting skin. Meanwhile Connie just lay on her back, occasionally making little comments.

"Ooh, that's where I go wee-wee. I'm sure *our* mummy and daddy don't do this." My supporting arm was being seared by pins and needles, I was feeling raw and yet still I poked and pushed, in a mood of growing despair. Each time Connie said, "I still don't get any feeling," I felt another ounce of my manhood slip away. Finally I had to rest. I sat on the edge of the bed to consider my hopeless failure, while behind me Connie propped herself up on her elbows. After a moment or two I felt the bed begin to shake with silent spasms and, turning, I saw Connie with tears spilling down her screwed-up face, inarticulate and writhing with choked laughter.

"What is it?" I asked, but she could only point vaguely in my direction and groan, and then she lay back on the bed, heaving and helpless with mirth. I sat by her side, not knowing what to think but deciding, as Connie quaked behind me, that another attempt was now out of the question. At last she was able to get out some words. She sat up and pointed at my still erect prick and gasped,

"It looks so ... it looks so ..." sank back in another fit, and then managed in one squeal, *"So silly, it looks so silly,"* after which she collapsed again into a high-pitched, squeezed-out titter. I sat there in lonely detumescent blankness, numbed by this final humiliation into the realization that this was no real girl beside me, this was no true representative of that sex; this was no boy, certainly, nor was it finally a girl – it was my sister, after all. I stared down at my limp prick, wondering at its hang-dog look, and just as I was thinking of getting my clothes together, Connie, silent now, touched me on the elbow.

"I know where it goes," she said, and lay back on the bed, her legs wide apart, something it had not occurred to me to ask her to do. She settled herself among the pillows. "I know where the hole is."

I forgot my sister and my prick rose inquisitively, hopefully, to the invitation which Connie was whispering. It was all right with her now, she was at Mummies and Daddies and controlling the game again. With her hand she guided me into her tight, dry little-girl's cunt and we lay perfectly still for a while. I wished Raymond could have seen me, and I was glad he had brought my virginity to my notice, I wished Dinky Lulu could have seen me, in fact if my wishes had been granted I would have had all my friends, all the people I knew, file through the bedroom to catch me in my splendorous pose. For more than sensation, more than any explosion behind my ears, spears through my stomach, searings in my groin or rackings of my soul – more than any of these things, none of which I felt anyway, more then than even the thought of these things, I felt proud, proud to be fucking, even if it were only Connie, my ten-year-old sister, even if it had been a crippled mountain goat I would have been proud to be lying there in that manly position, proud in advance of being able to say "I have fucked," of belonging intimately and irrevocably to that superior half of humanity who had known coitus, and fertilized the world with it. Connie lay quite still too, her eyes half-closed, breathing deeply – she was asleep. It was way past her bed-time and our strange game had exhausted her. For the first time I moved gently backwards and forwards, just a few times, and came in a miserable, played-out, barely pleasurable way. It woke Connie into indignation.

"You've wet inside me," and she began to cry. Hardly noticing, I got up and started to get dressed. This may have been one of the most desolate couplings known to copulating mankind, involving lies, deceit, humiliation, incest, my partner falling asleep, my gnat's orgasm and the sobbing which now filled the bedroom, but I was pleased with it, myself, Connie, pleased to let things rest a while, to let the matter drop. I led Connie to the bathroom and began to fill the sink – my parents would be back soon and Connie should be asleep in her bed. I had made it into the adult world finally, I was pleased about that, but right then I did not want to see a naked girl, or any naked thing for a while yet. Tomorrow I would tell Raymond to forget the appointment with Lulu, unless he wanted to go it alone. And I knew for a fact that he would not want that at all.

SUSAN MINOT

LUST

"Adolescence," said Proust, "is the only time in which we learn something." It is a painful learning. Who we are and what the world is are identities that change moment to moment, shifting in front of our eyes before they can be grasped. And all the while we are required to learn norms of conduct, scales of value, hierarchies of power – the entire conventional structure of our society, of which sex is only one devastating aspect. For the adolescent, the erotic language must be learned long before a sexual identity is recognized.

Susan Minot has made it her business to explore these learnings and their consequences. Her territory is family life; her method, the meticulous collection of details that will reveal, in their grouping, a truth about their subject. The details may seem trivial, fleeting, merely circumstantial: in fact they are the essence of the family experience itself, more wonderful and more horrible than we are often willing to acknowledge. Minot's talent, in this respect, lies in her compassionate sobriety; in having "gone so deep, so terribly deep into family life," as Alice Munro has remarked, "and done it so quietly."

In "Lust," one member is pulled out from the family circle and observed with that same depth and unobtrusiveness, but also with love and compassion.

LEO was from a long time ago, the first one I ever saw nude. In the spring before the Hellmans filled their pool, we'd go down there in the deep end, with baby oil, and like that. I met him the first month away at boarding school. He had a halo from the campus light behind him. I flipped.

Roger was fast. In his illegal car, we drove to the reservoir, the radio blaring, talking fast, fast, fast. He was always going for my zipper. He got kicked out sophomore year.

By the time the band got around to playing "Wild Horses," I had tasted Bruce's tongue. We were clicking in the shadows on the other side of the amplifier, out of Mrs Donovan's line of vision. It tasted like salt, with my neck bent back, because we had been dancing so hard before.

Tim's line: "I'd like to see you in a bathing suit." I knew it was his line when he said the exact same thing to Annie Hines.

You'd go on walks to get off campus. It was raining like hell, my sweater as sopped as a wet sheep. Tim pinned me to a tree, the woods light brown and dark brown, a white house half hidden with the lights already on. The water was as loud as a crowd hissing. He made certain comments about my forehead, about my cheeks.

We started off sitting at one end of the couch and then our feet were squished against the armrest and then he went over to turn off the TV and came back after he had taken off his shirt and then we slid onto the floor and he got up again to close the door, then came back to me, a body waiting on the rug.

You'd try to wipe off the table or to do the dishes and Willie would untuck your shirt and get his hands up under in front, standing behind you, making puffy noises in your ear.

He likes it when I wash my hair. He covers his face with it and if I start to say something, he goes, "Shush."

For a long time, I had Philip on the brain. The less they noticed you, the more you got them on the brain.

My parents had no idea. Parents never really know what's going on, especially when you're away at school most of the time. If she met them, my mother might say, "Oliver seems nice" or "I like that one" without much of an opinion. If she didn't like them, "He's a funny fellow, isn't he?" or "Johnny's perfectly nice but a drink of water." My father was too shy to talk to them at all unless they played sports and he'd ask them about that.

The sand was almost cold underneath because the sun was long gone. Eben piled a mound over my feet, patting around my ankles, the ghostly surf rumbling behind him in the dark. He was the first person I ever knew who died, later that summer, in a car crash. I thought about it for a long time.

"Come here," he says on the porch.

I go over to the hammock and he takes my wrist with two fingers.

"What?"

He kisses my palm then directs my hand to his fly.

Songs went with whichever boy it was. "Sugar Magnolia" was Tim, with the line "Rolling in the rushes / down by the riverside." With "Darkness Darkness," I'd picture Philip with his long hair. Hearing "Under My Thumb" there'd be the smell of Jamie's suede jacket.

We hid in the listening rooms during study hall. With a record cover over the door's window, the teacher on duty couldn't look in. I came out flushed and heady and back at the dorm was surprised how red my lips were in the mirror.

One weekend at Simon's brother's, we stayed inside all day with the shades down, in bed, then went out to Store 24 to get some ice cream. He stood at the magazine rack and read through *MAD* while I got butterscotch sauce, craving something sweet.

I could do some things well. Some things I was good at, like math or painting or even sports, but the second a boy put his arm around me, I forgot about wanting to do anything else, which felt like a relief at first until it became like sinking into a muck.

It was different for a girl.

When we were little, the brothers next door tied up our

ankles. They held the door of the goat house and wouldn't let us out till we showed them our underpants. Then they'd forget about being after us and when we played whiffle ball, I'd be just as good as they were.

Then it got to be different. Just because you have on a short skirt, they yell from the cars, slowing down for a while, and if you don't look, they screech off and call you a bitch.

"What's the matter with me?" they say, point-blank.

Or else, "Why won't you go out with me? I'm not asking you to get married," about to get mad.

Or it'd be, trying to be reasonable, in a regular voice, "Listen, I just want to have a good time."

So I'd go because I couldn't think of something to say back that wouldn't be obvious, and if you go out with them, you sort of have to do something.

I sat between Mack and Eddie in the front seat of the pickup. They were having a fight about something. I've a feeling about me.

Certain nights you'd feel a certain surrender, maybe if you'd had wine. The surrender would be forgetting yourself and you'd put your nose to his neck and feel like a squirrel, safe, at rest, in a restful dream. But then you'd start to slip from that and the dark would come in and there'd be a cave. You make out the dim shape of the windows and feel yourself become a cave, filled absolutely with air, or with a sadness that wouldn't stop.

Teenage years. You know just what you're doing and don't see the things that start to get in the way.

Lots of boys, but never two at the same time. One was plenty to keep you in a state. You'd start to see a boy and something would rush over you like a fast storm cloud and you couldn't possibly think of anyone else. Boys took it differently. Their eyes perked up at any little number that walked by. You'd act like you weren't noticing.

The joke was that the school doctor gave out the pill like aspirin. He didn't ask you anything. I was fifteen. We had a picture of him in assembly, holding up an IUD shaped like a T. Most girls were on the pill, if anything, because they couldn't handle a diaphragm. I kept the dial in my top drawer like my mother and thought of her each time I tipped out the yellow tablets in the morning before chapel.

If they were too shy, I'd be more so. Andrew was nervous. We stayed up with his family album, sharing a pack of Old Golds. Before it got light, we turned on the TV. A man was explaining how to plant seedlings. His mouth jerked to the side in a tic. Andrew thought it was a riot and kept imitating him. I laughed to be polite. When we finally dozed off, he dared to put his arm around me, but that was it.

You wait till they come to you. With half fright, half swagger, they stand one step down. They dare to touch the button on your coat then lose their nerve and quickly drop their hand so you – you'd do anything for them. You touch their cheek.

The girls sit around in the common room and talk about boys, smoking their heads off.

"What are you complaining about?" says Jill to me when we talk about problems.

"Yeah," says Giddy. "You always have a boyfriend."

I look at them and think, As if.

I thought the worst thing anyone could call you was a cockteaser. So, if you flirted, you had to be prepared to go through with it. Sleeping with someone was perfectly normal once you had done it. You didn't really worry about it. But there were other problems. The problems had to do with something else entirely.

Mack was during the hottest summer ever recorded. We were renting a house on an island with all sorts of other people. No one slept during the heat wave, walking around the house with nothing on which we were used to because of the nude beach. In the living room, Eddie lay on top of a coffee table to cool off. Mack and I, with the bedroom door open for air, sweated and sweated all night.

"I can't take this," he said at three A.M. "I'm going for a swim." He and some guys down the hall went to the beach. The heat put me on edge. I sat on a cracked chest by the open window and smoked and smoked till I felt even worse, waiting for something – I guess for him to get back.

One was on a camping trip in Colorado. We zipped our sleeping bags together, the coyotes' hysterical chatter far away. Other couples murmured in other tents. Paul was up before sunrise, starting a fire for breakfast. He wasn't much of a talker in the daytime. At night, his hand leafed about in the hair at my neck.

There'd be times when you overdid it. You'd get carried away. All the next day, you'd be in a total fog, delirious, absent-minded, crossing the street and nearly getting run over.

The more girls a boy has, the better. He has a bright look,

having reaped fruits, blooming. He stalks around, sure-shouldered, and you have the feeling he's got more in him, a fatter heart, more stories to tell. For a girl, with each boy it's as though a petal gets plucked each time.

Then you start to get tired. You begin to feel diluted, like watered-down stew.

Oliver came skiing with us. We lolled by the fire after everyone had gone to bed. Each creak you'd think was someone coming downstairs. The silver loop bracelet he gave me had been a present from his girlfriend before.

On vacations, we went skiing, or you'd go south if someone invited you. Some people had apartments in New York that their families hardly ever used. Or summer houses, or older sisters. We always managed to find someplace to go.

We made the plan at coffee hour. Simon snuck out and met me at Main Gate after lights-out. We crept to the chapel and spent the night in the balcony. He tasted like onions from a submarine sandwich.

The boys are one of two ways: either they can't sit still or they don't move. In front of the TV, they won't budge. On weekends they play touch football while we sit on the sidelines, picking blades of grass to chew on, and watch. We're always watching them run around. We shiver in the stands, knocking our boots together to keep our toes warm, and they whizz across the ice, chopping their sticks around the puck. When they're in the rink, they refuse to look at you, only eyeing each other beneath low helmets. You cheer for them but they don't look up, even if it's a face-off when nothing's happening, even if they're doing drills before any game has started at all.

Dancing under the pink tent, he bent down and whispered

in my ear. We slipped away to the lawn on the other side of the hedge. Much later, as he was leaving the buffet with two plates of eggs and sausage, I saw the grass stains on the knees of his white pants.

Tim's was shaped like a banana, with a graceful curve to it. They're all different. Willie's like a bunch of walnuts when nothing was happening, another's as thin as a thin hot dog. But it's like faces; you're never really surprised.

Still, you're not sure what to expect.

I look into his face and he looks back. I look into his eyes and they look back at mine. Then they look down at my mouth so I look at his mouth, then back to his eyes then, backing up, at his whole face. I think, Who? Who are you? His head tilts to one side.

I say, "Who are you?"

"What do you mean?"

"Nothing."

I look at his eyes again, deeper. Can't tell who he is, what he thinks.

"What?" he says. I look at his mouth.

"I'm just wondering," I say and go wandering across his face. Study the chin line. It's shaped like a persimmon.

"Who are you? What are you thinking?"

He says, "What the hell are you talking about?"

Then they get mad after, when you say enough is enough. After, when it's easier to explain that you don't want to. You wouldn't dream of saying that maybe you weren't really ready to in the first place.

Gentle Eddie. We waded into the sea, the waves round and plowing in, buffalo-headed, slapping our thighs. I put my arms around his freckled shoulders and he held me up, buoyed by the water, and rocked me like a sea shell.

I had no idea whose party it was, the apartment jam-packed, stepping over people in the hallway. The room with the music was practically empty, the bare floor, me in red shoes. This fellow slides onto one knee and takes me around the waist and we rock to jazzy tunes, with my toes pointing heavenward, and waltz and spin and dip to "Smoke Gets in Your Eyes" or "I'll Love You Just for Now." He puts his head to my chest, runs a sweeping hand down my inside thigh and we go loose-limbed and sultry and as smooth as silk and I stamp my red heels and he takes me into a swoon. I never saw him again after that but I thought, I could have loved that one.

You wonder how long you can keep it up. You begin to feel as if you're showing through, like a bathroom window that only lets in grey light, the kind you can't see out of.

They keep coming around. Johnny drives up at Easter vacation from Baltimore and I let him in the kitchen with everyone sound asleep. He has friends waiting in the car.

"What are you, crazy? It's pouring out there," I say.

"It's okay," he says. "They understand."

So he gets some long kisses from me, against the refrigerator, before he goes because I hate those girls who push away a boy's face as if she were made out of Ivory soap, as if she's that much greater than he is.

The note on my cubby told me to see the headmaster. I had no idea for what. He had received complaints about my amorous displays on the town green. It was Willie that spring. The headmaster told me he didn't care what I did but that

Casey Academy had a reputation to uphold in the town. He lowered his glasses on his nose. "We've got twenty acres of woods on this campus," he said. "If you want to smooch with your boyfriend, there are twenty acres for you to do it out of the public eye. You read me?"

Everybody'd get weekend permissions for different places, then we'd all go to someone's house whose parents were away. Usually there'd be more boys than girls. We raided the liquor closet and smoked pot at the kitchen table and you'd never know who would end up where, or with whom. There were always disasters. Ceci got bombed and cracked her head open on the banister and needed stitches. Then there was the time Wendel Blair walked through the picture window at the Lowes' and got slashed to ribbons.

He scared me. In bed, I didn't dare look at him. I lay back with my eyes closed, luxuriating because he knew all sorts of expert angles, his hands never fumbling, going over my whole body, pressing the hair up and off the back of my head, giving an extra hip shove, as if to say *There.* I parted my eyes slightly, keeping the screen of my lashes low because it was too much to look at him, his mouth loose and pink and parted, his eyes looking through my forehead, or kneeling up, looking through my throat. I was ashamed but couldn't look him in the eye.

You wonder about things feeling a little off-kilter. You begin to feel like a piece of pounded veal.

At boarding school, everyone gets depressed. We go in and see the housemother, Mrs Gunther. She got married when she was eighteen. Mr Gunther was her high school sweetheart, the only boyfriend she ever had.

"And you knew you wanted to marry him right off?" we ask her.

She smiles and says, "Yes."

"They always want something from you," says Jill, complaining about her boyfriend.

"Yeah," says Giddy. "You always feel like you have to deliver something."

"You do," says Mrs Gunther. "Babies."

After sex, you curl up like a shrimp, something deep inside you ruined, slammed in a place that sickens at slamming, and slowly you fill up with an overwhelming sadness, an elusive gaping worry. You don't try to explain it, filled with the knowledge that it's nothing after all, everything filling up finally and absolutely with death. After the briskness of loving, loving stops. And you roll over with death stretched out alongside you like a feather boa, or a snake, light as air, and you … you don't even ask for anything or try to say something to him because it's obviously your own damn fault. You haven't been able to – to what? To open your heart. You open your legs but can't, or don't dare anymore, to open your heart.

It starts this way:

You stare into their eyes. They flash like all the stars are out. They look at you seriously, their eyes at a low burn and their hands no matter what starting off shy and with such a gentle touch that the only thing you can do is take that tenderness and let yourself be swept away. When, with one attentive finger they tuck the hair behind your ear, you –

You do everything they want.

Then comes after. After when they don't look at you. They scratch their balls, stare at the ceiling. Or if they do turn, their gaze is altogether changed. They are surprised. They turn casually to look at you, distracted, and get a mild distracted surprise. You're gone. Their blank look tells you that the girl they were fucking is not there anymore. You seem to have disappeared.

YUKIO MISHIMA

RAISIN BREAD

"It is always difficult to judge a great contemporary writer," noted Marguerite Yourcenar in her book-long essay on Mishima. "We lack the proper distance." In the case of Mishima, she continues, the chances of misunderstanding him are compounded because the influences of both Western culture, which he so avidly absorbed, and that of his own cultural heritage mix in his work in different degrees. In many of his novels, he inscribes himself solidly in certain Japanese literary traditions; in many others, he is a contemporary of Sartre, of Heidegger, of Albert Camus.

The events of twentieth-century history left Japan with a morbid sense of despair; Mishima set out to chronicle that despair with documentary scrupulosity in stories such as "Raisin Bread," resorting to words but aware of his desire "to encounter reality in some field where words should play no part at all." Despair, the tedium of modern Japanese society, and the erotic become in Mishima's story three parallel worlds, each devoid of language – language which the writer must supply through inference, through allusion, through atmosphere.

No writer is ever successful to his or her satisfaction. Perhaps the failure, in Mishima's ears, to fill the silence with language, led him to commit suicide in the spring of 1970, leaving behind him a list of other literary suicides, amongst whom he named Socrates and Christ.

TURNING INLAND at eleven-thirty on an August night with his back to the white grinding of the waves on the beach, Jack began to climb the broad, sandy cutting that ran up beside the Yuigahama Hotel.

He had made it somehow from Tokyo by hitching rides. As a result, it was a good deal later than the time he'd been supposed to meet up with Peter and Keeko, in addition to which the truck had dropped him off at the wrong spot. But you could get to the meeting place this way too, though it was a long detour, and much farther to walk.

Peter, the girl, and the rest of them would have given him up long ago and gone straight on to the rendezvous.

Jack, twenty-two and made of some clear crystalline substance, had as his sole aim to become quite invisible.

Something of an expert in English, a translator in his spare time of science fiction stories, with a past that included an attempted suicide, he was slim, with a good face fashioned of ivory. It was the kind of face you could strike repeatedly without provoking any response; so no one ever struck it.

Someone in the modern jazz cafe had summed him up by saying that if you took a running jump at him, you'd find you'd gone straight through and out the other side....

The banks of the cutting loomed on either hand. Few stars were out; as he ascended the slope, the beating of the waves behind him and the roar of cars on the tollroad faded into the distance, and a dense silence took over everything. The sand ran off the insteps of his feet, bare in their rubber sandals.

Someone, somewhere, had tied up the darkness, he thought as he went: the bag of darkness had been tied at the mouth, enclosing within it a host of smaller bags. The stars were tiny, almost imperceptible perforations; otherwise, there wasn't a single hole through which light could pass.

The darkness in which he walked immersed was gradually pervading him. His own footfall was utterly remote, his presence barely rippled the air. His being had been compressed to the utmost – to the point where it had no need to forge a path for itself through the night, but could weave its way through the gaps between the particles of which the darkness was composed.

To become transparent, to be free of all things, Jack retained nothing unnecessary: no muscles, no fat, only a beating heart and the idea, like a white sugared candy, of an "angel"....

All of which was probably the effect of barbiturates. Before leaving his apartment, he'd taken five of them in a glass of beer.

The slope whose top he reached before long opened onto a spacious tableland, on the other side of which he saw two cars squatting on the firm sand like discarded shoes.

Jack broke into a run. "Running!" he reflected, pursuing himself in dismay. "Me, running! ..."

The broad path led to the far side of the plateau, which abruptly fell away to a deep gully on whose floor lay a pool of still denser darkness. Suddenly, Jack saw smooth flames flickering upward. It was as though the night, with a loud noise, were starting to disintegrate from that one point, just as a whole embankment begins to burst from one small hole.

Trampling through the dry undergrowth, Jack slipped and slid as he ran down sand that might or might not be a path, heading for the bottom of the gully. He felt rather like a fly slipping down into a sugar basin.

The confusion of human sounds at the bottom came closer, but with another twist in the interior of the gorge the great flames he had seen moments earlier vanished, and the voices came closer to hand, though still no human forms were visible. The stones beneath his feet grew more numerous; as in a dream, they would suddenly rear up, blocking his path, and as soon again become flat and indistinguishable from the sand.

Reaching a vantage point, Jack saw a group of giant shadows leaping up the slope opposite. At almost the same time, he saw the bonfire. But then the flames suddenly died down, so that the interweaving feet of the people moving to and fro on the rough terrain of stones and sand around it were left illuminated and their faces, surrounded by darkness, floated disembodied in the air.

The only thing he could identify was the shrill voice of Keeko, laughing.

At that moment, Jack stumbled against a mass of something

blacker than the darkness and, involuntarily putting a hand on it to steady himself, apologized to it. His hand had touched something sweaty yet smooth and unnaturally cold to the touch: the flesh of a shoulder that was like well-kneaded black clay.

"No problem," said Harry the black, giving a preliminary slap to the conga drum held between his knees, which sent a series of sluggish beats echoing around the surrounding hills.

The crowd that hung out in the modern jazz cafe had had the idea of giving summer a send-off by holding a party, a rather offbeat party, somewhere by the sea. There on the sand they would do the twist, and a whole roast pig would be served. They also felt there should be some kind of primitive dance ritual, even if it was inevitably of somewhat uncertain pedigree.

In great excitement, they had split up to search for a suitable place, finally settling on this uninhabited valley. The members of the group who'd gone out to a suburb of Tokyo to buy the pig had been short of funds, and had come back shouldering half a pig instead.

Who would have thought that here, not far from that tawdry beach where the boring bourgeoisie jostled each other in the water, they would find an untouched spot like this? For the ideal site they had pictured to themselves was, whatever else, no ordinary place, but one where their own frayed jeans would take on the luster of damask.

The site: it must be chosen, made clean, sanctified.... They were young people for whom neon signs, tatty movie posters, exhaust fumes, and car headlights had always served as substitutes for the light of the countryside, the scent of the fields, moss, domestic animals, wild flowers; so it was natural enough now that the stretch of sandy ground they envisaged should be like a carpet of the finest workmanship, that their ultimate starry sky should resemble a piece of jewelry of the utmost artifice.

To cure the world of its stupidity, the first requirement was a process of purification through stupidity: a thorough exaltation of what the bourgeoisie saw as stupid, even if it meant aping the bourgeois creed and its single-minded, tradesman's energy....

Such was the basic scheme, as it were, of the party for which thirty or forty had gathered here in the middle of the night – which to them meant business hours, their own all-important daytime....

The bonfire, having suddenly died down, was smoldering, then abruptly flaring up again. This was due, Jack realized, to fat from the pig, already being roasted on a thick spit; from time to time someone was basting it with a cheap red wine. The face of the person was unidentifiable, the hands alone appearing, detached amidst the flames, as they performed their task.

Harry the black's drum was still beating, and a number of figures on the sand were doing the twist. The sand was strewn with stones, so they planted their soles carefully, their dancing for the most part a slow swaying of the knees and hips.

Over by the bank stood crates of beer and orange juice. Some empty bottles lay among the stones, gathering the faint light of night to their surfaces.

Jack's eyes should have been used to the dark by now, yet he still couldn't identify anyone in the group. The low-creeping flames of the bonfire only made it more difficult. Here and there the brief flare of lighters and matches stabbed at the bounds of vision, making it still harder to distinguish things.

Nor did the voices help; loud laughter and excited cries alike were overwhelmed by the surrounding darkness, were themselves tinged with darkness. And all the while, the night was rent by the sound of Harry's conga drum and the shrill yells that so vividly suggested the pink cavity of his mouth.

Keeko's was the one voice recognizable. Letting it guide him, Jack went and grabbed an arm that was slender and insubstantial as the wick of a lamp.

"So you got here," she said. "You alone?"

"Right."

"The gang waited for you at Inamura-ga-saki Station. But then, we knew you're always changing your mind, so we came on ahead. It's a wonder you managed to find your way here." She pursed her lips in the dark. The movement of mouth and nearby cheek, and the gleaming whites of her eyes, were visible, so Jack greeted her in the usual way by planting his own lips on hers, applying a light friction, then withdrawing them. The effect was like kissing the inside of a piece of bamboo bark.

"Where's everybody?"

"Hymenara and Peter are both over there. Gogi's with them. Seems he's in a state because his girl hasn't turned up. You'd better not stir him up."

Jack had got used to his own nickname. As to what "Gogi" meant, he still had no idea.

Taking him by the hand, Keeko led him through the

dancers to the place beneath the bluff where the others were sitting by a big rock.

"Jack's arrived."

Hymenara responded by slowly and sleepily raising one hand. Even at this hour he was wearing dark glasses.

Deliberately, Peter lit his lighter and passed it to and fro across his own face. Blue lines were painted around the upper rim of his eyes, sweeping up at the corners to where silver dust glittered in the firelight.

"What the hell have you done to your face?"

"Peter's going to do a show later," explained Keeko, on his behalf.

Gogi, naked to the waist, was lolling sulkily against a nearby tree. Realizing it was Jack, however, he came writhing out of the darkness and, seating himself cross-legged on a patch of sand amid the undergrowth, hailed him with beery breath:

"Hi!"

Jack wasn't particularly taken with Gogi, but Gogi on his side was persistent in demonstrations of affection, and had once brought a girl with him to visit Jack in his room.

He went in for body-building, and was vain about his physique. He was almost aggressively muscular, the slightest movement of his limbs sending quick quivers of movement through chains of linked tendons. On the meaninglessness of life and the stupidity of human beings he and the rest were in theory agreed, but unlike the others he had gone to such lengths in building up a screen of muscles against the winds of despair that he had ended up fast asleep, asleep in that darkness of blind strength which is, essentially, what muscles are all about.

The thing that bothered Jack about this entity called Gogi was its non-transparent quality. Whenever it planted itself in front of him, it shut off his own view of the world, clouding with its sweaty, musky body the crystal that he always worked so hard to keep clear. Gogi's constant flaunting of his strength was intensely irritating. The insistent odor of his armpits, the hair that grew all over his body, the unnecessarily loud voice – everything made its presence as plain as filthy underwear even here in the darkness.

It was a similar disgust, oddly upsetting, that made Jack now come out with something he wouldn't normally have said:

"You know something? It was a night just like this when I tried to kill myself. Just about the same time the year before last. Today you could all have been attending my second memorial service. I mean it, really."

"If they cremated Jack," came the voice of Hymenara, tinged with a disagreeable mirth, "I guess he'd just melt, like a piece of ice...."

Either way, Jack was cured by now. He'd been mistaken in thinking that if he killed himself the sordid bourgeois world would perish with him. He'd lost consciousness and been taken to a hospital, and when he came to and surveyed his surroundings, the same world had been all around him, alive and kicking as ever. So, since the world seemed irremediable, he'd resigned himself to getting better....

After a while Peter got up and, leading Jack toward the bonfire, said:

"Do you know Gogi's girl?"

"No."

"She's a stunner, according to Gogi. Not that *that's* anything to go by. So long as she hasn't stood him up completely, she'll probably turn up sometime before morning."

"How do you know she's not here already? In this darkness you couldn't make out her lovely mug anyway, so her ladyship's idea is probably to let him discover her by the light of dawn. Much more effective."

A faint stirring of the air brought an unmistakable whiff of fat-smelling smoke, and the two of them averted their faces.

Jack set off to get some beer. Short though the way was, he stumbled over a variety of rocks, Boston bags, and recumbent forms that yielded to the touch. One couple that lay in a tightly wrapped bundle, lips joined, failed to stir even when one of Jack's rubber sandals flipped against them.

He wondered where Gogi's girl was. She might be one of that vivacious group of new faces; or again, she could be lurking behind that clump of undergrowth in the dark, or behind the smoke-wreathed stand of trees. Surely, though, if her looks were really so stunning, a faint glow would penetrate the darkness, indicating their whereabouts? Such a beautiful face ought to reveal itself by its own light, wherever it might be in that black valley or amidst the sea breezes that filled the starry sky....

"Right – the ceremony's beginning! The ceremony! We'll hand out the roast pig when the dancing's over, OK? Come on, stoke up the fire!" The bellowing voice, slurred as usual by barbiturates, belonged to Hymenara. His dark glasses were thrust close to the fire, the reflection of its flames forming two miniature paintings in the lenses.

The sound of the conga drum had stopped, since Harry was tightening its skin over the flame of a candle. For a moment, the people in the valley were silent too. Like fireflies, the glow of cigarettes swelled and shrank here and there in the shadows.

Having at last found a bottle of beer, Jack asked a stranger, a young man whose white teeth gleamed in the darkness near him, to open the bottle. He did it, expertly, with the same powerful teeth; white foam ran from his mouth down the front of his shirt, and the white teeth flashed once more in a triumphant smile.

The drum had started throbbing again, and was gradually speeding up. As Peter, in nothing but a pair of swimming trunks, began to run about the fire it blazed up, and the colored patterns and silver dust with which his body was daubed gleamed dully in its light.

Jack failed to understand Peter's excitement. Why, exactly, was he dancing? Because he was dissatisfied about something? Because he was happy? Or because it was at least better than killing himself? …

What exactly did Peter believe in, wondered Jack in his transparency, watching Peter's body dancing, glinting, in the light of the bonfire. Had it all been lies, then – what Peter had once told him of the misery that settled on him every night like a heavy, sodden wad of cotton? Why, when solitude howling like the sea bestrode the gaudy lights of the nocturnal city, should one proceed to *dance?*

That was the point, Jack himself was convinced, at which

everything stopped. He, at least, had stopped. And then, little by little, he had become transparent....

Yet after all, he reflected, dancing was a signal: an intermittent signal drawn out from somewhere deep inside human beings by some unknown agent. Peter was scattering such signals in the darkness about him now, as though scattering cards of many colors.... Before he realized it, Jack's own foot had begun to beat time.

As Peter's body bent backward, the white of an eye ringed with eye shadow shone in the flames like a great tear in the black night. Before long, a young man in a leopardskin loincloth appeared grasping a scimitar in one hand and dangling a live white chicken, trembling, from the other. It was Gogi.

The muscles of Gogi's sweaty chest moved lustrous into the firelight. Jack saw nothing but a dark shimmer of copper flesh, darker even than the night surrounding it.

"Hey, watch him go!" cried the people around him. What could Gogi be setting out to prove? By now, his brawny arm was forcing the chicken against a rock. The chicken struggled, scattering white down that swiftly, as in a dream, was caught up in the draft of the fire and whirled high into the air. The soaring of those feathers! How well Jack knew it, that weightless flight of the emotions at the moment of the body's agony....

Thus it happened without his seeing it. The callous sound came of the knife descending, and there on the stone, deaf to the cries, blind to the blood, the chicken lay twisted, its head and body parted.

Wildly plucking up the head, Peter rolled about on the sand: now, at last, Jack could appreciate his rapture. When he finally stood up again, a trickle of blood was clearly visible on the flat, boyish chest.

The head itself must have been puzzled to find things ending like this, in such a frivolous death, as part of a stunt. Its eyes no doubt, earnestly open, were full of inquiry ... but Jack didn't look. This jesting beatification, this chance glory that had befallen the chicken crowned with its red comb, had cast a faint, scarlet reflection within his own cold, utterly uncruel heart.

And yet – he told himself – I feel nothing. Nothing at all.

Still grasping the white bird's head, Peter got to his feet and began to dance, then whirl, in a widening circle, till finally he was up against the spectators, singling out the women and thrusting the head into their faces as he rotated.

Screams ran around the ring of onlookers. Why, Jack wondered, did women's cries all sound the same? Yet even as he wondered there rose to the starry sky, then died away, a cry conspicuous for its beauty, for its clarity, for an almost tragic quality. He couldn't remember ever hearing it before. And it seemed to him that the cry must, at last, have come from that "stunning" girl of Gogi's.

Jack was a sociable fellow.

That was why – half-awake, half-asleep – he stayed on the land or in the scrub till morning, was bitten by many mosquitoes, went swimming with the group in the daytime and, utterly exhausted, went back to his apartment in Tokyo, where he promptly fell into a deep sleep. When he awoke, his tiny room was dreadfully quiet. Why should the morning be so dark, he wondered, and looked at the clock. It was still eleven at night on the same day.

He had been sleeping with the window open, but not a breath of air came in, and his body was like a wet rag, soaked with sweat. Switching on the fan, he got his *Chants de Maldoror* from the bookshelf and lay, face down, on the bed to read.

He started to reread his favorite section, the one about the nuptials of Maldoror and the shark.

... *What is that army of sea monsters cleaving the waves at such speed?*

It was six sharks.

... *But what, again, is that commotion of the waters, over there, on the horizon?*

It was a huge, lone, female shark, the shark that was eventually to be Maldoror's bride.

The alarm clock placed by his pillow, undaunted by the humming of the fan, was marking off the time with a dull tocking. The clock was a sardonic embellishment to his daily life, for he had never once used it to wake him. His consciousness flowed on, day and night, like a murmuring brook; he was long used at night to maintaining himself transparent like crystal within it, and the alarm clock was the friend, the Sancho Panza, that turned the custom into a comedy on his behalf. The cheap sound of its mechanism was a splendid source of comfort: it made a farce of any continuity in him.

The clock, the eggs he fried for himself, the season ticket that had long ago run out – and then, the shark: yes, most definitely the shark, Jack thought forcibly....

The previous evening's pointless, and more than pointless, party came back to him.

The chicken's head, the charred pig ... and, most wretched of all, the dawn. They had all been hoping for a beautiful dawn, a splendid dawn, the kind of dawn you'd be lucky to see in a thousand years. But the reality, sad to say, had been a dawn too unsightly to bear contemplation, the very dregs of dawn.

As the first glimmerings of pale light illuminated the western side of their valley, they had seen that the trees adorning their untouched sanctuary were no more than a commonplace patch of the kind you could see anywhere, wilting in the salt breezes. Yet there was worse to come. As the light slowly slid down the western slope, it filled the gully with a bleaching-powder white that pitilessly laid it all bare – the wrecks of empty beer, juice, and Coke cans; the collapsed and smoldering bonfire; the ugly gnawings on the corncobs flung about the ground; the litter of bags of various kinds; the half-open mouths of the crowd sleeping in each other's arms by the rocks, in the scrub or on the sand; the sparse growth of moustache over some of those mouths and the sparse lipstick left on the rest; the scattered newspaper (how wretched here, though so poetic when blown about nocturnal streets!). The slaughtered remnants of a typical bourgeois outing....

Some of the crowd had vanished in the course of the night, and at dawn Gogi was nowhere to be seen.

"Gogi's not here," Peter had said. "I expect he cleared out because his girl never turned up. He worries about appearances a lot more than you'd think."

A time came, a cursed time, when I grew in beauty and innocence; all admired the intelligence and virtue of this divine adolescent. Many consciences blushed to behold the features, so transparent, in which his soul sat enthroned. None approached him but with veneration, for there was apparent in his eyes the gaze of an angel.

Jack's idea of an angel might well have been fostered by this passage from *Maldoror.* Tick-tock, tick-tock: the snickering of the bedside clock seemed to discourage any answer. A dim vision of roast angel came into his head. Perhaps he was hungry.

In the sea where wrecked ships lay sunk – in some sea, surely, lay that ship wrecked with its full cargo of the world's wealth, and love, and meaning of every kind.... Glass scales, tilting in the distant sky.... The gentle panting of three dogs along the sandy shore.... Just before his attempted suicide, Jack had felt that he held the world like a dice in the palm of his hand, shaking it. Was there any reason why a dice shouldn't be round? A single, round dice, turning up every number in rapid succession, so that decision was suspended and the game never consummated....

Jack *was* hungry. That explained it all. Standing up, he went and opened the cupboard. He didn't have a refrigerator.

Nothing to eat.

The swimming man and the female shark rescued by him face each other. For several minutes, they hold each other's gaze....

Quite suddenly, Jack felt he might starve if he didn't eat something. He shook the rice cracker can. Nothing but the faint sound of crumbs at the bottom. At the back of the shelf an orange lay rotting, caved in with green mold. Just then, he noticed a file of small red ants running along the edge of the cupboard. Squashing them carefully one by one, gulping down the saliva that gathered at the back of his tongue, he finally discovered, in the depths of the cupboard, half a loaf of raisin bread that he'd laid in, then forgotten all about.

Several of the ants had eaten their way into the bread between the raisins. Jack brushed them out without ceremony, then went and lay face down again on the bed, where he scrupulously examined the surface of the bread beneath the light of the lamp. He picked out two more ants.

When he sank his teeth into the bread, it tasted part bitter, part sour. He couldn't afford to let the taste bother him, so he began to gnaw into it from one end, a little at a time so as to conserve his provisions for the long night to come. The inside of the loaf was oddly soft.

They swam around in circles, never losing sight of each other, and each thinking: "I was wrong: here is another who is uglier than I."

Thus with one accord, beneath the water, they glided toward each other in mutual admiration, the female shark cleaving the water with her fins, Maldoror flailing the water with his arms....

Time passed.

For some while now there had been the clatter of still-shod feet in the corridor outside and the sound of bodies colliding with the thin wooden walls, but since the other inhabitants of the apartment house often came home late Jack had paid them no attention. He got up and went, still gnawing on the raisin bread, to open the door. As he did so a man and woman came collapsing into the room like a screen falling suddenly forward. The room gave a great shudder and the bedside lamp fell over.

Closing the door behind him Jack gazed down with little surprise at his nocturnal visitors. The boy was Gogi, his aloha shirt rucked up to reveal sturdy back muscles.

"You might at least take your shoes off," said Jack. At this, the couple stretched out hands toward each other, casually took off each other's shoes and flung them in the direction of the entrance, then shook with waves of laughter. Their breath spread a reek of alcohol throughout the tiny room. Jack gazed attentively at the girl's pallid face with its closed eyes and the smile playing around the mouth. She was a stranger to him, and she was incredibly beautiful.

The face, aware of being looked at despite the closed lids, was prim even in its intoxication, and the neat, well-shaped nose, though breathing heavily, retained a porcelain stillness. The hair, which covered half her forehead, fell in attractive waves. Beneath the slight swell of her closed eyelids the eyeballs moved secretly and sensitively, the long, regular lashes held profoundly closed. The lips were exquisitely fashioned and the dimples into which they narrowed at the ends were as pristine as though carved there a moment before. Yet the face as a whole had the kind of mature dignity that only a woman of twenty-four or -five could show.

So this was the "stunning" girl, thought Jack as he went on eating the raisin bread. Gogi must have spent the whole day searching for her and brought her all the way here just to recover lost face.

"I don't have any quilts. There are two or three cushions if you want them...." Gogi did not reply but smiled at the corners of his eyes. This, no doubt, was his evening for not saying anything.

Scraping three cushions together with his foot, Jack kicked them over behind Gogi's back, then returned to his bed, lay on his belly again, and went on eating and reading.

Sounds of protest soon came from the girl and gradually grew louder, so, putting down his book, Jack raised himself on one elbow and gazed in their direction. Gogi was already naked, the muscles moving beneath his damp, shiny skin. The girl, though down to her bra and panties by now, was still affecting delirious cries of resistance. Her body was a heap of smooth, gardenia-colored flesh.

After a while she became quiet, so Jack turned his back on them again and nibbled the raisin bread as he read.

Behind him, the expected small cries and heavy breathing failed to materialize. This eventually began to bother him. Taking another look, over his shoulder, he found that the woman was now quite naked. Locked together, the two of them were making breathy noises not unlike the grumblings of a steam train whose departure has been delayed. From Gogi's brawny back the sweat was dripping down onto the tatami.

Finally, Gogi turned his face in Jack's direction. The look of power had gone, replaced by an ambiguous, hazy smile.

"It's just no good. Lend a hand, will you, Jack?"

Nibbling the raisin bread, Jack stood up.

As he did so, he caught sight of the mark of his friend's masculinity, a half-dispirited lump of muscle. Lazily, like an indolent referee, he made his way around their heads to the other side.

"What am I supposed to do?"

"Keep tugging good and hard on her leg. That should do the trick somehow."

As though retrieving a fragment of a body run over by a

train, Jack grasped one of the girl's ankles and raised it up and out. Beyond its smooth whiteness he glimpsed something briefly, as a traveler glimpses the light of a distant hut. The leg, though not particularly sweaty, slipped in his hand, so turning around he took it in his right hand. Thus he found himself standing with his back to the two of them, facing a wall that was bare save for a beer brewer's calendar. As he gnawed at the loaf in his left hand, he passed the time reading the calendar:

August 5 Sunday
6 Monday
7 Tuesday (Dog Day)
8 Wednesday (First Day of Autumn, lunar calendar)
9 Thursday
10 Friday
11 Saturday
12 Sunday
13 Monday
14 Tuesday
15 Wednesday (Anniversary of End of World War II)
16 Thursday
17 Friday
18 Saturday
19 Sunday

As Gogi's and the girl's breathing started to vie with each other in what seemed to be a new lease of energy, the leg dangling from his hand moved busily, transmitting ripples of motion to him; it grew steadily weightier, with no sign of wishing to escape from its yoke. The raisin bread was bitter and sour as ever, and the more he ate the more it clung around his mouth.

After a while, Jack began to find it difficult to believe that the thing suspended from his right hand was really a woman's leg, so to make quite sure he took another look at it in the distant light of the bedside lamp. The red varnish on the toenails had peeled slightly, and the nail of the little toe was an oddly indeterminate shape, the nail itself half-buried in the flesh. A callus caused by wearing high-heeled shoes was in contact with Jack's middle finger.

Eventually, there were indications that Gogi had got up. Sure enough, a hand tapped him on the shoulder.

"That'll do," said Gogi. Jack let the leg fall to the floor.

Without further ado Gogi pulled on his trousers and, taking his aloha shirt in one hand, walked toward the door.

"So long, then," he said as he went. "Thanks. I'll leave the after-service to you."

Jack heard the door being closed. Looking down at the girl lying stretched on the floor, he put the last piece of raisin bread in his mouth and masticated dryly and at length. He touched the girl's inner thigh stealthily with his foot, but the girl was playing dead and didn't stir. He seated himself cross-legged between her parted legs. Like water from a burst main, meaninglessness came welling up from all sides with tremendous force. So he was supposed to see to the "after-service," was he? Trust Gogi to make such a comically condescending request! He bent to bring his face closer. Unnecessary obeisance: she might play dead, but her belly was rising and falling healthily, and Jack's alarm clock was marking the passage of time with a dreadfully vulgar tick-tock, tick-tock.

Arms and fins entwined the body of the loved one, embracing it with passion, while throats and breasts by now were but a blue-green mass that gave off an odor of seaweed....

Translated by
John Bester

ALBERTO MORAVIA

LOVE IN THE CHINESE RESTAURANT

More than any other Italian writer, Alberto Moravia's name has been associated with explicit sexual themes. His novels – The Woman of Rome, The Conformist, Two Women *and many others – and the films made from those novels have made it seem as if erotic Italian literature is Moravia's exclusive domain, and his readership has both benefited and suffered from this perception. It is true that he explored the erotic customs of society with intensity and honesty, but it is also true that his plots and characters are not merely excuses for sexual passages.* The Conformist *is, among other things, a reflection on political responsibility;* Two Women, *however obvious its sexuality, is a furious condemnation of the mindless brutality of war. It is often forgotten that, to Moravia's honour, his books were personally banned by Mussolini, who had them put on the Index in 1952.*

"Love in the Chinese Restaurant," a self-contained chapter from Moravia's novel The Voyeur, *depicts a relationship establishing its own fantastical rules of courtship. Moravia was, in the truest sense, a realist: that is to say, he was able to portray, in almost documentary fashion, the fantastical absurdities with which we try to lend structure to our hungers and thirsts.*

I'M IN the Chinese restaurant again, in a booth this time, sitting on a bench with my back to the wooden partition. Since I generally come early so as to be able to talk in peace with Silvia, the restaurant is deserted. Behind the wall of the booth I can hear rustling, footsteps and whispers that seem to come from the kitchen. While waiting for Silvia, I wonder how I should go about telling her that I've been to ask my father for help and that he immediately promised to give me back the flat. I am still convinced that Silvia left because she was disappointed about not having a place of her own, but at the same time, I am perfectly well aware that our future relationship will depend on the way I announce the unhoped-for solution to the problem that torments and divides us. Mentally, I go over what I should and should not do. One, I must not present the agreement with my father as a victory, but as a tactical retreat. Two, I must stress that I still think of my father as a representative figure of the society I have always rebelled against. Three, I must minimize the advantages of the agreement, say that it's only a temporary solution. Four, I must insist that we find a rented place as soon as possible and that I will then give up my mother's flat once again. As you can see, what worries me most of all is the image of valiant rebel that I would like Silvia to have of me. The curious side to this vanity of mine in my relationship with my wife is that I know perfectly well that Silvia really couldn't care less whether I was or still am a rebel. The truth is, I'm worried about what Silvia will think of me as about what I'll think she thinks.

But here comes Silvia. As on previous occasions, she's wearing her leather jacket, her long, thin, Modigliani neck rising out of it with wistful delicacy. She hasn't got a skirt on today though. Instead she's wearing a pair of bright red trousers, so tight they seem to be separating the lips of her sex between her legs with a neat, fine cut from which a score of straight creases radiate fan-wise like rays of a rising sun. I'm once again struck by Silvia's dual nature, the spirituality of her facial expression and then the sensuality of this certainly not unplanned exhibitionism. My gaze doesn't escape her. Squeezing with some difficulty between bench and table into the booth, she asks: "What are you looking at?"

"Your trousers. They're so tight. Don't they bother you?"

Good-humoured and provocative, she answers: "Not me, what about you?"

Quite suddenly, all my preparation, my calculations vis-à-vis the announcement of the agreement with my father, all go up in smoke. I reach out a hand to take hers and say emotionally: "You realize that I want you?"

"I know," she replies calmly, "I saw it in your eyes."

"I want you and can't have you."

She looks at me with an almost bureaucratic air of understanding, the way a polite shop assistant behind her counter will listen to the complaints of a customer. "I've already told you any number of times: come to my aunt's when she's not there. If you don't want to, that's your problem."

I ask: "But don't you think there's a contradiction between the fact that you don't want to live with me and this invitation to come and make love at your aunt's place?"

She answers serenely: "I don't see any contradiction. They are two different things that haven't got anything to do with each other."

I realize that going on with the argument won't get me anywhere and so, almost in spite of myself I announce the arrangement with my father: "It doesn't matter, I'll wait. In fact, while we're on the subject, I think the flat problem really is about to sort itself out."

"How?"

Silvia's tone of voice isn't encouraging, as if, deep down, she wanted to prolong our present pro tem relationship. In fact she adds: "You still think I left because of the flat. But I didn't. Even if you were to find a place tomorrow, I might decide to go on living on my own."

I try not to give much importance to her objection and push on: "Of course, you're free not to accept. But if you don't accept, you'll have to tell me why. If your reasons are sensible, I promise to respect them."

I think I've said everything. Everything, of course, bar the arrangement with my father, an arrangement I'm ashamed of and that even now I'd be glad not to have made. Silvia seems to sense my reticence because she remarks under her breath: "What a lot of introduction. I hope it's not a hole of a place with two rooms and a kitchen."

"On the contrary, it's a very big flat."

"So where is it?"

I realize that now, like it or not, I'll have to tackle the news of the agreement. Sure in the knowledge that Silvia isn't capable of understanding me, and that therefore it's not worth wasting time explaining, I reply: "The flat is on the third floor of our block. It was my part of my mother's estate. I had in fact refused the inheritance and passed it on to my father. I didn't need it and I didn't want to own property. But now that we're married everything has changed, so I decided to ask him to give it back to me."

Incredulous and vehement, Silvia bursts out: "You talked to your father about it?"

God knows why, but this unexpected reaction of hers provokes a similar reaction in me. In a different voice, I say: "Yes, I did, there was nothing else I could do. What would you rather I did? Rob a bank?"

She answers in exactly the way I don't want her to: "I think that given your political convictions you shouldn't have gone to your father."

I'm furious: "Why not? He may see things differently from me, but he's still my father."

"Ever since we met you've done nothing but run him down. And now you go and ask him to help you."

I explode: "And you of all people have the gall to come and tell me I'm a coward! It was you who forced me to go and play prodigal son, running off like that. You knew all along that my political beliefs made it impossible for me to go to my father without surrendering my self-respect! And now you come and criticize me for trying to satisfy your filthy goddammed sick craving to have a filthy goddammed roof owned exclusively by yourself over your head!"

I'm not shouting, but my low, angry voice has the intensity of a shout.

Silvia looks at me bewildered, then says in a desperate voice: "You know what I think? I think it'd be better if we stopped seeing each other."

My heart sinks. "But why?" I exclaim. "What's got into you now?"

My distress doesn't escape her. In a low voice she asks: "So you think it's sick to want to have a home?"

She is thus implicitly admitting that she did, as I've always thought, leave because of the flat problem. Still beside myself with anger, I retort: "No, but it is sick to let the problem destroy your relationship with your husband."

Perhaps she's had a moment to reflect and understand me. because in a contrite, reasonable voice she says: "I'm sorry, don't bother about me, go on. So you went to your father, and ..."

My voice is calmer too as I finish her sentence: "And spoke to him about our difficulties."

"And your father?"

I want to tell the whole truth now, not hide anything any more: "He said he'd never taken my decision to give up the inheritance seriously, just as, though this is my own personal impression, he never took any of the protest movement seriously. He simply looked after the flat for me and now he's giving it back to me. So, we can go and live there, right away if we want."

I think for a moment, then conclude with jarring irony: "In short, the prodigal son has come home and his father has slain the fatted calf."

Silvia says nothing, so I pick up again, trying to explain my father's behaviour this time: "Apart from the prodigal-son side, though, I did find him incredibly agreeable. Not that he's mean, but he's always been rather attached to things. I think he was ready to come to an agreement with me partly out of a delayed sense of guilt. He ought to have offered us the flat when we got married. Your running away must have made him feel ashamed of himself."

Silvia shakes her head: "Wouldn't it be simpler to put his behaviour down to affection?"

I shake my head: "I don't think my father really has any affection for me. If anything, the opposite. The other day, for example, I surprised him acting in – how can I put it? – making a gesture of sexual rivalry that wasn't exactly affectionate."

"Sexual rivalry? What are you on about?"

In a would-be superficial, conversational voice, I tell her the story of how he showed off his penis during the injection ceremony. I would like it to sound like an amused observation of idiosyncratic behaviour, nothing more. But Silvia listens seriously, without a smile. In the end, she says: "Perhaps he was just being careless and you mistook it for exhibitionism."

"One may be mistaken over ideas, but not with feelings and my feeling was that I was being confronted by an old man who was showing me his tool as if to say: 'mine's bigger than yours.'"

Silvia says nothing. She watches me with listless, motionless eyes. Finally she seems to make up her mind: "You talk about the flat in your block as if it was already decided I was going to live there. But that's not how things stand. The fact that you've found a flat doesn't mean that I'm coming back to live with you. Seeing as you can't or won't understand this, we'd better have it out once and for all."

I haven't followed any of this, but a sudden shiver runs down my spine and I feel thoroughly shaken: "What do you mean?"

She replies hurriedly: "I haven't got anything against living in this flat in theory, but you don't seem to want to understand that there's another reason why I'm not sure whether I'll accept your offer or not. The fact is I've got another man."

I'm already so worked up that this revelation arouses more amazement than anything else. Why on earth didn't I think of it before? Then, together with an aching sense of loss, I feel ashamed of my chatter about the flat and the story of my father's supposed exhibitionism. "But why didn't you tell me right away? Why did you let me go on and on about my father and his stupid flat?"

"I tried to make you see, but it was as if you were blind, and then maybe I was ashamed of admitting it."

"What's there to be ashamed about, admitting you love another man?"

Lowering her head, she says: "The fact is, I don't love this man." Then I realize to my surprise that this, for me, flattering response doesn't actually give me any relief at all. No, because this declaration of Silvia's has settled one question, why she left me, only to open another: if she doesn't love him, then why is this man so important as to have her leave the husband she does love? All at once I feel overwhelmed by a sick feeling of tiredness. I say coldly: "I don't want to hear any more, but since that's how things stand, it seems pointless for us to go on seeing each other."

Silvia doesn't speak. She stares at me from wide eyes, but seems not to see me. Then comes the explanation for this staring, dreamy gaze of hers: to my surprise, because I didn't expect it from someone so rational and unemotional as Silvia usually is, two very small, pinched tears run down from her eyes to stop and then lose themselves almost immediately in the upper part of her cheeks. It's a mysterious kind of crying, simply because there are so few tears, and I suddenly feel the same mixture of doubt and incredulity as the believer who, kneeling in the gloom of a church, thinks he has seen the statue of a madonna renowned for her miracles crying in the same uncertain way. Is Silvia crying, or is it a hallucination? To make sure, I ask her, "But why are you crying? What's wrong?" almost afraid that she'll tell me she isn't crying at all.

Instead she acknowledges her tears with an oddly resentful tone: "I'm crying because I'd like to go on seeing you."

"But if you've got another man?"

"If I go on seeing you, perhaps I'll finally make up my mind."

"Make up your mind about what?"

"To leave him."

"A few moments ago," I say, as though thinking aloud, "it was you who didn't want us to see each other any more. Now it's me. What should we do?"

"Go on seeing each other."

"And then?"

"Then, I don't know."

"What don't you know?"

"I don't know what will happen. I've got a crush on this man. Perhaps it'll go away."

I sense that the word "crush," a frivolous, juvenile expression for falling in love, is at once appropriate and inadequate. Appropriate because it indicates the short-lived nature of Silvia's infatuation; inadequate because it doesn't express its irresistible violence. "It seems to me," I hazard, "that 'crush' isn't the right word."

"So what would you call it?"

"I don't know. Passion."

"No, Dodo," she explains calmly, "it really is a crush, the kind you get at eighteen. The kind that when it's over you ask yourself, but how could I have gone and lost my head for a man like that?"

Cautiously, I suggest: "Crushes don't last very long. Whereas this . . ."

I'm hoping she'll tell me how long her betrayal has been going on. But she doesn't fall into the trap, just agrees vaguely: "Perhaps this won't last long either. But for the moment I've got it and I can't do anything about it."

"What do you mean you can't do anything? All you have to do is decide not to see him any more."

"Right, but that's exactly what I find it impossible to do. I've done my best to stop seeing him, really my very best. But then I run into him and . . ."

"And what?"

"And I'm back where I started. I can't help it."

"There's nothing we can't help. There mustn't be."

"Yes, I thought the same myself. But you know what happens? That exactly because you don't want to do certain things, you maybe find yourself enjoying them even more."

"Enjoying them more how?"

"It's as if you wanted to put out a fire only you make a mistake and instead of water you throw petrol over it. Perhaps I wouldn't go back to him if I didn't take it all so seriously, if I didn't swear to myself never to go back to him again."

She speaks with growing abandon and fluency and I'm struck by the humiliating suspicion that I'm serving as confidant to my wife in her adulterous relationship with an unknown lover. But the desire to know more, to know everything, gets the better of me and in the end, to quote Silvia's own words, I can't help myself.

I say: "But can't you at least tell me why this man you don't love turns out to be so irresistible?"

She shakes her head: "Look, I'd rather not talk about it. And then I wouldn't have mentioned it if you hadn't forced me to by going on about the flat thing. I only told you because you were so far from the truth and I felt bad about leading you on."

"No, I don't care, I want you to tell me everything. Who is he? What does he do? What's he like? Everything."

"But why?"

Exasperated, I shout: "But don't you understand that I'll only really be able to believe you love me and not him if you tell me everything about him?"

"And if I don't tell you everything?"

"Don't you remember what you said not long before we got married?"

"What?"

"'You're the man of my life,' you said."

"It was true. It's still true."

"Yes, but if you don't tell me everything, I'll think he's the man of your life now."

"It's not true, nothing's really changed between us."

"So what is he? The man you're betraying the man of your life with?"

With disconcerting reasonableness she accepts this: "It's a funny way of putting it, but probably that's the truth."

I'm furious: "And you tell me just like that?"

"How am I supposed to tell you?"

This time I say nothing, my head down. Silvia starts talking again in that intimate, confidential tone, which, like I said, humiliates me and automatically makes me what I don't, in any circumstances, want to be: the understanding friend a woman can confide in without embarrassment. "Everything, really everything, I can't tell you. There are some things you can't say, not just because one's ashamed of them, but because if you say them just like that, on their own, in isolation, they give an incomplete, false idea of what's going on."

Brusquely and angrily, I say: "I don't understand what the hell you're on about."

She looks at me and obviously realizes I'm suffering because her face assumes that expression of sorrow and pity typical of Silvia in her best moments. She protests: "But Dodo, why do you want to know all these things about the intimate side of life? It's difficult for me to tell you these things and it won't make you happy to hear them. So?"

"But what things?"

She looks at me a while, then in a condescending voice, like a schoolmistress with a particularly childish pupil, begins: "You asked for it, mind! Now let's imagine that someone were to ask me what happens between us at certain moments. What do you think this inquisitive person would think about the way you make love?"

"I don't know," I reply, a shade unsettled, "what's so special about the way we make love?"

"Not we. You," she corrects. "Nothing special at all until you get down to the details."

"But what are you talking about?"

"I think our inquisitive friend would think that you make love with your eyes."

Suddenly remembering Pascasie and her light-hearted insinuation that I was a voyeur, I exclaim: "Now you're accusing me of being a Peeping Tom."

Smiling, she says: "There, you see. You get worked up if I tell you you're a voyeur, and you're right to be worked up because there's more between us than just the fact that you watch me. And the same thing's true of my relationship with this man I've got the crush on. To say certain things would give a false and incomplete idea of the relationship."

At this point I want to hear more about my own way of making love, partly because I sense that through talking about this I'll get to know about "their" way. To encourage her, I remark: "You're the second person who's told me I'm a voyeur lately."

"Who's the other?"

"A friend. A woman."

She shows no interest in knowing who this woman is. "You see," she cries. "I'm not the only person who says so."

"Okay, but what is my way of making love, then?"

She eyes me for a moment, then explains: "You always make love the same way. You lie on your back and want me to climb on top. You see, just describing the way we make love, I've already given a false, incomplete, crude idea of it. But let's go on. Why do you want me to be on top and you below? I often used to wonder and then you told me yourself: so as to watch me better, in a more detached, more contemplative way. And in fact you sometimes tell me that while we're making love my face reminds you of the face of a madonna in a church your mother took you to when you were a boy. So what is all this, if not a kind of, maybe, mystic voyeurism? That's certainly the feeling I get: so much so that this sort of religious idea you have of me has quite an influence on the way I act when we make love. I sense that you *want* me to look like a madonna so I try not to show the pleasure I'm feeling and make an effort to keep my face serene, immobile and impassive, even though, if I let myself go, God knows what faces I might pull, the kind people do of course when they're making love! What an effort, though, pretending to be a madonna when the man you love is fucking you."

I'm not used to hearing Silvia use bad language and I start. She notices and adds: "I'm sorry, but it's the truth."

I protest: "So people who go to church and lift their eyes to the holy image while they're kneeling are voyeurs then?"

"In a certain sense, yes."

"But the voyeur spies on people. I don't spy on you when we're making love, like a voyeur would, to see if your face contorts in spasms of pleasure. On the contrary, I like to see you impassive, serene, without grimaces or spasms."

She shakes her head: "Maybe so. But madonna apart, my impression is that when you make love you do more looking than anything else." She thinks, then reaches out an affectionate hand and takes mine: "Dodo, when it comes to love, one needn't be ashamed of anything. You love through your eyes. That's all. And then sometimes I've enjoyed this eye-love and didn't disguise the fact. Even if you weren't looking at me in quite the way the faithful look at the madonna."

"But when?" I ask, faintly stirred.

She smiles: "Have you forgotten already? In Forte dei Marmi, before we knew each other, when you flirted with me from the window of your *pension.*"

I haven't forgotten at all. On the contrary, I remember very well. I was staying in a *pension* in the pinewood by the sea. It was very near another one and I could see a wall with a few windows, all closed except for the one exactly opposite mine. One afternoon, I'd gone to my room for a nap and was already closing the shutters when I noticed that the window opposite was wide open, giving me a complete view of the room. It was a room like any other, the sort they usually have in these small seaside hotels, but perhaps precisely because it was so common, I found it mysterious; it had that obscurely significant mystery that insignificant things do have. Most of all I remember the colours, every single one of them; they seemed gay and fresh, perhaps because I was looking at them so hungrily, as if to feed my famished vision. In the middle was the bed, painted green with a yellow coverlet. In one corner there was a red cupboard. The floor was tiled blue. At the foot of the bed was an ochre-coloured armchair. The seats and backs of the chairs were orange. The walls were whitewashed. What else? Oh yes, a big

Florentine straw hat, pale yellow with a black ribbon, hung from a coat hook; a pair of pink sandles with red heels were poking out from under the bed; a green-and-blue striped dressing gown had been thrown across the armchair. Finally, the bathroom door was a glaring ultramarine blue.

I had the impression of a scene at the theatre. The curtain had risen, but the actors, or rather the actress (because there could be no doubt that the occupant of the room was a woman), hadn't made her entry yet. So instead of closing the shutters, I just pulled them to and started to wait, standing there with my eye to the crack and with that somehow cruel patience of the hunter lying in wait for his prey. She had to come back to her room some time and I would wait just as long as it took, until evening if necessary, until the following day. It was very hot; you could hear the June bugs droning in the pine branches. Although aware that my watching amounted to snooping, I felt a happy sense of well-being, as if I were doing something I had a natural talent for. So much so that after a while I felt there was no need to hide any more and I opened the shutters wide. I didn't just want to see now, but to be seen as well, to be noticed while I watched.

Finally, after a wait of almost half an hour, the bedroom door opened and Silvia came in. Since the door was exactly opposite my window, she could hardly help but look back at me. Her face took on a half-surprised, half-puzzled expression and I imagined, logically enough, that her first move would be to close the shutters. With the result that I felt in advance a sense of frustration and guilt; she would shut the window in my face now, and automatically, I would become just the usual indiscreet and out-of-luck voyeur.

But it didn't turn out like that. Silvia moved across the room, threw me another glance, obviously aware I was there, then disappeared into the bathroom. She came out a few moments later and once again, with a by-now undisguised complicity, didn't go to close the shutters. All at once I was sure that she was responding to my voyeurism with a corresponding exhibitionism and my heart began to beat faster.

Silvia moved to and fro about the room, doing the most insignificant things with the concentration of the actress who senses she is being watched by a large and attentive audience. She moved to and fro and with every step her flowing yellow skirt flapped around her legs as if in a provocative dance. Finally, she stood in the middle of the room and with a brusque gesture, like a marionette, bent down, legs apart, took hold of the hem of her skirt and pulled it up and off over her head. From then on the game between us grew faster and faster, more and more arousing. And yet I wasn't feeling the kind of excitement people imagine a voyeur out for smut must feel. The truth is I had managed to create, almost immediately, a chaste, natural relationship between Silvia and myself, between my observation and her apparition. It was a relationship where love with its questions and answers, its surrender and trust, was already present.

So the show went on. Having taken off her skirt, Silvia threw it on the armchair, then went to the mirror over the dresser and, standing so as to show me her profile, slipped off her bra and curved her hands in two cups under her breasts, weighing them and pushing them up a little as if to study their shape and volume. Then she let them fall again and touched the nipples with her ringers in a delicate, contemplative way, as though checking their sensitivity. In short, by now she was no longer pretending to ignore me with an innocent naturalness; she was playing stripper with the obvious intention of producing certain effects rather than others. In fact every now and then she would throw me a quick sidelong glance as though to make sure I was still there and not unhappy with the performance.

The contemplation of her bust didn't end when she dropped two hands to her waist to roll down her pants. Dazed and thoughtful she went on looking at her breasts while distractedly exposing her crotch, as if she had something on her mind which only had to do with the upper half of her body. Almost immediately I understood what she was up to: she wanted to show me the thick, dark pubic hair that thrust out aggressively under the curve of her rump, and she wanted to show it in profile, because only in profile would I be able to see its curious bristling quality, like the hackles of a frightened cat. Not satisfied with that, she ran a hand through the hairs to fluff them up and have them bristle out after their long constriction under her pants. At this point the performance, so like a normal striptease, yet different because of our unexpected, mutual feeling of love, seemed to be over. Silvia pulled a chair into the middle of the room, picked up a guitar propped against the wall, and, bending her head over the instrument, began to strum some chords. The position reminded me of the viola-playing angels you sometimes see in old paintings; except that the angels keep one leg crossed over the other, while at the centre of Silvia's groin, in the brown bush of her hair, I could see the white of a cotton-wool tampon. Did Silvia know that apart from her naked body she was also showing me something men usually find repugnant? Of course she knew. But showing me the tampon must have been, for her, like an unconscious challenge to my incipient love. Because only love is capable of transforming repugnance into attraction.

But the exhibitionism aroused by my voyeurism had by now exhausted its invention. Silvia played the guitar for a while, then, as if suddenly bored, got up and, without hurrying, came to the window and closed the shutters.

The next day I looked for her on the beach, found her and had myself introduced by a friend we had in common. Thus, from the encounter of a casual exhibitionism with an unplanned voyeurism, was born a very normal love relationship, which, a year later, was to lead to our marriage.

At the end of this lightning recollection, I say: "I know, our love began with looking. But why were you so happy for me to look at you then, and so bothered by it now?"

"I don't know," she answers vaguely. "It was summer, it was very hot and I felt dazed by the heat. When I saw you watching me from your window, I thought: if it makes him happy, it doesn't cost me anything, why not?"

"Is that all? Didn't you feel anything yourself?"

"Yes, I did feel something perhaps. I liked you, Dodo. You didn't look like a voyeur at all, more like somebody at the theatre, watching the performance in a detached way. But you know what?"

"What?"

"After closing the shutters I lay down on the bed and masturbated."

"You never told me that!"

"You never asked."

She is quiet for a moment. "The next day, when you got yourself introduced, I had a strange sensation."

"What?"

"I said to myself in amazement: I feel like I've already made love with this man."

I feel reassured by this. I say gently: "Now that you've described my way of making love, tell me how you do it with him."

This time, I don't know whether out of tiredness or trust, she doesn't hold back, doesn't hesitate: with brutal frankness she says: "I know this will disappoint you, seeing as when we make love you always look at me as if I were the madonna, but I'm not the madonna."

She falls silent a moment, then goes on, staring right into my eyes: "I'm a pig, and I like to make love like a pig."

With an effort I ask: "How do pigs make love?"

"The animal way. I read it in an old guide for saying confession: *more ferarum.*"

"But which animals?"

"Dogs, horses: it was the first time I'd done it that way. It was a revelation."

"But why?"

"I don't know. Perhaps because I turn my back to him and he can't see me, so that I can pull all the faces I want; perhaps because, unlike you, he's the active one and I'm passive: perhaps because ..."

At this point Silvia breaks off and bows her head.

"Perhaps because what?" I insist.

She raises her head again to show me a smiling face: "Oh God, Dodo, why do you want to know everything, absolutely everything?"

"You know why," I reply angrily. "Because even if only in words I want you to betray him with me."

She doesn't seem to notice what I've said. After glancing round the restaurant, she says under her breath: "Okay, listen: right at the moment of climax, he says: 'Tell me you're my pig.' And I have to repeat: 'Yes, I'm your pig.'"

"Have to? You don't have to do anything. You like saying it and you say it, and that's that."

"No. I have to."

"But why?"

"Because he's on top of me: he forces my head down on the table and whispers in my ear: 'If you don't say it, I'll break your neck.'"

"Brutal, huh?"

"Some things seem brutal when you describe them straight off like this. But the voice that says those words isn't brutal."

"So what is it?"

"It's the voice of love."

"But do you love him?"

"I've already told you. I don't love him."

This time I fall silent. The roof has fallen in on my world and I'm in a state of near delirium searching through the ruins.

Silvia seems aware of my distress, because she reaches out a hand and says: "Come on, don't be so sad. After all, it's better to be treated like a madonna than a cow. I'm going through an animal phase, then I'll get back to being your sacred image, okay?"

She squeezes my fingers, a little excitedly, as if to rouse me into saying or doing something. Suddenly I say: "Let's make love, here, now."

"What?"

"Let's do it the way we did it the first time, by looking."

"By looking? What do you mean?"

"Let me see you."

This time Silvia understands and turns to glance round the restaurant. "Here? But how?"

"We are out of the way in this booth, no one can see us. You come and sit next to me, between me and the wall. You open your pants, just for a moment, and I'll look at you."

Taking pity, she asks: "You love me that much?"

I nod, unable to speak. Silvia looks round, then gets up, goes round the table and comes back in the booth on my side. I shift to the outside of the bench and she sits between me and the wall. Then she lies back, takes hold of her zip and pulls it right down with a single tug. Her hands go to widen the opening above pale-blue panties plump with a dark shadow. She pushes them down and arches back on the seat, her rump thrust upward. Out of her trousers, that strange pubic fleece of hers rears up like an aggressive crest, all the hairs standing on end as if in a fury. She says gently: "You can touch me if you want. But just for a moment."

"No, I only need to look."

She looks down at herself too and says: "Isn't it better the way other women have it? Flat and soft as velvet?"

"No. I like it like this, like a brush."

She says: "I'm going to touch myself now. Tell me something else it makes you think of."

I see her sink her hand between her legs: "It makes me think of the hackles of a frightened cat."

"And then?"

"Of a cock's crest."

"And then, quick, something else."

"The plume of a helmet."

"And another?"

"A Phrygian cap."

"Something else."

"The sun rising with all its rays."

"Yes, the sun's rays, yes."

Silvia sighs, stretches out some more and sighs again, lifting her stomach while her pubic hair thrusts stiffly upward. Finally she falls back, eyes closed, as if exhausted. I reach down and pull up her zip. Silvia opens her eyes. "Thanks," I tell her.

Silvia shakes her head as though still unable to speak. Then she manages to get out: "Thanks for what?"

"For doing what you did."

She gets up now and slips by me out of the booth, saying: "I've really got to be going."

"Do me a last favour."

"What?"

"Seeing as I've made love to you with my eyes, now close them."

"But how?"

"Pass a hand over them."

"But that's what you do to a corpse."

"Right."

She reaches out a hand and passes the palm quickly over my eyes. I lower my eyelids. When I open them again she has already disappeared leaving only the tinkling of the carillon.

Translated by
Tim Parks

ADOLF MUSCHG

GRANDFATHER'S LITTLE PLEASURE

Roland Barthes described the erotic as "the place where the clothing gapes," that is to say, the interstice, the crack, the fissure in the formal appearance. For that reason, that which is forbidden reinforces the erotic sense, because it draws attention to the zone that should remain covered, hidden from view, away from society's gaze.

For many years, Adolf Muschg has sought in these "gapings" his subject matter. Professor of German Language and Literature at the Swiss Institute of Technology in Zurich, he is the author of numerous stories, poems and novels (only one book, the short story collection The Blue Man, *has been translated into English) which successfully depict the rips in the fabric of polite society: the transgressions of incest, murder, madness. "Grandfather's Little Pleasure" ironically and poignantly describes one such transgression, both in word and deed, in the ultra-conventional setting of a family gathering.*

GRANDFATHER doesn't like talking about his visit to the brothel, but whenever we ask him nicely he gives in. He is the sturdiest in our family. When, on some mornings, we all stay in bed a little longer, he sits down at our bedside, dressed in his spotless uniform from the '70s. Tell us, we then say. He is living with us; in return he tells something. We pay close attention every time whether the story stays the same. The following is a summary of all the other stories which Grandfather, sitting at our bedside, has told us about his visit to the brothel.

One morning during his middle years, Grandfather, carrying his sample case with five pieces of artificial turf, arrived at the faraway railroad junction of Njesa.

It was 10:30 A.M.; the meeting with the president of the Athletic Club was not to take place until 3:00 P.M.

A sizable market had opened up around Njesa, surrounded by wooden churches and junipers. Grandfather had taken the sleeper car in the Forest-Heath-Express to be the first traveling salesman who would acquaint the Njesa district – which pervaded even the passing trains with the sweet smell of its lilacs – with artificial turf. What grew here, even on the athletic fields, was still the old, worn down and delicate green.

But when he stood there, at 10:30 and also at 10:35 A.M. in the square outside the Njesa railroad station, where the sun was already casting harsh shadows, all he could think of – looking up and down the high-storied houses – was that it was still too early for lunch. His mouth dry, he had stood there, facing the dirt-colored vagueness of Njesa, searching in vain for an appetite. All of a sudden he did not feel like entering a town where the cuisine, by and large, was still brutish.

Pot roast with sauce Remoulade! We call from the bed. In short, Grandfather had stepped from the station into the open, without a definite goal; the sample case weighed so little that he didn't resist the idea of a walk; so he crossed onto the shady side of the street and avoiding the open square he let himself be led by the first best row of houses. It ran parallel to the tracks, in the direction from which his train had come. The sidewalk was so narrow that he was unable to take a good look at the shadowy buildings he almost brushed with his shoulder. However, he had the impression of entering a district where only manual services of the rougher or noisier kind were located: auto repair shops where wind-driven ventilators turned lazily in the still air, a brewery with rundown, badly paved ramps, warehouses for tubeless tires and things of that sort, also barracks for foreign laborers, partially boarded up.

Go on, Grandfather, we say.

And always the trains in the corner of his left eye, clumsily maneuvering back and forth, rumbling into each other under drawn out whistles, while the heat was sizzling over the tracks. Gradually the landscape of tracks became larger and bleaker, and on his side too there were fewer buildings, only sheds by now, except for one single high structure, displaying on its blind wall a cocoa advertisement which, flashing white teeth, enhanced the sense of isolation.

A cocoa ad! we laugh.

Naturally, under the circumstances the sunny intervals between the shadows became more and more spacious, and to the same extent also the sky which in its glare seemed almost dark to the eyes.

Boy, does he keep us in suspense, we say, huddling in our blankets. Now he has begun to age, says Grandfather, but even then he wasn't all that young anymore. That's why all of a sudden he was aware of his legs and the sweat on his forehead; so he decided to turn back at the single house with the cocoa advertisement. One should always set oneself a goal in life. At the house he stopped for a moment to put his decision into practice, or to put it more simply: to turn around. From the front it was a house in the style of French apartment blocks which in turn were modeled – however faintly – on French chateaux (aha! we say at this point), with a gray faceted roof uncommon in this area, hidden until now by the billboard; and now too you could see the scaffolding holding up the board from the attic windows. There were no shutters, however; instead the mostly broken window frames and sills had a layer of pink paint over older yellow. These traces of elegance had an effect curiously enhanced by the isolated location of the house; part of the effect was also a faded brown sign on the facade, between the second and third floor, obviously outdated, naming in gothic script a certain Hartmuth Müller, Coal. He had to step back a few feet in order to decipher it, which the wide, even endless sidewalk now permitted. The strangely remote thundering of the trains at his back, the accelerating thumps of a steam locomotive unleashing themselves into the distance, the strain of having to squint into the sun, and the sudden weight of the sample case drove him back into the shade where he was going to turn back; and in this moment, an old doorman materialized, detached himself from the shade and extending his arm politely, left him no choice but to enter.

Here it comes, we say, stuffing our fists into our mouths.

The hall he entered, Grandfather goes on, remained empty for several seconds. Only the sensation of having chanced into some kind of hospital made the seconds pass, and probably the coolness too – emitted by the pastel walls and doors, imitation wallpaper and wood: emitted breathlessly, so to speak, because plastic doesn't breathe. He saw door upon door, as in a pigeon coop, a morgue or a nursery school; something hopelessly quaint lay in the air, reminding him of nothing, nothing at all, at best perhaps of an unknown loss.

But then a scantily dressed girl stepped up to him with an accommodating smile; opened lips as if about to speak when a second female figure moved into position, pushing her back a little; she seemed dressed for an old-fashioned ball and looked up to him with her ceremoniously painted face. He turned to her and asked with a faint smile if one could get something to drink there, that he really had no other desires but to spend a quiet hour in *intelligent* company. With the same smile and a glance at his sample case, the lady assured him that every client could do as he pleased, but that they were not permitted to serve alcoholic beverages. As for a bright little head, and she turned to the scantily dressed girl, he would certainly get his money's worth with this one, and by way of suggestion freed the space between them. He then asked what his expenses might be and got the answer: this would be between him and the girl. He repeated that he was looking only for a quiet chat and something to drink, but at that point the lady with the harshly painted face had already turned away and he actually found himself following the girl up the first steps of the staircase. What he could make out from her face was neither unpleasant nor enticing, a reminder of no one he'd ever known, at best perhaps the wife of an old friend whom he hadn't seen in years; there had not been a particular bond between him and this woman either, not even some special conversation. He climbed stair after stair, following the girl, and the distance between them increased. The staircase, too, was obviously washable, surfaces joined together without a speck of dust and, although existing in space, with no depth at all. He kept climbing after the girl in her red, ribbon-trimmed panties and brassiere, through pure *surfaces* and noticed suddenly that in these non-spaces there wasn't a glimmer of daylight. The bright lightbulbs in their decorative wire cages located at regular intervals on the staircase ceiling, smoothed away all edges. The gauze curtains which he had seen from the outside were presumably draped boards. He did feel a rise in temperature now, which was utterly different from the warmth outside, its faint oily smell took on a hint of cologne as they were climbing higher and higher and the house seemed infinitely higher on the inside than on the outside; it was a stale warmth, reminding him of hard times. And finally the girl, calling him "honey," opened a pink door in a light green corner, letting him enter into a really heavy warmth. She then, as on command, sat down on a chair by the wall, tapped a cigarette from her pack, lit it, while he remained standing there, not sure where to sit down.

Now we listen to Grandfather, holding our breath. He said that in this small room with artificial – but not unfriendly – lights, there had been a bed taking up the corner opposite the door; it had some kind of wooden frame around it on which souvenirs were crowded together, just like in a shooting gallery at some country fair. The bed itself did not seem to be made for use or even rest; it was barricaded, so to speak, by several heavy woollen blankets and secured by an enormous Bambi.

A Bambi? We ask.

A deer, says Grandfather.

Oh, a deer, we say and don't understand a word.

The thought alone of doing anything having to do with that bed required an effort. Behind the headboard the frame continued toward the door, extending into the flat top of a slightly higher cabinet, where two white plastic molds with flat eye sockets were standing, probably for the use of wigs. Above this cabinet hung a framed regulation listing an exit plan in case of fire. Behind the door a radiator completed the arrangement. Hard at the foot of the bed stood a table covered with a brown, fringed tablecloth; a few bright-colored magazines were on top, one of them called *The Courier.* The girl sat at the far end of the table, smoking hastily. Just opposite the girl, next to the door, stood a low shelf stuffed with jars, tubes and bottles. The larger spray cans on the top shelf were reflected in a mirror, which however did not take in all their bright colors; and yet it was neither tinted nor dusty. Next to this, by the closed window, diagonally across from the bed, was a cot with a raised headrest; its end was wrapped in pale plastic, evidently to protect against shoe marks; on the middle section of the cot lay a terry towel folded lengthwise.

He ought to have seen the house, said the girl, before the present owner had taken over and set it in order. A sleazy joint it was, one to be ashamed of. But that was before her time.

He, Grandfather, had nodded, still looking for a suitable seat. One thing was clear: any kind of settling down in this room would seem an overture to certain acts. To keep at least some kind of company with the girl there at the table, he had to use the edge of the bed; of course he had no room for his legs under the table but had to stretch them, one over the other, straight out into the little room. Only then did he put down his sample case. Now he was sitting with the girl at the same wall after all; if he had leaned back, Grandfather said, he would have upset the souvenirs on the frame. He repeated his request for something to drink, whereupon she repeated the word "honey" or "hon" and left the room very quickly. After a few minutes she put a glass in front of him, holding her cigarette in the same hand, and standing in the half open door, she opened the small bottle of lemonade by prying it with both hands against the door lock, squinting over the cigarette dangling from her mouth. After she had poured, Grandfather wondered if it was wise to drink from the glass. But later on he did anyhow. She had not brought a glass for herself. Then, as on the stairs when he had said it too softly, he asked her not to call him "honey." He shouldn't be upset, she said, it came naturally with her job. Later on she added that kind of talk hadn't been easy for her in the beginning, but since she was much in demand, it had become a habit, more or less. Every now and then Grandfather would bring the glass to his lips without actually touching it;

and so some of its contents dripped down on his trousers. A look at the many photographs of children on the bed frame provided the opportunity to ask about her family. As it turned out, the little girl was not *her* as a child but her *daughter,* now five years old. All the photographs portrayed the same child in different years. But in a color photo he also recognized her leaning against the fender of a car, one arm around the driver who, in turn, was holding on to the steering wheel with both hands. He was light blond, smiling a vague but pleasant smile, as one does in photographs. And there was the third figure of a mutual friend, slightly cut off by the margin.

To look at the pictures he had to get up again, which was no trouble since one did not sink down into the bed.

He walked about the room a little, asked permission to guess her age and, as it turned out, overestimated by three years.

But she didn't seem to mind. When asked about her background, she said she had been born in this city and grown up in a part of town beyond the railroad station and, in reply to another question – that she had been working here for the last two years. It hadn't been easy to find an opening, the owner was choosy – she was a studied woman and the city was very particular about the good reputation of the candidates. In another two years, she said, she hoped to have saved enough money for her own beauty parlor, said Grandfather. At that moment a terrible scream was heard throughout the house. In response to the raised eyebrows of our grandfather, still pacing aimlessly, the girl explained that the screaming woman was the oldest in the house, about forty-five already. She wasn't quite right in the head and sadly unable to do any other work. And yet she owned two luxuriously furnished apartments with many appliances – she hardly knew how to use any of them – she couldn't even fry an egg. Whenever the phone rang she was so scared she'd switch off the TV and all lights, hoping this way she would be less visible to the caller on the phone. Even after the phone stopped ringing she would sit in the dark for quite some time, just to be sure.

Ho ho, we say, and Grandfather thinks we're laughing.

It wasn't funny at all, he says, and he asked the girl if it wouldn't be detrimental to her beauty shop if people in town knew that she had worked here? He wouldn't believe, she replied, how few people knew about it. Except for her parents and her boyfriend, only her sister; and they had more or less resigned themselves to the fact. Grandfather asked if she had many out-of-town clients – Americans, for example? – and she replied that that wasn't the case, not really. Here he sensed a contradiction but tactfully refrained from pointing it out. As he was reading the brothel regulations on the wall which listed the details of permissible intercourse in this establishment, as well as the girls' fees and their responsibilities in compliance with the health authorities, he was reminded of a contemporary artist who had illustrated a similar document from another city with drawings which were more hilarious than risque. To direct their conversation onto a more personal level – and he felt some obligation to do so since her nervous smoking and cross-legged position on the chair began to make him feel uncomfortable – he asked her if she could give him some advice in a private matter.

Is this really true, Grandfather? all of us laugh.

Gentleman of the old school that he is, Grandfather never reacts at this point but continues more or less like this: the girl replied without the slightest hesitation that he had picked the wrong person for his question. She had never experienced it herself, neither with her boyfriend nor at any other time. She sometimes toyed with the thought of seeing a doctor, but it cost too much; besides, she wasn't missing anything and didn't see why she ought to have it. She was a person with a mind of her own. That she had a mind of her own she repeated more than once that morning, but she also admitted that there were some in this house who'd experience it now and then. They would say: if you're enjoying it, why not let yourself go – but they were a minority here. Did it bother her just to chat with him for a while, Grandfather then asked and she replied, no, not at all.

When he lay down beside her cradling her wig-covered head like a barren shrub in his arms, she stroked his back a few times which made him think of someone writing, without looking, on a board, with the tiniest piece of chalk in such a way, that the fingernails too grated along a little.

Hold it, we say. Haven't you left out something here?

We say this every time but never succeed in closing the gap in his memory. Not at all, he says every time; he had most certainly not left out anything, and he fills his pipe, blushing in the reflection of the match.

There are passages which you have suppressed, we say. Grandfather, it is a love story.

Oh, yes indeed, he did love us, Grandfather says, drawing like mad on his pipe.

All right, Grandfather, we say sternly through all the smoke. Up to this point you have been precise, almost punctilious, Grandfather, but now you're beginning to slip. We have information about cocoa advertisements in your time; even railroad stations can be imagined if need be; and artificial turf we have seen for ourselves. However, we are left in the dark about vast areas of private experience in your time; and don't forget: you are a source.

Grandfather begins to weep.

You can't fool us, Grandfather, we say. With all due respect to your memories, our curiosity, which is scientific, is at stake. There used to be certain copulation techniques, and you knew them, too. So out with it.

Grandfather tries hard to weep silently, but he doesn't fool us, the old man.

Today no peanut butter, tomorrow no TV special, we say. We too have our means.

Grandfather dries his tears. He had not left out anything then, he says. He tried to move, to reach that body bound only with two thin chains, one around her neck, the other around her hips, with a tinkling medallion on it.

A medallion, Grandfather? we ask, for inconspicuous finds often lead to the discovery of entire civilizations.

With a head on it, says Grandfather, there was the head of an emperor on the medallion.

Impossible, we say, the girl could not have been that old.

Grandfather says that he asked her if she was a Catholic, but she denied it vehemently.

Catholic or not, we say, where did you have your face, Grandfather?

Near her ear, says Grandfather.

Contradiction! contradiction! we cry. If you had your face near her ear, you could not have seen the medallion, Grandfather, since it was dangling from her hips – your so-called emperor was playing with her pubic hair, yes or no? We know pubic hair from the dictionary.

He could *feel* the medallion, Grandfather said – in those days one's belly was still sensitive. Besides, in the meantime he had had plenty of chances to look at it.

In the meantime? We act surprised. Well now, this is the first time we hear about it. What happened to this "meantime," Grandfather?

He had asked himself that question too; and that we could no longer understand it, says Grandfather, "because you are nothing but little colored blocks, hard little blocks in your little beds." That's how direct our grandfather can become when he feels cornered. You can hear his pipe snort.

Well, Grandfather, you tried to move the girl, we say magnanimously, because his opinion of us doesn't matter. And then?

Grandfather picks up his thread: the girl quivered all the time, it was a constant undercurrent quiver, apparently of a nervous nature, because it could neither be suppressed nor increased. It communicated itself much like shivering, as the result of a tense hopelessness or of some expectation all jammed up somewhere, and not even tact would loosen it again.

And there Grandfather goes again, weeping, and doesn't even take his pipe out of his mouth.

Tut, tut, Grandfather, we cluck, you and your tact, when you have no need for it.

That was precisely it, Grandfather swallows, he had no need for it, there had been no need for him to be there, and that was the reason he had been unable to rescue – better, tear away this girl who quivered so unnaturally. She, at least, had a beauty shop to show for herself, but he? Apart from a few pieces of artificial turf nothing but the fading wish to turn back at this house. Some heat over the railroad tracks wasn't good enough a reason. Nothing but coincidence had weighed on him when he entered there, in short, he had not felt any love, and therefore had no business being there and screwing.

That was quite a word, we cry, we found it in the dictionary, go on now, Grandfather, let's have it, we say, clapping our hands rhythmically to get Grandfather going; we finally want to see him squirm, the noble old gentleman. But he remains silent, at best he nods a little keeping time to our clapping, after all, he doesn't want to ruin our fun. He is biding his time until we get tired; we tire quickly, and he knows it. Even if we wanted to, we cannot deny him the peanut butter, because he is the one who brings it to our bedside – we have no one else. On the way he can lick his fingers as much as he likes. That is the misery of our age – it is still dependent on the older generation. But he lets us feel this on rare occasions only, he is still a gentleman. It is only when he tells a story that he does whatever he wants with us.

There were no "passages" in his story, he says. If we wanted "passages," we should go look them up in our dirty old books.

First of all, they are your books, Grandfather, we say; secondly, you lock them up wherever possible and thirdly, "passages" there are quite general, and love was something special in those days. You say so yourself, Grandfather, we say.

No, it wasn't anything special, Grandfather says, and no power of persuasion would prove the contrary. The girl kept answering with the same stubborn presence of mind, fixing her eyes firmly on the ceiling. At one time he touched her and tried to judge her weight, again too much, and again she didn't take offense, no offense at all; fat doesn't weigh much, she had said. And then, all of a sudden, as if he had put a coin into some slot machine, she had started wiggling about –

You see, Grandfather! we are triumphant; warm, Grandfather, press on, Grandfather!

– but then he had slapped her hand immediately and we never found out where she had her hand at that moment. Then she put her arms behind her head to prove to him that she had not wanted to set up a trap – that was another vague expression in Grandfather's report. His touchiness, however, prevented him from appreciating this little beauty of a moral gesture. Instead he was searching for her ear, to speak to it, first with his lips, then with his teeth. All he had wanted to do was *play,* Grandfather blurted out.

Now you have us, we say maliciously, little, hard, colored blocks.

That's true, Grandfather says sadly.

We are scientists and not inhuman, therefore we ask: what did you want to say into the girl's ear?

Nothing, Grandfather says, blushing again. Something kind, perhaps, about her little daughter, something about the weather in Njesa. But she would not be moved by him. Then, as he said earlier, he had grasped her ear with his teeth.

And then? we ask, because it is a beautiful passage every time.

Grandfather screams, losing his control altogether, but he can't get rid of us that easily.

It's all in our dictionary, we say, we want to know what it was like in reality.

Reality, always reality, Grandfather complains; reality in those days was beginning to come undone; you could tell, because children like us were born – *anaemic* creatures – and had multiplied by leaps and bounds. In the old days, tremendous efforts were made in the service of love, he says, entire generations of youth melted away over it. Decent people then still refused to believe that the human condition "was curable in one point alone." But in Grandfather's young manhood, certain varieties of feelings were already lost, for which a need was felt much later on, and then, quite naturally, one stopped missing them.

Traces of elements, we nod.

You acted only out of some undefined need, visited a brothel, for example, and now there were but a few left – period pieces, so to speak, reminding of a time when love had been something special. But he must be boring us, Grandfather says at this point in his story, which he elaborates more forcefully on some occasions than on others.

It doesn't matter, Grandfather, we say. Collect yourself. What did you do with the girl's ear?

He returned it, says Grandfather, and by and by finds his way back into his story; we let him, there's nothing more to be gotten out of him. At first it felt as if a sign of life might be drawn from this ear, she was even whispering now: no, please, no, and again: no, dammit. That sounded genuine, but only because he was really beginning to annoy her and she spitefully tossed her head back and forth. As if this ear with all the horse hair around it had been all that much fun. He, however, happy at last to see a reaction without wanting to know where it would lead and whether it was a reaction at all and not a struggle against it – presumably a struggle become routine long ago; after all, what hopes could she possibly set in him who had chanced into this place by coincidence, and most likely she had made it one of the rules of her life not to understand any signs for hope – where was he?

You, however, we said. He knows the words but we are good in grammar.

That's right, he, however, had clung for a few moments to this flesh numbed in its hopelessness, as if life could still be engendered here or its loss be made up.

Orgasm? We ask at this point.

Why not, says Grandfather, and doesn't blush anymore. It had no longer any significance.

Tell the rest, Grandfather, we say. We know him – nothing more to be squeezed out of him.

Although he was lying on top, he goes on, the impression therefore misleading, her body under and away from him had closed into a stubborn ball denying him all support, unyielding; in order not to slide off, he had to support his weight with his arms. In this position, but bent over, he had tried to fill her ear with a sound gentle enough not to be shaken out immediately. But, he says, she pressed her ear too into the ball her flesh had formed against him. So then he let go, screaming the rest into her breasts; those breasts were of an exhausted pointedness, which reminded him of home, perhaps of something knitted by his mother. With those breasts the girl's body seemed strangely *clothed,* however poorly, as if something here had to be treated with great care. When he finally raised himself on his arms to give her a chance to uncurl, an absolutely unequivocal gesture, she uttered a sigh of relief and, without giving him so much as a glance she repeated – that's the way she was, a person with a mind of her own. Honey, she added after a pause. And: Sorry.

Then they got right up, and there was no further need for a gratuitous gesture.

From the cot?

From the cot.

What a pity, we say. Actually we don't like such stories at all – as stories, that is; and as documentaries they remain too skimpy.

While he dressed slowly Grandfather watched as she first sprayed her private parts, then dried off with a resolute rub of the towel. The domestic appeal of this gesture prompted him once again – pushing his arms through his shirt sleeves, his shirt front still unbuttoned – to stroke her stiff, almost glazed hair. Honey, she said and no longer apologized for it. While he gave a look at his watch – almost noon – he asked her if she had to accommodate every client. On principle, every client, she answered, unless he was dirty or drunk, but Turks and Italians were, on principle, not permitted to undress completely. He opened his wallet asking how much he owed – 250 – which she tucked away in a small strong box on her bedframe. This box she had left open, by the way, during the two times she had left the room. He then took his sample case by the handle, it felt light once again. Despite his protest, says Grandfather, she accompanied him down all the stairs to the exit; it was customary in this house to do so, she explained. As he let her go ahead, he was aware for the last time of the undefined firmness of her flesh, constricted by tight-fitting panties and brassiere. The owner no longer showed herself – evidently a sign that no one was interested in his return.

You must be mistaken there, Grandfather, we say, but he doesn't want comfort.

He went in, says Grandfather, because twenty years earlier, as a youth, he had toyed with the idea; almost forty by this time, he could finally accept the fact that he had not entered before. In the open door he wondered if he should say goodbye to the girl with a bow, and he did.

And at this very moment the clock struck twelve. Twelve o'clock noon.

Huh, we say and give a frightened scream.

So that's the way it went in the brothels, we say.

No, says Grandfather, that's the way it went with me, and that was probably my fault.

And what about the artificial turf, Grandfather, we ask, and Njesa? and the athletic club?

Grandfather remains silent. Once he has finished his story or thinks he has, he wants no part of the artificial turf, he rolls it out only for the first move of that game. What was this eternal turf on which the Njesa Soccer Club won or lost, compared with the 0:0 score in the house with the cocoa advertisement, near the tracks and close to noon. It had been a long time ago, it had been nothing, or almost nothing, but something in itself.

We are fond of our grandfather. He is still capable of blushing, he is not of our time. But he still knows how to tell a story, he is still a storyteller.

Translated by
Marlis Zeller Cambon
and Michael Hamburger

ANAÏS NIN

MANDRA

To supplement a slim income, many writers have written erotic or pornographic books. The poet Apollinaire produced an erotic adventure novel, Les onze mille verges*; Oscar Wilde (perhaps not for economic reasons) is said to have been the author of a gay erotic novel,* Teleny. *Anaïs Nin, who after an American childhood returned to her native France and joined the surrealists' coterie, wrote in her early New York days a series of erotic vignettes which she eventually collected under the title* Little Birds. *"I became," she confesses, "what I shall call the Madame of an unusual house of literary prostitution. It was a very artistic '*maison,*' I must say, a one-room studio with skylights, which I painted to look like pagan cathedral windows."*

*Writers, all poor, frequented her "*maison*" and were fed Quaker Oats "because it was the cheapest thing to make." Most of the erotica – such as "Mandra" – was written on an empty stomach. "My real writing," says Nin, "was put aside when I set out in search of the erotic. These are my adven-*

tures in the world of prostitution. To bring them into light was at first difficult. The sexual life is usually enveloped in many layers, for all of us – poets, writers, artists. It is a veiled woman, half-dreamed."

THE ILLUMINED SKYSCRAPERS shine like Christmas trees. I have been invited to stay with rich friends at the Plaza. The luxury lulls me, but I lie in a soft bed sick with ennui, like a flower in a hothouse. My feet rest on soft carpets. New York gives me a fever – the great Babylonian city.

I see Lillian. I no longer love her. There are those who dance and those who twist themselves into knots. I like those who flow and dance. I will see Mary again. Perhaps this time I will not be timid. I remember when she came to Saint-Tropez one day and we met casually at a café. She invited me to come to her room in the evening.

My lover, Marcel, had to go home that night; he lived quite far away. I was free. I left him at eleven o'clock and went to see Mary. I was wearing my flounced Spanish cretonne dress and a flower in my hair, and I was all bronzed by the sun and feeling beautiful.

When I arrived, Mary was lying on her bed cold-creaming her face, her legs and her shoulders because she had been lying on the beach. She was rubbing cream into her neck, her throat – she was covered with cream.

This disappointed me. I sat at the foot of her bed and we talked. I lost my desire to kiss her. She was running away from her husband. She had married him only to be protected. She had never really loved men but women. At the beginning of her marriage, she had told him all sorts of stories about herself that she should not have told him – how she had been a dancer on Broadway and slept with men when she was short of money; how she even went to a whorehouse and earned money there; how she met a man who fell in love with her and kept her for a few years. Her husband never recovered from these stories. They awakened his jealousy and doubts, and their life together had become intolerable.

The day after we met, she left Saint-Tropez, and I was filled with regrets for not having kissed her. Now I was about to see her again.

In New York I unfold my wings of vanity and coquetry. Mary is as lovely as ever and seems much moved by me. She is all curves, softness. Her eyes are wide and liquid; her cheeks, luminous. Her mouth is full; her hair blond, and luxuriant. She is slow, passive, lethargic. We go to the movies together. In the dark she takes my hand.

She is being analyzed and has discovered what I sensed long ago: that she has never known a real orgasm, at thirty-four, after a sexual life that only an expert accountant could keep track of. I am discovering her pretenses. She is always smiling, gay, but underneath she feels unreal, remote, detached from experience. She acts as if she were asleep. She is trying to awaken by falling into bed with anyone who invites her.

Mary says, "It is very hard to talk about sex, I am so

ashamed." She is not ashamed of doing anything at all, but she cannot talk about it. She can talk to me. We sit for hours in perfumed places where there is music. She likes places where actors go.

There is a current of attraction between us, purely physical. We are always on the verge of getting into bed together. But she is never free in the evenings. She will not let me meet her husband. She is afraid I will seduce him.

She fascinates me because sensuality pours from her. At eight years old she was already having a Lesbian affair with an older cousin.

We both share the love of finery, perfume and luxury. She is so lazy, languid – purely a plant, really. I have never seen a woman more yielding. She says that she always expects to find the man who will arouse her. She has to live in a sexual atmosphere even when she feels nothing. It is her climate. Her favorite statement is, "At that time, I was sleeping around with everybody."

If we speak of Paris and of people we knew there, she always says, "I don't know him. I didn't sleep with him." Or, "Oh, yes, he was wonderful in bed."

I have never once heard of her resisting – this, coupled with frigidity! She deceives everybody, including herself. She looks so wet and open that men think she is continuously in a state of near orgasm. But it is not true. The actress in her appears cheerful and calm, and inside she is going to pieces. She drinks and can sleep only by taking drugs. She always comes to me eating candy, like a schoolgirl. She looks about twenty. Her coat is open, her hat is in her hand. Her hair is loose.

One day she falls on my bed and knocks off her shoes. She

looks at her legs and says, "They are too thick. They are like Renoir legs, I was told once in Paris."

"But I love them," I say, "I love them."

"Do you like my new stockings?" She raises her skirt to show me.

She asks for a whiskey. Then she decides that she will take a bath. She borrows my kimono. I know that she is trying to tempt me. She comes out of the bathroom still humid, leaving the kimono open. Her legs are always held a little apart. She looks so much as if she were about to have an orgasm that one cannot help feeling: only one little caress will drive her wild. As she sits on the edge of my bed to put on her stockings, I cannot withhold any longer. I kneel in front of her and put my hand on the hair between her legs. I stroke it gently, gently, and I say, "The little silver fox, the little silver fox. So soft and beautiful. Oh, Mary, I can't believe that you do not feel anything there, inside."

She seems on the verge of feeling, the way her flesh looks, open like a flower, the way her legs are spread. Her mouth is so wet, so inviting, the lips of her sex must be the same. She parts her legs and lets me look at it. I touch it gently and spread the lips to see if they are moist. She feels it when I touch her clitoris, but I want her to feel the bigger orgasm.

I kiss her clitoris, still wet from the bath; her pubic hair, still damp as seaweed. Her sex tastes like a seashell, a wonderful, fresh, salty seashell. Oh, Mary! My fingers work more quickly, she falls back on the bed, offering her whole sex to me, open and moist, like a camellia, like rose petals, like velvet, satin. It is rosy and new, as if no one had ever touched it. It is like the sex of a young girl.

Her legs hang over the side of the bed. Her sex is open; I can bite into it, kiss it, insert my tongue. She does not move. The little clitoris stiffens like a nipple. My head between her two legs is caught in the most delicious vise of silky, salty flesh.

My hands travel upwards to her heavy breasts, caress them. She begins to moan a little. Now her hands travel downwards and join mine in caressing her own sex. She likes to be touched at the mouth of her sex, below the clitoris. She touches the place with me. It is there I would like to push a penis and move until I make her scream with pleasure. I put my tongue at the opening and push it in as far as it will go. I take her ass in my two hands, like a big fruit, and push it upwards, and while my tongue is playing there in the mouth of her sex, my fingers press into the flesh of her ass, travel around its firmness, into its curve, and my forefinger feels the mouth of her anus and pushes in gently.

Suddenly Mary gives a start – as if I have touched off an electric spark. She moves to enclose my finger. I press it farther, all the while moving my tongue inside her sex. She begins to moan, to undulate.

When she sinks downwards she feels my flicking finger, when she rises upwards she meets my flicking tongue. With every move, she feels my quickening rhythm, until she has a long spasm and begins to moan like a pigeon. With my finger I feel the palpitation of pleasure, going once, twice, thrice, beating ecstatically.

She falls over, panting. "Oh, Mandra, what have you done to me, what have you done to me!" She kisses me, drinking the salty moisture from my mouth. Her breasts fall against me as she holds me, saying again, "Oh, Mandra, what have you done . . ."

I am invited one night to the apartment of a young society couple, the H's. It is like being on a boat because it is near the East River and the barges pass while we talk, the river is alive. Miriam is a delight to look at, a Brunhilde, full-breasted, with sparkling hair, a voice that lures you to her. Her husband, Paul, is small and of the race of the imps, not a man but a faun – a lyrical animal, quick and humorous. He thinks I am beautiful. He treats me like an objet d'art. The black butler opens the door. Paul exclaims over me, my Goyaesque hood, the red flower in my hair, and hurries me into the salon to display me. Miriam is sitting cross-legged on a purple satin divan. She is a natural beauty, whereas I, an artificial one, need a setting and warmth to bloom successfully.

Their apartment is full of furnishings I find individually ugly – silver candelabra, tables with nooks for trailing flowers, enormous mulberry satin poufs, rococo objects, things full of chic, collected with snobbish playfulness, as if to say "We can make fun of everything created by fashion, we are above it all."

Everything is touched with aristocratic impudence, through which I can sense the H's fabulous life in Rome, Florence; Miriam's frequent appearances in *Vogue* wearing Chanel dresses; the pompousness of their families; their efforts to be elegantly bohemian; and their obsession with the word that is the key to society – everything must be "amusing."

Miriam calls me into her bedroom to show me a new bathing suit she has bought in Paris. For this, she undresses herself completely, and then takes the long piece of material and begins rolling it around herself like the primitive draping of the Balinese.

Her beauty goes to my head. She undrapes herself, walks naked around the room, and then says, "I wish I looked like you. You are so exquisite and dainty. I am so big."

"But that's just why I like you, Miriam."

"Oh, your perfume, Mandra."

She pushes her face into my shoulder under my hair and smells my skin.

I place my hand on her shoulder.

"You're the most beautiful woman I've ever seen, Miriam."

Paul is calling out to us, "When are you going to finish talking about clothes in there? I'm bored!"

Miriam replies, "We're coming." And she dresses quickly in slacks. When she comes out Paul says, "And now you're dressed to stay at home, and I want to take you to hear the String Man. He sings the most marvelous songs about a string and finally hangs himself on it."

Miriam says, "Oh, all right. I'll get dressed." And she goes into the bathroom.

I stay behind with Paul, but soon Miriam calls me. "Mandra, come in here and talk to me."

I think, by this time she will be half-dressed, but no, she is standing naked in the bathroom, powdering and fixing her face.

She is as opulent as a burlesque queen. As she stands on her toes to lean towards the mirror and paint her eyelashes more carefully, I am again affected by her body. I come up behind her and watch her.

I feel a little timid. She isn't as inviting as Mary. She is, in fact, sexless, like the women at the beach or at the Turkish bath, who think nothing of their nakedness. I try a light kiss on her shoulder. She smiles at me and says, "I wish Paul were not so irritable. I would have liked to try the bathing suit on you. I would love to see you wearing it." She returns my kiss, on the mouth, taking care not to disturb her lipstick outline. I do not know what to do next. I want to take hold of her. I stay near her.

Then Paul comes into the bathroom without knocking and says, "Miriam, how can you walk around like this? You mustn't mind, Mandra. It is a habit with her. She is possessed with the need to go around without clothes. Get dressed, Miriam."

Miriam goes into her room and slips on a dress, with nothing underneath, then a fox cape, and says, "I'm ready."

In the car she places her hand over mine. Then she draws my hand under the fur, into a pocket of the dress, and I find myself touching her sex. We drive on in the dark.

Miriam says she wants to drive through the park first. She wants air. Paul wants to go directly to the nightclub, but he gives in and we drive through the park, I with my hand on Miriam's sex, fondling it and feeling my own excitement gaining so that I can hardly talk.

Miriam talks, wittily, continuously. I think to myself, "You won't be able to go on talking in a little while." But she does, all the time that I am caressing her in the dark, beneath the satin and the fur. I can feel her moving upwards to my touch, opening her legs a little so I can fit my entire hand between her legs. Then she grows tense under my fingers, stretching herself, and I know she is taking her pleasure. It is contagious. I feel my own orgasm without even being touched.

I am so wet that I am afraid it will show through my dress. And it must show through Miriam's dress, too. We both keep our coats on as we go into the nightclub.

Miriam's eyes are brilliant, deep. Paul leaves us for a while and we go into the ladies' room. This time Miriam kisses my mouth fully, boldly. We arrange ourselves and return to the table.

STAN PERSKY

EROS AND CUPID

"I marvel at this rarest of gifts," wrote Stan Persky in Buddy's, *"the literal truth." In the erotic context it is almost impossible to read* literally, *without allegory or metaphor. Persky writes in the tradition of Montaigne, for whom the literal truth serves as the starting-point of meditation. In* Buddy's, *the literal truth is the existence of a gay bar, Buddy's, in Vancouver from 1982 to 1988. The bar is the territory Persky sets out to explore, with its local customs, myths and particular cast of characters. From there, Persky takes off on an erratic and intelligent conversation in which anecdotes, stories, reflections become a metaphorical language to discuss the intricacies of homoeroticism.* Buddy's *is a collection of stories ("Eros and Cupid" is one of them), of essays, of aphorisms, of memories, a treatise on gay aesthetics, a meditation on love.*

Buddy's *appeared in 1989; in 1991, when the paperback edition came out, Persky included an epilogue in which the characters correct, add or simply comment on the book, becoming thereby readers who in turn are read by further readers, like mirrors within mirrors.*

On Condition

IN PARIS, long ago, a French boy my own age, about nineteen, a hustler, whom I had asked to sleep with me, replied, "...*à condition.*" I have ever since retained the sense in which all of life is presented to us "on condition." We slept together many times.

Eros

It's probably not a good idea to see either of them at their best. Blinding Eros; charming Cupid. Better to catch them off-guard, as they do us.

For an instant, they stand revealed in the merciless fluorescence of a public building, or their voices grasp at optic fibres. For instance, B., scruffy, unshaven, stoned to the eyeballs, making me drive him to the airport through rush-hour traffic, and then getting the flight info all wrong, forgetting his i.d., etc., so I have to use my credit cards for his fool's errand across the mountains. Or M., phoning collect in the middle of the night from some other time zone, with an incomprehensible tale of loss. So, one starts, and moans, as did Jack Spicer:

What have I gone to bed with all these years?
What have I taken crying to my bed
For love of me?

But there is no denying how they marked us, broke our hearts, wrinkled our souls. One even left a blue anchor tattooed on my forearm.

The first time I saw B. was in the Ambassador pub. I can't remember the time of year, but it must have been sometime during the rainy season because it was pouring outside.

I cajoled my drinking crony Mr Stevens, who had a special talent for such chores, to intercede on my behalf with a blond, curly haired sprite sitting several tables away. *Mis*ter Stevens was the camp name of this thin, fortyish man with pale, thinning hair and wire-rimmed glasses that corrected only about a third of his myopic sight. Because I was the member of our troupe most identifiable as "political," he liked to subject me to Tory diatribes, the intensity of which were directly correlated to the level of alcohol in his blood.

I rather preferred Mr Stevens' drunken and savage self-caricatures to his attacks on human equality. "Well, what am I?" he would wail, and then pathetically answer himself, "A third-rate hag in a fifth-rate faggot bar in a ninth-rate town." I appreciated in this the grain of half-truth that applied to all of us. In fact, we made a rather comic duo. Squinting behind inadequate spectacles at a hazy youthful shape, he'd ask, "How about that one?" It was like cruising with Mr Magoo, the short-sighted cartoon character likely to mistake a tank for a toad-stool. I felt like a seeing-eye dog reporting in, "No, not him."

He was not, however, without his redeeming features. Simone de Beauvoir once wrote, "Sometimes man seeks to find again upon the body of young boys the sandy shore, the velvet night, the scent of honeysuckle." Some nights in the bar, only Mr Stevens could adequately verify this text by his rapturous description of teenage flesh – someone he had slept with the night before – as he ran his feathery fingers over my own forearm to illustrate his story.

Mr Stevens returned alone from his mission, dropping into a vacant armchair alongside me at the terrycloth-covered circular table several of us were clustered around. "He'll be over in a minute," Mr Stevens said.

This is perhaps the most tremulous moment in desire, equal even to the first sight of the desired one nude. The madly entertaining or boring evening is about to go on without me. Lolo, heavy-lidded and magisterial, is grumbling his displeasure over Mr Stevens and my lascivious gossip, his hopes for a literary turn in the conversation dashed. Mr Stevens, by now, is listening to a plaintive anecdote by Ed T., an accountant. As Norman, the waiter, glides down the aisle with a trayful of beer, B. pulls up a chair at a tangent to our crude circle. On my lips the unimaginable yet utterly banal language which will cloak the arrangements for a startling intimacy. Equal even to the first touch; say, a hand placed around the curve of his side, just above the waist.

"Look, I'll be blunt," B. began, without preliminaries, but half-apologizing in advance for the commercial proposition he was about to make. I unhesitatingly agreed to the terms of the contract.

However, once we were out in the streets – we had quickly collected our things, made our farewells to our respective friends; "I'll call you," I yelled to Mr Stevens, as if we were erotic scientists and I was promising to report my findings from the laboratory/bedroom – and had walked about a block and a half in the driving rain toward my parked car, B. surprised me by confessing he was too drunk, stoned or otherwise out of sorts for sex.

I was taken by his candour. Instead of our agreed-upon destination, B. requested a ride to the other side of town where he proposed to spend the night at a friend's house. Although this was something of a violation of the code governing such affairs – i.e., it suggested a relation based on respect – I acceded, having long ago been persuaded by my father's example that courtesy was a true virtue. In any case, I could enjoy the anticipation of our next meeting.

Almost needless to say, even in such arranged circumstances, there is an element of seduction. At first, B. was a casual pleasure.

That is, I became immediately unconscious of what had initially possessed me, Eros. But I sought to entice him, laying myself bare, openly admiring his evident charms, initiating a discourse of admissions. Soon he delighted me by the frankness of his expressions of pleasure.

B. was from a rural town upcountry. There was a monstrous but typical family: younger brothers in Prince George, alcoholic and physically dangerous father, a sister in Edmonton. B.'s sexual tastes were distinctly bifurcated. Presently, he was at the tail-end of a deteriorating relationship with a man in the suburbs, a salesman with whom, by B.'s own account, he had fallen in love – this casual acknowledgement itself opened a horizon.

Like many others his age, B. was living more or less by his wits and the welfare system. Capitalism, or more specifically, its disemployment of youth, rendered B. economically powerless. And as ridiculous as it often seemed, the world – or at least that part of it known as the media – was for the moment demanding of me an almost daily exercise of minor intellectual authority. I was called on, often at dawn, by the local radio station, for ceaseless commentary on a range of current issues, including the economy and the high rate of unemployment, especially among youth.

I'd have to be particularly obtuse – more so than in my dimmer moments – not to recognize the inequities in class power between B. and myself. Worse, there's also, as it's known in Marxist argot, a cash nexus, which poses its own set of inescapable culpabilities, but I think I'll save that one for a rainier day. Nonetheless, as I began seeing B., I was struck by how the structure of the homoerotic tends to even out the standard imbalances in relationships – class, age, education, whatever. Partly, it is the forbidden character of this desire that accounts for its egalitarian current, that causes its relations to be fundamentally a collusion, a conspiracy, a project. But, more: in the sex of homosexuality, how often those who are, by definition, the dominated, become the dominant.

I'm not saying that homosexuality eradicates differences, just that it reshuffles the cards one is holding. It may seem as if I'm claiming some sort of superiority for gay relations and, perhaps – if somewhat sneakily – I am, but I also know better. I've seen enough heterosexualities that are sufficiently dense, tangled and constructed of sub-basements of charged feeling, that I'm little tempted to engage in a bidding war. Nonetheless, among the pleasures of that celebrated homoerotic sexual preference, then, are its *equalities, reciprocities, reversals.*

I once saw a movie called *Trading Places* – an update of the old prince and pauper fairy tale – with a boy named Michael. When it ended, as we were about to go home for sex, I suggested that we could "trade places" also. He was immediately enthused by this verbal play and the ease with which it could be enacted.

Similarly, the assumptions one makes about many stereotypical sex roles are often surprised by a reversal: one night in Numbers, a Davie Street gay bar, Mr Stevens and I were taking pleasure in viewing the affectations of a faggoty but exceptionally pretty youth as he played up to various men in the room – "outrageous" gestures, poses, swoons. Yet, how often these effeminate youngsters startle us later in the evening with the certainty of their desire.

In sum, I succeeded in arousing a hitherto unexplored

region – a utopia – of B.'s ardour. I can't say, I *gave* B. power. The very presumption is arrogantly self-defeating. The most that can be claimed of my volition is that I *enticed* us to an edge, or perhaps, since it all occurs within the boundaries of a code, I conducted us to, not a play-within-a-play, but rather, a reality-within-a-play, occurring within the sexual drama itself. Herein, a reversal which offers the possibility of counteracting the endemic will-to-possess. This also happens to be the key to sadomasochism: the apparent exaggeration of possession harbours the abandonment of the will-to-possess. In all this, for Sade as for Socrates, the consideration is ultimately moral, or else it is without interest.

B., from our first encounters, sought to diffuse the boundaries of the code, to make them ragged as a fjord, invoking ambiguous borders between coded and open relationships, in sex as well as within economic matters. In bed, one or the other of us "fully impaled," as pornographic purple prose has it, it was soon mutually obvious that we were engaged in "something more" than a protocol. And how often he transformed monetary transactions, for his own sake as much as mine, with the utterance, "You're helping me out," as though it was but a munificent loan whose return was not pressing.

The recurrent spatial metaphor for me is "beneath" – beneath the arena of the code, under the stairway, in the basement, where a friend and I, as adolescents, fantasized "initiating" another boy whom we desired.

However, just as I began to acquire the illusion, like Proust's Charlus, that my life would become considerably easier were B. to enter it on a more permanent basis, he announced a brief visit to his sister in Edmonton, which, instead, turned out to be a temporary disappearance.

When B. phoned one crisp morning in early December – the beloved has the uncanny ability to announce himself or appear out of nowhere – I was in the backyard, seated on a kitchen chair in front of the Japanese plum tree, working (... well, pontificating) before a television camera, constituting myself as an imaginary being.

I hadn't seen him in three months. In the meantime I had discovered Buddy's, where I often brooded in contentment after a day's work on the book I was writing about local politics, and had even met a faggoty young man there with whom I was having an affair. The young man was one of those wonderful people from another planet, interested in clothes, haircuts, interior decoration – a devout reader of *Gentlemen's Quarterly* – but who thought sex rather messy, sticky, smelly. In contrast, B. loved to get in and unpretentiously rut. Indeed, he appeared within the hour, stripped, announced his "horniness," which was formidably visible, and promptly, to paraphrase the Homeric poets, entangled me in his limbs. In the hazy enchantment of afternoon, the room grew languorous with smoke and recumbent flesh.

B. had changed, or certainly wanted to be seen by me, among others, as having changed. Nonetheless, it was his relatively unchanging "essence" that was of interest to me. He was at that naissance of adulthood when it seemed urgent that his identity become more comprehensible. He wanted to "get it together," as if he saw his life as a scattering of fragments that he now sought to gather into one place or link into a network. B. had returned to school and had decided, apparently, that there was a role for me in this scenario as unofficial tutor. To all this I found myself sympathetic, because it was B. of course, but perhaps also as a characteristic of getting older: increasingly, as I observed human striving from the minuscule distance of imagined immortality, it seemed to me that what people wanted was often reasonable, even modest. At the same time, the charnel-house of a society in which they sought to realize their ambitions appeared ever more appalling.

In those days, not yet in love, I would arrive upstairs at Buddy's around 9:30 or so for our rendezvous. B. was already there, perhaps shooting pool with someone. There is an instant, seconds prior to greeting each other, which nurtures Eros. He is across the room, engrossed in triangulating a shot. I've just passed through a blur of men below. Like no other feeling, desire conveys with immediacy the *otherness* of the other person. He could be an utter stranger who happens to bear a pleasing resemblance to my favourite hockey player on TV.

In this pure glimpse preceding recognition, one also sees what might be called his other*li*ness. One afternoon B. and I agreed to meet in a straight pub not far from where he was living. He was having a beer with a friend when I arrived. The stripper had just come on and both of them were immersed in her act. I took a table some distance away to wait until it was over, casually observing B., seeing him not only as an other (so, too, am I, as Rimbaud celebratedly noted), but a degree beyond that in which there appears the chasm that separates everyone, in which would-be lovers see in the beloved, as if by foresight, the limited duration of their love, in which we see not merely otherness, which prompts us to respect the independence of his being, but otherliness, which tells us of the impossibility of knowing him, and a shudder passes through the body, echoing as the longing for "transparence." The stripper exits, and I approach; or B. misses a shot, and glances up from the table. For an even briefer microsecond, I'm thoroughly startled by beauty, as if I'd never known it before. Then we see each other. With a look, he lets me know the game will be over in a minute; he'll join me for a drink; we'll go home together.

For perhaps six months, I was in love with B. In a sense, I was almost the last to know. At first, I found myself mentioning B. to my intimates. I think this is more than casual, I'd say as casually as possible to my house-mate Lanny. Letters to George: B. carefully placed in a seemingly throw-away line. Or with Tom in the sauna, after a morning of racquetball, I'd obliquely hint that "something" was going on. "Maybe I'm a little infatuated," I told myself with the same innocent enthusiasm with which the Trojan horse was first greeted.

Then for several months I was subject to the *figures of love,* as they're sometimes called; at once, a continuous meditation, a constant reading of minuscule ambiguous signs, an incessant imaginary discourse about, with, directed toward, the beloved.

"The body makes for the source from which the mind is pierced by love ... So, when a man is pierced by the shafts of Venus, whether they are launched by a boy with graceful limbs or a woman radiating love from her whole body, he strives toward the source of the wound and craves to be united with it and to transmit something of his own substance from body to body. His speechless yearning is a presentiment of bliss" (Lucretius, *The Nature of Things*).

Far from being blunt, as he had originally proclaimed, B. was evasive, Ariel-like, mercurial, moody, "hyper," panic-prone, goony. The capacity of youth for solipsism should not be underestimated. It was weeks, perhaps months, before it occurred to me that I was often but a character in an *internal* drama of his own, one which my own actions did not necessarily affect, variously appearing as wished-for-father, friend, trick/sugar daddy, sanctuary, "mature" man he liked/sexually desired.

Arriving home from work some afternoons I'd find B. in a T-shirt and cotton jogging sweats, listening to thunderous rock, having become horny. Raising his eyebrows, batting his lashes, in what looked like a parody of seductiveness but, I later realized, wasn't, he'd ask with a leer, "Do you wanna get fucked?" Yet, openness to the infinite degree is so rare among men that, despite the near-certainty with which he could expect my heartfelt "yes," I knew what it cost him to casually toss out that question, and was moved by the glee with which he shucked those baggy exercise pants to display the fine blond down of his thighs and hard cock toward which I inclined my head.

On the receiving end, he urges me on, uttering confessions one would whisper only to God.

Afterwards, from across the room as he pulls up his jeans, B. says, "I needed that." Then unaffectedly adds, "Thanks."

"Really?" I ask.

"Yes."

In bed, one night, B. suddenly cries out, "I no longer feel young." He is momentarily inconsolable over his loss.

Occasionally, I see him anew, through someone else's eyes. George and I arrive at my place. B. is curled up on the couch, watching TV, in three-quarters view, wearing only my kimono-like mock-velour robe (underneath, tan briefs). He turns to be introduced to George; involuntarily, I imagine I'm seeing him for the first time as George might see him. I'm struck by B.'s fragility, the way in which he resembles one of those delicate pale blue-and-white Chinese vases.

His inconstancy: disappearances, journeys, imperative missions, casual fucks, an affair with a woman, instant friends acquired during drunken afternoons in the pubs. Erotic adventures that leave me breathless with lust when he recounts them: B. and a friend, Sticks (but I hear "Styx," the gloomy river between us and hell), are taken to dinner at a fashionable restaurant by three men, who afterwards suggest that all of them return to one of their houses. "It was supposed to be a party," B. says, "but *we* were the party." He shrugs at the inevitability of the ways of the world: B. blown three times in the course of the evening, and no doubt gives head in return ("but I told them I wouldn't get fucked"); Sticks fucked by all and sundry: "You should have seen him this morning; he was walking around bow-legged."

Enough idylls. Proust: Marcel "measured his pleasure in seeing him by the immensity of his desire to see him and by his grief at seeing him go; for he enjoyed his actual presence very little."

It's almost over. I phone his former lover. He's seen B., who disappeared a week ago. The ex's cheery tones, my strained timbre. We're close to the last straw. I assemble the prosecutor's final summation: an imaginary speech studded with coolly delivered ultimatums, uttered in the tragicomic mode I learned while attending the medieval court of an early lover.

Around dawn, a racket of crows, and then they fall silent. I wake desolate, having dreamt of B.

Memory: B.'s boast that the more he exposes of his body the easier it is to catch rides. Hitchhiking along the summer highway, clad only in gym shorts, a tiny knapsack at his calf. But one Sunday morning he phones in; I have to drive all the way up the Fraser Valley to rescue my stranded friend at a roadside restaurant. I'm touched by the thought that his beauty – so obvious it fairly cries out for notice with or without his efforts – is somehow invisible to almost everyone but me.

Weeks later, after it's over, I'm in Buddy's with George, who's in town for the weekend. We make our way through the crowded bar, up the stairs, into an even denser pack of bodies. Suddenly B. By the faint light of the cigarette machine, under the deafening music, jostled by passing forms, it is yet possible – our mouths in turn necessarily pushed close to each other's ear – to declare our mutual undiminished love. The crowd separates us. I'm with George and we're joined for a drink by the beguiling beauty, Michael. Past him, I see B. in the background.

And after we have exhausted these snapshots, how can we proclaim: This passed through me, like a torrent, staining the cells of my bloodstream ...?

If I'm shocked at the less than attractive sight of him (much later, in an airport), it is because Eros has left this body. The existence of the gods is immaterial; rather, they are a provisional answer to a mystery. Those in whom Eros once dwelled, now "sag a bit/As if five years had thickened on their flesh."

Cupid

From the first, I recognized Cupid, the god(let) presiding over crushes, infatuations, tricks, one-night stands, brief liaisons, and other lesser affairs of the heart.

He was stripped down to the minimum for hustling on a hot summer afternoon, sitting on a low stone wall in front of the church at the corner of Broughton and Pendrell, crossroads of the most notorious erotic zone in Vancouver's West End. For this incarnation, he appeared in brief cut-off jeans, white gym socks and runners. The rest was well-tanned, firm, nineteen-year-old flesh, on display for passing motorists.

The dazzling smile he flashed as I drove through the neighbourhood brought me back around the block where I parked opposite him beneath a pastel apartment tower. He crossed the street and leaned in through the car window. It was three o'clock in the afternoon. His name was M. We made a date to meet at a gay bar later that evening.

As usual, I was unprepared for fateful encounters. In fact, I carried the anticipation of M. as little more than a talisman to see me through the appointed rounds of a crowded day. Notwithstanding that our little corner of the globe is locally known as Lotusland, its citizens are, it must be admitted, a disputatious lot. It so happened we were once more in the midst of a familiar political crisis pitting the people against the state. We were about to take to the streets again, thus occasioning a familiar flurry of phone calls, committees, coalitions, and the gossip necessary to fuel such endeavours. When I met M., I was en route to one such assembly.

Nor was the temper of the present times the extent of my preoccupations. I'd lucked into a new teaching job, due to start in days, which required that I expound upon, among other things, ancient political thought. At the moment I was scrambling to augment my shaky understanding of the Roman republic, hardly expecting to run into one of its mischievous minor deities.

That night the August moon was at the top of Robson Street as I entered Neighbours, a raucous excuse of a bar, to find M. A mirrored globe slowly twirled over the dance floor, casting pieces of light across the men. From the crowd, I caught a glimpse of a busboy named Jason familiarly running his hand over M.'s ass as he passed behind him, and immediately knew that they were lovers.

The short-lived fashion of the season was khaki battle fatigues and other bits of jungle paraphernalia. M. wore a trendy military camouflage cap, leather jacket, blue T-shirt, and tight-ass jeans. "I have to peel 'em off," he said, as he did so, once we were home. His white jockstrap – which he claimed to have donned solely to surprise me (needless to say, it succeeded) – glowed against his tanned groin. As his massive, uncut cock sprung hard out of the pouch, it didn't require remarkable foresight to intuit I was at the initiation of what might be more than a passing fancy. When I deep-throated him, a groan of pleasure echoed up from the bottom of M.'s throat.

At Buddy's toga party a few nights later, M. arrived in the guise of a Roman slave, attired solely in sandals and a loin cloth, which was about the size of a pocket handkerchief. Most of the bar's patrons who had consented to go along with this outing contented themselves with laurel wreaths and pieces of bedsheet draped and pinned in the form of white togas. The prettier ones bared a summer-bronzed shoulder. Even the more priggish clientele who remained in civvies (myself included, alas) had to admit that the scene was delightful.

There was a prize for the best costume. It was destined for a gargantuan good-natured queen named Tiny who tended bar at a neighbouring establishment. He was decked out in the gear of a Roman centurion, complete with polished breastplate and crested helmet. M. was one of the contestants. The finalists formed a tableau on the little stage in the mainfloor bar as the M.C., one of Buddy's managers, imitating a TV game show host, maintained a bright patter while soliciting audience applause to determine the victor. When he got to M., the M.C. pretended to peer under his loin cloth, joking, "That's what pays the rent," as he flashed an exaggerated leer to the Roman mob. Stern faggotry, unyielding in its standards, refused, however, to award the triumph to mere Beauty; it favoured the centurion, on grounds of "artistic" merit.

As I stood in the white toga'd ranks of the condo gentry at this auction of the flesh, M. seemed to me heartbreakingly vulnerable in offering himself thus, subjected to public quips about his streetcorner activities. He, however, was indifferent to these indignities, apparently satisfied by the prior arrangement with management that his near-naked performance would be rewarded with an evening's free drinks, or perhaps content with the sighs elicited by the sight of his bare flesh, still warm with the day's sun, as he passed through the senatorial crowd.

Cupid, in addition to igniting the affairs of others, is himself, of course, constantly enamoured. It was a part of the old story I'd forgotten, or perhaps nobody had noticed before – Cupid carousing, having casual sex, stormily breaking up with his lover, discovering that all his boyfriends like him *too* much, etc. We only picture him presiding over our little tempests, forgetting he has a life of his own to disorder.

M. was lured by Jason's "butch *GQ*" looks (as he characterized them), though, I must admit, on the few occasions I ran into the object of M.'s affections, usually at Buddy's, I failed to appreciate the attraction. Rather, I instantly spotted Jason as a closet case, distrusting his hearty handshake and hail-fellow-well-met style.

On first sight and in public view, he had cupped M.'s butt in the hollow of his palm with the casualness of dominance or confident possession, but appearances, as usual, were deceiving. It was true that M. was in his most boyish phase, which often had a pleasantly effeminate aspect, even a touch of faggotiness – in contrast to Jason's studied manly ruggedness. Thus the fantasies of the voyeuristic chorus, consisting perhaps only of myself, imagined Jason driving his substantial dick (M. had already put in a good word for cock size) up M.'s ass.

But, in fact, as M. recounted it to me in a succession of nights that quickly stretched into the rainy season, their amorous games, which included a few scenes of mild bondage, weren't entirely predictable. It was Jason, although vigorously denying it even as he squirmed with his wrists tied behind him with a leather thong, who longed to be helplessly penetrated by his youthful partner, ejaculating simply from the combination of the friction of his cock against the sheets and the pressure on his prostate from M.'s well-timed thrusts into his asshole. Indeed, M. cleverly manipulated the situation to the point where he could issue ultimatums to Jason to bend over and take it. And Jason did, which seemed to me a rare point in his favour.

Naturally, such brutal intimacy could only contribute to the unsmooth course which true love must run. Jason resented M.'s working the streets, and responded with unfaithfulness in kind, barely troubling to disguise his adventures. Jason's preferred lubricant for sexual congress was Vaseline Intensive Care Lotion. One night, M. told me, he arrived home hot for Jason, wrenching his boyfriend's white jockeys from his hips, but even as he pressed forward to lick Jason's cock, his olfactory sense was assaulted by the smell of Vaseline Intensive Care, indisputable proof that Jason had earlier in the evening betrayed him with a rival from their handsome circle of friends, and then added insult to injury by not bothering to shower away the tell-tale evidence. It was that refusal to observe the protocols of deception that M. regarded as infuriatingly vulgar.

But then, M. was not exactly a paragon of monogamous virtue himself. First, of course, there was the business of hustling. Though Cupid is traditionally scorned for his cupidity, and it is true that he must make his way in the world, his behaviour is hardly, as his detractors would have it, a form of greed. M.'s views on hustling oscillated wildly, depending on the shaky state of his relationship with Jason. In his more maudlin moments – which, nonetheless, were rescued by his sincerity – he imagined himself and Jason living happily ever after in conjugal devotion, and vowed to abandon the street, sparing himself no recriminations for his whorish refusal to attain that blissful state. On less mopey occasions, M. admitted with an impish smile that, economics apart, he liked the "charge" hustling provided. Second, there was the possibility of erotic adventures of his own with members of the fraternity of his co-workers.

But what of myself in this scheme of things? Especially since a friend notes, "Most will perforce identify your beautiful young men with 'whores,' and most men who 'go with' whores don't love them or want to hang around them." I had never thought of it that way.

When I was eighteen and in the navy, stationed outside Naples, I often went into town with the guys, where we hung out with the women at the Black Diamond Bar. Our foreignness exempted us from certain taboos of manliness – within whose code, for example, one was ordinarily shamed by "paying for it." Though I was mainly engrossed, even then, in barracks romances, and only infrequently sampled the pleasures at the Black Diamond, I was interested in those affairs between sailors and women which went beyond the terms of the contract. For both parties, there was something of a game – but also, more than a game. To cause such a woman to love you was considered a sign of ultimate sexual prowess. For her part, the object was matrimony. I noted that a law of averages appeared to regulate – and even ensure a modicum of "justice" in – the outcomes of these unconventional pairings.

My role model was Dooley, a wiry nineteen-year-old Boston Irishman. Never, then or later, have I seen such awe-inspiring purity of passion. In the middle of a desultory pinochle game in the barracks, Dooley would think of a woman he had seen in the Black Diamond, but had yet to sleep with. As Barthes notes, in a slightly different context, "Desire is no respecter of objects. When a hustler looked at A., A. read in his eyes not the desire for money but just desire – and he was moved by it." Dooley, rising from his chair, suddenly possessed, would conjure up this apparition before us, and then, gritting his teeth and lashing out an arm above his head at the end of which he would split the air with a snap of his bony fingers, cried out to his gods, *"Just one time!"* And he was off, making a dash for the last bus to Naples, leaving us to thumb through our guidebooks to the ancient Roman ruins of nearby Paestum.

But the prosaic and simple truth of the matter is that M., and the others, are persons. I saw him as a boy, as a young man. When you win his love, it is not the sex he loves, since he is already a past master of that, but *you* – for yourself, and for treating him as a human.

In any case, with M., I was caught up in the comic mechanics of desire. He wisely insisted on condoms, and soon I was in the drugstore, feeling exactly as I had at sixteen, confronting a vast display – made more confusing by the advances in technology that had taken place since my last shopping expedition – of "lubricated" and "regular," "ribbed" and smooth, "spermicidals," "snug-fitting," and a litany of brand names, such that you practically needed a degree in biology to buy a rubber.

What's more, I had momentarily discovered the secret of happiness, namely: life is imperative. The meeting begins in half an hour! I have a date with M. at 10! The notes for "Tricks" *must* be finished! I need more whipped cream for the chocolate mousse, *now*!

Meanwhile, a seventeen-year-old hustler, oddly named L'Amour, or perhaps L'Amoreaux (I never did get it quite right, though I was later to know him), had developed a crush on M. Soon he was courting M. in that charming way younger boys have, bringing little presents to the streets where they waited for johns. M., wearing a sliver chain around his neck that he'd received from this youth, and positively glowing, described in detail his enthusiastic deflowering of L'Amour, fucking him not once, but several times, thus perpetuating the myth of youth's relentless potency.

But what about Jason? I asked. M. shrugged helplessly, anticipating the impending domestic disaster. Cupid's genre, naturally, is bedroom farce. And since Cupid is the only immortal moved by boredom (a vastly underestimated emotion, as my friend George points out), inevitably L'Amour was introduced to Jason. The three of them were promptly cavorting in the same waterbed. My imagination reached a point of raw exhaustion. For a final twist, as M. and Jason quarrelled, L'Amour moved in with, of all people, Jason, testimony, once again, to Jason's unseen but nonetheless formidable powers. This was spitefully convenient for Jason, since he could revert to the dominant stereotype he preferred to identify with, now that M. was no longer around to hold up to him a mirror of his actual desire. Our mildly bereaved Cupid drowned his sorrows in the readily available libations and bodies, and bought tickets for – where else? – Christmas in Hawaii.

In all this, I'm affectionately bemused. After a string of debaucheries, M., nude, towelling off from a shower just before we head out for dinner and a movie, innocently announces, "I've got a lot of growing up to do." He squeezes by me on the way to his wardrobe, his flesh brushes my fingers, he tries on half a dozen tops, gazes in the full-length mirror, asks, "Do I look butch?"

These moments remain: one evening, M. amused me by casually glancing at one of those atrocious seventeenth-century representations of Cupid which happened to be lying on my night table. Like someone complaining that a photograph of himself "doesn't look like me," he criticized its ugliness. "Yes," I readily agreed, "it doesn't do you justice."

Or: he asked, more than once, if I might write about him. I was curious as to what advantage he saw. Well, just as letters are better than phone calls, he sensibly replied, the written word is preferable to memories. "You can read it again, you can *have* it," M. said. Votary of Cupid, his wish is my command.

And this: we mate by candlelight. Its flicker throws the shadow of his erect cock, enlarged, upon the wall. Delighted, he points it out to me as I lay under him. The illusion of its enormity amuses him as he enters me and it disappears, giving way to the giant shadow of our conjoined bodies.

On the coldest full-moon night of the year, M. calls from Waikiki. He'd gone with a blond friend he knew from the streets, Skip, who now lived on one of the islands. The sole glimpse I'd gotten of this slim, faggoty, striking beauty one crowded night in Buddy's was sufficient to pique my interest. But it hadn't quite worked out. Though M. had planned to earn his way as he went, there apparently wasn't much demand in Honolulu for black-haired, native-looking, well-endowed nineteen-year-olds. The men thought blond Skip a more exotic sight. M. was lonely – for Jason, even though they'd split up, and he missed me and his friends at Buddy's. He even idly suggested that I might fly out. My temperamental caution, however, spared me that particular temptation of middle age, whose foolishness is quite distinct from that of young and old fools.

When M. returned early to rainy, cold British Columbia, he brought me a souvenir pineapple, and we resumed our sociable round of going to the movies – we preferred quasi-mythological tales of mermaids, Neanderthal men frozen in the ice, remakes of *Tarzan* – followed by dinners at Japanese restaurants, and sex by candlelight to the accompaniment of Pink Floyd and hashish. But he was pining for Jason, who was working at a winter resort in the Rockies. I empathized with M.'s lovesick condition, since I suspected I was coming down with a slight case of flu myself.

I went with M. to the shops in the underground mall where he picked out a beautiful sweater to take to Jason in Banff. "The amorous gift is sought out, selected and purchased in the greatest excitement … we calculate whether this object will give pleasure, whether it will disappoint … seem too 'important,' whether it will *perfectly* suit his desire" (Barthes). The box was encased in a special wrapping paper whose design consisted of Jason's name repeated endlessly, which M. could absently caress as the train took him into the Rockies.

Two weeks later M. calls from Edmonton in the middle of the night. I met him at the airport the next day. As one might have expected, it was a fiasco. Jason had met a young woman. I knew he was a desperate closet case from the moment I saw him. Not only are M.'s hopes rebuffed, but he is consigned to sleep on the sofa, while in the next room Jason beds down in comfort with his new inamorata. Nor does Jason refrain from pointing out to M. the advantages of social acceptability that accrue to him from this more conventional arrangement.

Of course, it doesn't end there. Resilient M. quickly acquires a new lover, a slim, muscular, mustachioed man in his mid-twenties with whom he'd had a brief previous fling. As usual, I fail to understand M.'s taste in lovers. This young businessman ran a frame shop with one of those cutesy names – "Picture Perfect," I think – thus providing M. with part-time employment and the opportunity to be built into his paramour's newly purchased condo. The man's only redeeming feature, apparently, was a rather terrifying and simultaneously thrilling piledriver/jackhammer style of fucking. But this virtue had little utility since M., in his mastery of Jason, had come to prefer being a "top."

Obviously, this affair on the rebound can't last. Indeed, by Valentine's Day, Cupid's own national holiday, M. and I were having dinner in Buddy's. M., seeking my professional advice as a writer, showed me the lengthy text of a proposed letter to Jason, offering him chance number 3,408. I savour the irony of being consulted on a Valentine composed by Cupid himself.

So it goes. But enough of infinite variations; let us hasten to the epilogue that assigns each one to his fate. Jason and M. tried it again, broke up, coupled, split. Eventually, Jason came to a deservedly cruel – well, not end, but – middle as the kept young man of a wealthy Californian and was last seen, stoned on cocaine, at the wheel of an expensive car, either in L.A. or New Orleans, imagining himself happy. As for Jason's short-lived girlfriend, she became friends with M., who once spent several days with her and her girlfriend in Montreal.

Notwithstanding my conceit of M. as Cupid, he was, of course, simply M. Which is to say, he was, in addition to his basically adorable self, the adopted child of an upstanding, Christian fundamentalist, monogamous, etc., Edmonton couple.

At various times, M. would lament, "I'm almost twenty and still a virgin," much to my astonishment that he would reserve that category for such quaint usage. At his worst, he would deliver a depressing programmatic speech filled with reactionary and repentant avowals. I think this was in the spring, after a ship's engineer with whom he occasionally tricked got M. a job aboard an icecutter in the Beaufort Sea, part of the Arctic drilling fleet based at Tuktoyaktuk, and just before he obtained a devoted new boyfriend named Kevin. He would give up his degenerate existence, avoid the fate of "lonely, old men sitting in gay bars," go to school, get married, have kids, attend church, the whole package. This, from someone who, just the other night it seemed, was causing men to drool as he pranced among them in the near-altogether. I could've wept. Happily, these declarations dissipated like a sudden squall at sea.

Nor was I forgotten in these dispensations. Fortune, Cupid's capricious cousin, occasionally smiled. For instance, M.'s friend from Hawaii, Skip, was passing through town, and M., amused by my smitten sighing, intervened on my behalf. Soon I was driving through the rainy streets to pick up this attractively fey blond – one of the perks, apparently, of moving in charmed circles.

Fortunately, I fell in love with Cupid only briefly. M. had taken up with Kevin – once more I missed the erotic point of this choice, though I had to admit that the new boyfriend, who diligently held down two jobs as a waiter in the downtown hotels, was an improvement in character over those who had gone before. M. would return from a weekend romp with Kevin, triumphantly announcing, "We fucked our brains out," or, "We went through a whole box of rubbers."

I moped, either in person, or by mail when M. was at sea for his six-week stint. M. was quite gallant about it all. Once, when I was being particularly lachrymose at dinner, and he could barely conceal his annoyance, he gently pointed out that he was putting up with this ridiculous comportment only because it was me, and we were friends. When I received his letters signed "I miss you and love you," and rather bitterly asked George "What does that mean?", my guru replied, "It means he misses you and he loves you." This was confirmed by the ship's engineer who had gotten M. his job, an interesting, articulate man in his own right, who I eventually met in Buddy's and with whom I had avuncular conversations about our protégé. Alas, dejected lover though I momentarily was, it had to be admitted there was no flaw in M.'s affection. In contrast to Eros, Cupid's touch is light; rather than heartbreaking, the pain he inflicts but pricks the skin, almost as a reminder that the body is alive.

Though we are charmed by Cupid, it would be a sentimental mistake not to recognize his streak of less-than-well-intentioned mischief. According to legend, he empties his quiver under contract to Venus; in fact, he does considerable freelancing. Consider Cupid's geometry: M. is bored with his live-in boyfriend Kevin, and still wants to fool around with his ex-boyfriend Jason, so he brings in another hot number, Derek, to spend the night, though nothing overt occurs during the evening's party. As planned, M. groggily wakes up hungover on the morrow in an undulating waterbed to find Kevin and Derek getting it on. This provides a pretext to feign anger with Kevin for unfaithfulness – even though he was only going down on Derek in obedience to M.'s injunction to be less "clingy" – and simultaneously to deny he is angry. "Why should I be angry?" he ingenuously declares on the phone to a worried Kevin. Why indeed? He's already made a separate arrangement to see Derek. All of this to get Kevin disgusted enough to move out and thus permit M. to get it on in good conscience with Jason, who, unlike the predictable, faithful and loving Kevin, excites M. by being surprising, disloyal and aggressive. Naturally, none of these manoeuvres quite works out – pieces of a jigsaw puzzle that don't fit – and M. laments the human condition as he prepares to climb into bed with me.

Or, one rainy season, M. seems to be systematically seducing all my friends and former lovers. Since I'm already going with Pat, I can hardly complain. Soon, he's seen at the opera with my friend Tod. He's spent the night with Ron. Once, at 4:30 in the morning, Terry wakes me, needing a bed. "Well, climb in," I groan. "No, I've got someone with me," Terry says. "Who?" "M." Since they both have boyfriends at their respective homes, they need a place to fuck. And since it was raining, and they're half-pissed, they decided it would be nice to come over and drive me crazy. I suggest a threesome, a fantasy M. himself had conjured up several months ago, but now he wants Terry to himself. Actually, my proposal was quite innocent this time – I merely wanted to watch a master at work. Subsequently, I'm required to suffer M.'s sulky criticism of me for having failed to be a generous host, despite the fact that Terry proved not all that interesting to him, though the latter, on a separate occasion, offers a fairly enthusiastic account of having been ploughed by M.

Finally, some parting glances: M. has moved into a little ground-level suite in my neighbourhood, and has just disposed of his latest boyfriend, when I arrive to visit. Wrapped around his neck and torso is his latest acquisition, a two-metre boa constrictor. He shows me his fish-tank, which contains some colourful, swimming cannibals, and enthusiastically describes his intention to purchase a pet tarantula and, in fact, to assemble an entire bestiary, one of each phylum. I see M.'s boyfriends, sex partners, lovers, tricks, including me, as a *hominary.* One morning, he arrives at my place, just as Pat and I are getting up. Pat is in the bathroom, washing his face. M. has his snake under his shirt, its head and flicking tongue peeking up out of M.'s chest. He sneaks into the bathroom and stands behind Pat, who is facing the mirror. I hear Pat's yelp.

Friends for about four, five years now, though we see each other less frequently, M. occasionally still drops by. Always in the latest style, he's wearing cyclist's skin-tight mid-thigh spandex shorts, and parks his mountain bike in the kitchen. He's rather bored with the young doctor he's living with in a fashionable False Creek condo. He picked up a seventeen-year-old innocent while riding in Stanley Park and introduced him to the sublime. There's a young man in his mid-twenties, but who "looks nineteen" and has a splendid ass and kinky habits. I feel my breath getting shorter. There are various oldies but goodies. He reels off their names. Plus, he has a videotape of one of his enemies masturbating, shot when the boy was seventeen, which M. is taking pleasure in showing around in revenge for various imaginary offences committed by said monster, who is very blond, very pretty, and very everything in his one on-screen performance. As long as the VCR is already on, we allow ourselves to be accompanied in our own ministrations by some imaginary beings practising porn on another planet.

Long after its haunting streetcorner figures have been dispersed to other districts of the city, its "property values" safely restored, the neighbourhood now cloaked in middle class tranquillity, I sometimes drive slowly through that place where I was first entranced by M.'s impish grin.

Where Eros cries out in his own desire, Cupid offers the enigmatic smile of the master of technique. Eros opens himself; the art of the lesser Roman deity is to place his pointed shafts well. Cupid is amused as his arrows are transmuted into our errors of affection.

I come back to our Roman winter. Gruff Cato, worthy Cicero. All day I traced the doings of Pompey and Caesar in the last days of the Republic. Sure enough, as I'm having a drink at Buddy's that night, the air is afresh with rumours of return. Later, M. wakened me out of sleep, calling collect from Edmonton. The amorous existence is a matter of comings and goings. Again, it is time to meet him at the airport.

Amorous Despair

Just on the other side of my life I found myself, deep in the night, sleeping not in my body but in my corpse, still contorted with pain from my dying. Is it to evade this unspeakable terror that I've slid my palm along the inside of a thousand thighs? knowing full well that the habituating use of desire for this purpose would raise an insuperable barrier to the realm of love?

ELENA PONIATOWSKA

PARK CINEMA

After the remarkable literature of the Aztecs and Mayas, the first Latin American writer of distinction is a Mexican nun, Sor Juana Ines de la Cruz who, after joining the Hieronymite order in 1669, began composing extraordinary poems and plays. Her superiors commanded her to give up her writing "as unbefitting a nun and a woman." Sor Juana responded with an Answer to Sor Filotea *in which, with grace and intelligence, she defends women's rights to learning and attacks a society dominated by men. More than four centuries later, Mexican women writers must still battle the same patriarchal society.*

The daughter of a Polish nobleman, Elena Poniatowska, born in France and living in Mexico since the age of ten, confronted the resistance to a literary career first by working as a journalist, and then by writing realistic fiction inspired by her experience in Mexico's poorer quarters. Her novel Dear Diego, *a love story told singly from the woman's point of view, made her known to the Anglo-*

Saxon public when it was translated into English; in the same vein is "Park Cinema," also a love story, but here Poniatowska's erotic phantasm is conjured up by a man.

SEÑORITA:

As of today, you will have to strike my name from the list of your admirers. Perhaps I ought not to inform you of this decision, but to do so would be to betray a personal integrity that has never shied away from the exigencies of the Truth. By thus divorcing myself from you, I am acting in accordance with a profound change in spirit, which leads me to the decision never again to number myself among the viewers of your films.

This afternoon – or rather, this evening – you have destroyed me. I do not know whether this matters to you, but I am a man shattered to pieces. Do you understand what I am saying? A devotee who has followed your image on the screens of first-run houses and neighborhood theaters, a loving critic who would justify the very worst of your moral behavior, I now swear on my knees to renounce you forever, though a mere poster from *Forbidden Fruit* is enough to shake my resolve. As you may see, I am yet a man seduced by appearances.

Comfortably ensconced in my seat I was one in a multitude, a creature lost in an anonymous darkness, who suddenly felt himself caught up in a personal sadness, bitter and inescapable.

It was then that I was truly myself, the loner who suffers and now addresses you. For no brotherly hand reached to touch mine. While you were calmly destroying my heart on the screen, all those around me stayed passionately true. Yes, there was even one scoundrel who laughed shamelessly while I watched you swoon in the arms of that abominable suitor who dragged you to the final extremes of human degradation.

And let me ask you this, señorita: Is he worthless whose every ideal is suddenly lost?

You will say I am a dreamer, an eccentric, one of those meteorites that fall to earth against all calculated odds. You may dispense with your hypotheses: it is I who is judging you, and do me the favor of taking greater responsibility for your actions, and before you sign a contract or accept a co-star, do consider that a man such as I might be among your future audience and might receive a fatal blow. It is not jealousy that makes me speak this way, but, believe me: in *Slaves of Desire,* you were kissed, caressed and assaulted to excess.

I do not know whether my memory makes me exaggerate, but in the cabaret scene there was no reason for you to half-open your lips in that way, to let your hair down over your shoulders, and to tolerate the impudent manners of that sailor who yawns as he leaves you, who abandons you like a sinking ship after he has drowned your honor on the bed.

I know that actors owe a debt to their audience; that they, in a sense, relinquish their free will and give themselves up to the capricious desires of a perverse director; moreover, I know that they are obliged to follow point by point all the deficiencies and inconsistencies of the script they must bring to life, but let me state that everyone, even in the worst of contingencies, retains a minimum of initiative, a fragment of freedom – and you could not or chose not to exercise it.

If you were to take the trouble, you might say in your defense that the very things I am accusing you of today you have done ever since your screen debut. True, and I am ashamed to admit that I cannot justify my feelings. I undertook to love you just as you are. Pardon – as I imagined you to be. Like anyone who has ever been disillusioned, I curse the day that linked my life with your cinematographic destiny. And I want to make clear that I accepted you when you were an obscure newcomer, when no one had ever heard of you, when they gave you the part of that streetwalker with crooked stockings and worn-down heels, a part no decent woman could have accepted. Nonetheless I forgave you, and in that dirty and indifferent theater I hailed the birth of a star. It was I who discovered you, I was the only one who could perceive your soul, immaculate as it was despite your torn handbag and your sheepish manner. By what is dearest to you in the world? Forgive the bluntness of my outburst.

Your mask has slipped, señorita. I have come to see the vileness of your deceit. You are not that creature of delights, that tender, fragile dove I had grown used to, that swallow innocent in flight, your face in my dreams hidden by a lacy veil – no, you are a tramp through and through, the dregs of the earth, a passing fancy in the worst sense of the word. From this moment on, my dear señorita, you must go your way and I mine. Go on, go, keep walking the streets, I have already drowned in your sewer like a rat. But I must stress that I continue to address you as "señorita" solely because, in spite of the blows you have dealt me, I am still a gentleman. My saintly old mother had instilled in my innermost being the importance of always keeping up appearances. Images linger, my life as well. Hence … señorita. Take it, if you will, as a sort of desperate irony.

I have seen you lavish kisses and receive caresses in hundreds of films, but never before did you receive your fortunate partner into your spirit. You kissed with simplicity like any good actress: as one would kiss a cardboard cutout. For – and I wish to make this clear once and for all – the only worthwhile sensuality is that which involves the soul, for the soul surrounds our body as the skin of the grape its pulp, as the peel contains the juice within. Before now, your love scenes did not upset me, for you always preserved a shred of dignity albeit profaned; I was always aware of an intimate rejection, a last-minute withdrawal that redeemed my anguish and consoled my lament. But in *Rapture in the Body,* your eyes moist with love, you showed me your true face, the one I never wish to see again. Go on, confess it: you really are in love with the scoundrel, that second-rate flash-in-the-pan comedian, aren't you? What avails an impudent denial? At least every word of mine, every promise I made, was true: and every one of your movements was the expression of a spirit that had surrendered itself. Why did you toy with me the way they all do? Why did you deceive me like all women deceive, wearing one different mask after another? Why would you not reveal all at once, in the beginning, the detestable face that now torments me?

This drama of mine is practically metaphysical, and I can find no possible solution. I am alone in the nighttime of my delirium. Well, all right, my wife does understand me completely, and at times she even shares in my distress. We were still revelling in the sweet delights appropriate to newlyweds when, our defenses down, we saw the first of your films. Do you still remember it? The one about the dumb athletic diver who ended up at the bottom of the sea because of you, wetsuit and all. I left the theater completely deranged and it would have been futile effort to try to keep it from my wife. But at least she was completely on my side, and had to admit that your deshabilles were truly splendid. Nor did she find it inconvenient to accompany me to the cinema six more times, believing in good faith that the enchantment would be broken by routine. But, alas, things grew worse with every new film of yours that opened. Our family budget underwent serious modifications in order to permit cinema attendance on the order of three times a week. And it goes without saying that after each cinematographic session we spent the rest of the night arguing. All the same, my mate did not get ruffled. For after all, you were but a defenseless shadow, a two-dimensional silhouette, subject to the deficiencies of light. And my wife good-naturedly accepted as her rival a phantom whose appearance could be controlled at will, although she wasted no opportunity to have a good laugh at our expense. I remember her pleasure on the fatal night when, due to technical difficulties, you spoke for a good ten minutes with an inhuman voice, almost that of a robot, going from a falsetto to deepest bass. And while we're on the subject of your voice, I would have you know that I set myself to studying French because I could not resign myself to the abridged subtitles in Spanish, colorless and misleading. I learned to decipher the melodious sound of your voice, and with that accomplishment came the intolerable scourge of hearing atrocious words directed at your person or issuing from your very lips. I longed for the time when these words had reached me by way of a priggish translation; now, they were slaps in the face.

The most serious aspect to this whole thing is that my wife is showing disquieting signs of ill-humor. Allusions to you and to your on-screen conduct are more and more frequent and ferocious. Lately she has concentrated on your intimate apparel and tells me that I am talking in vain to a woman of no substance. And sincerely now, just between ourselves, why this profusion of infamous transparency, this wasteful display of intimate bits of filmy acetate? When the only thing I want to find in you is that little sparkle, sad and bitter, that you once had in your eyes … But let's get back to my wife. She makes faces and mimics you. She makes fun of me too. Mockingly, she echoes some of my most heart-rending sighs. "Those kisses that pained me in *Unforgettable You* still burn me like fire." Wherever we may be, she is wont to speak of you; she says we must confront this problem from a purely rational angle, from a scientific point of view, and she comes up with absurd but potent arguments. She does no less than claim you are not real and that she herself is an actual woman. And by dint of proving it to me, she is demolishing my illusions one by one. I do not know what will happen to me if what is so far only a rumor should turn out to be the truth: that you will come here to make a film, that you will honor our country with a visit. For the love of God, by the holiest of holies – stay where you are, señorita!

No, I do not want to go see you again, for every time the music dies away and the action fades from the screen, I am overwhelmed. I'm speaking of that fatal barrier represented by the three cruel letters that put an end to the modest measure of happiness of my nights of love, at two pesos apiece. Bit by bit I have relinquished the desire to stay and live with you on film, and I no longer die of pain as I am towed away from the cinema by my wife, who has the bad habit of getting up as soon as the last frame has passed. Señorita, I leave you here. I do not even ask you for an autograph, for should you ever send me one I would be capable of forgetting your unpardonable treason. Please accept this letter as the final act of homage of a devastated soul, and forgive me for including you in my dreams. Yes, more than one night I dreamt about you, and there is nothing that I have to envy those fly-by-night lovers who collect a salary to hold you in their arms and ply you with borrowed eloquence.

Your humble servant

P.S. I had neglected to tell you that I am writing from behind bars. This letter would never have reached your hands, had I not feared that the world would give you an erroneous account of me. For the newspapers (which always twist things around) are taking advantage of this ridiculous event: "Last night, an unknown man, either drunk or mentally deranged, interrupted a showing of *Slaves of Desire* at its most stirring point, when he ripped the screen of the Park Cinema by plunging a knife in the breast of Françoise Arnoul. In spite of the darkness, three members of the audience saw the maniac rush towards the actress brandishing a knife, and they got out of their seats to get a better look at him so they could identify him at the time of arraignment. This was easily done, as the individual collapsed once the crime had been committed."

I know that it's impossible, but I would give anything for you to remember always that sharp stab in your breast.

Translated by
Teres Mendeth-Faith
and Elizabeth Heinicke

GLORIA SAWAI

THE DAY I SAT WITH JESUS ON THE SUN DECK AND A WIND CAME UP AND BLEW MY KIMONO OPEN AND HE SAW MY BREASTS

Certain writers achieve fame through no particular book but through the creation of an entire world: Balzac and Trollope come to mind. Others are known to readers because of a single novel, or story or poem. Most of us might be hard put to name a poem by Edward FitzGerald other than The Rubaiyat of Omar Khayyam, *or one of Bram Stoker's many novels other than* Dracula. *Gloria Sawai is blessed (or cursed) with the fame of a single story, "The Day I Sat With Jesus ...," which has been included in countless anthologies.*

The mystical experience is, according to most accounts, best told in terms of physical sexual encounters. The ecstasy of the saints appears to common mortals like the ecstasy of love; sacred texts speak of the union with the godhead as the union with a lover; nuns are referred to as the brides of Christ. St Mary Margaret Alacoque wrote that, when complaining to Christ about the pains of mystical love, He said to her: "Let me do my pleasure. There is a time for everything. Now I want you to be the plaything of my love, and you must live thus without resistance, surrendered to my desires, allowing me to gratify myself at your expense." It is in this same guise that Jesus shows himself to Sawai's protagonist in her deservedly famous story.

WHEN an extraordinary event takes place in your life, you're apt to remember with unnatural clarity the details surrounding it. You remember shapes and sounds that weren't directly related to the occurrence but hovered there in the periphery of the experience. This can even happen when you read a great book for the first time – one that unsettles you and startles you into thought. You remember where you read it, what room, who was nearby.

I can remember, for instance, where I read *Of Human Bondage.* I was lying on a top bunk in our high school dormitory, wrapped in a blue bedspread. I lived in a dormitory then because of my father. He was a religious man and wanted me to get a spiritual kind of education: to hear the WORD and know the LORD, as he put it. So he sent me to St John's Lutheran Academy in Regina for two years. He was confident, I guess, that's where I'd hear the WORD. Anyway, I can still hear Mrs Sverdren, our housemother, knocking on the door at midnight and whispering in her Norwegian accent, "Now, Gloria, it iss 12 o'clock. Time to turn off the lights. Right now." Then scuffing down the corridor in her bedroom slippers. What's interesting here is that I don't remember anything about the book itself except that someone in it had a club foot. But it must have moved me deeply when I was sixteen, which is some time ago now.

You can imagine then how distinctly I remember the day Jesus of Nazareth, in person, climbed the hill in our backyard to our house, then up the outside stairs to the sun deck where I was sitting. And how he stayed with me for a while. You can surely understand how clear those details rest in my memory.

The event occurred on Monday morning, 11 September, 1972, in Moose Jaw, Saskatchewan. These facts in themselves are more unusual than they may appear to be at first glance. September's my favourite month, Monday my favourite day, morning my favourite time. And although Moose Jaw may not be the most magnificent place in the world, even so, if you happen to be there on a Monday morning in September it has its beauty.

It's not hard to figure out why these are my favourites, by the way. I have five children and a husband. Things get hectic, especially on weekends and holidays. Kids hanging around the house, eating, arguing, asking me every hour what there is to do in Moose Jaw. And television. The programs are always the same; only the names change! Roughriders, Stampeders, Blue

Bombers, whatever. So when school starts in September I bask in freedom, especially on Monday. No quarrels. No TV. The morning, crisp and lovely. A new day. A fresh start.

On the morning of 11 September, I got up at 7, the usual time, cooked Cream of Wheat for the kids, fried a bit of sausage for Fred, waved them all out of the house, drank a second cup of coffee in peace and decided to get at last week's ironing. I wasn't dressed yet but still in the pink kimono I'd bought years ago on my trip to Japan – my one and only overseas trip, a $300 quick tour of Tokyo and other cities. I'd saved for this while working as a library technician in Regina, and I'm glad I did. Since then I've hardly been out of Saskatchewan. Once in a while a trip to Winnipeg, and a few times down to Medicine Lake, Montana, to visit my sister.

I set up the ironing-board and hauled out the basket of week-old sprinkled clothes. When I unrolled the first shirt it was completely dry and smelled stale. The second was covered with little grey blots of mould. So was the third. Fred teaches junior-high science here in Moose Jaw. He uses a lot of shirts. I decided I'd have to unwrap the whole basketful and air everything out. This I did, spreading the pungent garments about the living-room. While they were airing I would go outside and sit on the deck for a while since it was such a clear and sunny day.

If you know Moose Jaw at all, you'll know about the new subdivision at the southeast end called Hillhurst. That's where we live, right on the edge of the city. In fact, our deck looks out on flat land as far as the eye can see, except for the backyard itself, which is a fairly steep hill leading down to a stone quarry. But from the quarry the land straightens out into the

Saskatchewan prairie. One clump of poplars stands beyond the quarry to the right, and high weeds have grown up among the rocks. Other than that it's plain – just earth and sky. But when the sun rises new in the morning, weeds and rocks take on an orange and rusty glow that is pleasing. To me at least.

I unplugged the iron and returned to the kitchen. I'd take a cup of coffee out there, or maybe some orange juice. To reach the juice at the back of the fridge my hand passed right next to a bottle of dry red Calona. Now here was a better idea. A little wine on Monday morning, a little relaxation after a rowdy weekend. I held the familiar bottle comfortably in my hand and poured, anticipating a pleasant day.

I slid open the glass door leading to the deck. I pulled an old canvas folding-chair into the sun, and sat. Sat and sipped. Beauty and tranquillity floated toward me on Monday morning, 11 September, around 9:40.

First he was a little bump on the far, far-off prairie. Then he was a mole way beyond the quarry. Then a larger animal, a dog perhaps, moving out there through the grass. Nearing the quarry, he became a person. No doubt about that. A woman perhaps, still in her bathrobe. But edging out from the rocks, through the weeds, toward the hill, he was clear to me. I knew then who he was. I knew it just as I knew the sun was shining.

The reason I knew is that he looked exactly the way I'd seen him 5000 times in pictures, in books and Sunday School pamphlets. If there was ever a person I'd seen and heard about, over and over, this was the one. Even in grade school those terrible questions. Do you love the Lord? Are you saved by grace alone through faith? Are you awaiting eagerly the glorious day of his Second Coming? And will you be ready on that Great Day? I'd sometimes hidden under the bed when I was a child, wondering if I really had been saved by grace alone, or, without realizing it, I'd been trying some other method, like the Catholics, who were saved by their good works and would land in hell. Except for a few who knew in their hearts it was really grace, but they didn't want to leave the church because of their relatives. And was this it? Would the trumpet sound tonight and the sky split in two? Would the great Lord and King, Alpha and Omega, holding aloft the seven candlesticks, accompanied by a heavenly host that no man could number, descend from heaven with a mighty shout? And was I ready? Rev. Hanson in his high pulpit in Swift Current, Saskatchewan, roared in my ears and clashed against my eardrums.

And there he was. Coming. Climbing the hill in our backyard, his body bent against the climb, his robes ruffling in the wind. He was coming. And I was not ready. All those mouldy clothes scattered about the living-room, and me in this faded old thing, made in Japan, and drinking – in the middle of the morning.

He had reached the steps now. His hand touched the railing. His right hand was on my railing. Jesus' fingers were curled around my railing. He was coming up. He was ascending. He was coming up to me here on the sun deck.

He stood on the top step and looked at me. I looked at him. He looked exactly right, exactly the same as all the pictures: white robe, purple stole, bronze hair, creamy skin. How had all those queer artists, illustrators of Sunday School papers, how had they gotten him exactly right like that?

He stood at the top of the stairs. I sat there holding my glass. What do you say to Jesus when he comes? How do you address him? Do you call him *Jesus*? I supposed that was his first name. Or *Christ*? I remembered the woman at the well, the one living in adultery who'd called him *Sir.* Perhaps I could try that. Or maybe I should pretend not to recognize him. Maybe, for some reason, he didn't mean for me to recognize him. Then he spoke.

"Good morning," he said. "My name is Jesus."

"How do you do," I said. "My name is Gloria Johnson."

My name is Gloria Johnson. That's what I said, all right. As if he didn't know.

He smiled, standing there at the top of the stairs. I thought of what I should do next. Then I got up and unfolded another canvas chair.

"You have a nice view here," he said, leaning back against the canvas and pressing his sandaled feet against the iron bars of the railing.

"Thank you," I said. "We like it."

Nice view. Those were his very words. Everyone who comes to our house and stands on the deck says that. Everyone.

"I wasn't expecting company today." I straightened the folds of my pink kimono and tightened the cloth more securely over my knees. I picked up the glass from the floor where I'd laid it.

"I was passing through on my way to Winnipeg. I thought I'd drop by."

"I've heard a lot about you," I said. "You look quite a bit

like your pictures." I raised the glass to my mouth and saw that his hands were empty. I should offer him something to drink. Tea? Milk? How should I ask him what he'd like to drink? What words should I use?

"It gets pretty dusty out there," I finally said. "Would you care for something to drink?" He looked at the glass in my hand. "I could make you some tea," I added.

"Thanks," he said. "What are you drinking?"

"Well, on Mondays I like to relax a bit after the busy weekend with the family all home. I have five children you know. So sometimes after breakfast I have a little wine."

"That would be fine," he said.

By luck I found a clean tumbler in the cupboard. I stood by the sink, pouring the wine. And then, like a bolt of lightning, I realized my situation. Oh, Johann Sebastian Bach. Glory. Honour. Wisdom. Power. George Frederick Handel. King of Kings and Lord of Lords. He's on my sun deck. Today he's sitting on my sun deck. I can ask him any question under the sun, anything at all, he'll know the answer. Hallelujah. Hallelujah. Well now, wasn't this something for a Monday morning in Moose Jaw.

I opened the fridge door to replace the bottle. And I saw my father. It was New Year's morning. My father was sitting at the kitchen table. Mother sat across from him. She'd covered the oatmeal pot to let it simmer on the stove. I could hear the lid bumping against the rim, quietly. Sigrid and Freda sat on one side of the table, Raymond and I on the other. We were holding hymn books, little black books turned to page one. It was dark outside. On New Year's morning we got up before sunrise. Daddy was looking at us with his chin pointed out. It meant be still and sit straight. Raymond sat as straight and stiff as a soldier, waiting for Daddy to notice how nice and stiff he sat. We began singing. Page one. Hymn for the New Year. Phillip Nicolai. 1599. We didn't really need the books. We'd sung the same song every New Year's since the time of our conception. Daddy always sang the loudest.

The Morning Star upon us gleams; How full of grace and truth His beams,
How passing fair His splendour. Good Shepherd, David's proper heir,
My King in heav'n Thou dost me bear Upon Thy bosom tender.
Near – est, Dear – est, High – est, Bright – est, Thou delight – est.
Still to love me, Thou so high enthroned a – bove me.

I didn't mind, actually, singing hymns on New Year's, as long as I was sure no one else would find out. I'd have been rather embarrassed if any of my friends ever found out how we spent New Year's. It's easy at a certain age to be embarrassed about your family. I remember Alice Olson, how embarrassed she was about her father, Elmer Olson. He was an alcoholic and couldn't control his urine. Her mother always had to clean up after him. Even so, the house smelled. I suppose she couldn't get it all. Anyway, I know Alice was embarrassed when we saw Elmer all tousled and sick-looking, with urine stains on his trousers. Actually, I don't know what would be harder on a kid – having a father who's a drunk, or one who's sober on New Year's and sings *The Morning Star.*

I walked across the deck and handed Jesus the wine. I sat down, resting my glass on the flap of my kimono. Jesus was looking out over the prairie. He seemed to be noticing everything out there. He was obviously in no hurry to leave, but he didn't have much to say. I thought of what to say next.

"I suppose you're more used to the sea than to the prairie."

"Yes," he answered. "I've lived most of my life near water. But I like the prairie too. There's something nice about the prairie." He turned his face to the wind, stronger now, coming toward us from the east.

Nice again. If I'd ever used that word to describe the prairie, in an English theme at St John's, for example, it would have had three red circles around it. At least three. I raised my glass to the wind. Good old St John's. Good old Pastor Solberg, standing in front of the wooden altar, holding the gospel aloft in his hand.

In the beginning wass the Word,
And the Word wass with God,
And the Word wass God.

All things were made by him;
And without him wass not anything made
That wass made.

I was sitting on a bench by Paul Thorson. We were sharing a hymnal. Our thumbs touched at the centre of the book. It was winter. The chapel was cold – an army barracks left over from World War 2. We wore parkas and sat close together. Paul fooled around with his thumb, pushing my thumb to my own side of the book, then pulling it back to his side. The wind howled outside. We watched our breath as we sang the hymn.

In thine arms I rest me, Foes who would molest me
Cannot reach me here; Tho' the earth be shak – ing,
Ev – ry heart be quak – ing, Jesus calms my fear;
Fires may flash and thunder crash,
Yea, and sin and hell as – sail me,
Jesus will not fai – l me ...

And here he was. Alpha and Omega. The Word. Sitting on my canvas chair, telling me the prairie's nice. What could I say to that?

"I like it too," I said.

Jesus was watching a magpie circling above the poplars just beyond the quarry. He seemed very nice actually. But he wasn't like my father. My father was perfect, mind you, but you know about perfect people – busy, busy. He wasn't as busy as Elsie though. Elsie was the busy one. You could never visit there without her having to do something else at the same time. Wash the leaves of her plants with milk or fold socks in the basement while you sat on a bench by the washing-machine. I wouldn't mind sitting on a bench in the basement if that was all she had, but her living-room was full of big soft chairs that no one ever sat in. Now Christ here didn't seem to have any work to do at all.

The wind had risen now. His robes puffed about his legs. His hair swirled around his face. I set my glass down and held my kimono together at my knees. The wind was coming stronger now out of the east. My kimono flapped about my ankles. I bent down to secure the bottom, pressing the moving cloth close against my legs. A Saskatchewan wind comes up in a hurry, let me tell you. Then it happened. A gust of wind hit me straight on, seeping into the folds of my kimono, reaching down into the bodice, billowing the cloth out, until above the sash, the robe was fully open. I knew without looking. The wind was suddenly blowing on my breasts. I felt it cool on both my breasts. Then as quickly as it came, it left, and we sat in the small breeze of before.

I looked at Jesus. He was looking at me. And at my breasts. Looking right at them. Jesus was sitting there on the sun deck, looking at my breasts.

What should I do? Say excuse me and push them back into the kimono? Make a little joke of it? Look what the wind blew in, or something? Or should I say nothing? Just tuck them in as inconspicuously as possible? What do you say when a wind comes up and blows your kimono open and he sees your breasts?

Now, there are ways and there are ways of exposing your breasts. I know a few things. I read books. And I've learned a lot from my cousin Millie. Millie's the black sheep in the family. She left the Academy without graduating to become an artist's model in Winnipeg. A dancer too. Anyway, Millie's told me a few things about body exposure. She says, for instance, that when an artist wants to draw his model he has her either completely nude and stretching and bending in various positions so he can sketch her from different angles. Or he drapes her with cloth, satin usually. He covers one section of the body with the material and leaves the rest exposed. But he does so in a graceful manner, draping the cloth over her stomach or ankle.

Never over the breasts. So I realized that my appearance right then wasn't actually pleasing, either aesthetically or erotically – from Millie's point of view. My breasts were just sticking out from the top of my old kimono. And for some reason that I certainly can't explain, even to this day, I did nothing about it. I just sat there.

Jesus must have recognized my confusion, because right then he said, quite sincerely I thought, "You have nice breasts."

"Thanks," I said. I didn't know what else to say, so I asked him if he'd like more wine.

"Yes, I would," he said, and I left to refill the glass. When I returned he was watching the magpie swishing about in the tall weeds of the quarry. I sat down and watched with him.

Then I got a very, very peculiar sensation. I know it was just an illusion, but it was so strong it scared me. It's hard to explain because nothing like it had ever happened to me before. The magpie began to float toward Jesus. I saw it fluttering toward him in the air as if some vacuum were sucking it in. When it reached him, it flapped about on his chest, which was bare now because the top of his robe had slipped down. It nibbled at his little brown nipples and squawked and disappeared. For all the world, it seemed to disappear right into his pores. Then the same thing happened with a rock. A rock floating up from the quarry and landing on the breast of Jesus, melting into his skin. It was very strange, let me tell you, Jesus and I sitting there together with that happening. It made me dizzy, so I closed my eyes.

I saw the women in a public bath in Tokyo. Black-haired women and children. Some were squatting by faucets that lined a wall. They were running hot water into their basins, washing themselves with white cloths, rubbing each other's backs with the soapy washcloths, then emptying their basins and filling them again, pouring clean water over their bodies for the rinse. Water and suds swirled about on the tiled floor. Others were sitting in the hot pool on the far side, soaking themselves in the steamy water as they jabbered away to one another. Then I saw her. The woman without the breasts. She was squatting by a faucet near the door. The oldest woman I've ever seen. The thinnest woman I've ever witnessed. Skin and bones. Literally. Just skin and bones. She bowed and smiled at everyone who entered. She had three teeth. When she hunched over her basin, I saw the little creases of skin where her breasts had been. When she stood up the wrinkles disappeared. In their place were two shallow caves. Even the nipples seemed to have disappeared into the small brown caves of her breasts.

I opened my eyes and looked at Jesus. Fortunately, everything had stopped floating.

"Have you ever been to Japan?" I asked.

"Yes," he said, "a few times."

I paid no attention to his answer but went on telling him about Japan as if he'd never been there. I couldn't seem to stop talking about that old woman and her breasts.

"You should have seen her," I said. "She wasn't flat-chested like some women even here in Moose Jaw. It wasn't like that at all. Her breasts weren't just flat. They were caved in, as if the flesh had sunk right there. Have you ever seen breasts like that before?"

Jesus' eyes were getting darker. He seemed to have sunk farther down into his chair.

"Japanese women have smaller breasts to begin with, usually," he said.

But he'd misunderstood me. It wasn't just her breasts that held me. It was her jaws, teeth, neck, ankles, heels. Not just her breasts. I said nothing for a while, Jesus, too, was not talking.

Finally I asked, "Well, what do you think of breasts like that?"

I knew immediately that I'd asked the wrong question. If you want personal and specific answers, you ask personal and specific questions. It's as simple as that. I should have asked him, for instance, what he thought of them from a sexual point of view. If he were a lover, let's say, would he like to hold such breasts in his hand and play on them with his teeth and fingers? Would he now? The woman, brown and shiny, was bending over her basin. Tiny bubbles of soap drifted from the creases of her chest down to her navel. Hold them. Ha.

Or I could have asked for some kind of aesthetic opinion. If he were an artist, a sculptor, let's say, would he travel to Italy and spend weeks excavating the best marble from the hills near Florence, and then would he stay up night and day in his studio, without eating or bathing, and with matted hair and glazed eyes, chisel out those little creases from his great stone slab?

Or if he were a curator in a large museum in Paris, would he place these wrinkles on a silver pedestal in the centre of the foyer?

Or if he were a patron of the arts, would he attend the opening of this grand exhibition and stand in front of these white caves in his purple turtleneck, sipping champagne and nibbling on the little cracker with the shrimp in the middle, and would he turn to the one beside him, the one in the sleek black pants, and would he say to her, "Look, darling. Did you see this marvellous piece? Do you see how the artist has captured the very essence of the female form?"

These are some of the things I could have said if I'd had my wits about me. But my wits certainly left me that day. All I did say, and I didn't mean to – it just came out – was, "It's not nice and I don't like it."

I lifted my face, threw my head back, and let the wind blow on my neck and breasts. It was blowing harder again. I felt small grains of sand scrape against my skin.

Jesus lover of my soul, let me to thy bosom fly.
While the nearer waters roll, while the tempest still is nigh …

When I looked at him again, his eyes were blacker still and his body had shrunk considerably. He looked almost like Jimmy that time in Prince Albert. Jimmy's an old neighbour from Regina. On his twenty-seventh birthday he joined a motorcycle gang, the Grim Reapers to be exact, and got into a lot of trouble. He ended up in maximum security in PA. One summer on a camping trip up north we stopped to see him – Fred and the kids and I. It wasn't a good visit, by the way. If you're going to visit inmates you should do it regularly. I realize this now. Anyway, that's when his eyes looked black like that. But maybe he'd been smoking. It's probably not the same thing. Jimmy Lebrun. He never did think it was funny when I'd call him a Midnight Raider instead of a Grim Reaper. People are sensitive about their names.

Then Jesus finally answered. Everything seemed to take

him a long time, even answering simple questions.

But I'm not sure what he said because something so strange happened that whatever he did say was swept away. Right then the wind blew against my face, pulling my hair back. My kimono swirled about every which way, and I was swinging my arms in the air, like swimming. And there right below my eyes was the roof of our house. I was looking down on the top of the roof. I saw the row of shingles ripped loose from the August hail storm. And I remember thinking – Fred hasn't fixed those shingles yet. I'll have to remind him when he gets home from work. If it rains again the back bedroom will get soaked. Before I knew it I was circling over the sundeck, looking down on the top of Jesus' head. Only I wasn't. I was sitting in the canvas chair watching myself hover over his shoulders. Only it wasn't me hovering. It was the old woman in Tokyo. I saw her grey hair twisting in the wind and her shiny little bum raised in the air, like a baby's. Water was dripping from her chin and toes. And soap bubbles trailed from her elbows like tinsel. She was floating down toward his chest. Only it wasn't her. It was me. I could taste bits of suds sticking to the corners of my mouth and feel the wind on my wet back and in the hollow caves of my breasts. I was smiling and bowing, and the wind was blowing in narrow wisps against my toothless gums. Then quickly, so quickly, like a flock of winter sparrows diving through snow into the branches of the poplar, I was splitting up into millions and millions of pieces and sinking into the tiny, tiny, holes in his chest. It was like the magpie and the rock, like I had come apart into atoms or molecules, or whatever it is we really are.

After that I was dizzy. I began to feel nauseated, there on my canvas chair. Jesus looked sick too. Sad and sick and lonesome.

Oh, Christ, I thought, why are we sitting here on such a fine day pouring our sorrows into each other?

I had to get up and walk around. I'd go into the kitchen and make some tea.

I put the kettle on to boil. What on earth had gotten into me? Why had I spent this perfectly good morning talking about breasts? My one chance in a lifetime and I'd let it go. Why didn't I have better control? Why was I always letting things get out of hand? *Breasts.* And why was my name Gloria? Such a pious name for one who can't think of anything else to talk about but breasts. Why wasn't it Lucille? Or Millie? You could talk about breasts all day if your name was Millie. But Gloria. Gloria. Glo-o-o-o-o-o-o-o-oria. I knew then why so many Glorias hang around bars, talking too loud, laughing shrilly at stupid jokes, making sure everyone hears them laugh at the dirty jokes. They're just trying to live down their name, that's all. I brought out the cups and poured the tea.

Everything was back to normal when I returned except that Jesus still looked desolate sitting there in my canvas chair. I handed him the tea and sat down beside him.

Oh, Daddy. And Phillip Nicolai. Oh, Bernard of Clairvaux. Oh, Sacred Head Now Wounded. Go away for a little while and let us sit together quietly, here in this small space under the sun.

I sipped the tea and watched his face. He looked so sorrowful I reached out and put my hand on his wrist. I sat there a long while, rubbing the little hairs on his wrist with my fingers. I couldn't help it. After that he put his arm on my shoulder and his hand on the back of my neck, stroking the muscles there. It felt good. Whenever anything exciting or unusual happens to me my neck is the first to feel it. It gets stiff and knotted up. Then I usually get a headache, and frequently I become nauseous. So it felt very good having my neck rubbed.

I've never been able to handle sensation very well. I remember when I was in grade three and my folks took us to the Saskatoon Exhibition. We went to see the grandstand show – the battle of Wolfe and Montcalm on the Plains of Abraham. The stage was filled with Indians and pioneers and ladies in red, white and blue dresses, singing "In Days of Yore From Britain's Shore." It was very spectacular but too much for me. My stomach was upset and my neck ached. I had to keep my head on my mother's lap the whole time, just opening my eyes once in a while so I wouldn't miss everything.

So it felt really good having my neck stroked like that. I could almost feel the knots untying and my body becoming warmer and more restful. Jesus too seemed to be feeling better. His body was back to normal. His eyes looked natural again.

Then, all of a sudden, he started to laugh. He held his hand on my neck and laughed out loud. I don't know to this day what he was laughing about. There was nothing funny there at all. But hearing him made me laugh too. I couldn't stop. He was laughing so hard he spilled the tea over his purple stole. When I saw that I laughed even harder. I'd never thought of Jesus spilling his tea before. And when Jesus saw me laugh so hard and when he looked at my breasts shaking, he laughed harder still, till he wiped tears from his eyes.

After that we just sat there. I don't know how long. I know we watched the magpie carve black waves in the air above the rocks. And the rocks stiff and lovely among the swaying weeds.

We watched the poplars twist and bend and rise again beyond the quarry. And then he had to leave.

"Goodbye, Gloria Johnson," he said rising from his chair. "Thanks for the hospitality."

He leaned over and kissed me on my mouth. Then he flicked my nipple with his finger. And off he went. Down the hill. Through the quarry, and into the prairie. I stood on the sun deck and watched. I watched until I could see him no longer. Until he was only some dim and ancient star on the far horizon.

I went inside the house. Well, now, wasn't that a nice visit. Wasn't that something. I examined the clothes, dry and sour in the living-room. I'd have to put them back in the wash, that's all. I couldn't stand the smell. I tucked my breasts back into my kimono and lugged the basket downstairs.

That's what happened to me in Moose Jaw in 1972. It was the main thing that happened to me that year.

SARAH SHEARD

EUGENIA

In 1985 Sarah Sheard published a perfect little novel called Almost Japanese, *in which she chronicled the birth, growth and final dissolution of a falling in love. The lover was an adolescent Canadian girl; the loved one, a man, a Japanese orchestra conductor. The union of opposites, which the alchemists saw as necessary to any given creation, becomes in Sheard's novel a game with mirrors, one dark, one light, East, West, male, female. The voice that leads us through that game is, however, unmistakably a woman's.*

In spite of the advances of feminist ideology, women's erotic voices still struggle to make themselves heard. The old stereotypes seem as strong as ever, even though they are now pronounced in the name of civil liberties and sexual freedom. "In the course of history," wrote Rosalind Miles, "to be a woman had been a sin against nature and a crime against God. Now it has become an ideological deviance into the bargain." Sheard makes no apologies for her erotic explorations and in stories such as "Eugenia" extends them beyond all such historical strictures.

THE SMOKE in the room was ferocious. In spite of that and my pre-party resolution not to, I cadged a cigarette from the stranger next to me and lit up in self-defense. *Défense de fumer.* It was a Gitane. And suddenly I recalled Eugenia, the taste of that tobacco on her tongue, its incense clinging to her hair. She, who moved inside a pitchy Balkan aura, smudge pot of London train stations and Paris cafés. Each time I brought my hand to my mouth, our mad, bad school days were carried back to me …

Eugenia, standing before the mirror, turned this way and that to study her new shirt, a man's and very large. "What do you think?"

I shrugged. "Why so big?" She undid the buttons, one, two, three, until her breasts fell into view, then she doubled the shirt into pleats and tucked it into the waistband of her skirt, reaching up from underneath to pull the cloth taut. She dropped her crucifix over her head and the black beads rolled into the hollow between her breasts. The cross itself knocked inside her shirt like a heartbeat as she walked across the room and fell onto the bed beside me, exposing her flawless neck sliced into a V by the shirt, her face framed by a twist of hair as wiry and waxen as a horse's tail, that I caught and coiled into my hand. It was January but her skin still showed the faint striations left from a summer of halter tops and shorts.

Where'er she walks ... To school and back. Branches of forsythia foaming into blossom at her approach, dropping seed in her wake.

Her hips sloped gracefully into a strong ass, curved and classic, womanly in spite of her age. The gores of her skirt clung to her haunches then flared out below like water pouring off a swimmer.

She enjoyed putting her clothes on me although our bodies were very different. We touched each other at first only as friends, in generic places, our hands instructing like mirrors. Look. This is how your hair should fall. Now tie this scarf around your waist. Knot it here, just once and let's see what the colour does for your skin. Good. Stand up straight. No, not that way. I'll show you. Let your breasts rise and part, now drop your shoulders a bit.

We took inventory of one another's bodies, composed the ideal collage of our best features – her breasts and hair, my waist, her ass, my legs, her eyes, my shoulders and definitely her mouth. We went through a time of stealing small gifts for one another from cosmetic counters, indicating by signs what it was we wanted, then dropping the item inside our clothing, lingering a moment at the next counter before shamelessly strolling out.

We were never caught.

I liked to steal cigarettes just for the pleasure of watching Eugenia catch the tab of cellophane between her teeth and tear it apart, extract a tube with her nail and light it, her eyes on mine as she lifted her chin to exhale, lost in pleasure. I inhaled the forbidden in the air around her.

It was July. The last summer of high school.

Eugenia and I sat on my front porch cooling our feet in the night air. We'd missed the bus after our movie and had walked home instead, all the way across town. My father didn't come off shift for hours so I nipped a bottle of his beer from the fridge, opened it and carried it out to the porch where Eugenia sat tapping her ashes into a tiny cairn at her feet. We passed the bottle back and forth without talking, watching a bolus of midges swarm under the streetlamp. In that hour something shifted inside me. The affection I was accustomed to feeling for Eugenia intensified into a kind of inexplicable yearning, like hunger but more urgent. I realised I was inhaling her breath.

"Eugenia, do you feel sleepy?" I whispered, my lips against her ear.

She shook her head. "Not yet."

We sat in silence. She lit another cigarette. It was all I could do to keep from wrapping myself around the lamp post and baying at the moon.

She took a last pull on the beer and then threw me a look – with those heavy-lidded eyes – one with which I'd seen her drench strangers in movie lobbies, bus drivers, our gym teacher. I was struck dumb, my heart roaring inside my ears. I adored her, felt so tender I could have bitten her in two. It was curious and confusing – I couldn't get out a sound, barely draw breath against the repressed excitement I felt.

She flicked her cigarette into the darkness, picked up the empty bottle and disappeared into the house. I followed, carrying our shoes. In the kitchen she turned and handed me the bottle and I dropped it into the carton of empties on the back stoop, making an effort to appear calm.

We were going upstairs to lie down. It was late. Eugenia was tired. She would stay the night. We'd often done that, shared the same bed together countless nights, chastely and without premeditation. But tonight she lit a candle and watched me from the bed as I undressed and when I undid my hair and sank onto the mattress beside her she pulled me tight to her, whispered my name and didn't turn away when I touched my mouth to hers, softly at first, not sure how to – but she opened her lips gently and the tip of her tongue slid out and touched mine and the wet taste of her, the tobacco and the ghost of beer flooded me with pleasure. I began to explore her mouth as her fingers slid down my back to steady me in the narrow bed, her ass against the cool plaster wall, I palmed it, suddenly realising I'd longed to for months – and of course had, but only through cloth, brushing her skirt smooth, not like this, my hand sliding across her cool flesh, across the small of her back, her tiny waist ebbing away below the ribcage she was panting softly I could hear my own heart, the excitement in my clogged blood, my body a mattress of flesh thrown up against her, sharp fingernails scratching across my back, coming up in front, claws sheathed to cup each breast she looked me straight in the eye then bent her head to crush each nipple against her teeth sending a scorching ache down between my legs I squeezed them tight, shuddering involuntarily and her hand moved over my belly and parted my legs she knew her own body, that was how she – and the liquid awaiting her drew a gasp. She seized my hand and directed it to the same place in her, thickly furred and also wet, there was a sound of my fingers sliding against her, the slick froth as she rocked against my hand, squeezing it between her thighs, letting out a moan, a shudder when a creak from downstairs –

Immediately we froze – ears cocked for footsteps on the stairs – but we had hours yet we were safe, her hip pressed to bring me back, my fingers so slippery I was losing her I blotted them against the sheet and slid them back quickly before she lost pleasure, her breasts pressed to mine, spreading, cool and so unimaginably soft – the bonelessness of her against me her fingers twisting my nipple my mouth anxious to taste her elsewhere but the rocking I didn't want it to stop, when suddenly –

She came, making sounds I'd never heard her – and then rolled onto her back with a sigh and I slid down and drew my cheek across her belly, her navel, following the line of hairs that divided her abdomen until my cheek came to rest on her pillowed bone the salty smell of her was – so sweetly intimate I opened her legs gently and began to tongue her there and both her hands clutched my head suddenly in a fury of sharp pleasure. I slid my tongue into her folds and she froze against my tongue, twisted aside for an instant, then brought herself back for more. I slid up and down its ridge, then off down one side into rain shadow and she moaned and arched, pulling my head up sharply by the hair. I torched her, broke off, lit her again until she began growling in her throat a purely animal sound and my own hips began to pulse against the bedclothes in time, blood rising just to think of her coming in my mouth like this, my Eugenia – she gasped once and I trilled my tongue against her then froze and in that instant she erupted, holding my head and jerking once, twice, spasms wracking her in waves and I reached down and stroked myself quickly to climax, our spines fusing we locked hips until the convulsions melted away too small to count.

We drew apart from each other slightly to release our prickly heat, listening to the sounds of the house, the ticking of the room, our ears straining for the particular step of my father's below our window, muttering in search of the key, the slam and scrape as he came into the kitchen below, a grunt, as each boot was tugged off and flung behind the door.

He would undoubtedly notice Eugenia's Gitanes on the kitchen table, our shoes and satchels piled in the corner, would open the fridge, count the empties, note our theft …

I prayed we'd be asleep long before he returned and chanced upstairs, peered into our room and, God forbid, approached our bed, drawn by the mysterious scent of our passion to investigate, the ghostly imprint of the act hovering just above our sleeping bodies like a sneeze left by a leopard or a guardian angel.

HELEN SIMPSON

FOUR BARE LEGS IN A BED

Eros or Love, Hypnos or Sleep and Thanatos or Death are siblings; in Greek iconography, the tomb is sometimes called thalamos *or bridal chamber, and the bed in which we sleep we also make love. But Eros also has its own existence in our dreams: from adolescent wet dreams to the sexual fantasies of adult life, Eros invades our sleep as much as our waking hours.*

Literature has invented for the erotic dream a series of extraordinary myths: the legend of the incubus and the succubus, male and female demons who copulate with us while we sleep; the story of Maia, mother of Buddha, who, while asleep, is assaulted by a six-tusked white elephant with a ruby-coloured head; the episode of the mirror in the vast eighteenth-century Chinese novel, The Dream of the Red Chamber, *in which Chia Jui is given a magic mirror by whose power he can make love to the seductive Lady*

Phoenix in his dreams, and is found dead in the morning, lying on soiled sheets. Giving these stories a new, wickedly funny turn, in "Four Bare Legs in a Bed" Helen Simpson has imagined a different method of erotic dreaming.

When you draw the curtains in the morning you stand in front of the window like a black dog. I am brought down to earth with a bump. It isn't fair.

"Where were *you* last night?"

You ask, even though you *know* we were sitting side by side over a shepherd's pie in front of *World in Action.* I sip my tea and blink at the little azure Chinaman fishing from his pagoda.

"*Well*?" you insist.

I channel vertically under the sheet to hide my blushing neck, muttering demulcent nothings. Goats and monkeys.

What can I say, after all? I can hardly admit that I had a most colourful and stimulating night, thank you, lying bear-hugged with your squash partner skin to skin, dissolving in an exchange of slow damp kisses.

Don't let on to the Old Man, but I think I can safely say I have slept with all the men and boys of my acquaintance, including the grey-beards and one-way homosexuals and those towards whom I had not thought I felt an iota of oestrus.

Only two nights ago I was lying on a riverbank with the other girls, and beside me knelt a boy of about fourteen or fifteen, a childish little chap. A boatload of his schoolfriends in their uniforms drifted past. They wore straw hats, but the sun beat up from the river to make crescents of light flick like sticklebacks over their faces. As they floated by, their smarmy teacher unleashed on us a particularly obsequious grin. His teeth were snaggled and tarnished. Ooh, we all giggled, revolted, and my little boy showed himself in sympathy. I gave him a kiss and a hug; there was a beam of envy from the schoolmaster. I gave him more hugs and kisses, and a generous warmth spread through me, tantalising and lovely.

"You're only fourteen, aren't you, darling," I teased, pressing his head to my bosom, pretending to be motherly. I woke describing circles, and I was laughing.

When we were first married, all of six months ago, he used to bring home large men in suits who laughed loudly, drank beer from tins and said outlandish things in suddenly solemn voices: for example, "It's time to put your cock on the block," and, "We are talking serious megabucks." After a couple of months he stopped inviting them. I missed the flick of their eyes, but by then of course we were talking serious monogamy.

A couple of nights before the wedding we met for a drink on Eel Pie Island. We stood in the long grass staring upstream, watching the Thames flow by on either side, dividing just before it reached us and meeting again behind us. I looked back down half-a-dozen years and saw my secret self at thirteen or fourteen. I had never felt incomplete alone, nor had I ever trembled for security. Now I had a premonition that my privacy and self-possession, which harmed nobody and were my only important treasures, would be things of the past the day after tomorrow. My saying yes to a wedding appeared in this illuminated instant as self-betrayal. A tide of shame and terror crept over my skin, moving fast like spilt wine. I stammered some thin wedge of these thoughts to my future husband, thinking (with an early marital shudder at the predictability), he will say no man is an island.

"No man is an island," he said.

Incidentally, marriage gave his words the lie, since it made an island of every man except himself. Conjugal life correctly conjugated reads: libido libidas libidat libidamus libidatis libiDON'T. Goodbye to the pure uncomplicated glee which can spring up between strangers, leading them out of their clothes and towards each other in a spirit of, among other things, sunny friendship.

The girls at school had a quasi-religious conviction that once you felt the right way about a man, that was *it.* He was the other half who would make you whole, he was the only possible father of your children. I meet Rhoda every once in a while for a slice of cauliflower quiche, and she still subscribes to all that.

"Either it's Animal Lust, which doesn't last," says Rhoda, "or it's the Real Thing, which means Marriage." Rhoda likes things cut and dried. Recently she became engaged to the only possible father of her children. She took him shopping for a ring, hauled him past the windows of Hatton Garden, and he expressed nothing but ridicule at the prices. Next time he went to tea with Rhoda's parents, he was sitting on the edge of the sofa balancing a plate of flapjacks on his knee when his prospective mother-in-law produced a tray of unpriced rings and demanded that he choose one. She said her daughter Rhoda was not to be shamed by a naked finger. He chose, and of course it turned out to be the second most expensive, over a thousand. There is a moral in that somewhere.

Sometimes I slide my ring off before we go to a party, but he makes me put it on again. That left-handed ring finger is the weakest of the ten, always the first to let you down during a vigorous scherzando; there are sets of arpeggios based exclusively round strengthening its feebleness. It is also the most sensitive, the one women use when following such instructions as, Pat this featherweight creme lightly into the fragile skin tissue which surrounds the eye area.

Lily-livered, swathed in white from head to foot, I said, "I will." Willing and waking may come to the same thing, but sleep is another matter. I am only properly alone now when I'm asleep, such is the encroachment. Well, sleep is a third part of life so I suppose I mustn't grumble.

You don't even have a right to your own bed when you're married. There is no escaping the mildmint breath toothpasting its way across the pillows. I am lying cool and straight in my bed when *he* climbs in with a proprietorial air, and I catch myself thinking, "How dare you." I never achieve the old full secrecy now, I never properly escape him, not until I've lost consciousness altogether. And even then ... The other night as I lay waiting for sleep – almost there – I felt his fingertips on my eyelids, and I knew he was testing whether the eyeballs were moving in order to tell whether I was dreaming or not.

My husband is older than me; not so much older that he thanks his lucky stars for me, but sufficiently older to create the distance of a demi-generation gap between us. He is a Management Consultant and he thinks he's got me taped. He probably has, except for my nocturnal life. He has a square leonine head with icy blue-green eyes. I don't know what he thinks about – "If only he could talk," as old people say of their pets.

You could say we rushed into it, but then, why *not* repent at leisure. How dismal are those long-term liaisons where, the seven years and a day being up, no nerve is left to take the plunge. On our honeymoon near St Ives, there was one late wordless picnic down on the beach when I stared at his cleanly minted profile against the night sky and worshipped the silence. Out last week at some busy new restaurant, however, we sat dumbly over plates of chilli-spiced pomfret fish until in the end, to stop the water-drops leaping, I lowered my eyes, staring hard at his tee-shirt, on which was traced a detailed map of half a square mile of the Outer Hebrides, and savagely wished myself there.

His worst failing so far is jealousy. The last time I rang him at the office, his secretary said earnestly, "I haven't seen hare nor hound of him." But if *he* rings *me* and I don't answer, there is likely to be an inquisition. Last week it got beyond a joke. I had taken the phone off the hook because Mr Pembleton had come round to give me my clarinet lesson and at nine pounds an hour I don't like to take any chances on being interrupted. Anyway, towards the end of the lesson we were deep into a passage of Albinoni, quite transported by its bosky rills, and Mr Pembleton's eyebrows were leaping in time to the rhythm as always, when in burst my bellowing pinstriped husband. It was very embarrassing. I was furious. Mr Pembleton was almost crying as he slunk off, not even given enough time to pack away his clarinet properly.

I shall have to be more careful in future.

Sometimes I have a dream that tears through me like a

hurricane and leaves me shaking, the sort of dream that used to be explained away as the work of devils. There were sleepy female demons who gave out such heat that even in midwinter the soporific lettuce seeds sprouted when they walked by, the mere rustle of their skirts made frosty rosebushes blossom into full-blown crimson. Such a succuba would descend in a hot dream upon a sleeping man with an appetite so violent that by the time she had finished with him even the densest-bearded would wake quite exhausted and feeling as though his bones had been dislocated. My own hurricanes would no doubt have been described as the work of that cocky male devil the incubus, whose nocturnal interference was held responsible for the births of mutants and monsters.

Occasionally, at the end of some mad sparkling quarrel, he clubs me down at last with that spiteful threat: "What *you* need is a baby. *That* would sort you out." Oh yes, that would be the end of this road and no mistake. They're all on his side, of course: First, it was ordained for the procreation of children, etc.

Do you think it possible that a dream confluence – put it more bluntly, fusion with a chimera – might result in a phantom pregnancy? Or does the waking self give up the ghost?

My dreams have been with me from the edge of childhood, mostly the sort of dream in which every courtesy is maintained and every permission given; but I never knew before I married what it was to be a quarreller. Our rows are like the weather, there is no control over them and very little warning, sometimes none at all. We might be basking in the sunshine when a squall appears from nowhere and within seconds develops into a howling tornado. At the same time and with equal speed we hurtle back down the decades, transformed into giant infants stamping and frowning and spouting tears of rage.

"Don't talk to me then! See if I care!" rings out with playground simplicity.

I slap his arm and burst into tears of rage and disappointment. I follow him into the next room. "What about the time you left me stranded by the Albert Memorial," I yell.

"You sound just like a scratched old record," he hisses. He follows me upstairs. Insults cramp my throat. I find the best one and aim it carefully like a dart. I watch the pupils disappear to pin-points in the great excited aquamarine irises of his eyes.

"Go away! Go away!" I shout, turning to the wall as he approaches and whamming my forehead against it.

Every time this happens I am astonished at the pack of devils let loose.

We fall into bed like two nasty children. He says things so hard that I feel little shooting spasms in sexual places, so then I feel they *must* be true. I am quiet. I think about them. Then I slap out at him and he thumps me, so I scratch and bite. He says my name after I've turned out the light but I don't answer. We lie awake in that sort of long dead silence when all future life is Arabia Deserta.

We still behave fairly normally in public, avoiding the little bitternesses which longer-established married couples automatically bat to and fro without self-consciousness. Recently we had to go to a dinner party given by one of my husband's grateful clients. Towards the end of the meal, the client's wife ran in from her kitchen bearing a Baked Alaska alight with blue rum-based flames. In case you don't know about Baked Alaska, it is a nightmare of a pudding which only a fool would try to make, a large lump of ice cream covered with heavily whipped sugar-stiffened raw egg-whites sitting on a sponge cake. This structure is cauterised in a scorching oven for three minutes, during which time the ice cream is supposed to stay frozen while the meringue bakes to brown peaks. It is what you might call the Ur-recipe for disaster.

The client and his wife were a fairly tense couple anyway, but the stealthy sniping with which they had seasoned the early part of the meal was now given culinary fulfilment.

"Knife, darling." His voice rose to shrillness. "*Sharp* knife."

"I *know,* darling, but cut it faster than you did last time," she urged. "You remember what happened *then.*"

"It's *melting,* darling," he barked.

"You're not cutting it *fast* enough," she said. A slice shot across the waiting tea-plate, and ice cream slopped onto the tablecloth.

"Come on, come *on*!" Her brows were knitting furiously, and she was dancing a little jig at his side.

"It's been in too long," he said as the second slice collapsed.

"Three minutes and not a second more, on my mother's grave," she said with hatred. "It's *you.* You're so *slow.*"

The table had fallen silent, no chit-chat being possible at the borders of such a scene. I looked on with what I thought of as a sort of Olympian compassion at first, until, like a tuning fork, I shuddered, catching certain unmistakably *married* reverberations.

This morning when I wolf-whistled him as he emerged shaggy and glistening from the shower, he clapped his hands over himself and said, "That's not exactly very feminine, is it."

He has beautiful hands, fine as earth, rough and warm like brown sand. Sometimes he lets me wash his back and shoulders, which is when I get the *marvelling* feeling most strongly. I have never told him about this.

I first felt helpless admiration when I watched him come off the court after a game of tennis, pulling off his shirt as roughly as a child would, his sweat drops white and pearly in the sun. His face was brighter than silver, sunburnt to coppery patches on the cheekbones, his florid shoulders weathered almost to the colour of claret. Let me love you, I said silently as we went to bed that night for the first time, let me stroke your shadows with my fingers and inhale your skin's smell of honey and air; let me love you before you heave ho my hearty.

At night, in pyjamas (which did not appear until after the wedding), he curled to me like a striped mollusc, with the long curving back of a prawn. My little crocodile, I said maliciously as he draped his length against me in bed. When he whispered in my ears (which he still does sometimes) then he caused trembling while my fingers and toes turned to sparklers. It made him groan like a wood-pigeon before falling asleep, though usually I was chortling away for some time afterwards.

Then, my mind was a sunny prairie of contentment; my body was quick, god-like, with a central line of stars. There was the scarcely-dare-believe-it hope that marriage might even mean years of this ahead, safeguarding a life of such subterranean holiday in perpetuity. Yes, yes, there is more to marriage that *that,* I know that now; but surely there is nothing as good.

About six months ago, a week or two after the marrying event, we were walking along the edges of some stubbled cornfields when we came to a solitary house in a field of its own. We looked through the windows – some of which were broken – and there was no furniture inside, so we didn't feel like intruders when we lifted the latch of the garden gate. Concealed by its hedge from the gaze of idle ramblers was a menagerie of topiary, wild-looking peacocks, boars sprouting long leafy green bristles, one or two blurred heraldic hounds. It was hot, late in the afternoon, and we lay down on a bed of box clippings at the end of the garden. I could see horse-chestnut trees nodding beyond the hedge. The densely knit noise of bees came from a nearby tangle of blackberries. I slipped out of my clothes, we lay together on his shirt, we concentrated suddenly for a while on a time of intense and escalating delight. Afterwards I was wicked with pleasure, and we shared the bread roll and apples saved from our pub lunch. I remember noticing the red and green striations on the apples' skins and the miraculous honey-combed structure of the bread. Then we fell asleep.

I dreamed an urgent heated dream of the sort which sometimes follows hard on the heels of satisfaction.

I was walking down the High Street in Bakewell with a modest strong young man. He was quite tall; as he talked to me, he turned his head slightly and tipped his glance down to shoulder level. He was telling me how he made all his own bread, how easy it was, just two or three loaves a week, or four when he felt unusually hungry.

"How on earth do you find the time," I said. "All that kneading and proving."

"Oh, you can fit that in round other things in the odd few minutes here and there," he assured me.

He showed me his current mass of dough, throwing it lightly from hand to hand like a goal-keeper. Then he wore it as a vast damp pliable boxing glove, deftly pulling at it and pummelling it with his other hand.

"You try," he said. I found the glove-trick manipulation too difficult, so instead I kneaded away enthusiastically. It grew and grew, elastic and cirrus-streaked, until I felt worried.

"Have I spoiled the loaf?" I asked anxiously.

"Not at all," he said. "It'll be even better than usual." We continued our walk, his arm round my shoulder as friendly as could be.

When I woke up it was almost evening, warm and still. I watched his crumpled face a foot away coming out of sleep, the lids flickering, light clearing the eyes and then a wreath of smiles.

We used to be *friends* then.

He upends me, he takes no notice of anything above the waist. How would *he* like it, that's what *I'd* like to know. And after some farmyard activity, while *I'm* still inside my night-dress, very often, he cages me in his big arms and legs and disappears with a snore.

"How did you sleep?" My husband has started to make casual enquiries. "Did you have any interesting dreams?" I found a rubbishy paperback calling itself a Dictionary of Oneirology in his briefcase the other night when I was looking for *The Times*. How fascinating to learn that in Islam dreams of shrews are always related to faithless wives; I wonder if that works the other way around. And dreams of being infected with vermin are often the equivalent for pregnancy, it says here. No flies on *me*. Soon he will be cross-questioning me about the possible appearance of daggers, snakes, nail-files and umbrellas in my night pictures.

What does worry me is that I am finding it increasingly difficult to tell the difference between dreaming and awake. I often feel quite astonished when I turn out of a dream into the morning. I shout or laugh in dreams and wake my husband. I dream I am dreaming; or I dream I have woken up. I try to test whether a dream is a dream by cutting a plate of sardine sandwiches; I scoff the lot and am none the wiser. Recently I tried biting my hand in a dream to see if I was awake. Next morning there were toothmarks, so where does that leave me?

I was very late back one night last week, and crept up the stairs hoping he would have fallen asleep. No such luck. He was propped up against the pillows, and closed *Anna Karenina* with a bang as I came into the room.

"It took ages to find a taxi," I said. "They seem to dry up after eleven."

"Why didn't you catch the train? The last one doesn't go until eleven-thirty."

"I know, but Rhoda and I were having such an interesting discussion in the wine bar. The film was very thought-provoking."

"What was it again?"

"*Battleship Potemkin.*" Surely he wouldn't have seen that. *I* certainly hadn't.

"Ah. What was it about?"

"Oh, you know, the nature of war, particularly at sea."

"And you and Rhoda sat till past midnight discussing naval tactics over the Liebfraumilch."

"Along with related matters. Look, you can just stop being so suspicious. I'm sick of your bullying. I'm going to get changed." I stormed off to the bathroom with my nightdress.

"Stay here," he called. No fear, I thought as I bolted the bathroom door. That way he would see that, at the particular request of Mr Pembleton, I had uncharacteristically left off my bra. I took a quick cold shower using Coal Tar soap, and went back into the bedroom with an innocent smile.

"Where did you find a taxi?" he said.

"Oh, don't start again."

"I want to know."

"Waterloo Bridge."

"But you say you met Rhoda at the Barbican."

"Yes, I did, but the wine bar was a little way off, and then there are no taxis in the City late at night. So we carried on walking because we knew there are always taxis on Waterloo Bridge."

"It's miles to Waterloo from the Barbican."

"I *know*, and that's why I'm so tired and cross and longing for bed. And if that's all the sympathy you can show, I wish I'd never married you." I burst into tears at last, and finally convinced him of my blamelessness, so much so that he apologised and kissed me goodnight.

Then I woke up, and the crocodile tears were still trickling down my cheeks. I looked at the clock – five a.m. – and at the sleeping bulk beside me, remembering how we had spent the previous evening in front of the fire playing chess. You see how confusing it can be.

He beat me at that game of chess as he usually (though not invariably) does. When I was putting the pieces away, thinking about them one by one, I said, "I like the knight best. I like his L-shaped hopping."

"You would," said my husband, *bitterly.* The funny thing was, I understood exactly how he felt.

When I catch him in some detail of his body, whirling his little finger round an ear rim or squeezing a pore on the wing of his nose, our eyes meet coldly and he looks away. These fugitive glimpses of hatred between us are frighteningly hearty.

Yesterday, on my way to the shops, I was standing waiting to cross at the busy corner by Marchmont Drive, when a blue plumber's van flew by. The driver's window was open and, although he must have been doing fifty, I caught a long moment of his burnished shoulder and beautiful naked arm with the underarm tuft like the beard of a mussel. There was a blast of music – "Get Out of My Dream and Into My Car" – as potent as a rogue whiff of jasmine, then it was all gone. I almost cried; I still had a lump in my throat by the time I reached the dry-cleaners. You're not saying that means nothing.

Recently I have noticed a disturbing change. Disapproving of my keeping any secrets from him, my husband has started appearing at precisely the wrong moment in places where he doesn't belong. Last night I was lying in a tipped-back chair while the dentist puffed some sort of dizziness around me until I was only half-conscious. He approached and stroked me, removing his white coat, holding me, pressing me to him; and then my husband appeared in the doorway and said, "Excuse me, I'll take over now."

I woke furious to his unconscious weight at my side. I felt like hitting him, but subsided, snarling. When I got back again I was by the sea and it was warm luminous evening. The light was so rare, the sky and sea of such a strange icy blue-green, that I knew I was further north than usual. I walked a few steps along sibilant shingle and quietly plosive bladderwrack, noticing that both a red sun and a yellow moon were in the sky, though the sun was very low. Now, running lightly down the dunes of marram grass appeared some sort of fisherman or sea-gypsy; I was only able to take in the black eyes with their oblique gleam.

He was beside me and the sides of our faces touched; his felt like the skin of a starfish and mine like the lining of a shell. I was both aware of existing in my own body – the mild drumming of my pulses, the gentle maritime roar in my ears – and of being able to see myself and this other figure standing on the shore.

He took a small mother-of-pearl box from his trouser pocket and gave it to me, watching intently as I nodded my thanks. Then his arm lifted at the elbow and he slid his finger under a strand of hair which had stuck to my forehead. I saw my face and neck flood with colour just as the disappearing sun set fire to a stripe of sea. He slid his hand suddenly through the deep armhole of my dress and his fingers curled to the shape of my breast. I lost all power and was beached onto his shoulder.

Time makes a little leap. We are in a house built of driftwood and pine branches. The windows show oblongs of brine-blanched aquamarine; there are bubbles and knots in the glass. He is stoking the sea-coal fire. I stand waiting and hot salt tears brim up. He draws me gently into him again. I feel the extreme heat of his body; it radiates through his clothes like the sun. The middle of my own body bucks softly, gratefully. We stare at each other with reluctant half-smiles, and from our stiff breathing you might think we are about to fight.

We lie down together on the bed by the wall. I close my eyes, curiously at rest now, floating. His violent hand plucks me from my suspension in the middle air and I hug him with equal violence. We rock together as though it seems our ribs must crack.

But when at last it comes to it, clipped in the warm frame of his arms, thighs enfolded in his tangle, at this moment I happen to glance across his shoulder and so spoil everything. It has been going swimmingly but now there will be no conclusion. I sit up, spit words of refusal, glare across the room.

He has done it again. This second invasion *proves* he has broken my cover. Now I will never more be private, even in the slumbering third part of my time. There at the window, his face like a censorious turnip, my husband is staring in.

ARMONIA SOMERS

THE FALL

For the Greeks, the Romans, the Hindus, the Aztecs and countless others, the gods were subject to the same passions and desires as humankind. The Judeo-Christians forbade their deity any carnal commerce, and even though their mystical experience was steeped in erotic imagery, the erotic act itself was regarded as beneath the dignity divine. The Africans who were brought to the New World as slaves and were forced to hide their religions under the theological trappings of their masters were less emphatic. For example, Oxala, identified with Christ, and Iemanja, identified with the Virgin Mary, enjoyed a vigorous sexual life among Afro-Brazilians. Armonia Somers's deities belong to this latter pantheon.

For many years now, since the publication of The Naked Woman *in 1950, a novella which caused a scandal in Uruguay at the time, Armonia Somers has written erotic fiction while at the same time pursuing a career in education, mainly as the director of the National Education*

Museum in Montevideo. Of her stories, "The Fall" is perhaps the best crafted and the most daring.

STILL RAINING. Damn you, Holy Virgin, damn you. Why, why is it still raining?" Too dark a thought for his black voice, for the soft saliva-tasting humble black sounds. That's why he had only imagined the words. He could never allow them to escape, into the air. And even as a thought they were something wicked, something bad for his white negro conscience. He had always prayed, spoken, differently; like a lover:

"Help me, my Lady, white Rose of the rose-bush. Help this poor nigger who killed the big brute of a white man, who did just that, today. My only Rose, please help him, my Heart of sweet almond, bring this nigger a little good luck, my bright garden Rose."

But not tonight. It was cold and it was raining. His bones were drenched to the point where the cold hurt the bone. He had lost one of his shoes walking in the mud, and his toes had come out through the other one. Every time a sharp stone lay in his path, the bare toes would hit against it violently, against that stone and not another, never against a smooth round stone. And the blow on the toes was hardly painful compared to the savage pain that soared up the branches of his body and then fell back again, back to his toes, gripping onto them, hard, painfully hard. It was at times like these that he felt unable to understand his white, white Rose. How could She do this to him? Because the sweet Lady should have warned him that the stone was there, in his way. She should also have made it stop raining so hard, so hard and cold.

The black man kept his hands stuffed into his pockets, his hat pulled down to his shoulders, the old suit buttoned up as far as the few buttons allowed. But the suit was no longer a suit; it was a rag, sodden, shining, as slippery as spit. The body was shaped under the cloth, showing perfect, harmonious black curves. And also – he kept saying to himself – She should have made night fall faster. He had needed night so much throughout the day. There was not a single hole left out there to hide this nigger's fear, in the blazing light. And only now had the white Rose sent him the gift of night.

The black man's tread was slow, persistent. Like the rain, it neither quickened nor slackened its pace. At times he and the rain seemed to know each other too well to be enemies, fighting one another, but not wounding their opponents. Also, the rain made music.

He arrived at last. How he had longed for this place! A short distance from paradise his eyes would not have shone as bright. Yes: the ramshackle house stood there alone, in the night. He had never been inside, but he had heard of it. More than once he had been told about this "safe place," but that was all.

"My rose-white Lady!"

This time he called Her with a full voice. A bolt of lightning cut out his figure, bony and long and black, against the night. Then a blast in the sky, a rough, painful blow, sharp like the one against his toes. He touched his thighs through the ripped lining of his pockets. No, he hadn't vanished into the ground. He felt suddenly happy, humbly and tenderly happy to be still alive. And the bolt had allowed him to see the house clearly. He could have sworn he had seen it move during the blast. But the house had steadied itself, like a woman recovering from a fainting spell. All around the house were ruins, where they had swept away those shacks by the river. Prostitution had made its nest there some time ago, but now all that was left was rubble, these walls left standing because of some unexplained whim. He saw it all, admiring the beautiful hovel, its lost loneliness, its locked-in silence. Now he not only saw it; he could almost touch it if he wanted to. But then, just like someone who is about to reach what he most wants, the black man felt he did not dare. He had walked so long, suffered so much to get here, that it all now seemed unreal, inviolate. The house. On both sides were bits of wall, desolate heaps of rubbish, piles of mud. With each flash of lightning the house appeared again. Everywhere he could see vertical cracks. Also a low door, and two windows, one at the front, one at the side.

The black man, with almost sacrilegious terror, knocked on the door. His fingers hurt, stiff, petrified by the cold. The rain kept falling. He knocked a second time; still no one came to open. He wanted to seek cover, but the house had no eaves, nothing hospitable on the outside. It had been different, walking under the rain. It had seemed different to brave the drifting heavens, out there. The real rain was not like this. The real rain was the one borne by the toes, the stones, all anchored things. It was only then that one could say it rained within, that the liquid world weighed down, destroyed, dissolved. For the third time he knocked with cold, stone fingers, black onyx fingers with tender yellow rose-tips. The fourth time he used his fist. And here the black man made a mistake; he thought they had come to open because he had knocked louder.

The fourth time was the number of the code established by the house. A man appeared carrying a shaded lamp.

"Master, master, let this poor nigger in."

"Go on, damn you, get in!"

He closed the door behind him and lifted the lamp, black with soot, as high as he could. The negro was tall, as if on stilts. And the other man, damn it, was short. He could see his face. It was white, wrinkled vertically, like plaster scratched with nails. From the corner of his lips to the edge of his left eyebrow ran a savage scar of unmistakable origin. The scar followed the line of the lips, the thin lips, making the whole mouth look enormous and lopsided, all the way up to the eyebrow. The eyes were piercing and small, with no lashes, and the nose was Roman. The black man snapped out of the gaze and said in a honeyed voice:

"How much, master?"

"Two prices, you choose. Quickly, nigger. Ten for the camp bed, two for the floor," came the reply, harsh, while the man shielded the lamp with his hand.

That was it. Ten cents and two. The bed, the luxury, the solitary bed lay almost always empty.

The black man looked at the floor. Full. From the bodies rose a unified snore, heaving like sounds from a midnight swamp.

"I'll take the two cents one, master," he said humbly, bending over.

The man with the scar lifted his lamp once more, and wound his way back among the bodies. The black man followed him along the twisting path, like a dog. For the time being, the white man did not care whether the visitor had money with him or not. He would find out once the negro fell asleep, even though the search was usually fruitless. Only someone who had been tricked would arrive here with money. The house was a tramp's establishment, the last refuge on a doorless night. He could not remember whether he had ever rented out the bed. Now it had become the owner's own.

"There you are. Lie down," he said at last, stopping, his voice as sharp and cold as the cut on his face. "Naked or as you are. You're lucky, you'll be between these two heaps. But if another one arrives you'll have to make room for him. This ditch is large enough for two, or three, or twenty."

The black man looked down from his height. In the broken floor, no one knew why, was a kind of valley, soft and warm like the space between two bodies.

He was about to take his clothes off. He was about to become part of the sea of heaving backs, stomachs, snores, smells, ghoulish dreams, sighs, moans. It was then, after the white man had blown out the light next to the single bed, that he discovered the image of the white Rose Herself, with a small flickering flame burning in oil, high upon a shelf on the wall he was supposed to be facing.

"Master, master!"

"Will you shut up?"

"Tell me," he asked, ignoring the order, "do you believe in the white Lady?"

The raw laugh of the scarred man on the bed cut through the air.

"Me? Believe? You ignorant nigger! I've got Her there just in case She's in charge, eh? That way She can see to it that the roof doesn't fall down on me."

He was about to laugh again, that laugh so like his face, but he couldn't finish it. A blast of thunder that seemed to come from underneath the earth shook the house. It was different in here, thought the black man. It drummed inside his guts, deep inside him. Then the rain, the wind, whipped up again. The side window was being furiously beaten; it seemed to shake in an epileptic fit.

Above the sounds, the black man's strong smell took over. It seemed to drown them, the sounds, the other smells, as if fighting against them all.

Sleep. But how? If he kept his clothes on, it would be like sleeping in water. If he took them off, the skin on his bones would feel drenched. He chose the skin, thinking that it would somehow lend warmth to the icy puddles. And he let himself fall into the ditch, stark naked. The light of the Virgin's lamp began to turn softer, clearer, as if the shadows had fed the oil, black as the black man's skin. From the Virgin's wall to the wall opposite someone had hung a dirty gauze, flapping obsessively, swinging in the seeping wind. It was a sample of the ancient weaving that had grown within the house. Every time the wind grew stronger, the gauze's dance became more dazzling, maddening. The black man covered his ears and thought, "If I were deaf I still wouldn't be free of the wind. I'd see it, Holy Mother, in that spider's web, I'd see it, and I'd die from seeing it."

He began to shiver. He touched his forehead; it seemed on fire. At times his whole body seemed to burn. Then it would fall into ice, shaking and sweating. He wanted to wrap himself up in something, but what? No use. He'd have to brave it naked, powerless, in the ditch. How was he to stand the shivering, the sweating, the helplessness, the cold? No way of knowing. And the pain in his back was stabbing him. He tried to close his eyes, to sleep. Perhaps in sleep he'd forget it all. There was much to forget, not only his body. What he had done that day with these, his hands, now part of the pain in his flesh....

But first he tried looking at the Lady. There She stood, tender, soft, white, watching over the sleepers. The man had a dark thought. How could She be there, among so many lost souls, in the midst of that dirty human mass from which a strong stench arose, a filthiness of bodies and rags, fetid breath, crimes, vices, bad dreams? He looked at the strong mixture of men, sins and lice, spread out on the floor, snoring, while She, on Her shelf, kept on quietly shining.

And he? He thought about himself, saw his own nakedness. He was the worst of the lot. The others at least didn't show their flesh to the Virgin as he did, their uncovered shame. He should hide that, not offend the Immaculate Eyes, cover it somehow. He tried. But he couldn't bring himself to do it. Cold, heat, shivers, a stab in the back, dead will, longing for sleep. He couldn't, perhaps he would never be able to, ever again. He'd lie forever in this ditch, unable to cry out that he was dying, unable to pray to the Good Lady, beg Her forgiveness for his coal-black nakedness, his jutting bones, his overpowering odour, and worse, for what his hands had done.

It was then that it happened. The white Rose began to climb down from Her shelf, very slowly. Up there She had seemed to him as small as a doll – small, compact, shapeless. But as She descended She grew – carnal, sweet, alive. The black man felt he was dying. His fear and his surprise were larger than himself, outgrew him. He tried to touch his own body, make sure of his presence, simply to believe in something. But he couldn't. Outside his pain and shivering, he felt nothing. Everything seemed impossible, faraway, like another world lost in another time. Except for this: the approaching Woman.

The white Rose wouldn't stop. Her descent was something decisive, like running water, like rising light. But the most terrible thing about it was the direction of Her movement. Could one doubt that She was coming towards him, towards *him,* the most naked and filthy of men? Now She was almost by his side. He could see Her dainty shoes of golden glazed earthenware, the rim of Her pale blue cloak.

The black man tried to get up. Useless. His terror, his trembling, his shame, had nailed him with his back to the ground. Then he heard the voice, the sweetest honey life can offer:

"Tristan...."

Yes, he remembered being called that in a faraway time on the other side of that door. It was therefore true; the Lady had come down, Her earthenware feet were real, the trimming of Her cloak was true. He would have to answer or die. He would have to speak, acknowledge the arriving Flower. He tried to swallow. Thick, bitter, insufficient spit. But it helped, a little.

"You, white rose-bush Rose...."

"Yes, Tristan. Can you move?"

"No, my Lady. I don't know why. Everything stays up here, in the thoughts, and won't go down to my body. I can't believe it's You, my clear Pearl, I can't believe it."

"It is true, Tristan. Don't doubt Me."

Then, incredibly, the Virgin knelt by his side. It had always been otherwise; now the Virgin humbled Herself before a black man.

"Holy Mother of God, don't do that! No, my solitary Rose on the bush, don't do that!"

"Yes, Tristan, and not only kneel, which hurts Me terribly. Other things I'll do tonight that I never dared do. And you will help Me."

"Help You, Water Lily? With these hands that will do nothing now, but that today.... Oh, I can't tell You, my Lady, what they've done! Rose of amber, forgive this good nigger who turned bad on this black day!"

"Give Me that hand you killed with, Tristan."

"How do You know it was a nigger who killed that man, my Lady?"

"Don't talk like an unbeliever, Tristan. Give Me your hand."

"I can't lift it...."

"Then I will come to the hand," She said with a voice that seemed to grow less vague, more alive.

And now a new impossibility occurred in that descent. The Virgin pressed Her waxen lips against the hard, bony hand of the black man, and kissed it.

"Holy Mother of God, I can't resist it!"

"Yes, Tristan. I've kissed the hand you killed with. And I will tell you why. It was I who told you the words you heard inside you: *Don't stop, press harder, finish with him now, don't hesitate!*"

"You, Mother of the Child!"

"Yes, Tristan, and you have said the word. They killed my Child. They would kill Him again, were He to return. I won't go on. I want no more pearls, prayers, tears, perfume, songs. Someone had to be the first to pay; you helped Me. I've waited peacefully, but now I've understood that I must begin. My Child, my poor and sweet Child, sacrificed in vain! How I cried, how I soaked in tears His torn and mangled body! Tristan, you don't know the worst."

"What, Little Mother?"

"I could never cry after that day for His loss. Since I was made marble, wax, sculpted wood, gold, ivory, I've had no tears. I had to carry on living this way, with a lie of stupid smiles painted on My face. Tristan, I was not what they have painted. I was different, certainly less beautiful. And I have come to tell you something."

"Yes, my Lady. Tell this nigger."

"Tristan, you will be frightened by what I am about to do."

"I am dying of fright, my Lily, but I am still alive."

"Tristan," said the Virgin, Her voice more sure, almost more human. "I will lie by your side. Didn't the white man say there was room for two here in the ditch?"

"No, no, Little Mother! My tongue is fainting, I can hardly ask You any longer not to do it!"

"Tristan, do you know what you are doing? You are praying, ever since you saw Me. No one has ever prayed like this to Me before...."

"I'll sing You a sweeter tune, I'll sing and cry like the reeds, but please, please don't lie by the side of this bad nigger!"

"Yes, Tristan, I am doing it. Watch Me do it."

And the black man saw how the figure lay down by his side with a rustle of silk and necklaces, with Her smell of time and virginity mingled in Her hair.

"And now comes the most important part, Tristan. You must take these clothes off Me. Start with the shoes. They are instruments of torture, as if made of rigid iron, destroying My feet on which I must stand throughout the centuries. Take them off, Tristan, please. I can bear them no longer."

"Yes, I will free Your feet in pain with these sinner's hands. That, yes, clear Lady."

"Oh, Tristan, the relief! But you haven't finished, Tristan. See how ridiculous they look, My feet. They are made of wax: feel them, made of wax."

"Yes, my Lady of the waxen feet, they are of wax."

"But now you will learn something important, Tristan. Inside the waxen feet I have got feet of flesh and blood."

"Holy Mother, You are killing me!"

"Yes, I am flesh and blood under the wax."

"No, no, Little Mother. Go back on the shelf. This nigger doesn't want the Holy Mother of flesh to lie by his side in the dark. Go back, sweet Rose, go back to Your place of roses!"

"No, Tristan, I'm not going back. When a Virgin has left her site She can never go back to it. I want you to melt My wax. I cannot be the Immaculate; I am the true Mother of the Child they killed. I need to walk, hate, cry on this earth. I need to be of flesh, not cold and lifeless wax."

"And how can I, sweet Lady, melt the wax?"

"Touch me, Tristan, fondle Me. A moment ago your hands

would not answer. Since I kissed them they are moving. You understand what your touch will do. Start now. Touch My waxen feet, you will see how the cast melts."

"Yes, my wonderful Pearl, that, yes. Your feet must be set free, in spite of stones. And I will touch them, there. And I can feel it happening, Little Mother. Look, look how the wax melts in my fingers...."

"And now touch my real feet, Tristan."

"They are two live gardenias, two feet made of flowers...."

"But that is not enough. Go on and free My legs."

"The Rose's legs? No, I can't, I can't go on melting. That frightens me. This nigger is very frightened."

"On, Tristan, on."

"I can feel the knee, my captive Lady. And that is all. Here I stop this savage deed, this nigger deed.... I swear I'll stop. Cut off my hands, sweet Mother of the Blond Child, cut them off. And make this nigger forget he ever had these hands, forget he touched the Holy Flower's stem. Cut them off, with a knife sharpened in blood."

A furious blast thundered through the night. The windows beat against their frames, shaking. The house quivered like a ship.

"Have you heard, have you seen how things are tonight? If you don't continue melting, everything will be over for Me before morning. Go on, hurry, finish melting My thighs. I need My whole legs to be Mine once again."

"Yes, soft thighs, terror of this lost nigger. Here they are, warm and silky, like lizards under a winter's sun. But no more, Little Virgin. See how I cry. These tears are my blood aching inside this nigger."

"Have you heard, Tristan, and seen? The house is shaking once more. Don't be afraid of My thighs. Go on, go on melting."

"But we are near the golden bud, my Lady. The locked garden. I can't, I shouldn't!"

"Touch it, Tristan, touch that, especially that. When the wax there melts you need go no further. Then the wax on My breasts, on My back, on My belly, will melt on their own. Do it, Tristan. I want you to do it."

"No, my Lady. Not the golden bud. That I can't."

"It will still be the same, Tristan. Do you think it will change because you've touched it?"

"But it is not only touching it. It is that one can want it so much, with one's blood, with this crazy nigger blood. Have pity, my Lady. This nigger doesn't want to lose himself forever. With tears I beg You to leave him."

"Do it. Look Me in the eyes and do it."

Then the black man lifted his eyes up to the Virgin and saw two forget-me-nots sparkling with celestial fire, like the breath of a chimera. He could no longer disobey. He felt She would consume him.

"I knew it, I knew it. Why did I do it? Why did I touch it? Now I want to enter, now I want to sink into the dampness of that garden. Now this poor nigger can stand it no longer. Look, forbidden Lady, how this nigger's life is trembling, how his mad blood is rising to choke him. I knew I should not have touched it. Let me enter that tight ring, my captive Lady, and then kill this nigger trapped in his own disgrace."

"Tristan, you won't, you won't. You have achieved something greater. Do you know what you've done?"

"Yes, sweet Palm Tree of this nigger's dreams. Yes, I know the terrible thing I've done."

"No, you don't know all of it. You have melted a Virgin. What you now want is unimportant. It is enough for a man to know how to melt a Virgin. That is a man's true glory."

"That's too hard for this poor nigger's head. That's for the clear head of One Who comes from Heaven."

"Tristan: another thing you don't know. Tristan: you're dying."

The black man sank his head between the Woman's breasts, among the smell of blossoming flowers.

"I had forgotten, Little Mother!" he suddenly cried out, as if possessed. "It has come back to me, here, in Your Childless milk! They want to lynch me! I have touched one of their creatures! Let me go, sweet Lady, let me get away! Let me escape! Let me go, Little Mother, let me go!"

"Not so loud, Tristan, the others on the floor will wake up," said the Woman softly, as in a lullaby. "Keep quiet. Nothing can touch you now. Can you hear? The wind. This house hasn't fallen because I am here. But something worse could happen to it, even with Me under its roof. Be sure."

"What? What could that be?"

"I'll tell you. They have hunted all day. Only this place remains; they left it till the last, as usual. In a few seconds they'll be here. They will come because you killed that brute. And they won't care if you're dying naked in this hole. They will trample the others, they will fall on you. They will drag you outside by an arm or a leg."

"Little Mother, don't let them!"

"No, I won't let them. How could I? You are the one who

helped Me come out of My wax. I won't forget you."

"How will You stop them from catching me alive?"

"I only have to leave by that window. Now I have feet that move; you gave them to Me," She said in a secret whisper. "They will knock. You know how many times they must knock. At the fourth knock the white man will leave his bed. They will come to get you. But I won't be there. If you were not dying I'd take you with Me, We'd jump through the window together. But in these cases Our Father can do more than I can. You cannot escape your death. All I can do is stop them catching you alive."

"And then, Holy Mother?" said the black man, kneeling up in spite of his weakness.

"You know, Tristan, what will happen without Me in this house."

"Listen.... They're knocking. That's the first time...."

"Tristan, upon the second knock We will hold each other tightly," the Woman whispered, also rising to Her knees.

The man with the scar heard the knocking and stood up. He lit the lamp.

"Now, Tristan."

The black man held the Virgin tight. He sniffed Her real hair, real woman's hair, then pressed his face against Her human cheek.

The third knock on the door. The scarred man moved among the sleepers on the floor. This was not the usual kind of knocking, the kind he recognized. This was a knocking with a full stomach, with a gun in the hand.

At that very moment the Woman opened the side window. Thin and light like a half-moon, She needed barely the slightest gap to escape. A sad, languid wind carried her away into the night.

"Mother, Mother, don't leave me! That was the fourth knock! I remember what their death is like! Any death, except theirs!"

"Shut up, you stupid nigger!" said the white man. "I bet it's because of you they're here. You swine! I thought as much!"

Then it happened. They entered like flung stones, full of eyes. They went straight towards the black man, holding their lamps ahead of them, treading, kicking the others like rotten fruit. An infernal wind followed them in. The house began to shake again, as it had done several times that night. But the Virgin was no longer in the house. There was a crack, like a skeleton snapping. Then, a world falling apart – the rumble that can be heard before something crumbles down, before a fall.

It happened. Suddenly. Over everyone, over the dead man and over the ones who had come to drag him out.

Of course the rain had stopped. The wind seemed freer, harsher and more naked, licking up the dust, the dust of annihilation.

Translated by
Alberto Manguel

MARIO VARGAS LLOSA

CANDAULES, KING OF LYDIA

"Ever since I wrote my first short story, people have asked if what I wrote 'was true,'" wrote Vargas Llosa in an essay on fiction as the art of lying. "Though my replies sometimes satisfy their curiosity, I am left each time, no matter how sincere my answer, with a nagging sense of having said something that's not quite on target." Vargas Llosa's early novels – The Green House, Conversation in the Cathedral *– depict a reality that demands from the reader a belief in their social or political "truth." His later work, however, shifts to a more dangerous zone in which the reader is asked to be constantly aware of the fiction he or she is reading.* In Praise of the Stepmother, *written in 1988, and which contains the story "Candaules, King of Lydia," is one such book. Dona Lucrecia, the stepmother of the title, and Don Rigoberto, her husband, entertain one another with stories woven around a series of erotic paintings. Which is true? The conjugal conversation, or the painted tales? The reader is drawn from one truth to*

the other without the assurance of an answer.

"Candaules, King of Lydia" is based on a painting by the Flemish painter Jacob Jordaens, assistant to Rubens, in which the king is showing the physical beauties of his wife to his delighted prime minister.

I AM CANDAULES, King of Lydia, a little country situated between Ionia and Caria, in the heart of that territory which centuries later will be called Turkey. What I am most proud of in my kingdom is not its mountains fissured by drought or its goatherds, who, if need be, do battle with Phrygian and Aeolian invaders and Dorians come from Asia, and rout bands of Phoenicians, Lacedaemonians, and the Scythian nomads who come to sack our borders, but the croup of Lucrecia, my wife.

I say and repeat the word. Not behind, or ass, or buttocks, or backside, but croup. For when I ride her the sensation that comes over me is precisely this: that of being astride a velvety, muscular mare, high-spirited and obedient. It is a hard croup and as broad, perhaps, as it is said to be in the legends concerning it that circulate throughout the kingdom, inflaming my subjects' imaginations. (These accounts all reach my ears, but rather than angering me, they flatter me.) When I order her to kneel and touch her forehead to the carpet to kiss it, so that I may examine her at will, the precious object attains its most enchanting volume. Each hemisphere is a carnal paradise; the two of them, separated by a delicate cleft of nearly imperceptible down that vanishes in the forest of intoxicating whiteness, blackness, and silkiness that crowns the firm columns of her thighs, put me in mind of an altar of that barbarous religion of the Babylonians that ours expunged. It feels firm to my touch and soft to my lips; vast to my embrace and warm on cold nights, a most comfortable cushion on which to rest my head and a fountain of pleasures at the hour of amorous assault. Penetrating her is not easy; painful, rather, at first, and even heroic, in view of the resistance that those expanses of pink flesh offer to virile attack. What are required are a stubborn will and a deep-plunging, persevering rod, which shrink from nothing and from no one, as is true of mine.

When I told Gyges, the son of Dascylus, my personal guard and minister, that I was prouder of the feats performed by my rod with Lucrecia in the sumptuous, full-sailed vessel of our nuptial bed than of my valorous deeds on the battlefield or of the impartiality with which I mete out justice, he whooped with laughter at what he took to be a jest. But it was not; I truly take more pride in such exploits. I doubt that many inhabitants of Lydia can equal me. One night – I was drunk – I summoned Atlas, the best endowed of my Ethiopian slaves, to my apartments, merely to confirm that this was so. I had Lucrecia bow down before him and ordered him to mount her. Intimidated by my presence, or because it was too great a test of his strength, he was unable to do so. Again and again I saw him approach her resolutely, push, pant, and withdraw in defeat. (Since this episode vexed Lucrecia's memory, I then had Atlas beheaded.)

For it is beyond question that I love the queen. Everything about my spouse is soft, delicate, by contrast to the opulent splendor of her croup: her hands and her feet, her waist and her mouth. She has a turned-up nose and languid eyes, mysteriously still waters troubled only by pleasure and anger. I have studied her as scholars ponder the ancient volumes of the Temple, and though I think I know her by heart each day – each night, rather – I discover something new about her that touches me: the gentle curve of her shoulders, the mischievous little bone in her elbow, the delicacy of her instep, the roundness of her knees, and the blue transparency of the little grove of her armpits.

There are those who soon tire of their lawfully wedded wife. The routine of married life kills desire, they philosophize: what illusory hope can swell and revive the veins of a man who sleeps, for months and years, with the same woman? Yet, despite our having been wed for so long a time, Lucrecia, my lady, does not bore me. I have never grown weary of her. When I go off on tiger and elephant hunts, or to make war, the memory of her makes my heart beat faster, just as in the first days, and when I caress a slave girl or some camp follower so as to relieve the loneliness of nights in a field tent, my hands always experience keen disappointment: those are merely backsides, buttocks, rumps, asses. Only hers – O beloved! – is a croup. That is why I am faithful to her in my heart; that is why I love her. That is why I compose poems to her that I recite in her ear and when we are alone prostrate myself to kiss her feet. That is why I have filled her coffers with jewels and precious stones, and ordered for her, from every corner of the world, slippers and sandals, garments, priceless ornaments she will never get around to wearing. That is why I care for her and venerate her as the most exquisite possession in my kingdom. Without Lucrecia, life would be death to me.

The real story of what happened with Gyges, my personal guard and minister, bears little resemblance to the idle rumors that have made the rounds concerning the episode. None of the versions I have heard comes even close to the truth. That is always the way it is: though fantasy and truth have one and the same heart, their faces are like day and night, like fire and water. There was no wager or any sort of exchange involved: it all happened quite spontaneously, on a sudden impulse of mine, the work of chance or a plot by some playful little god.

We had attended an interminable ceremony on the vast parade ground near the Palace, where vassal tribes, come to offer me tribute, deafened our ears with their brutish chants and blinded us with the dust raised by the acrobatic tricks of their horsemen. We also saw a pair of those sorcerers who cure ills with the ashes of corpses and a holy man who prayed by twirling around and around on his heels. The latter was impressive: impelled by the strength of his faith and the breathing exercises that accompanied his dance – a hoarse panting that grew louder and louder and appeared to be coming from his very guts – he turned into a human whirlwind and, at one point, the speed he attained was such that it caused him to vanish from our sight. When he again assumed corporeal form and ceased whirling, he was sweating like a war-horse after a cavalry charge and had the dull pallor and the dazed eyes of those who have seen a god, or a number of them.

My minister and I were speaking of the sorcerers and the holy man as we savored a cup of Greek wine, when good

Gyges, with that wicked gleam that drink leaves in his eyes, suddenly lowered his voice and whispered to me:

"The Egyptian woman I've bought has the most beautiful backside that Providence has ever bestowed upon a woman. Her face is imperfect, her breasts are small, and she sweats excessively; but the abundance and generosity of her posterior more than compensate for all her defects. Something the mere memory of which dizzies my brain, Your Majesty."

"Show it to me and I'll show you another. We'll compare and decide which is better, Gyges."

I saw him lose his composure, blink, part his lips to speak, and yet say nothing. Did he believe that I was speaking in jest? Did he fear he had not heard right? My guard and minister knew very well who it was we were speaking of. I had made that proposal without thinking, but once it was made, an irksome little worm began to gnaw at my brain and rouse my anxiety.

"You haven't uttered a word, Gyges. What is troubling you?"

"I don't know what to say, sire. I'm disconcerted."

"So I see. Go on, give me your answer. Do you accept my offer?"

"Your Majesty knows that his desires are mine."

That was how it all began. We went first to his residence, and at the far end of the garden, where the steam baths are, as we sweated and his masseur rejuvenated our members, I scrutinized the Egyptian woman. A very tall woman, her face marred by those scars with which people of her race dedicate pubescent girls to their bloodthirsty god. She was already past childhood. But she was interesting and attractive, I grant. Her ebony skin shone amid the clouds of steam as though it had been varnished, and all her movements and gestures revealed an extraordinary hauteur. She showed not the slightest trace of that abject servility, so common in slaves, aimed at attaining the favor of their masters, but, rather, an elegant coldness. She did not understand our language, yet she immediately deciphered the instructions transmitted to her by her master through gestures. Once Gyges had indicated what it was we wanted to see, the woman, enveloping the two of us for a few seconds in her silken, scornful gaze, turned around, bent over, and lifted her tunic with both hands, offering us her backside. It was indeed notable, a veritable miracle in the eyes of anyone save the spouse of Lucrecia, the queen. Firm and spherical, gently curved, the skin hairless and fine-grained, with a blue sheen, over which one's gaze glided as over the sea. Bliss, and bliss likewise for my guard and minister, as the owner of such a sweet delight.

In order to fulfill my part of the offer, we were obliged to act with the greatest discretion. That episode with Atlas, the slave, had been deeply shocking to my wife, as I have already recounted: Lucrecia acquiesced because she satisfies my every whim. But I saw her so overcome with shame as Atlas and she did their best, to no avail, to act out the fantasy which I had woven that I swore to myself not to subject her to such a test again. Even now, when so long a time has passed since that episode, when there must be nothing left of Atlas but bones picked clean in the bottom of the stinking ravine teeming with vultures and hawks into which his remains were flung, the queen sometimes awakens at night, overcome with terror in my arms, for in her sleep the shadow of the Ethiopian has once again burst into flame on top of her.

Hence, this time I arranged matters so that my beloved would not know. That was my intention at least, though on reflection, delving into the chinks of my memory in search of what took place that night, I sometimes have my doubts.

I took Gyges through the little garden gate and introduced him into the apartments as the maidservants were disrobing Lucrecia and perfuming her and anointing her with the essences that it pleases me to smell and savor on her body. I suggested to my minister that he hide behind the draperies of the balcony and try not to move or make the slightest sound. From that coign, he had a perfect view of the splendid bed with carved corner posts, bedside steps, and red satin curtains, richly decorated with cushions, silks, and precious embroideries, where each night the queen and I staged our love matches. And I snuffed out all the lamp wicks, so that the room was lighted only by the crackling tongues of flame in the fireplace.

Lucrecia entered shortly thereafter, drifting in dressed in a filmy semitransparent tunic of white silk, with exquisitely delicate lacework at the wrists, neck, and hem. She was wearing a pearl necklace and a coif, and her feet were shod in felt slippers with high wooden platform soles and heels.

I kept her there before me for a fair time, feasting my eyes upon her and offering my good minister this spectacle fit for the gods. And as I contemplated her and thought of Gyges doing the same, that perverse complicity that united us suddenly made me burn with desire. Without a word I advanced upon her, pushed her onto the bed, and mounted her. As I caressed her, Gyges' bearded face appeared to me and the idea that he was watching us inflamed me even more, seasoning my pleasure with a bittersweet, piquant condiment hitherto unknown to me. And Lucrecia? Did she surmise that something was afoot? Did she know? Because I think I never felt her to be as spirited as she was that time, never so eager to take the initiative, to respond, never so bold at biting, kissing, embracing. Perhaps she sensed that, that night, it was not two of us but three who took our pleasure in that bedchamber turned a glowing red by candlelight and desire set aflame.

When, at dawn, as Lucrecia lay sleeping, I slipped out of bed and went on tiptoe to guide my guard and minister to the gate leading out of the garden, I found him shivering with cold and astonishment.

"You were right, Your Majesty," he stammered, ecstatic, tremulous. "I have seen it and it still seems to me that I merely dreamed it."

"Forget all about it this very minute and forever, Gyges," I ordered him. "I have granted you this privilege in a strange access of passion, without having expressly planned it, because of the esteem I have for you. But watch your tongue. I would not be pleased if this story were to become tavern gossip and marketplace tittle-tattle. I might regret having brought you here."

He swore to me that he would never say a word.

But he did. If not, how did there come to be so many stories about what happened? The various versions contradict one another, each of them more absurd and more untrue than the next. They reach our ears, and though they annoyed us in the beginning, they amuse us now. It is something that has come to be part of this little southern kingdom of that country which centuries later will go by the name of Turkey. Like its bone-dry mountains and its churlish subjects, like its wandering tribes, its falcons, and its bears. After all, I am not displeased at the idea that, once time has gone by, swallowing everything that now exists and surrounds me, the one thing to come down to future generations on the waters of the shipwreck of Lydia's history will be, round and solar, bountiful as spring, the croup of Lucrecia the queen, my wife.

Translated by
Helen Lane

VICKI VIIDIKAS

DARLINGHURST PORTRAIT

Prostitution has flourished throughout the ages in most societies. In Greece and Rome, prostitutes of either sex were made to wear distinctive clothing and paid huge taxes. The Jews of Moses' time allowed prostitutes as long as they were foreigners. In ninth and tenth century India, the Devadasi or Handmaids of the God served as prostitutes in the temples and pilgrims were blessed by their commerce. Both encouraged and reviled, the female prostitute plays a dual role in most literary traditions, as temptress and as saviour. In the Christian tradition, she is embodied by Mary Magdalene, patron saint of penitents.

The Athenian courtesan Thaïs who induced Alexander the Great to burn down the Palace of Persepolis, Marguerite Gautier or the Dame aux Camélias, *Zola's Nana, Balzac's Esther Gobseck tell of the male fascination with the prostitute and her powers; women writers – Colette for instance – have been more cautious in their assessment of the prostitute's role. Vicki Viidikas's*

"Darlinghurst Portrait" (Darlinghurst is one of Sydney's liveliest neighbourhoods) refuses the glamour and the glory, and prefers instead to lend her character a sort of compassionate irony.

BIG NOSE, big lips, small but definite waist, what a case. The body sustains its incongruities – like the mouth dropped open as if in a state of permanent surprise, the big lips parted all shiny with Burlesque Red. She's notorious for those lips, which can suck so damn hard it's a wonder they don't get blisters, shiny lips which gape at remote horizons, enigmatic lips to pass the body through (her speciality is "French"). That's the lure, she's Egyptian or Eastern somewhere, and claims her name means "Big Treat" in Arabic. That's exotic for Australia, for the streets anyway.

Shukala has tremendous staying power – she can hang onto a bleak wet morning when the other girls have left their beat, and pick up some tired man on his way home from work, and turn a trick which empties his wallet before he's even decided.... She pumps him dry with amazing vigour, before he's noticed her Islamic nose, or flat little tits all mainly nipple, or lack of height (she rarely takes her highheels off) which brings her to the level of an average man's armpit. She can tuck in under one shoulder which makes a client feel powerful and protective. With the kind of sob stories she regularly uses, that's very important. Protection. Support. Defence system. What everyone must have.

She can repeat her movements as easily as a donkey taking a familiar mountain path, without blinking, just forward, going over the contours of a man's body as if no other location ever existed. Instincts have a way of taking root in specific desires, racial memories have flavours all of their own. Her new found customer is so glad to be relieved of his ambiguity, he accepts her olive complexion and rapid-fire techniques. Her way of conversation is unique, her movements unexpected. He never quite focuses on how short she is (4' 10"), or the fuzziness of her hair which has been carefully hennaed. What amazes him is the fact he's made it with a Muslim – there's no doubt about that, her pubic hairs all shaved away, along with underarms and complete smooth legs. Australian girls mostly shave their legs up to the knee and that can feel pretty strange. There's no doubt that her big lips are wet all the time, she has licked him dry. Instinct tells him that this odd little Easterner is more hot than any local girl. Sheilas, well, they often only flash what they've got, they don't drop a bald snatch directly over your face. Cripes. He'll be back to see this one again with an "extra heavy load."

Shukala has it all over the other "workers." She's direct, all the way, with plenty of imaginative suggestions. She only discusses one thing: sex, with a thousand different ways of how to enjoy it with her. Her time means money, you don't mess around. You pay all the way, with extensions of technique which cost you extra. Each time you cum a few more redbacks are handed over. A bestial position here, a lean over the bedstead there, a putting on or off of knickers, a "69" with twenty-five minutes allocated for the job. She opens that big mouth of hers like a well-honed razor, and splices her way through questions to get to the immediate need – desire, the nature of it, and how quickly to take the edge off it. No unresolved actions, she'd be as kinky as her hair so long as it earned her a few thousand dollars a week. She was, as they say, in the oldest profession in the world.

"Big Treat" meant business, all her clients said so, and were faint hearted by her tenacity, her intensity of purpose. What a challenge. No cowboy would quit the saddle until he'd ridden himself mad. She never concealed the fact she was on drugs permanently, vast quantities of them as big as her eyes, black edged with kohl, and all smokey with euphoria. Drugs kept her working, she gave herself to the nights and bags of white powder, till both of them ran out and she was forced to sleep. Her clients didn't dare argue with her habit – it was taboo, a purdah which made her more exotic. To see her contorting that muscley body of hers, with the eyelids heavy and so dark, was to feel like living a tale from the *Arabian Nights*. Spicy, wet, and weird, an original fable enacted in the twentieth century.

Her lack of tits don't matter. She has a brilliant arse which fits neatly into bright coloured shorts, cut away at the sides to accentuate her strong thighs. No one else can tilt forward like that over the cars and gutters of Darlinghurst, their bum thrust out as surely as a hard boiled egg. Any man could fantasise about being squeezed by her thighs, those slightly bandy legs turned inwards.... Australians had to suffer to get skin the colour of hers, and it was fascinating to watch beads of sweat break out across her forehead, tiny drops glinting along the creases of her body. The customers didn't realise it was the overload of drugs in her system which made her sweat that way. To see her pink tongue run over those big lips was enough to suggest delirium.

Shukala has to be fully "on the tilt" before she'll do business at all. She can spot a mug five blocks away, and size up how much money he's carrying before he's even approached her. Those enormous brown eyes could outstare any psyched-up arrogance or challenge the meanest stance. Determined to satisfy, like a good shot in the arm, she wasted nothing, just kept stuffing her wallet with notes (she liked the grey ones best). Her future gaped in front of her like those blasé yawns which defined a man's hunger – that enigma of gratification which gave the illusion of "forever." She was girl/woman, demon/tonic, a pint-sized female of gall and nerve....

Her trademark is a black glove with the fingertips cut out of it, an alluring detail which suggests intrigue or violence. With her gloved hand she can squeeze a penis, a syringe, a full wallet or a set of insecure balls, she can squeeze until exhaustion is total – this is the real meaning of staying power. Her naked fingertips beckoning from that black glove could entice an old man back to memories of his youth, some rare moment of sensation like tasting that first Turkish delight.

When the Buddhists say "all sensations are temporary," they obviously haven't experienced "Big Treat" at her best, pouring her energy into a sexual act so intense, the memory of it can reinforce a lifetime. Each man felt like a virile lion as he roared away inside her, buried up to the hilt in a dream of horny woman. She was here, at last, tangible under his hands. She wrapped her legs around him in everything from a sailor's knot to a serpent's twist, panting in a fury while the minutes ticked away. Another knock on the brothel's door only increased his sense of power, never mind if it cost an extra $50. She demanded his seed and wouldn't let up until sperm dribbled from her mouth, or between her legs. Those lips were swollen with desire only for him. She made a man feel he'd been robbed of strength if he ejaculated too many times, just like Samson getting his hair cut off by Delilah. As if virility ever had to do with the outgoing of bodily fluids.... What did the flowing of blood from a woman mean other than she was fertile?

Big lips, proud hips, what an arse. The mouth dropped open like a doorway to blind ecstasy. Pleasure equalled alluring repetition. Enigma of desire. Endless variation of intimate performance. Burial and resurrection. The challenge of Shukala's need. Encounter without commitment. Belief – this satisfaction of hunger. Miracle – this unexpected doing of one's most secret cravings. Love – this exchange of skin blurring into skin. Return to the deep root. Instinctive capacity for infinite pleasure. The thrill of forgetting all obligation. No remands or revenge. Special. French or Egyptian or the Muslim unveiled. "Big Treat" – what a case, worth blowing every cent.

EIMI YAMADA

THE X-RATED BLANKET

Because Eros is transient, because Eros is fugitive, because Eros is moody and brittle, we long to hold him, chain him, turn him to stone or ice or salt, objectify him, in the hope that like Eurydice preserved in a rock or Hyacinth rooted to the ground as a flower, Eros will never leave us. The risk is that, trapped, Eros is no longer Eros but becomes nothing but a voice, a name, a hand, a foot, a breast, a pair of eyes.

"Eroticism," wrote the poet Bernard Noël, "is the art of making last in the body that which merely made it tremble." Eimi Yamada, one of the most outstanding figures of Japan's younger literary generation, describes in "X-Rated Blanket" one such attempt. For the woman whose lover's name "is the key that opens my body," lovemaking becomes an agonizing process from which she cannot escape – a process in which the loved one ceases to exist as an individual being and becomes instead an extension of the lover herself, a second skin.

WHEN I SAY I want a man, I mean this man; if it's not that man, then it just won't do for me. George. The name alone twists open a faucet inside my body. Twisted, I am wet; water floods high enough to wet my eyes. That's how I clearly recognize my own desire when I look in the mirror.

Powdering myself, applying lipstick, I suddenly halt my hand, remembering many things. These memories frighten me a little because they so resemble flashbacks – the final-stage symptoms suffered by drug addicts. The name George is the key which opens my body. I whisper that name, and my legs open of themselves; I place my hand there, inside, churning what is about to ooze out. I blend this self, a self excited by a finger. And so in a delicious state a delicious concoction is served up; how wasteful that George is not here. I close my eyes in distress.

Ever since I met George I am always starved and wretched. No matter how often I hold him, or how much I am held, the next moment brings fresh desire for George. He never extinguishes the spark of desire inside me. He was the first man to impart memory to my body itself. My skin retains the sensation of becoming saturated by his; I can always remember this clearly. This astonishes me. That the physical can imprint so strongly on the physical. I didn't realize until then that a specific man's body could become an essential for a woman.

I think that George experiences me in the same way. The doorbell rings; I fly to the door. The knob rattles noisily with my impatience as I open the door. Together with the outside air George's eyes nestle into my body. I receive, catch his tumbling gaze. Before being touched by fingers or lips, all of me is licked by his eyes.

George does not push me down. In spite of that my body collapses weakly into a shape mirroring the space between his arms. Like mine, his body caves and coils. When my skin makes a depression, his skin touching that spot rises to fill it in. When my nipples are erect they are buried by his body. We love each other exactly like liquids. Feeling that we both are entwined together in everything, I am overtaken with a desire to weep. That we are each others' perfecting part. I cannot separate this man from myself.

All we ever do is make love. Maybe I will suffer divine punishment for calling it love. But we cannot do anything about it. We cannot endure not dissolving into one another when we are separated, and of course when together we simply must shed our clothes rapidly. We become crazed with impatience. From the first time we shared a bed our bodies have been tugging against each others' – webs sweet as honey. We live dragging this dripping pleasure, a pleasure that can never be sated.

I dress myself so George may desire me at any moment. I even wash carefully between my toes so that he may, at any time, take them in his mouth. Of course I polish my toenails. I wonder if I am the only woman to go as far as perfuming her toes. I labor to make myself into a delicious treat for him. He might want to bite my neck sometime, so I take special care of it. Baked to a soft brown in the sun, prepared in advance ready to be eaten any time. I always adorn my earlobes with gold pierced earrings so that his tongue may savor them. When putting on my makeup I agonize over such details as which lipstick, which blush will make me the most beautiful as I lie in George's arms. This is how I serve him.

Sometimes we talk frankly.

"All we do is make love."

"We can't help it. We have to make love."

"Why do we have to make love?"

"Because I love you."

George's eyes are already moist as he answers. His lips close firmly to prevent his desire from spilling out. I think: he wants me. Even as I am wondering if he does, already my body is encompassed by his skin. Warm, heavy. I feel peaceful. Reassurance awakens my sensuality, and I am hot down to my tiptoes.

I think that using the phrase "in love" is appropriate. I believe that it is OK to use such lofty words for something that is an absolute necessity. If I were not enwrapped by George's body, my life would probably be ruined by my fretfulness. Even if I am left breathless by the onslaught of pleasure, without him I could have no tranquillity.

Maybe people will say we are like animals. But do animals

desire their partners like this? Can they know the art of feeling the flesh tingle with desire even as one is satisfied? Every bit of him is enveloped in smooth skin. There, in that core, he is. Can an animal hunger to taste that, as though sipping broth? I want George. I want only him.

Wrapped in his two arms I am helpless. Although he is never violent, I find it hard to breathe. I search around in desperation, as if I were drowning. If there is a pillow, I seize the pillow; if the sheets have wrinkled, I cling to them. Sometimes, during such moments I catch sight of his hands. Bony, thick fingers. The thought of the largeness of his fingernails makes me shiver uncontrollably. I realize that this body draped over mine is a completely different type of body. I move my hips, raise my voice, trying to transform his type into the same type as mine.

George likes whispers. His voice is always cool. That troubles me. I express my pleasure openly; he is not like that. It excites me more and more. A man who is without a modicum of rationality in bed will disillusion a woman. At such times a woman likes to be treated with a touch of unkindness. Even though she is completely absorbed, she enjoys a bit of teasing, a little naughtiness.

In those moments his whispering voice contains fingers and arms, even a tongue. It has a genius for everything: pinching my ears, opening my pores, tickling my sides. This, crowned with sweet words or vulgar queries, seizes my heart and reduces me to tears. At these times the word "love" by itself turns into a tool which moves the lower half of my body. It is his words, even more than his penis, that turn into a naughty toy which makes me wild, makes me salivate. This is loving. My artless mind thinks so: the grinding of naked bodies against each other, leaking, sparking, blending, all of this. Is there any finer way to love? Crying, yelling, laughing. These things all happen at once; is there anything else so preposterous? George's whispers make me crazy. The tone of his delicate voice, incongruous with his large body, makes me do all things. As soon as his low, soft voice passes into and through my ears, it is transformed to a yell of desperation. The cool whisper of a man dampens a woman's ears, still and quiet, where it becomes a broadcast. He can do that. Only through me as filter.

I think I need redden only my lips. He will do the rest for me. He stains me red here and there. My skin turns red in those spots where he bites and sucks. He pulls up hot blood from inside me and leaves it floating, revealed, on the surface of my skin. I wonder if he wants to eat me up, speeding the pounding in my breast. Little by little my whole body is colored. I will take care of the lips on my face by myself, but the rest of me I will leave to him, and then, at that moment when words fail me, he is probably dying red those lips which hold his penis. By the time droplets drip down on me from his sweat-soaked brow, my entire body has already been colored. Perfect physicality is, in this way, fully consummated. As the sensation of satiation fills me – the satisfaction of having at last become one – I savor an intense pleasure tinged already with the mingling of a new, ongoing hunger.

George's voice flows on composedly as always, like the strains of a southern melody, but I am sure that he feels just as good as I do. I know this because his skin is puckered with gooseflesh even though his body is scorched with heat. This is evidence of a physical response, specific to human beings who have been touched by keen emotion. I then stroke George's body as though I were comforting a child who has put on a display of bravery. Just like a child who, desperately enduring loneliness, will burst into tears at a single gentle word, he, unable to resist, breathes a single deep sigh. Precious George. Precious me. I stroke his back for a while, savoring our shared satisfaction. In his satisfaction he allows the strength to go out of his body, temporarily defenseless. It is only then that I feel again and accept the heaviness of his body. Beloved. I love him. Too precious to strip off, he is like my blanket.

Translated by
Nina Cornyetz

Notes on Contributors

Allende, Isabel. Chilean novelist and short-story writer (1924-). Her novels include *The House of the Spirits* (1982), *Of Love and Shadows* (1984) and *Eva Luna* (1987). She has also published *The Stories of Eva Luna* (1991). She now lives in California.

Baldwin, James. Born in Harlem, New York (1924-1989). He is the author of novels: *Go Tell It on the Mountain* (1953), *Giovanni's Room* (1956), *Another Country* (1962); short stories: *Going to Meet the Man* (1965); plays: *Blues for Mr Charley* (1964), *The Amen Corner* (1964); and essays: *Notes of a Native Son* (1955), *Nobody Knows My Name* (1961), *The Fire Next Time* (1963) and *The Devil Finds Work* (1976).

Balzac, Honoré de. French novelist (1799-1850). In his *Human Comedy*, a vast cycle of novels and stories published between 1842 and 1848, he attempted to portray the whole spectrum of French society. He also published several plays, a collection of *Droll Tales* (1832-37) and the posthumous *Letters to the Foreigner* (1899-1906), his correspondence with his mistress, Mme Hanska.

Bataille, Georges. French writer (1897-1962). His novels, many of which were banned at different times, include *Story of the Eye* (1928), *Blue of the Sky* (1935), *Madame Edwarda* (1941) and *My Mother* (1966). Among his literary studies are *On Nietzsche* (1946), *Literature and Evil* (1949), *Eroticism* (1958) and *The Tears of Eros* (1961).

Billat, Anne. Palestinian writer (1957-1990). Her only published work is a collection of short stories, *The Blue Dress* (1985). She committed suicide at the age of thirty-three, leaving behind her a large number of unpublished texts, including the one included in this anthology.

Brodkey, Harold. Born in Staunton, Illinois (1930-). He is the author of two collections of short stories, *First Love and Other Sorrows* (1958) and *Stories in an Almost Classical Mode* (1988). Harold Brodkey has twice won the O. Henry Short Story Award.

Coover, Robert. American novelist and short-story writer (1932-). He won the William Faulkner award for his novel *The Origin of the Brunists* (1965). Other novels include *The Universal Baseball Association, Inc., J. Henry Waugh, Prop.* (1968), *The Public Burning* (1977) and *Spanking the Maid* (1981). His short stories are collected in *Pricksongs and Descants* (1969) and *A Night at the Movies* (1987).

Dixon, Stephen. Born in New York (1936-). Among his many books are *No Relief* (1976), *Too Late* (1978), *14 Stories* (1980),

Time to Go (1984), *Love and Will* (1989), *All Gone* (1990), *Frog* (1991) and *Moon* (1993).

Dörrie, Doris. German short-story writer (1955-). Her books include *Love, Pain and the Whole Damn Thing* (1987), *What Do You Want From Me?* (1989), *The Man of My Dreams* (1991) and *For Ever and Ever* (1991).

Heker, Liliana. Born in Argentina (1943-). Her short-story collections include *Those Who Beheld the Burning Bush* (1966), *Aquarius* (1972) and *The Pears of Evil* (1982). Her two novels to date are *A Radiance Died Out in the World* (1977) and *Fracture Zone* (1988). None of her books has appeared in English.

Indiana, Gary. American writer. His books include *Roberto Juarez* (1986), *Scar Tissue and Other Stories* (1987), *White Trash Boulevard* (1988) and *Horse Crazy* (1989).

Kamondy, László. Hungarian short-story writer and dramatist (1928-1972). He is the author of two plays, *Lover's Tree* (1960) and *Indictment and Magic* (1963), and several short story collections: *Decimated Joys* (1964), *Adam's Father* (1968), *Conditional Confession* (1969) and *Married Lovers* (1973).

Karapanou, Margarita. Greek writer (1946-). After studying philosophy and cinema in Paris, Karapanou settled in Athens. Her fiction has appeared in English translation in *Anteus*, *Shenandoah* and the *Tri-Quarterly Review*. The collection *Kassandra and the Wolf* was published in 1974.

Kawabata, Yasunari. Japanese novelist (1899-1972). His books include *The Izu Dancer* (1927), *Snow Country* (1948), *The Lake* (1954), *The Master of Go* (1954) and *The House of Sleeping Beauties* (1960). He was awarded the Nobel Prize for literature in 1968. Kawabata committed suicide in 1972.

Kundera, Milan. Czech writer and dramatist (1929-). Since 1975 he has lived in exile in France. His novels include *The Joke* (1967), *Life is Elsewhere* (1969), *The Book of Laughter and Forgetting* (1979) and *The Unbearable Lightness of Being* (1984). His short stories were collected in *Laughable Loves* (1984).

Lawrence, D.H. English novelist, poet and short-story writer (1885-1930). Among his great novels are *The White Peacock* (1911), *Sons and Lovers* (1913), *The Rainbow* (1915), *Women in Love* (1920), *The Plumed Serpent* (1926) and several versions of *Lady Chatterley's Lover* of which the final version was privately printed in Florence in 1928.

Law-Yone, Wendy. Born in Mandalay, Burma. Since 1973 she has lived in the United States. She has published one novel, *The Coffin Tree* (1988); her stories have appeared in both *The Atlantic* and *Grand Street.*

Lessing, Doris. British novelist and short story writer (1919-). Born in Persia, moved to Southern Rhodesia at the age of five, and to England in 1949. Her books include *The Grass is Singing* (1950), her five-novel cycle *Children of Violence* (1952-1969), *The Golden Notebook* (1962), *Briefing for a Descent Into Hell*

(1971), the science-fiction series *Canopus in Argus Archives* (1979-1983) and *The Fifth Child* (1988).

Li Ang. Born in Taiwan (1952-). Li Ang was a journalist and social worker before becoming a full-time writer. She has published two novels, *Flower Season* (1969) and *The Butcher's Wife* (1983), and three collections of short stories: *Their Tears, Mixed Chorus* and *The Mundane World.*

Mamleyev, Yuri. Russian short-story writer and novelist (1931-). His collection of short stories, *The Sky Above Hell,* was published in 1980. He teaches Russian Literature at Cornell University.

Mandiargues, André Pieyre de. French poet, novelist and short-story writer (1909-). He has published *Le Musée Noir* (1946), *Soleil des Loups* (1951), *La Marge* (1967) and many others. Mandiargues translated into French the works of Yukio Mishima and W.B. Yeats.

Martin, Valerie. American novelist and short-story writer (1948-). Among others, she has published *Alexandra* (1991), *The Consolation of Nature and Other Stories* (1989) and *Mary Reilly* (1990). She teaches at the University of Massachusetts.

Matheson, Richard. American novelist, short-story writer, and screenwriter/producer. He has written and produced over five hundred episodes for such television shows as "Hill Street Blues" and "Amazing Stories," and has written over fifty short stories. His collection *Scars and Other Distinguishing Marks* appeared in 1988; a novel, *Created By,* was published in 1993.

McCormack, Eric. Born in Scotland, he emigrated to Canada in 1966 (1938-). He has published two books: *Inspecting the Vaults* (1987), a collection of short stories, and *The Paradise Motel* (1989), a novel.

McEwan, Ian. English novelist and short-story writer (1948-). He is the author of two collections of short stories, *First Love, Last Rites* (1976) and *In Between the Sheets* (1978), and several novels: *The Cement Garden* (1978), *The Child in Time* (1987), *The Comfort of Strangers* (1981), *The Innocent* (1990) and *Black Dog* (1992).

Minot, Susan. American novelist and short-story writer (1956-). She has published one novel, *Monkeys* (1986), and one collection of short stories, *Lust* (1989). Minot has been praised as one of the most talented writers of her generation.

Mishima, Yukio. Japanese novelist, playwright and short-story writer (1925-1970). His books include *Confessions of a Mask* (1949), *The Thirst for Love* (1951), *Forbidden Pleasure* (1952), *The Temple of the Golden Pavilion* (1956), *The Sound of Waves* (1954), *Sun and Steel* (1970). He delivered to his publisher the final volume of his tretralogy, *The Sea of Fertility*, on the morning of his ritual suicide.

Moravia, Alberto. Italian writer (1907-1990). Pseudonym of Alberto Pincherle. His many books include *The Time of Indifference* (1929), *The Epidemic* (1944), *The Woman of Rome* (1947), *The Conformist* (1951), *Two Women* (1957), *Boredom* (1960) and *The Voyeur* (1985).

Muschg, Adolf. Swiss novelist, short-story writer and poet (1934-). His many books include *Baiyun or The Friendship Society* (1980), *The Blue Man* (1983), *The Light and the Key* (1984), *The Weathervane and Other Love Stories* (1987) and *An Unfaithful Bookkeeper and Other Stories* (1991).

Nin, Anaïs. French writer (1903-1977). Brought up and educated in New York, she moved to France where she lived most of her life. Her most famous works are her diaries. Her fiction includes *The Four-chambered Heart* (1950), *A Spy in the House of Love* (1954), *Seduction of the Minotaur* (1961), *Collages* (1964) and the posthumously published *Delta of Venus* (1977).

Persky, Stan. Born in Chicago, Persky settled in Canada in 1965 (1941-). His books include *Wrestling the Angel* (1977), *Son of Socred* (1979), *The House That Jack Built* (1980), *At the Lenin Shipyard* (1981), *America, the Last Domino* (1984), *Buddy's* (1989) and *Mixed Media* (1992).

Poniatowska, Elena. Mexican writer born in France (1923-). She came to Mexico at the age of ten with her father, a Polish aristocrat. Her novels include *Till Never, Dear Jesus* (1952), *Massacre in Mexico* (1971) and *Dear Diego* (1978).

Sawai, Gloria. Canadian writer born in Minneapolis (1932-). Her short stories have appeared in numerous anthologies. *Neighbour: A Play for Children* was published in 1991.

Sheard, Sarah. Canadian writer (1953-). She is the author of two novels, *Almost Japanese* (1985) and *The Swing Era* (1993).

Her stories have been published in magazines both in Canada and the U.S.

Simpson, Helen. English writer. She is the author of one collection of short stories, *Four Bare Legs in a Bed* (1990), one novella, *Flesh and Grass* (1990), and two cookbooks.

Somers, Armonia. Born in Uruguay (1918-). Pseudonym of Armonia Etchepare de Henestrosa. Her books include *The Naked Woman* (1950), *The Fall* (1953), *The North Wind Street and Other Stories* (1963), *From Fear to Fear* (1965), *All the Stories* (1967), *Rebellion of the Flower* (1988). Only a few of her stories have been translated into English.

Vargas Llosa, Mario. Peruvian novelist (1936-). His many books include *The Cubs and Other Stories* (1958), *The Time of the Hero* (1963), *The Green House* (1966), *Conversation in the Cathedral* (1969), *Aunt Julia and the Scriptwriter* (1977), *The Real Life of Alejandro Mayta* (1984) and *In Praise of the Stepmother* (1988).

Viidikas, Vicki. Australian writer (1948-). Her poetry and prose have been published in over twenty anthologies. Among her own books are *Condition Red* (1973), *Knabel* (1978), *Wrappings* (1974) and *India Ink* (1984).

Yamada, Eimi. Japanese writer (1959-). Her novels, for which she was nominated for three Akutagawa awards, include *Bedtime Eyes* (1985), *Jessy's Backbone* (1986), *Butterfly's Foot-Binding* (1987) and *Soul Music-Lovers Only* (1989).

Sources

Every effort has been made to contact copyright holders. In the event of an inadvertent omission or error, the editor should be notified at Macfarlane Walter & Ross, 37 A Hazelton Avenue, Toronto, Canada M5R 2E3.

Allende, Isabel, "Wicked Girl," from *The Stories of Eva Luna* by Isabel Allende, copyright © 1989 by Isabel Allende, translated from the Spanish by Margaret Sayers Peden. English translation copyright © 1991 by Macmillan Publishing Company. Reprinted by permission of Atheneum Publishers, an imprint of Macmillan Publishing Company, New York.

Baldwin, James, "Just Above My Head," from *Just Above My Head* by James Baldwin, copyright © 1979 by James Baldwin. Reprinted by permission of Doubleday, a division of Bantam Doubleday Dell Publishing Group, Inc., New York.

Bataille, Georges, "The Dead Man," from *My Mother, Madame Edwarda and The Dead Man* by Georges Bataille, copyright © 1989 by Marion Boyars Publishers Inc., translated by Austryn Wainhouse. Reprinted by permission of Marion Boyars Publishers, New York and London.

Billat, Anne, "How Ishmael and Isaac Came to Be Born," copyright © Nigel Gauvin Editeur/Les Feuillets Roses. This translation copyright © 1993 by Alberto Manguel.

Brodkey, Harold, "Innocence," from *Stories in an Almost Classical Mode* by Harold Brodkey, copyright © 1966-88 by Harold Brodkey.

Reprinted by permission of Alfred A. Knopf, New York.

Coover, Robert, "You Must Remember This," from *A Night at the Movies* by Robert Coover, copyright © 1987 by Robert Coover, published by Linden Press/Simon and Schuster, a division of Simon and Schuster Inc. Reprinted by permission of Georges Borchardt, Inc. for the author.

Dixon, Stephen, "Milk Is Very Good for You," from *14 Stories* by Stephen Dixon, copyright © 1980 by Stephen Dixon, published by Johns Hopkins University Press. Reprinted by permission of the author.

Dörrie, Doris, "What Do You Do While I'm Gone?" from *What Do You Want From Me?* by Doris Dörrie, copyright © 1991 by Alfred A Knopf, Inc., translated by John E. Woods. Reprinted by permission of Alfred A. Knopf, Inc., New York.

Heker, Liliana, "Jocasta," from *Evening Games*, edited by Alberto Manguel, copyright © by Liliana Heker, published by Penguin Books. This translation copyright © 1986 by Alberto Manguel. Permission granted by the Lucinda Vardey Agency, Toronto, on behalf of the author.

Indiana, Gary, "Dreams Involving Water," from *High Risks*, edited by A. Scholder and I. Silverberg, copyright © by Gary Indiana, published by Plume Books, an imprint of Penguin Books. Reprinted by permission of the author.

Kamondy, Lázló, "The Student and the Woman," from *Hungarian Short Stories*, edited by Paul Varnai, copyright © 1983 by Lázló Kamondy. Reprinted by permission of Exile Editions, Toronto.

Karapanou, Margarita, "Kassandra and the Wolf," from *Kassandra and the Wolf* by Margarita Karapanou, copyright © 1976 by Harcourt Brace Jovanovich, translated by N.C. Germanacos. Reprinted by permission of Harcourt Brace Jovanovich, Orlando.

Kawabata, Yasunari, "One Arm," from *House of the Sleeping Beauties* by Yasunari Kawabata, published by Kodansha International Ltd., copyright

© 1969 by Kodansha International Ltd., translated by Edward Seidensticker. Reprinted by permission. All rights reserved.

Kundera, Milan, "The Hitchhiking Game," from *Laughable Loves* by Milan Kundera, copyright © 1974 by Alfred A. Knopf, Inc., translated by Suzanne Rappaport. Reprinted by permission of Alfred A. Knopf, Inc., New York.

Law-Yone, Wendy, "Drought," from *Slow Hand*, edited by Michelle Slung, copyright © by Wendy Law-Yone. Reprinted by permission of HarperCollins Publishers, New York.

Lessing, Doris, "Each Other," from *A Man and Two Women* by Doris Lessing, copyright © 1963 by Doris Lessing. Reprinted by permission of Jonathan Clowes Ltd., London, on behalf of Doris Lessing.

Li Ang, "Curvaceous Dolls," from *Yellow Silk Journal*, 1990, copyright © 1987 by Li Ang, translation copyright © 1987 by Howard Goldblatt. Reprinted by permission of *Yellow Silk Journal*, Albany, California, and Howard Goldblatt.

Mamleyev, Yuri, "The Last Trace of Spinoza," from *The Sky Above Hell and Other Stories* by Yuri Mamleyev, copyright © 1980 by Yuri Mamleyev, translated by H.W. Tjalsma. Reprinted by permission of Taplinger Publishing Company, Inc., New York.

Mandiargues, André Pieyre de, "The Tide," from *Descant*, No. 54, Fall 1986. This translation copyright © 1986 by Alberto Manguel. Reprinted by permssion of *Descant*, Toronto.

Martin, Valerie, "Sea Lovers," from *The Consolation of Nature* by Valerie Martin, copyright © 1988 by Houghton Mifflin Co. Reprinted by permission of Houghton Mifflin Co. and the Nicki Smith Agency.

Matheson, Richard, "Arousal," from *Alien Sex*, edited by Ellen Datlow, copyright © 1990 by Richard Christian Matheson, published by ROC/Penguin Books, New York. Reprinted by permission of the author.

McCormack, Eric, "Birthday Present," copyright © 1992 by Eric McCormack. Permission granted by the author.

McEwan, Ian, "Homemade," from *First Love, Last Rites* by Ian McEwan, copyright © 1975 by Jonathan Cape Ltd. Reprinted by permission of Jonathan Cape Ltd./Random Century Group, London.

Minot, Susan, "Lust," from *Lust and Other Stories* by Susan Minot, copyright © 1989 by Susan Minot. Reprinted by permission of Houghton Mifflin Co./Seymour Lawrence, Boston. All rights reserved.

Mishima, Yukio, "Raisin Bread," from *Acts of Worship* by Yukio Mishima, published by Kodansha International Ltd., copyright © 1963 by Yoko Mishima. The anthology copyright © 1989 by Kodansha International Ltd. Reprinted by permission. All rights reserved.

Moravia, Alberto, "Love in the Chinese Restaurant," from *The Voyeur* by Alberto Moravia, copyright © 1986 by Secker and Warburg, translated by Tim Parks. Reprinted by permission of Gruppo Editoriale Fabbri, Bompiani, Sozogno, Etas SpA, Milan.

Muschg, Adolf, "Grandfather's Little Pleasure," from *The Blue Man and Other Stories* by Adolf Muschg, copyright © 1983 by Adolf Muschg, translation copyright © 1983 by Marlis Zeller Cambon and Michael Hamburger. Reprinted by permission of George Braziller, Inc., New York.

Nin, Anaïs, "Mandra," from *Little Birds* by Anaïs Nin, copyright © 1979 by Rupert Pole as Trustee under the Last Will and Testament of Anaïs Nin. Reprinted by permission of Harcourt Brace Jovanovich Inc., Orlando.

Persky, Stan, "Eros and Cupid," from *Buddy's* by Stan Persky, copyright © 1989 by New Star Books. Reprinted by permission of New Star Books, Vancouver.

Poniatowska, Elena, "Park Cinema," is reprinted with permission of the publisher from *Short Stories by Latin American Women: The Magical and the Real,* translated by Teres Mendeth-Faith and Elizabeth Heinicke (Houston: Arte Publico Press-University of Houston, 1990).

Sawai, Gloria, "The Day I Sat With Jesus on the Sun Deck and a Wind Came Up and Blew My Kimono Open and He Saw My Breasts," copyright © Gloria Sawai. Reprinted by permission of the author.

Sheard, Sarah, "Eugenia," copyright © 1992 by Sarah Sheard. Reprinted by permission of the author.

Simpson, Helen, "Four Bare Legs in a Bed," from *Four Bare Legs in a Bed* by Helen Simpson, copyright © 1990 by Helen Simpson. Reprinted by permission of William Heinemann Limited, London, and Peters, Fraser & Dunlop Ltd., London.

Somers, Armonia, "The Fall," from *Other Fires,* edited by Alberto Manguel, copyright © by Armonia Somers, published by Lester & Orpen Dennys, Toronto.

Vargas Llosa, Mario, "Candaules, King of Lydia," from *In Praise of the Stepmother* by Mario Vargas Llosa, copyright © 1990 by Farrar, Straus & Giroux, translated by Helen Lane. Reprinted by permission of Farrar, Straus & Giroux, New York.

Viidikas, Vicki, "Darlinghurst Portrait," from *The Babe is Wise,* edited by L. Harwood, *et al,* copyright © 1987 by Vicki Viidikas. Reprinted by permission of Pascoe Publishing Pty. Ltd., Australia.

Yamada, Eimi, "X-Rated Blanket," from *New Japanese Voices,* edited by Helen Mitsios, copyright © 1991 by Helen Mitsios. Reprinted by permission of Atlantic Monthly Press, New York.

This book is set in Garamond, a typeface designed in 1545 by Claude Garamont, a punch cutter in Paris. Garamond gained popularity in the early seventeenth century. It is light in colour, delicate in design, and yet smoothly legible. It is one of the finest old styles ever cut.

Book design by Gordon Robertson